Those Who Write for Immortality

H. J. JACKSON

Those Who Write for Immortality

ROMANTIC REPUTATIONS AND THE DREAM OF LASTING FAME

Yale UNIVERSITY PRESS
New Haven &
London

Published with assistance from the foundation established in memory of Calvin Chapin of the Class of 1788, Yale College.

1 0 0 7 4 7 6 3 5 7

Yale University Press books may be purchased in quantity for educational, business, or promotional use. For information, please e-mail sales.press@yale.edu (U.S. office) or sales@yaleup.co.uk (U.K. office).

Set in Sabon type by Westchester Book Group.
Printed in the United States of America.

Library of Congress Cataloging-in-Publication Data
Jackson, H. J.
Those who write for immortality : Romantic reputations and the dream of lasting fame / H. J. Jackson.
 pages cm
  Includes bibliographical references and index.
  ISBN 978-0-300-17479-3 (alk. paper)
1. English literature—19th century—History and criticism. 2. Romanticism—England—History—19th century. 3. Authorship—England—History—19th century. 4. Authors and readers—England—History—19th century.
5. Authors, English—19th century—Appreciation. 6. Fame—History—19th century. 7. Reputation—England—History—19th century. 8. Influence (Literary, artistic, etc.)—History—19th century. I. Title. II. Title: Romantic reputations and the dream of lasting fame.
  PR468.R65J33 2015
  820.9'008—dc23   2014023095

A catalogue record for this book is available from the British Library.

This paper meets the requirements of ANSI/NISO Z39.48-1992 (Permanence of Paper).
10 9 8 7 6 5 4 3 2 1

For
Robin,
in memoriam

Contents

Preface

This is a book about writing—specifically, about the relationship between seeking lasting fame as an author and getting it. It did not begin that way. Originally I thought it might be interesting to work out how it could be that two writers whose works appeared practically indistinguishable to their contemporaries, such as Jane Austen and Mary Brunton or John Keats and Barry Cornwall, have come down to us as so radically different from one another that one is now a household name while the other is virtually unknown.[1] Was there a difference there all along that took time to manifest itself, or was the difference somehow constructed? If the latter (as seemed more likely, now that we are used to the idea of the social construction of everything), by what process? In order to maintain some control, I wanted a set of writers of the same period so that the conditions of their afterlives would be roughly similar, and I chose the Romantic period for a variety of reasons, though it could have been any other from the Elizabethan to the postmodern. Theirs is the period I know best. They have had their century—the lapse of time after the death of the author that is supposed to allow for sound judgment of her or his worth. As a cohort, they have proved to be the most successful in English literature, with more canonical writers in thirty years or so than most of the centuries before them. A new school curriculum proposed for England, announced in 2013, has only two really specific requirements: one play by

Shakespeare and "a selection of representative Romantic poetry" (also, more generally, "at least one 19th-century novel," which could well be one by Austen).[2] Furthermore, the question of literary fame was so actively debated at the time that it is sometimes described as a turning point, when the rules of the game changed dramatically, though I think that in fact they underwent only minor modifications. Reception studies are seldom comparative—they tell the story, usually, of just one figure—but pairing authors offered a reality check, while multiplying the number of pairs would gradually expand the scope of the experiment and progressively test its conclusions. The proposed study was to be called "Romantic Reputations." One of my colleagues, a Victorianist with a lurid imagination, nicknamed it "the lost twins."

As I worked with the twins, however, it became so difficult to resist the impulse to polarize that I tried adding a third figure. That complicated the process and meant there were more variables to deal with, but it also increased the number of cases overall in a useful way and it seemed to temper the contrasts, adding shades of grey to the original black and white. In keeping with current trends in book history and cultural studies, the plan was to go beyond the traditional analysis of publication history and critical history (what professional reviewers and scholars have had to say) and to try, as far as possible, to take into account other, more "popular" aspects of reception, such as adaptation, illustration, and evolving cultural resonance. That was the task I set myself, with Lucasta Miller's brilliant book about the Brontës as a model to aspire to.[3] But again, as the work progressed, it took an unforeseen turn. The writer's own conception of his or her task came to seem as important a factor as the external forces of the reviewing system, the schools, or the book trade—and as variable. Historically, this was interesting because of recent attention to "the Romantic concept of authorship," which turns out to be less uniform, less revolutionary, and less tied to one period than I had been led to believe it was.[4] It also opened up the study as a whole, since it introduced a cluster of ideas that are not only historically significant but also still operative in the modern world.

In 2010, when the Library of Congress announced that it would be preserving and storing all the messages on the social networking site Twitter, one of the babbling heads on TV said an odd thing: he said that some messages were more momentous than others and that "we do want to save those tweets for posterity."[5] It's a notable mental leap, from saving tweets to saving "for posterity." These short statements, the epitome of impulse and ephemerality, are going to be preserved, and therefore they must be preserved for a purpose, which must be the benefit of posterity. Somehow a secondary industry will have to be developed to study, assess, organize, and promote the better tweets, with a degree of rivalry among contending gatekeepers. Such a profound change in the conditions of tweeting will transform—may already have transformed—the mental approach of all parties. When senders have to consider the way they will appear to the unknowable readers (and gatekeepers) of the future, not just to their peers, they will pick their subjects and attend to their style in a different way; their writing will become more self-conscious, more guarded, more artful, less like birdsong. The attitude of addressees is liable to be affected too; they will be more inclined to evaluate the messages they get in comparison with one another. In general, the possibility of preservation introduces a measure of worth and discrimination: is this tweet (that I am sending or receiving or having passed on to me) one that, more than others, deserves to be kept?

The mindset of writing to last, with attendant implications for writers, readers, publishers, and critics, is the central subject of this study now. The common word "posterity" and the idea of being kept "for" posterity, however, encompass a range of meanings and motives. In the case of the tweets, they might begin with the comparatively neutral significance of being available for readers in the future.[6] They might then come to imply the positive merit of being worthy of longevity, as the pundit's remark indicated (some tweets being more momentous than others). Quite often, though, they have critical or negative connotations: writers with their sights set on a distant readership might well disregard or even despise that of the present day, thinking of contemporary failure as the price they pay for triumph later. They might even court failure in the short term, gambling for success in the long run. In a book that covers some of the same ground as this one, Andrew Bennett has argued that the attitude of looking to the future for recognition *instead of* to the present—as though they were mutually exclusive—arose in the Romantic period and defines its theories of poetry insofar as they are distinctively "Romantic." "The appeal to a posthumous reception," he maintains, "is central to the project of Romantic poetics."[7] Bennett's work has been very helpful to me, not least because it begins by gathering and analyzing statements about posterity from many poets and essayists of the period. I accept the proposition, first expressed by Leo Braudy, that the myth of neglect which underpins what Bennett calls "the culture of posterity" came to the fore in the early nineteenth century. (Braudy describes it as "the era's special turn on the old Horatian paean to posterity.")[8] Only I question whether it was new in or peculiar to that period. Can it even be said to have been dominant then? There might have been a change of emphasis, but was there a fundamental shift in the concept of authorship?

As far as I can see, the attitudes of writers toward their present and future audiences, and thus toward their own work, were not all that different in

Romantic Britain from what they had been in Western literature for centuries before, and are still.[9] Authors would have had an array of options to choose from—had they been making conscious choices, though most of them were not. With this conviction, I cast my net wider than I had once intended, aiming to investigate the reception of a cohort of Romantic writers, mainly poets but also some novelists, with special attention to their views about their goals in writing; and then to see whether in actuality their goals were met. Did they get what they expected as they expected; if not, why not? In order to explain the goals themselves, it was necessary to look back to classical models and to the most influential versions of those ideas in the generation preceding the early Romantics: that is the ground covered by the first chapter. I wanted to avoid the narrow and negative focus on "posterity" and therefore settled on the larger notion of literary "immortality," adopting a phrase of Samuel Johnson's for my title.

The framework of this book may thus be a set of ideas associated with writing for immortality, but the bulk of it consists of case studies in the reception of a dozen authors. Though I prepared and made some headway with several others, it seemed better to retain plenty of grassroots evidence than to base conclusions on generalizations that readers would have to take on trust. For that reason, the core sample remains quite small. I wish there had been room for more. I gave up most reluctantly the idea of a chapter bringing together Byron, Moore, and Wolcot ("Peter Pindar," the most popular satirist of his day); perhaps, if the methods I have used here appeal to other scholars, someone else will write it another day.

What follows is a serious scholarly study with lessons, potentially, for writers and readers outside the academy; it was written with that wider audience in mind. I assume general knowledge of four major authors (Wordsworth, Austen, Keats, and Blake), including firsthand acquaintance with one or more of their works, but not necessarily deep study. I assume, too, that readers have access to online reference sources for basic information not provided here. Matters of debate among specialists are kept mainly to the endnotes, where information is supplied for anyone interested in further reading. As to the other less familiar writers, I provide introductions to their careers and some account of the character of their work, in addition to the survey of the afterlife that is at the heart of each case study; suggestions for further reading are listed in this book's appendix, with texts available in full on a dedicated website at http://hdl.handle.net/1807/65448. The result may seem uneven, but the intent was to restore balance, not distort it.

A more serious risk is the appearance of prejudice against the great and beloved: if the evidence I bring forward suggests that Wordsworth, Austen,

Keats, and Blake achieved their present-day pinnacles in part or even mainly because of adventitious circumstances, does it mean that we should give them up and turn to Leigh Hunt and Robert Southey? Of course not. Even if they had not been surpassingly good writers, we have come too far with them for that to be practical, as the chapter on Keats tries to demonstrate. We are historically invested in them. The conclusion, however, makes some positive proposals for giving the Hunts and Southeys another chance, as it was also mainly because of adventitious circumstances that they fell by the wayside. Between the introductory first chapter and the conclusion, four chapters highlight different aspects of the process of becoming famous in the nineteenth and twentieth centuries: first concepts of authorship and audience; then the problem of popularity; then the small question of merit; and finally mechanisms of recovery.

The topics of this study overlap with several areas of recent or current interest for which there is a quite extensive secondary literature: for example, celebrity studies, canonization, the definition of Romanticism, recovery projects, authorship, and audiences. Within recent months, what is called "failure"—the dark side of glory—seems to have become a topic of special interest in popular media, as witness the movies *Inside Llewyn Davis* and *Twenty Feet from Stardom,* both about the world of live music. The works I found most useful are indicated in the notes, as are those relied on for the histories of individual authors. If I have scanted any area—and I have no doubt that I have scanted them all for the sake of my particular perspective— the notes and bibliography should enable readers to fill in the gaps themselves. Other limitations will also be obvious. I deal with only a dozen authors, most of them poets, most of them male, and all of them British. Very little is made of their reception outside Britain and North America (and there is not much even on North America), though resources are available. Many aspects of the posthumous careers of Romantic writers—the role of musical settings of their works, for instance, or adaptation for radio and cinema—are barely touched on or are neglected altogether. Perhaps these deficiencies—casualties of not having world enough or time, like the abandoned Byron chapter—will provoke someone else to correct the record.

This book has been a long time in the making, and many people have contributed to it in different ways, with fruitful hints and constructive criticism—last and most effectively, my editors at Yale University Press, where I count it a piece of rare good fortune to have been able to work for a third time with Phillip King. A band of graduate students, over the years, put in hours sifting through magazines and periodicals, and through the catalogues of libraries and archives. If I haven't incorporated all the data they provided, if the labor doesn't show, it is not because it failed to make an impression. Thanks especially to Rebecca Walker, Jennifer O'Kell, Kate Trebuss, Christopher Laxer, and Elizabeth Dickens. Christopher Laxer also undertook the invaluable service of being the first reader of the draft version. The University of Toronto has a large Department of English with exceptional strength in the Romantic period, and I have benefitted greatly from discussions with Alan Bewell, Dan White, Jane Millgate, and Deidre Lynch; for expertise in American, Victorian, and Modern areas I have been fortunate in being able to consult especially Eleanor Cook, Jill Matus, Michael Millgate, Jeannine DeLombard, and Melba Cuddy-Keene. Staff at the Pratt Library of Victoria College and at the Thomas Fisher Rare Book Library have given me outstanding support. In Ottawa, Ina Ferris generously read and commented on a draft of the opening chapter and added some shrewd observations about Walter Scott. Farther from home, Lindsay Duguid, John Murray-Browne, and Christopher Coope left their marks in ways that might surprise them.

Some of the observations about Brunton in chapter 3 originally appeared in an essay written for the "Commentary" section of the *Times Literary Supplement* of April 7, 2006. An early version of the Wordsworth material in chapter 2 was delivered as the John Coffin Lecture at the Institute of English Studies in the University of London in 2007, and the section on Johnson's *Lives of the Poets* in chapter 1 is based on a lecture given at a symposium in Madison, Wisconsin, that was published later in *Age of Johnson* 19 (2009): 9–20. For substantial research support in the early stages of this project, between 2005 and 2008, I am very grateful to the Social Sciences and Humanities Research Council of Canada.

The Fame Tradition

The desire for fame is so ubiquitous among writers that it is sometimes described as "innate" in them.[1] Certainly they write and talk about it a lot. Apparently they always have: the literature of fame is abundant in the Western world. But the familiarity even to tedium of the theme and the simplicity of the word mask a complex reality. What does "fame" mean? Where did the idea come from? How has it evolved? Does it have the same significance for writers as it does for other ambitious people? And if writers now, or in the past, seem to have been obsessed with it, were they all (it seems unlikely) of one mind about it? Did they all mean the same thing when they embraced or denounced it? Though the coming-to-fame of Romantic writers provides the main content of this book, this opening chapter, unlike the others, contains no reception history. It aims simply to set the scene by introducing a traditional cluster of ideas about fame—descended from ancient writings, domesticated in the Christian world, transmitted to generation after generation of schoolboys through the classical curriculum, and so widely disseminated as to seem second nature by the end of the eighteenth century when Blake, Wordsworth, Austen, and Keats were born. Given that the idea of *literary* fame emerged out of debates about fame in general, I start with a wide perspective and gradually narrow down. In the interest of brevity, and wanting besides to remain faithful to the earliest formulations, I have resisted the temptation to add illustrations from Romantic and modern sources, but they are legion.[2]

Present and Future Fame

Though "fame" is hard to improve on as a general term for being widely known, its multiple meanings need to be disentangled from one another. "Fame" stems from Greek and Latin words meaning "to speak": those who are famous are often spoken about; their names are in many mouths. Hence we have the tradition of fame as Rumor (Pheme or Fama), a powerful and fearsome goddess personified in Virgil's *Aeneid* and Ovid's *Metamorphoses*.[3] She has many eyes, ears, and tongues; she heedlessly mixes truth and lies. She is a creature of the present moment, a vehicle of contemporary opinion, notoriously fickle. Moralists and common sense alike warn against getting involved with her, and yet the desire for recognition and approval is so strong, and the rewards are so gratifying, that there has never been a shortage of contenders jostling for her attention.

Present fame, fame in one's lifetime, has much to recommend it—not least the material benefits of success, such as wealth and honors. Even serious thinkers allow that the seemingly universal, unquenchable urge to be known and talked about motivates great efforts and exceptional achievements and is thus, as ambition, a stimulus to emulation and progress in all areas of endeavor. According to Xenophon, Agesilaus the Spartan king "was in love with glory and won more of it than any man of his age," confident that if he were a good king he would "gain high renown both in life and after death."[4] "'Rivalry is good,'" said Pliny the Younger, applying a phrase from Hesiod to the human condition, "when friends stimulate each other by mutual encouragement to desire immortal fame."[5]

For the purposes of this study I shall be using "renown" to refer to present fame and "reputation" for the posthumous kind. (The distinction is familiar and significant nowadays, especially in a literary context, though it was not always so.) "Fame" itself can then be used, in keeping with common practice, as an umbrella term denoting either or both. Of other terms that have been used for ephemeral, present, or what might be called "mortal" fame, "notoriety" too often implies being known for wrongdoing. "Celebrity" is heavily freighted with Hollywood associations, and in any case is—with perhaps two exceptions, Byron and Scott—too strong a word to use for the status of writers during the Romantic period, no matter how successful they were.[6] "Popularity," on the other hand, is not strong enough, though it does convey an important truth, which is that fame depends on numbers, a critical mass of persons to whom the name is known outside the private circle of acquaintance. The famous are public figures. It might seem obvious that there should be a direct correlation between numbers and success—the more the better—but conventional wisdom has swung the other way, as we shall see, favoring a substantial but smaller body of expert judges. One reason for the preference for smaller numbers is embedded in the etymology of "popularity": it comes from *populus*, the mass of ordinary or common people, a concept that easily shades over into *vulgus*, meaning likewise ordinary or common people but with more negative attributes—the ignorant, the uneducated, the lower classes, whose good opinion is not worth having. But the numbers issue is perennially and interestingly contentious, and social class is not the only concern.

Present fame or "renown" might or might not be worth striving for; it is in any case very often elusive. Those who, like Agesilaus, achieved it to a high degree could expect the continuing reward of memorialization after their deaths. But even those who failed in the contest might entertain the possibility of posthumous recognition. History celebrates many who were unappreciated or even persecuted by their contemporaries—saints, prophets, pioneers. Socrates, for instance: in the first century, Phaedrus declared that he would not refuse to die Socrates' death if he could achieve Socrates' after-fame and vindication. He also said that if envy should deprive him in his lifetime of the honors won by his model Aesop, still he would find comfort in the consciousness of having deserved them and the hope that eventually Fortune would put things right.[7] So from very early on, faith in the future offered consolation for disappointment in the present.

In the *Tusculan Disputations* of 45 BCE, Cicero used this kind of calculation about the future as evidence in favor of the immortality of consciousness, speculating that the soul after death might continue to be aware of goings-on on earth. So many illustrious men have given their lives for their country, he observes. Would they have done so without "good hope of immortality" based on "a sort of deeply rooted presentiment of future ages"? They must have expected that their names would live on and that they would be aware of the fact. Nor is it only soldiers and statesmen who think this way: he is able to give examples of poets and artists whose work bears signs of the same expectation. Nay, even philosophers "inscribe their names upon the actual books they write about contempt of fame."[8] Cicero concludes that "inasmuch as all the best characters do most service for posterity [*maxime posteritati serviat*], the probability is that there is something of which they will have sensation after death."[9]

"Posterity" is a key word here—with continuing resonance, as indicated in this book's preface. Those who deliberately seek lasting fame look beyond their own time and the people of their own time for a final judgment, in a kind of posterity worship that is paradoxically allied to ancestor worship (insofar as they find inspiration in famous people of remote generations whose names continue to be recognized and revered). Classical writers generally conceived of winning fame as an organic process in which the relatively narrow circles of recognition in one's lifetime widened steadily after death, renown growing into reputation as a name continued in circulation—though in some cases the process might not start early enough for the subject to enjoy it. Martial urged his friend Faustinus to publish his writings and not hesitate "to let Fame in when she is standing at the door"; after all, "Glory comes late to the grave."[10] Cicero frankly courted both present and future glory when he encouraged Lucceius to write about him, and Pliny reveled in the prospect of being celebrated by Tacitus, which would be to his immediate advantage as well as giving him a share in the immortality he prophesied for Tacitus himself.[11] It was also Pliny who described supreme happiness as residing "in the foretaste of an honest and abiding fame, the assurance of being admired by posterity, the realization, while yet alive, of future glory," and who admitted that the desire for an immortal reputation spurred him to work hard rather than spend his life at ease.[12] Ideally—even normally—then, renown and reputation would form an unbroken continuum, but if they did not, if fame did not emerge in one's lifetime, looking to the future kept ambition burning.

Cicero and Public Glory

Reflecting on fame throughout his illustrious career, Cicero adopted various perspectives, from austere contempt to positive encouragement. His works form the root of a vigorous line of thought in political theory and were standard reading for many generations of statesmen and public figures.[13] One of the most familiar passages occurs in "Scipio's Dream," where he expresses the belief that the soul, which is immortal, is released from the body at death into a transcendent realm "where eminent and excellent men find their true reward."[14] Rather than pursue worldly success, then, the great man will aim to do right for its own sake. The spirit of Scipio Africanus urges the dreamer to "keep your gaze fixed upon these heavenly things, and scorn the earthly. For what fame [*celebritatem*] can you gain from the speech of men, or what glory that is worth the seeking?" In conclusion he reiterates the lesson: "Therefore, if you will only look on high and contemplate this eternal home and resting place, you will no longer attend to the gossip of the vulgar herd [*sermonibus vulgi*] or put your trust in human rewards for your exploits. Virtue herself, by her own charms, should lead you on to true glory."[15] The chief point here is that the values and ambitions of earthly life appear trivial in belief systems that include a spiritual afterlife; earthly glory, whenever it might come, before or after death, is not the real thing. The persistence of this position, neatly summed up by Leo Braudy as "bad fame on earth and good fame in eternity," is a reminder that the idea is deeply invested in supernaturalism. Without denying Richard Terry's point that it can be seen as a secular alternative and therefore as a threat to orthodox religion, I would argue that insofar as the nexus of ideas mimicked that of orthodoxy and ran parallel to it, fame is a faith-based concept.[16]

An important endorsement of Cicero's idea of "true glory" dating from the second century is that of Marcus Aurelius. He describes different degrees or levels of fame—none, or lifetime renown, or a measure of posthumous reputation, or "everlasting remembrance"—but then marks a difference not of degree but of kind between worldly glory and the reward for doing right for its own sake:

> For all things quickly fade away and become legendary, and soon absolute oblivion encairns them. And here I speak of those who made an extraordinary blaze in the world. For the rest, as soon as the breath is out of their bodies, it is *Out of sight, out of mind.* But what, when all is said, is even everlasting remembrance? Wholly vanity. What then is it that calls for our devotion? This one thing: justice in thought, in act unselfishness and a tongue that cannot lie and a disposition ready to welcome all that befalls as unavoidable, as familiar, as issuing from a like origin and fountainhead.[17]

But the position adopted by Marcus Aurelius and by Cicero in "Scipio's Dream" is not necessarily at odds with the one quoted earlier from the *Tusculan Disputations*. "Scipio's Dream" offers an idealized view of human conduct, the *Disputations* a realistic one. The two can be reconciled by accepting that if it is too much to ask that people should act upon the principles of virtue for their own sake, the motive of desire for fame (present or future) may still, as second best, stimulate them to great achievements. That is precisely the compromise proposed in the final dialogue of Cicero's *De finibus*, that "whereas the Wise . . . make right action their aim, on the other hand men not perfect and yet endowed with noble characters often respond to the stimulus of honour [*gloria*], which has some show and semblance of Moral Worth." Juvenal echoes this idea in his tenth satire, giving it a sardonic twist: "how much more intense is the thirst for fame than for goodness." And Pliny, who freely acknowledged his appetite for fame, at the same time admitted that if he were a better man, he would labor for the sake of virtue alone, for fame is ideally the product, not the purpose, of good conduct.[18]

The sublime message of "Scipio's Dream" exposes some of the flaws in the concept of reputation or "immortal" fame. No less than its supposedly inferior counterpart, renown, it reflects the opinions of mere mortals, albeit mortals of ages yet to come. It presumes a kind of stability in the future that is unknown to the present; why should it? And its favorite epithets of "immortal" and "eternal" misrepresent even the best possible outcome, for if fame depends upon human witness, mortals sustain it, and they will die. Put the case that mortals collectively could be said to be immortal, as Keats's nightingale, "not born for death," can be addressed as "immortal bird" (the race living on though individuals die off); even so, the race could come to an end, and there would be an end to fame with it. In the human realm, then, "immortal" and "eternal" are hyperbolical epithets—figures of speech, remnants of supernaturalism in the natural world.

Horace and Literary Fame

Writers were comparative latecomers to the hope of an eternal reward in this world. First up were saviors of their country and benefactors of their race, particularly monarchs and military heroes. In the oral tradition that produced the *Iliad,* it was the warrior Hector who anticipated eternal renown for himself. His exploits would be reported over and over again, and the tales of those who had died at his hands would reinforce the message: "my fame will be kept alive forever."[19] The name lives on and is carried around the world. Reputation is thus a substitute for personal immortality, and the fame system either complements or competes with other supernatural beliefs. Eventually, the promise could be extended to heroes of lower ranks and to peacetime virtues, for words had the power to immortalize statesmen and lovers as well as kings and queens. Homer could be said to have led the way, though with a legendary character: in the *Odyssey,* the spirit of Agamemnon prophesies of Penelope that "her glory will not fade with the years, but the deathless gods themselves will make a song for mortal ears, to grace Penelope the constant queen." Centuries later, Ovid addressed a poem to his loyal wife, offering her consolation from his place of exile: "so far as my praise has power, thou shalt live for all time in my song."[20] Virgil likewise had Aeneas respond gallantly to Dido's offer of hospitality: "While rivers run into the sea . . . ever shall thy honour, thy name, and thy praises endure." But still it was the words and the subject of the words that were expected to live; the writer was merely the mortal instrument of that process. Writers had to see their own kind greatly honored before they could aspire to eternal life themselves.

That moment came in Rome in the first century BCE, when writers were elevated to a place among the immortals, notably in works by Cicero, Virgil, Horace, and Ovid that came to form the core of the school curriculum, so that their ideas spread as received wisdom into the general population. After their deaths, a well-known essay by Plutarch entitled "Were the Athenians More Famous in War or in Wisdom?" (or more simply "The Glory of the Athenians") asked whether it could be right to celebrate writers as much as military heroes, and answered firmly that it couldn't. All writing, Plutarch notes, is secondary to action. Men of action keep writers in business, so writers at best enjoy only a reflected glory. Poets and writers of fictions such as myths, epics, and tragedies are inferior to historians, who at least tell the truth; poetry is no more than "a childish pastime" in comparison with war.[21] Critics disagree with one another about whether Plutarch held these views seriously. Perhaps he was just trying them out. Nevertheless, the very fact that he wrote against the idolization of writers is a sign that it was already happening—as it was, for example, during his lifetime through the set of lives of the poets in which Suetonius included Virgil, Horace, and Ovid.

Fame for writers, literary fame, was not altogether an easy fit with preexisting models of greatness and memorialization. The problem was not just that it was a latecomer, but that it was a special case.[22] In the first place, literary prowess is harder to gauge than success in war or government. What would be the writerly counterpart to winning a battle, or even to an eminent act of virtue? In the absence of clear-cut proofs, how were great writers to be distinguished and rewarded—and by whom, who was to judge them? What course were ambitious writers to follow; whom should they aim to please; what policies or practices gave them the best chances of securing lasting fame? The rewards system might also prove to be problematic where writers were concerned. The customary indicators of success (prizes, triumphs, statues, monuments, shrines) were not obviously appropriate, and less tangible but more durable forms of memorialization through the words of historians, biographers, and poets might appear compromised, since writers already dominated the realm of language that is the ultimate medium of fame.

In a more significant mark of difference, the works that writers produce are perennially available as evidence of their talent; in consequence, literary fame is not wholly of the past, as other celebrated achievements are. If the works continue to be read, they continue to leave a mark on their readers, as the writer's words infiltrate other people's minds and temporarily become their thoughts. Great deeds, no matter how meritorious, can never be experienced at first hand again, but thoughts can. So writers of all kinds (philosophers, historians, poets) and eventually certain other categories of creative artist could look forward to a supplementary, distinctive kind of fame: not only the conventional after-the-fact celebration in historical narrative and memorialization, but also a continuing competitive viability in the present, as new generations reevaluated works that they experienced afresh at first hand.[23] Whether or not they enjoyed renown in their own day, writers could hope for both reputation and renown in the future. That is to say, they have potentially two ways of being famous, whereas most people have only one: they can be celebrated for something they have done that is over, or for something they have done that is still current. Or both.

As Cicero set a standard for statesmen, so Horace did for writers. He established the foundation of a theory of literary fame. Lowly born but well educated, a friend of Virgil and protégé of Maecenas, he moved in privileged circles, enjoying the approval of the leaders of society and the envy of less successful authors. His poetry consistently and memorably expresses the pride and power of authorship, and a very high proportion of all the tags and maxims associated with the idea of literary fame come from his works, for he seems to touch all the bases. Horace reveals himself as greedy for fame, present and future alike. He is gratified by the recognition of his contemporaries: other ways of achieving renown might have passed him by, he says—he is not a boxer, not a rider, not a soldier—but he is known as a lyric poet "pointed out by passers-by," and other people repeat the hymns that he has composed.[24] (According to Suetonius, Virgil used to duck into buildings to avoid his fans on the street.)[25] Horace declares that the true poet is divinely endowed; his art comes from Apollo and his words are more effective than marble statues at keeping the exploits of heroes alive. Indeed, poetry alone possesses the power to confer immortality on its subjects: "Many a brave man lived before Agamemnon; but all lie buried unwept and unknown in the long night, because they lack a sacred bard. In the grave there is little to distinguish unrecorded valour from forgotten cowardice."[26] Horace goes well beyond conventional claims about the memorializing powers of poetry and the practicality of staying on the right side of the poet, when he attaches the immortalization of the subject to the apotheosis of the poet himself. In two great odes, he exultingly anticipates the afterlife that he will enjoy through the dissemination of his works. He will not die but will be transformed into a tuneful swan, visiting the most remote realms: "the Spaniard will become educated by reading my works, and so will he who drinks the Rhone."[27] When he describes himself as having built a monument more lasting than bronze, it is explicitly a monument to *himself* that he has constructed, immortality that he has earned and will continue to earn with his works. I shall not entirely die, he declares, but "shall continue to grow, fresh with the praise of poster-

ity" (*ego postera / crescam laude recens*).[28] In a bravura passage at the end of
the *Metamorphoses,* his slightly younger contemporary Ovid makes a similar
prediction:

> And now my work is done, which neither the wrath of Jove, nor fire, nor
> sword, nor the gnawing tooth of time shall ever be able to undo. When it will,
> let that day come which has no power save over this mortal frame, and end
> the span of my uncertain years. Still in my better part I shall be borne im-
> mortal [*perennis*] far beyond the lofty stars and I shall have an undying [*in-
> delebile*] name. Wherever Rome's power extends over the conquered world,
> I shall have mention on men's lips, and, if the prophecies of bards have any
> truth, through all the ages I shall live in fame.[29]

Horace writes about not entirely dying, Ovid about a "better part" of himself
that carries on after the death of the body. These passages express a central
mystery of the cult of literature and serve as a reminder of the origins of these
theories in religious societies, namely the notion that the spirit of the writer is
embodied in the written work so that as long as the work continues to be read,
the author survives with it. It is an appealing thought, though baffling at first.
Granted that the gift that came from Apollo, immortal in origin, should not
die with its mortal vehicle, all the same why should any part at all of the *vehicle* be expected to survive? Mysteries are by definition immune to reason,
but the notion that the gift and the person become intertwined—the gift taking
form according to the character and circumstances of the author, the author
acquiring spiritual authority from visitations of the gift—makes a kind of sense,
with the corollary that their fortunes, too, are intertwined. It is not simply
that the author may be memorialized while the work continues to contend
for renown in the present; both benefit from both kinds of fame. The reputation of an author can keep afloat works that would have sunk by themselves,
and the continuing viability of a work can keep an author's name in circulation. Horace does not dwell much on the issue of the relationship between
the writer and the work; it would never have crossed his mind that an author
might become famous for his life and personality apart from his writings. He
accepted the fact that the work carried the mark of its maker, and declared
that he wanted posterity to know what he was like—short, prematurely grey,
quick to anger, and so on—just as his contemporaries did when they recognized him in the street. But he expected to be honored after death as he was in
life, for his art.

How was that posthumous honor to come about, exactly? Ideas about the
mechanisms of literary fame are scattered throughout Horace's work, often
phrased in such a way as to reveal that he was taking part in an ongoing

discussion. There might be general agreement in the literary world about the supreme value of enduring fame, but the way to achieve it was subject to debate. On the important questions about what constitutes merit and who gets to decide what works are meritorious (who are the gatekeepers?), Horace's views were consistently elitist: only the best poets are worth reading,[30] and only the best readers are trustworthy judges. What constitutes "best"? In the poet, technical mastery factors as a matter of course, but so does originality, not in the sense of having necessarily been the first ever to write in a certain way, but in the sense of breaking new ground and becoming a leader. This is Virgil's point also, in the third book of the *Georgics*. Other themes are trite, so he will find a new one. "I must essay a path [*temptanda via est*] whereby I, too, may rise from earth and fly victorious on the lips of men."[31] The great writer thus sets himself apart. Horace defended himself fiercely against charges of being a mere imitator. "I walked not where others trod," he writes. "Who trusts himself will lead and rule the swarm."[32]

In the reader, what counted (according to Horace) was cultivated literary taste. He did not usually object to being widely read—on the contrary—but he declares repeatedly that there is no point in paying attention to the opinions of the masses or their teachers, the schoolmaster class of *grammatici*. The masses might be right, but they might not; they are unreliable and fickle (*populus levis, ventosa plebs*).[33] The wise writer will not try to please everyone but will aim to satisfy the small group of cognoscenti: "'Tis enough if the knights applaud me," he proclaims defiantly, quoting an actress who had been hissed by her audience—and goes on to name the people whose opinions he despises, as well as those few whose opinions he values. "Let but Plotius and Varius approve of these verses," he writes, "let Maecenas, Virgil, and Valgius; let Octavius and Fucus, best of men; and let but the Viscus brothers give their praise!"[34] Horace worked under what now appear as unusual circumstances, at a time when literature was the preserve of a coterie, and his views reflect those conditions; but the fact that he raised these issues at all, and the vehemence with which he made his case, suggest that he was well aware that other people disagreed and that other authors might choose, as he did not, to court the approval of the masses or of literary professionals. A century or so later, Pliny, for instance, suggested that in the prepublication audience, diversity might be more important than expertise: "any work must be revised more than once and read to a number of people if it is intended to give permanent and universal satisfaction."[35] He for one took it for granted that writers who aspired to please the unknown readers of the future would have to be broad in their appeal.

On other issues too, Horace expressed his opinions forcefully. He objected to the prejudice in favor of dead writers (the longer dead the better), as though merit as well as fame magically increased after death so that a mediocre writer of the distant past might be rated above a first-class modern one like himself, in a process that he described as "valu[ing] worth by years, and admir[ing] nothing but what the goddess of funerals has hallowed."[36] In this early version of the quarrel between the Ancients and Moderns and our own recent canon wars, Horace vented his frustration by making fun of what came to be called "the test of time" (the 100-year rule), dismissing it as irrelevant: merit, for him, was what counted, and writers of the past should not be protected from having to compete with their successors. Survival due to merit was one thing, survival due to blinkered nostalgia another.[37]

Horace's assumption about the undifferentiated nature of fame, which seems to have been widely shared at the time—the view that there was no disjunction between present and posthumous fame, and that once properly earned, it might continue to spread like floodwater—had practical consequences in the counsel he offered to aspiring writers, which was, essentially, to be a leader, not a follower; but to make an effort to please the best judges, whose taste set a reliable standard for all time. His was an optimistic creed: he trusted that the criteria of art were fixed and that outstanding merit would be rewarded with steadily increasing success, both financial and critical. Hence the well-known formula for winning over readers in all ages, the *utile dulci* of the "Art of Poetry": "He has won every vote who has blended profit and pleasure, at once delighting and instructing the reader. That is the book to make money for the Sosii [booksellers]; this is the one to cross the sea and extend to a distant day its author's fame."[38] Advice to authors who have set their sights on posterity does typically take the form of generalizations such as these, which might seem so vague as to be pointless and which yet condition the choices that writers have to make, guiding them in one direction rather than another and, over time, reinforcing the lesson. Horace's memorable dictum, backed up by his own obvious success, closed off alternative paths—segregating instruction from pleasure, for instance—for many writers who aspired to match or to displace him.

At the end of the second century, then, writers had a choice between two ways of thinking about fame in general, adopting either the negative or, at best, ambivalent attitudes of Cicero and others, or those of the warm advocates of the fame motive such as Horace. But they would have to take into account also the fact that there was more at stake for them, as writers, than there was for other candidates for fame, since they could hope for continuing viability as well as respectful memorialization. The ideas continued to be debated, but it was hardly an equal contest. What would rising above the fray and doing good for its own sake—as Cicero and others had advised—entail in the writers' world? Who would propose that they should take no action to make their works endure? Besides, the Horatian theory addressed the peculiar condition of writers directly and eloquently, and so the Horatian tradition prevailed.

Eighteenth-Century England

Fast-forward fifteen hundred years, and the framework of ideas established in Augustan Rome had changed surprisingly little despite seismic shifts in society and technology. Apollo was gone; Latin had been sidelined; the printing press had arrived and settled in; aspiring authors could, as it were, review the future that Horace had anticipated and might have noticed that things had not turned out quite as he had anticipated. Nevertheless, they continued to invoke his theory of fame in their own vernacular versions and continued to believe that exceptional merit must win the prize of an unending readership, with a smooth transition from renown in the author's lifetime to sustained posthumous reputation. In a *Spectator* paper of 1712, for example, Joseph Addison explained how the system was generally understood to work: praise leads to fame, which leads to posthumous glory in a continuous process. "This Praise, which arises first in the Mouth of particular Persons, spreads and lasts according to the Merit of Authors, and when it thus meets with a full Success, changes its Denomination, and is called *Fame*." Death, which puts an end to envy, allows the process to continue unhindered. The spirit of the author survives in the works, which achieve still greater glory, "and they continue pleasing and instructing Posterity from Age to Age."[39]

Writers in English naturally inherited debating points and alternative views about fame (literary or general) along with the conventional position, and when they exercised their verbal skills on the subject, not all of them chose Horatian orthodoxy. For example, it was the Rumor figure of Virgil and Ovid that provided the chief model for Chaucer's *The House of Fame* and Pope's updating of it in *The Temple of Fame*. (Six writers—Homer, Virgil, Pindar, Horace, Aristotle, and Cicero—occupy the places of highest honor in Pope's temple.) Shakespeare's sonnets prophesied immortality for the verse and for the subject praised, but stopped short of claiming it, as Horace had done, for the author himself. In a rare gesture of concession to the actual collective experience of literary history, Spenser represented himself as channeling the spirit of Chaucer at a time when, on account of the evolution of the language, Chaucer's own words could no longer reach the audience he deserved.[40] Milton, much occupied by the theme of fame and not strictly of one mind about it, adopted a Ciceronian position in *Lycidas,* in which the desire for fame (which keeps the young poet at his work rather than sporting with Amaryllis in the shade) is memorably described as the "last infirmity of Noble mind," and in which "Jove" in heaven is to be the final arbiter, not any mortal court of opinion. In a passage of his earnest *Night Thoughts* (1742–45), Edward Young also followed the lead of Cicero: he described the life of virtue as a perpetual contest, rewarded with a heavenly crown. (A detail from William Blake's illustration for that passage appears on the cover of this book.) But by and large, Horace ruled.

The Horatian theory prevailed presumably because people *wanted* to believe in it; it gave them something they needed. Indeed, it had—still has—many virtues. It conveyed a hopeful message to writers, assuring them that their worth would be recognized and providing advice about how to make that happen. It gave readers and critics an instrument by which to gauge quality: can this work last, was it a pathbreaker, does it combine instruction and delight, is it the best of its kind? It represented a powerful myth about the course of literary history, telling how the greatest works rise to the top and stay there, perennially outshining the competition. It affirmed a form of universal justice. And for all its dogmatism, it had enough elasticity to adapt to altered circumstances. Over time, some features of the system came to be emphasized more than others, and some latent divisions opened up, with an overall trend toward simplification and codification, as a set of opinions hardened into dogma.

The most obvious source of division was commerce. Horace, whose livelihood depended on the favor of his patron Maecenas, could write about the best works indefinitely earning money for the booksellers and glory for their authors, implying no incompatibility, only a difference, between the money motive and the fame motive. By the eighteenth century, however, the difference had become a contradiction. Abraham Cowley's poem "The Motto," published in 1656, which begins with an allusion to Virgil's phrase about finding his own path (the motto for Cowley's volume as a whole), and which dramatizes the writer's struggle to break new ground, clearly sets the two at odds: "In this Scale *Gold,* in th'other *Fame* does ly." In *The Spectator,* Addison offered the view that literature was of a higher order than the plastic arts, for "The Artist finds greater Returns in Profit, as the Author in Fame."[41] In the opening chapter of book 13 of *Tom Jones,* Fielding cheekily invokes the opposing goddesses, Fame and Gold, both at once. Formulas were found. Boswell records a quotation from the French historian Thuanus (de Thou) in praise of a worthy scholar who wrote outstandingly well in spite of the fact that he wrote *fami non famae,* out of hunger and not for fame.[42] Laurence Sterne's English version works the other way round: he says the scholar wrote "not to be *fed* but to be *famous.*"[43] Alliteration highlighted antithesis. So Pope described Shakespeare as an anomaly, a man who had written "for gain, not glory" but who, improbably, "Grew immortal in his own Despight"; Samuel Johnson likewise described him (Shakespeare) as satisfied with "present popularity and present profit."[44] There was a developing consensus that—at least under normal circumstances—writers chose one track or the other and could be categorized accordingly. Giving up the prospect of a fortune would improve their chances of everlasting fame; chasing a fortune would more or less rule them out of the contest.

Modern publishing had created a class division between hack writers who were obliged to do as they were told and independent ones who supposedly served nobler aims. When Johnson, who worked as a freelancer with booksellers all his life, defiantly declared that no one but a blockhead ever wrote except for money, he might have been being deliberately contrary, he might have been striking a blow in the war on cant, but he was also on the defensive. It was much more usual for authors to claim that they wrote in the public service, or at the insistence of friends, or for the intangible benefits of fame—in short, for anything less crass than cash. Boswell's dissenting comment on this "strange" but fixed opinion of Johnson's was that "numerous instances to refute this will occur to all who are versed in the history of literature," and if he meant that there were plenty of counterexamples of great writers saying that they did not write for money, that is an understatement.[45] I don't know quite what to make of the fact that Grub Street, synonymous with writing for hire, was renamed Milton Street in 1830. In what spirit was that done? It might be taken to epitomize proud rejection of the mercenary role.

The opposition between commercial motives and immortal fame brought out a pattern of polarities in other, related aspects of the Horatian tradition without changing the essentials. The true poet endowed by Apollo and thus distinguished from the herd of false ones was recast as an original genius, still leading the pack. (Young's *Conjectures on Original Composition,* of 1759, defined genius as a "god within.")[46] The views that Horace had aired about suitable judges became redefined as a choice between a large popular audience and a smaller, more cultivated and discriminating one. (Milton's phrase in *Paradise Lost* 7:31—"fit audience find, tho' few"—reworks Horace's line about the knights.) The unequal contest between ancients and moderns that Horace had so bitterly complained about moved gradually toward a truce with the establishment of separate spheres for dead and living authors, in which longevity, the opposite of fashionable novelty, could be taken as proof of merit in the dead authors' league without prejudice to the pretensions of those who were still living. The process of constructing a national canon, which began in the seventeenth century (arguably, even earlier), though it was clearly a work in progress, had by the middle of the eighteenth century firmly established four literary giants—Chaucer, Spenser, Shakespeare, and Milton—who began to be given the kind of editorial and scholarly attention that had previously been reserved for classical and biblical literature. They set a standard to aspire to.[47]

These developments constituted no more than minor adjustments to the Horatian tradition, which still easily dominated conventional wisdom in the late eighteenth century, when most of the writers whom we call Romantic were born and educated. By the emergence of the four writers accepted as titans, literary history tended to confirm the pattern Horace had predicted, according to which the best rise slowly but inevitably to the top. But that is not to say that conventional wisdom was not questioned and quarreled about, nor that everyone brought up on these beliefs fully accepted them. For a comprehensive, intelligent, challenging theory of literary fame that directly affected the next generation, I turn to the writings of Samuel Johnson.

Samuel Johnson

On fame per se and writing as a moralist in works such as "The Vanity of Human Wishes" and *The Rambler,* Johnson invariably stressed the futility of earthly aspirations. On *literary* fame, however, his views were more complex and unconventional. Though scattered among occasional writings, they appear to have been consistent throughout the course of his long career, with a few favorite themes repeated over and over again; they arrived at a peak of theoretical coherence in his last extended work, *The Lives of the Poets.*

Several papers in *The Rambler* of 1750–52 took up the subject of literary fame, meaning fame for writing of any kind, especially contributions to learning. In these essays, Johnson drew on common knowledge but also on his command of literary history and his deep understanding of the book trade. He noted sympathetically how hard it can be for a new writer to attract attention, since there is only so much of it to go round, and people are busy: "no man can be formidable, but to a small part of his fellow-creatures," he wrote, and "it seems not to be sufficiently considered how little renown can be admitted in the world."[48] Literary fame in particular is "of very uncertain tenure." The lesson of history is that most writers, however celebrated they might have been in their own time, are quickly forgotten or, if their names are still on record, their works are lost and thus the second, superior form of fame—the one writers really care about—is no longer possible: "If we look back into past times, we find innumerable names of authors once high in reputation, read perhaps by the beautiful, quoted by the witty, and commented by the grave; but of whom we now know only that they once existed."[49] Every writer dreams of "unfading laurels, and immortal reputation," but the fact is that very few, in any age, will achieve them.[50]

Johnson's thoughts about the vain hopes of authors and the actual mechanisms of fame are presented with particular cogency in *Rambler* 106.[51] Here he makes short work of fantasies about neglect and deferred recognition. He begins by observing that writers love to be flattered by promises of future recognition; they want to be told soothing stories about "the neglect of learning, the conspiracies against genius, and the slow progress of merit" in which they themselves play heroic roles as figures "who encounter poverty and contempt in the cause of knowledge, and trust for the reward of their labours to the judgment and gratitude of posterity." But as he demonstrates in the rest of the essay, they are sadly mistaken. Practically all of them are destined to be forgotten, and the best they can do is lower their sights and aim to be useful by discharging "the duty which Providence assigns." Though Johnson's subject is, as usual, the efforts of learned men, he quotes Horace's well-known ode on literary achievement, and what he has to say could be applied to writers of any kind. "No place affords a more striking conviction of the vanity of human hopes, than a publick library," he writes, because these books, produced with difficulty and received, in many cases, with acclaim, are now read no longer. Some may have been without merit in the first place; others that did have merit proved to be "weak in the foundation" and could not stand up against "the saps of time" (here he is playing with Horace's image of the monument more lasting than bronze). He toys with the idea of different kinds of literary fame measured by duration, as Marcus Aurelius and others had done before him. Some works might start well but die off early, while others last longer and a few go on forever: "Parnassus has its flowers of transient fragrance, as well as its oaks of towering height, and its laurels of eternal verdure."

Two unusual features of Johnson's theory of fame are conspicuous in this essay. The first is his skepticism about reasons for renown or fame in one's own time, which he sees as tainted by personal interest and partisanship, as well as by the vagaries of fashion. Specious novelties are not to be confused with genuine originality, and writings on topical subjects that might attract a lot of attention for a time will die off when the public turns to something else. Beware "the bubbles of artificial fame," he warns, "which are kept up a while by the breath of fashion, and then break at once and are annihilated." And do not unquestioningly accept the praise we hear of past works either, because their initial reception must have been subject to the same sorts of bias: "The learned often bewail the loss of ancient writers whose characters have survived their works; but perhaps, if we could now retrieve them, we should find them only the Granvilles, Montagues, Stepneys, and Sheffields of their time, and wonder by what infatuation or caprice they could be raised to notice." Johnson's warning goes beyond Horace's rejection of the opinions of the general public, for it suggests that even the best judges could be misled by "infatuation or caprice."

The flip side of the comprehensive skepticism with which Johnson approaches contemporary judgment, however, is his faith in that of future generations. In the passage just quoted, he assumes that if he and his fellow readers had access to the lost works of those highly praised ancient writers (who were known only in the way that any historical figures might be famous, their names associated with past achievements and their "characters" detached from their works), they would be able to assess them correctly. Once personal interest and partisanship are at an end, the process of impartial evaluation can begin and be repeated until general agreement emerges.[52]

In his advice to authors who hoped to be favored in the future, Johnson broke decisively with the Horatian norm. High art alone is not sufficient, he contends. Nor can original thought guarantee continuing readership, because "the general reception of a doctrine obscures the books in which it was delivered." (Or, as he would observe in his life of Dryden, "A writer who obtains his full purpose loses himself in his own lustre.")[53] One of Johnson's examples here is the chemist Robert Boyle, whose "name is, indeed, reverenced; but his works are neglected." In contrast to Boyle he cites Bacon, who correctly predicted that it would not be his scientific writings that continued to be read but rather work that cost him much less labor: his essays. Johnson approves: of all who dream of lasting fame, "He who has carefully studied human nature, and can well describe it, may with most reason flatter his ambition."[54] He advises writers contending for audiences of the future to choose a subject that is (he believes) hardly susceptible of mutation or misconstruction, namely shared human emotions and experience; and to address posterity in the same way as they would address a contemporary audience.

In *The Rambler* and elsewhere, Johnson accepted the idea that continuing to be read was the writer's ultimate goal. He shared Horace's conviction that merit or what he and his contemporaries referred to as "genius" would prevail and that it would do so in a seamless way, starting with contemporary recognition that continued to grow over time, though he stressed the odds against it. But unlike Horace, he frequently expressed skepticism about the reasons for renown, suggesting that there could be no direct correlation between the level of fame in one's own time and prospects for the future; and his recipe for success in the long term rested on egalitarian premises that Horace had deliberately rejected.

After *The Rambler,* these values were aired even more explicitly in the 1765 "Preface to Shakespeare," which begins with a direct challenge to the familiar Horatian complaint that "praises are without reason lavished on the dead, and that the honours due only to excellence are paid to antiquity."[55] Johnson acknowledges cases in which it might be true—there can be bad reasons for venerating works of the past—but the bad reasons, he argues, are decisively outweighed by good ones. Since literary merit is relative, not absolute, the works that last have to have proven themselves by meeting the standard of repeated comparison, and so have earned the reverence "due" to them. His criteria are "length of duration and continuance of esteem."[56] (The books on the library shelves in *Rambler* 106 would not have qualified: they had duration but not esteem.) How long is long enough? Johnson proposes the very figure that Horace had scoffed at, the 100-year test of time. His subject is Shakespeare, who had "long outlived his century" and whom Johnson presents as not so much an anomaly as a test case in the fame stakes. Shakespeare may not have striven for the regard of posterity—he didn't even take the trouble of seeing to it that his plays were collected and published, though he had the time to do it—but he won it all the same in what Johnson takes to be the best and only reliable way, that is by creating "just representations of general nature."[57]

Johnson's analysis of Shakespeare—his presumed goals, his achievement, his wide appeal, his reputation and the judges responsible for it—is all of a piece. His (Johnson's) bedrock principle is the constancy of human nature, which in turn depends on a concept of soul or spirit. If the inner life of humankind does not change, then representations of it will always be understood, changes in outward circumstances notwithstanding. By the same token, all readers will be capable of assessing these representations against their own experience, and the collective judgment of the aggregate of readers must be the final court of appeal. This is, at least, one way—surely the most serious and significant way—in which Johnson embraces the "common reader."[58] The theory that led to this conclusion rests on humanist and egalitarian principles, though also on a respect for numbers. As with his calculations in *Rambler* 106 about the scarcity of renown and the odds against most writers' achieving it, Johnson emphasizes the practical importance of being able to reach a lot of readers, as opposed to a coterie or select group. The numbers are not important in the way that votes are, however (the candidate with the largest number taking the parliamentary seat); they are important because they confirm the permanent validity of the writer's observation of humankind. Johnson points out that learned editors and commentators such as himself are subject to fashions in learning; they come and go. But the plays of Shakespeare are impervious to critical trends because they "please many, and please long."[59] They please many, not just the cognoscenti or literary professionals, and they are able to do so generation after generation because they represent characters that are "natural, and therefore durable" in language that strikes a middle way between the polite and the vulgar, "above grossness and below refinement," expressing "human sentiments in human language."[60] Unlike Addison's *Cato*, a favorite play of educated critics, Shakespeare's work is accessible to everyone, for "Addison speaks the language of poets, and Shakespeare, of men."[61]

Shakespeare, then, is the outstanding example in English of a dead author praised with good reason. Johnson anticipates objections and exceptions to his summary of the general character of Shakespeare's work, and hence to his own critical principles, by conceding that Shakespeare had weaknesses and that the plays are uneven. He also reflects, in passing, on the literary equivalent of what has come to be called "cumulative advantage" (the way in which those who are already ahead advance at an accelerated pace),[62] when he acknowledges that readers do not bestow their approval always or only for the best reasons, and that the reputation of Shakespeare might well include traces of the prejudice that Horace objected to: "Yet it must be confessed, that as we owe every thing to him, he owes something to us; that, if much of his praise is paid by perception and judgment, much is likewise given by custom and veneration. We fix our eyes upon his graces, and turn them from his deformities, and endure in him what we should in another loathe and despise."[63] Culturally transmitted "custom and veneration" do weigh along with literary excellence when older writers are considered. Nevertheless, on balance, Johnson makes the strongest possible case for Shakespeare this side idolatry and holds him up as a model for all times.

Johnson had a more complicated task in *The Lives of the Poets*, the set of biographical and critical prefaces that he wrote to accompany a collection of the works of British poets since the Restoration. Though the collection included no living poets, by 1781, when the last of the *Lives* was published, only five of the fifty-two had reached the centenary of their deaths, and the outcome of posthumous assessment was in nearly every case still uncertain. Johnson did not himself choose the writers to be included—that was the decision of the publishers and depended in part on ownership of the copyrights—though he made a few suggestions. The fact that reputations were yet to be made may be one reason for the attention he devoted to the signs and mechanisms of fame; he was estimating these authors' chances of survival. Johnson gradually reveals the terms on which he believed lifetime renown and post-humous reputation were to be had by telling the story of one literary career after another, and thus the *Lives* incorporates a full-blown theory of literary fame that may be all the more compelling for being presented not as theory but as history.[64]

The basic components of the system are the same as those in Horace and Ovid and Addison and Pope. It is taken as given that the writer's highest goal is immortal fame, which only the brightest geniuses can attain—and *do* attain, Johnson clearly supporting the view that eventually merit would out. Living or dead, writers contend for public attention. But there are different kinds of fame varying in duration, and not all authors aim for the greatest prize. Returning to the plant imagery he had called on before, Johnson uses the ludicrous metaphor of a deciduous laurel when he describes the style of Cowley: "His character of writing was indeed not his own: he unhappily adopted that which was predominant. He saw a certain way to present praise, and not sufficiently enquiring by what means the ancients have continued to delight through all the changes of human manners, he contented himself with a deciduous laurel, of which the verdure in its spring was bright and gay, but which time has been continually stealing from his brows."[65]

Two factors, at least, are at play in this rather contemptuous remark. Cowley is represented as having fallen short by settling for present praise, that is, by trying to please his contemporaries—and in the *Lives,* as elsewhere, Johnson harps on his theme of the unreliability of contemporary judgment.[66] But Shakespeare had also, apparently, been content with present praise, and that in itself was not enough to hold him back.

The other factor, however, is lack of originality: Cowley is said not to have had a style of his own but to have adopted one that was readily available. "The highest praise of genius is original invention," as Johnson writes of Milton.[67] Johnson valued originality as much as Horace or anyone else, but like other critics, he took advantage of its loose definition. He was able to present Shakespeare as an original genius even though he took his stories from printed sources, by declaring that he had his observations of life, at least, at first hand; *Othello,* for example, is "the vigorous and vivacious offspring of observation impregnated by genius."[68] So "originality" need not be a matter of absolute priority; it might also be detected in style, or subject, or relative lack of indebtedness. *Paradise Lost* cannot be called the best epic poem "only because it is not the first," Johnson observes, but of all the imitators of Homer, Milton is "perhaps the least indebted."[69] A humbler instance of originality supplied the title for this book: in his life of Samuel Butler, describing Butler's way of keeping a notebook not for extracts from his reading but for ideas of his own, "thoughts that were generated in his own mind, and might be use-fully applied to some future purpose," Johnson comments, "Such is the la-bour of those who write for immortality."[70]

If ever anyone wrote for immortality, it was Alexander Pope, who adopted the mantle of Horace, took his precepts to heart, and reiterated them in his own criticism. But according to Johnson's way of thinking, Pope did not al-ways go about it in the right way. Johnson wrote enthusiastically about *The Rape of the Lock,* defending its originality against detractors and pointing out that "readers of every class, from the critic to the waiting-maid" loved it.[71] Pope's translation of the *Iliad,* likewise, was a popular success: though Addi-son and the wits might have favored a rival translation, Johnson approvingly quotes Pope's riposte that he had "the town, that is, the mob" on his side.[72] On the other hand, *The Temple of Fame,* adapted from Chaucer, was in Johnson's opinion doomed to failure. Not in any sense original, set "in remote ages," and having "little relation to general manners of common life," as he reports, "it never obtained much notice, but is silently turned over, and seldom quoted or mentioned with either praise or blame."[73] It was too bookish. In such judg-ments as these we encounter again Johnson's hallmark doctrine of the com-mon reader, a category that includes "readers of every class" (where "class" refers primarily, if not exclusively, to levels of literacy). He himself, a man of learning and a critic whose opinion might sometimes be at odds with theirs, bows to their collective wisdom, notably in his tribute to Gray's *Elegy:* "In the character of his Elegy I rejoice to concur with the common reader; for by the common sense of readers uncorrupted with literary prejudices, after all the refinements of subtilty and the dogmatism of learning, must be finally decided all claim to poetical honours. The *Church-yard* abounds with images which find a mirrour in every mind, and with sentiments to which every bosom returns an echo."[74] For Johnson, numbers count because they demonstrate wide appeal, and wide appeal matters as confirmation of truth to nature, or universal validity.

Johnson's faith in the nonspecialist reading public and his conviction that numbers trump the opinions of the elite in any age are all the more remark-able in light of the awareness of the importance of the role of professional mediators—booksellers, editors, reviewers, and critics—that he exhibits in *The Lives of the Poets.* While they live, he says, writers have primary responsibility for their own publicity and must make an effort to keep their names before the public. Edmund Waller, for instance, "did not suffer his reputation to die grad-ually away, which may easily happen in a long life, but renewed his claim to poetical distinction from time to time."[75] They are likely to be assisted in this effort by friends and supporters in the kind of partisan struggle that Pope encountered with his Homer, the wits coming out for Addison and the town for himself; also by friendly critics, who are "the distributors of literary fame," as Johnson puts it.[76] Once they are dead, however, the task falls to other people. It's all very well for Milton to have aspired to writing something so good that the world would "not willingly let it die," but keeping it alive requires human agency—readers to read it and middlemen to get it to them in the first place.[77] Someone has to write the life, reprint the works, oversee the collected edition, and periodically reassess the author's merit. Johnson points out that Pope's executors ought to have been able to "extend his fame" by bringing out some of his unpublished writings in the period immediately after his death, while his name was still current, but they did not do so.[78] In his lifetime, Elkanah Settle had been considered a serious rival to Dryden, but fifty years and more after his death, his works had "not yet been thought to deserve the care of collecting them."[79] Though the writings of Milton were said to have suffered a period of neglect after his death, Johnson denied it, arguing that if the number of readers was small at first, it was because the proportion of the population capable of reading had been small at the time, but that *Paradise Lost* held its own under circumstances that would have been difficult for any writer not writing for the royal court.[80] Nevertheless, in a time of expanded literacy, Addison was able to do something remarkable for Milton by turning a respected work into a popular one: "by the blandishments of gentleness and facility he has made Milton an universal favourite, with whom readers of every class think it necessary to be pleased."[81] A really able critic, then, has the power to *make* a writer's reputation.

From these patterns of careers and from incidental remarks about the world of publishing in *The Lives of the Poets,* there emerges a generic profile of success in authorship. Writers whose work displays genius, originality, and insight into human nature may or may not be adequately rewarded in their own day, but they are unlikely to be altogether unappreciated, and they may reasonably hope for continuing posthumous recognition in the form of new and collected editions, continuing sales, and the support of publishing professionals—all of which will contribute to maintaining and expanding their readership. Their work will be enjoyed, admired, and talked about by many people for many generations, perhaps forever. On the other hand, once lesser writers and their immediate allies are dead, their work will fade into oblivion.

Like generations before him, Johnson had been schooled in the traditional doctrine of fame and retained much of it in his own theory, including—perhaps surprisingly—its optimism; but he dissented from tradition in significant ways. Broadly speaking, his theory emphasizes the social aspects of immortalization, and I should have liked to call it a "social" or "egalitarian" model of authorship by contrast with Horace's "elite" or "independent" model, but for two considerations. First, Margaret Ezell has already adopted "social authorship" in a different context, with a different meaning. But second, I am deterred by the positive associations of "social" and the negative vibes of "elite" these days. "Social" has become the new "green." So I shall describe the Johnsonian model as "assisted" authorship, allowing the traces of stigma still attached to ideas of weakness, debility, and dependence as in "assisted living" or even "assisted suicide," by way of incorporating resistance.[82]

Whereas Horace relied on the good taste of a few contemporary judges to approve his work and see it on its way, Johnson questioned the impartiality of contemporaries and the prejudices of specialists, and he counted (literally) on the general public to separate the wheat from the chaff, their collective reiterated judgment growing steadily stronger and more reliable over time. His notion of the winning formula also depended on shared characteristics and social behavior, the "general manners of common life" that hardly change from one generation to the next. Whereas Horace celebrated the divine powers of the true poet, Johnson in a pragmatic, modern way emphasized the continuing role of other human agents in the process of transmission and evaluation. His was the homegrown version of the dream of literary fame that British writers of the Romantic period grew up with and, in some cases, reacted against.

A Heroic Model of Authorship

In 1815, in a fit of pique, William Wordsworth published a "sketch of my own notion of the constitution of Fame," in which he fought back against two powerful professional critics: Francis Jeffrey of the *Edinburgh Review* in his own time, and Samuel Johnson in the previous generation. (Jeffrey, who was still alive and dangerous, could not be named, but Johnson was.) The "Essay, Supplementary to the Preface," manifestly self-serving though it might be, was and is a defiant declaration of independence for the artist.[1] Even when the circumstances that had provoked the essay changed and Wordsworth became as honored in his own time as he could surely have wished, he never repudiated or appeared to regret it, and he continued to have it reprinted in collections of his work to the end of his life. He let it stand. It spoke for the wounded feelings and conscious pride of many writers before and since and has become a locus classicus for Romantic literary values. Indeed, the Romantic cult of genius so widely attacked by postmodern cultural criticism (but yet to be effectively snuffed out) is primarily a Wordsworthian cult.[2] This chapter describes the important features of Wordsworth's model and then tests it against the history of the actual reception of his work after his death, comparing his fate with that of two contemporary writers. As the architect of what is to this day the dominant theory of literary immortality and at the same time a prime example of it, Wordsworth demands detailed treatment, and his section of the chapter will be longer than usual. His essay provides a direct public statement of authorial ambition, and his example a benchmark against which others can be measured. A version of his theory of audiences, furthermore, will be a recurring motif in subsequent chapters.

Martha Woodmansee, who identifies Wordsworth's essay as fundamental to modern theories of authorship, is careful not to say that Wordsworth stood alone; rather, she describes the essay as the "fruition" of an evolving process.[3] Indeed, the ideas that he espoused seem to have been already widespread. Johnson might have been sarcastic in *The Rambler* about the consolation that unsuccessful authors may find in stories about the slow progress of genius; in *The Lives of the Poets* he might have questioned the legend that for many years *Paradise Lost* had no audience; but the seductive narrative of neglect gained ground in spite of his efforts and had become entrenched by the early nineteenth century. The fate of one young poet who had recently suffered rejection could have been a catalyst. Thomas Chatterton, a child prodigy, produced faux-medieval poems under the name of Thomas Rowley. Before he died by suicide in 1770 at the age of seventeen, it had been common enough for writers to indulge in self-pity over the difficulties of making their way. Boswell suggests that Johnson himself spoke feelingly when he recited the line "Slow rises worth, by poverty depressed" in his poem *London*. James Beattie's proto-Wordsworthian *The Minstrel; or, The Progress of Genius* opens with a plaintive stanza about "how hard it is to climb / The steep where Fame's proud temple shines afar."[4] These are conventional laments: Johnson's line is explicitly an updated rendering of Juvenal's *res angusta domi*, "narrow circumstances at home."[5] But they do not go so far as to blame society for failing to recognize talent. The editors and commentators who presented Chatterton's works in the 1780s did, and so a legend grew up about a brilliant boy driven to despair by neglect but subsequently recognized as a genius.[6] (John Hunter's doggerel history of poetry in four cantos, *A Tribute to the Manes of Unfortunate Poets*, which had at least two editions in 1798, started with Homer and ended with Chatterton.) Leo Braudy identifies the "concept of neglected genius" as the distinctive contribution of the Romantic period to the general theory of fame.[7] Evidently, since Johnson mocked it, the concept antedated Romanticism by many years; but it acquired respectability and prominence in Britain during the Romantic period.

Derivative reference books with no claims to fresh thinking sometimes speak better for the standards of a period than its front-runners, and Henry Kett's *Elements of General Knowledge* (1802), aimed at students in the upper classes at school or the early stages of university, reliably represents the state of received wisdom at the time. Kett starts his section on "polite literature and the arts" with an essay on taste that endorses both the myth of neglect and the test of time. Immortality is the proper reward of genius, he writes, but "public opinion seldom fixes the stamp of permanent approbation upon works of genius before a considerable time has elapsed," and "early fame is seldom the harbinger of future glory."[8] The best and brightest are commonly overlooked at first: "The animosity of party-spirit for a long time obstructed the reputation of the Paradise Lost; and the productions of Shakespeare and Racine obtained their just estimation, not from their contemporaries, but from the generations that succeeded them."[9] (The fact that even Shakespeare could be presented as a case of neglect suggests how powerful the myth had become.) This is precisely the position that Wordsworth adopted in the "Essay, Supplementary," where present and future or contemporary and posthumous fame are conceived of as mutually exclusive—and necessarily so.

Wordsworth made no secret of his lifelong ambition to rank among those whom he referred to, in a letter of 1824, as "the great poets of our country, who have stood the test of ages"—that is, Chaucer, Spenser, Shakespeare, and Milton.[10] In the 1800 "Preface" to *Lyrical Ballads,* in a passage that remained unchanged in all the collected editions, he presented his unconventional work as an attempt to introduce a new "class of Poetry . . . well adapted to interest mankind permanently"; at the end of the *Prelude* (1850), the poet entering upon his vocation dreams of "building up a work that shall endure"— something that Wordsworth had every reason to believe he had accomplished by the time of his death.[11] The reception of *Lyrical Ballads* had been reasonably encouraging: in the 1800 "Preface" Wordsworth acknowledged that he had "pleased a greater number, than I ventured to hope I should please." Even the unfriendly *Edinburgh Review* described that work as "unquestionably popular."[12] As early as 1820, when he was fifty, Wordsworth was being acclaimed as "a genuine English classic" more familiar than Milton to most readers, and public recognition improved steadily from then on. Honorary degrees were bestowed, he accepted the position of poet laureate, and tourists pestered him at home in Grasmere.[13] But in the low period from 1807 to 1815, his new publications were met with contemptuous criticism and sales were sluggish. A particularly harsh *Edinburgh* review, the notorious "This will never do" review of *The Excursion* (1814), was the last straw, and Wordsworth responded with the "Essay, Supplementary."

The general purpose of the essay is to stand up for the author of original genius against the prevailing taste of the age. Its underlying logic is as follows: writers who are truly original offer the public of their day something that has not been seen before; most readers will reject their work because it is unfamiliar and therefore difficult for them, and even literary specialists may be incapable of accepting something so new; therefore the original genius is bound to be disliked or disregarded by the majority of his or her contemporaries, and will have to wait until enough time has passed for the strangeness to have worn off and the value of the work to be properly appreciated.[14] Conversely, the lesser talent who pleases the audiences of the day with either conventional work or work of specious novelty, pandering to existing tastes, cannot last long. The "original Genius of a high order" must therefore accept sole responsibility for "*creating* the taste by which he is to be enjoyed." This task is so difficult that Wordsworth sees the author as a heroic figure, likening him to Hannibal crossing the Alps.[15] But the specific goal of the essay (as opposed to its general purpose here described) was self-defense. According to the line of reasoning that he has developed, if Shakespeare and Milton were underappreciated in their day while shams like Ossian were wildly popular in theirs (these are among the examples offered), it is only to be expected that the work of Wordsworth should be being vilified; but by the same token, when Ossian has been forgotten, "the products of my industry will endure."[16]

Two seldom-discussed parts of this "wrong-headed and tendentious" but interesting essay are especially relevant to the theme of writing for immortality.[17] In the historical survey in which Wordsworth gives examples of great writers being overlooked and bad ones overrated, he responds explicitly to Johnson's *Lives of the Poets*. He spends one long paragraph attempting to refute Johnson's objections and thus reaffirm the legend about the neglect of *Paradise Lost*, and another expressing astonishment and horror at the set of poets chosen for the edition with Johnson's collusion: not Chaucer, not Spenser, not Sidney nor Shakespeare, but "Roscommon, and Stepney, and Phillips, and Walsh" and so on, inept practitioners whose success only goes to show "what a small quantity of brain is necessary to procure a considerable stock of admiration, provided the aspirant will accommodate himself to the likings and fashions of his day."[18] And these overt references to the *Lives* are just the tip of the iceberg, for Wordsworth's model of authorship and reception, with its embattled genius, uncomprehending public, and licensed critical assassins, is antithetical to Johnson's—probably unconsciously so, since Wordsworth usually treats Johnson with respect. Wordsworth's heroic model does away with both the common reader, the "many" in pleasing many and pleasing long, and the middlemen, the literary professionals who play such a crucial role in Johnson's scheme. It replaces the interdependencies of the marketplace as Johnson described them with solitary grandeur: in one unintentionally comical aside, Wordsworth even imagines Shakespeare sighing over the bustle of his life in the theater.[19] The author, in Wordsworth's view, has sole responsibility for getting through to the individual reader, creating the taste by which he is to be enjoyed. Critics only get in the way, "for to be mistaught is worse than to be untaught," and professional pride is liable to produce (naming no names) "critics too petulant to be passive to a genuine poet."[20]

Turning his back on Johnson's version of the fame system, Wordsworth reverted to that of Horace—who is never mentioned, probably because he did not need to be. Wordsworth even exaggerated features of the Horatian tradition when he declared posthumous glory to be incompatible with popularity in one's lifetime. Horace expected posthumous fame to be the greater, indeed, but thought it would be based on fame in one's lifetime; the two were, as far as he was concerned, essentially undifferentiated and continuous. In other ways, however, Horace and Wordsworth are in accord with one another. Both affirm the "divine origin" of the poetic gift, the independence of the true poet, his role as original and leader, his spiritual authority, and the importance of combining instruction and delight.[21] So Horace's established model underwrites Wordsworth's heroic concept of authorship. Even that one marked departure from Horatian tradition, the stark separation of contemporary and posthumous fame, may be rooted in Horace (as well as reflecting commonplace opinions, as the passage from Kett indicates), for Wordsworth's influential theory of authorship is based on a theory of audiences.

Horace had recommended writing for a select audience while ignoring the opinions of the masses and the *grammatici*. The opening pages of Wordsworth's essay propose a theory of audiences on the analogy of four stages of human development.[22] Young people, he writes, as they are prone to love, read poetry ecstatically as lovers; but in due course, under the pressures of adult life, their love, tamed down, becomes only an "occasional recreation" or amusement. As they grow older yet, some of them turn to poetry in a new way, as they might turn to religion, for comfort among the afflictions of life. But others revert to the love of their youth and get to know it better: they make a study of it. These four hypothetical stages represent four modes of reading and four possible critical approaches: critics, Wordsworth notes rather bitterly, "abound in all" stages. The first three (ecstatic, recreational, and consolatory), representing the great majority of readers, have obvious limitations. Only the last—the mature, methodical, judicious, informed view—has reliable predictive power or, as Wordsworth puts it, can be "depended upon, as prophetic of the destiny of a new work."[23] Even within that group, many readers have to be disqualified because although they are now mature, their tastes have not evolved; or because they were educated on false principles in the first place. Hence it follows that genuinely original work is bound to suffer rejection at first. But as the small body of competent readers (Horace's metaphorical "knights") remains loyal to the meritorious work, as word spreads and converts are gained, as its influence is felt and the sense of novelty wears off, and as ephemeral fads pass away, the work of genius will come into its own. No intermediaries will be needed as the spirit of the dead author, embodied in the work, takes possession of receptive readers—"a conquest, made by the soul of the poet," reiterated in age after age.[24]

That is what Wordsworth believed—probably throughout his adult life— would happen to him. His determination to write works that would endure undoubtedly affected artistic decisions such as his rejection of fashionable poetic diction and his commitment to long poems. (Chaucer, Spenser, Shakespeare, and Milton were not famous for lyrics.) As his career developed, he came to present even his short poems as parts of a larger whole and strove to produce a work of epic proportions. And his works and name *have* endured, thus appearing to justify his faith in them as well as in the theory that underlies them. If the "Essay, Supplementary" had been written by Henry James Pye or Thomas Hood, it would most likely have been dismissed as a case of sour grapes. But associated as it was with Wordsworth, it was taken seriously and today is considered to be, as we have seen, the "fruition" of a long public debate about authorship.

Winner's Progress

Wordsworth is one of three or four clear winners in the Romantics' immortality stakes; the progress of his reputation defines the *cursus honorum,* the appropriate sequence of honors, for his generation. Received at first with skepticism or downright rejection, his work won widespread recognition even in his lifetime, when "Wordsworthian" began, quite early, to appear both as adjective and noun.[25] Editions proliferated, including legal but unauthorized overseas printings in North America and on the Continent, and outright piracies. He sat for the customary trophies of fame, the "wretched picture, and worse bust" that Byron ruefully refers to in the first canto of *Don Juan.* A William Westall engraving, for example, shows Wordsworth looking prosperous and respectable at home in 1840 (fig. 1). Upon his death, with the body of work completed and closed, he was honored with a substantial biography and a collected edition and thereafter with the usual spin-offs, such as specialized volumes of selections and entries in anthologies and reference books. The dissemination of his name and works gained momentum. Centenaries and other anniversaries were marked with exhibitions, celebrations, and new publications. A society named for him watched over his interests. Given the central place of literature in the school curriculum and, in time, in universities around the world, there was a call for textbooks and for scholarly editions not only of the published works

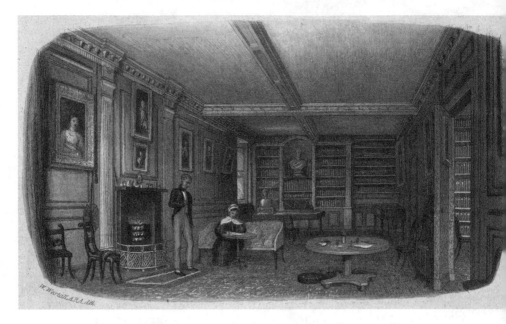

Fig. 1. "Room at Rydal Mount." Uncolored engraving, by William Westall (1840). By Permission of The Wordsworth Trust, Grasmere.

but also of secondary documents such as letters and journals. This scholarly literature made possible ever more detailed research and criticism, fueling debate and generating further writings, reviews, dedicated journals, conferences, and websites. After two hundred years he is known as the preeminent poet of his generation: the twentieth century gave his name to the whole period of his maturity: the Age of Wordsworth, 1798–1830.[26] But a closer look at the reception of Wordsworth's work tells a somewhat different story.

Wordsworth correctly predicted the overall result of his efforts but not the specific mechanisms that brought it about—small wonder, in some cases, since they did not exist in his own time—nor, more important, the reasons for his lasting success. He would probably be dismayed to find on what terms he has achieved worldwide fame. The following summary draws on histories of the critical and cultural reception of Wordsworth's work in the nineteenth and twentieth centuries, as well on primary materials, and describes certain publishing trends that played a part in keeping his name in circulation.[27] Rather than track his afterlife decade by decade, it takes up one topic at a time and brings them together in a general conclusion.

In the first place, the contemporary audience cannot properly be said to have been neglectful if *Lyrical Ballads* did reasonably well from the start and if Wordsworth was idolized after 1820. He had bad reviews and poor sales for a few years during the Napoleonic period, which was a time of hardship throughout Britain. But he also had warm supporters, including several reviewers (for *Blackwood's* and lesser periodicals) who took up his cause. As Coleridge reported in *Biographia Literaria* in 1817, "year after year increased the number of Mr. Wordsworth's admirers," their admiration distinguished by an almost "*religious* fervour" which, as he pointed out, was probably fanned by the controversies in the press.[28] Coleridge, like Wordsworth, was equally uneasy about negative partisan criticism and misguided admiration, and he strove to lay the foundations of a more balanced appreciation. But the history of the reception of Wordsworth's poetry exhibits what can be expected of any writing that has a very long run, which is that even if the same works continue to be read generation after generation, they are not read in the same way: every age reinterprets them through the lenses of its own concerns and values.[29] Stephen Gill observes, to take one small example, that "*Lyrical Ballads* was rightly viewed by Jeffrey as subversive, but by the 1840s the early poems were being read as universal statements of a Christian's humanitarian duty."[30] The Queen's chaplain, Stopford Brooke, lectured (not preached) on Wordsworth's "theology" in 1872.[31] In the 1860s and 1870s, schoolchildren were being made to parse and paraphrase; a hundred years later, Wordsworth's poems were being reinterpreted from various perspectives—biographical, political, ecological—and looked quite different.[32] Ideas that were at first considered religious came to be discussed later in the context of spirituality or psychology or cognitive science. So Wordsworth's analysis of what he considered to be subjective errors in reading could be extended from individuals to groups and from period to period without end. Interpretations seldom settle into consensus. Lack of consensus fuels discussion, however, and thus furthers the cause of fame.[33]

Furthermore, the audiences of Wordsworth's future did *not* always read the same works. He and his admirers pinned their hopes on his most ambitious philosophical poem, *The Excursion,* as "the work to which future ages will turn as the grand luminary of its era."[34] The Victorians for the most part also expected *The Excursion* to prevail, and until about the end of the nineteenth century it did, but it is known only to specialists today. In the 1890s, students at King's College London were being examined on *The White Doe of Rylstone.*[35] Now *The Prelude* is accepted as Wordsworth's masterpiece, though even it survives mainly in the universities (the "last retreats of fame," according to *Rambler* 146), where academic critics wrangle over versions. The wider public for the most part lost interest in long poems during the Victorian period (with notable exceptions, Tennyson especially). But it worked to

Wordsworth's advantage that, since he had continued to write throughout a long life and since he tried out various paths, his body of work is large and miscellaneous. Where some parts ceased to please, others might succeed, and all alike are "Wordsworth."

Two Victorian collections contributed in important ways to repositioning him as a lyric poet, as opposed to one known for either narrative or philosophical verse. One was *The Golden Treasury* of 1861, one of the great best sellers of all time, which devoted more pages to Wordsworth than to any other poet and which is said to have sold about ten thousand copies a year for almost a century. The other was Matthew Arnold's 1879 selection of Wordsworth's poetry in Macmillan's "Golden Treasury" series, which sold seventeen thousand copies in ten years and proved to be Arnold's greatest "popular success," according to Bill Bell.[36] Wordsworth's work continued to reach large numbers of readers, but it did so through anthologies and volumes of selections that presented him as a lyric poet.

Editors select, it's their job, and they do so usually with the aim of pleasing their own publishers and readers, not to promote the self-image of a dead poet. Thus Wordsworth was readily refashioned as a regional and national writer of lyric verses—which is not the way he would himself have presented his work. The jacket blurb of Stephen Hebron's standard introduction, published in 2000, expresses the familiar commonplaces of today: "Inspired by England's Lake District, William Wordsworth (1770–1850) created some of the best-loved poems of the Romantic Period." This sentence no doubt does sum up the popular image of Wordsworth and his works in recent times, though grossly oversimplifying. (A general introduction is hardly the place for nuance—that's what makes it useful.) The purist or disciple could point out that *Descriptive Sketches* (1793) is about the Swiss Alps; the original *Lyrical Ballads* were set in the West Country; *The Prelude* includes descriptions of Paris, London, and Wales; the *White Doe* (1815) belonged to Yorkshire; *Memorials of a Tour on the Continent* (1820) was set outside the British Isles; and *Yarrow Revisited* (1835) dealt mainly with scenes in Scotland. A cynic might say that besides the "best-loved" poems, Wordsworth wrote hundreds of unloved ones. But the quintessential Wordsworth is identified, for now, by these external features of lyric form and Lake District imagery, in a development of interpretation and publicity that began quite early. A typical illustration from 1866, for example, shows recognizably Lake District scenery (fig. 2).

Victorian publishing cultivated the symbiosis of literature and tourism through guidebooks and travel writing, and so it came about that the association of Wordsworth's name with the Lake District gave his work an accidental advantage. The Lakes had been publicized before Wordsworth moved

THERE WAS A BOY.

The vale where he was born : the Churchyard hangs
Upon a slope above the village-school ;
And there, along that bank, when I have passed
At evening, I believe that oftentimes
A long half-hour together I have stood
Mute—looking at the grave in which he lies !

Fig. 2. "There Was a Boy." Illustration by Birket Foster showing the "Islands of Winander,"
in *Poems of William Wordsworth*, ed. R. A. Willmott (London: Routledge, 1866). Courtesy
of The Thomas Fisher Rare Book Library, University of Toronto.

there, and he himself published a travel guide in 1810, but *literary* tourism on a large scale was a slightly later development.[37] In the 1830s Wordsworth found himself becoming one of the sights. After his death the family plot in Grasmere Churchyard and the Wordsworths' early home, Dove Cottage, took over as places of pilgrimage. By 1911 Eric Robertson could refer to the district without mockery as "Wordsworthshire," and the traffic has not diminished over the past century. Dove Cottage was opened to the public as a museum in 1891 and expanded, over the years, to the museum and library of today, run by the Wordsworth Trust and affiliated with the University of Lancaster; Rydal Mount was purchased by a descendant and opened in 1969. Wordsworth took Lake District names into his poetry, and his name in turn is now plastered all over the Lake District.

One of the key figures in the development of literary tourism was Wordsworth's friend William Howitt, who published a number of extraordinarily successful books about rural England and domestic travel, in most of which Wordsworth plays a significant part, from *The Book of the Seasons* and *The Rural Life of England* in 1831 and 1838, respectively, to the trend-setting *Homes and Haunts of the Most Eminent British Poets* of 1847, which was regularly reprinted for over half a century, leaving its mark in many similarly titled imitators and in a Library of Congress classification heading. *Homes and Haunts* blends biography, criticism, and description—typically, detailed and quite dramatic description of the walks leading to the homes. Though Howitt says of Rydal Mount that "there is, perhaps, no residence in England better known than that of William Wordsworth," for the sake of armchair travelers he describes the approach to and the views from it: "As you advance a mile or more on the road from Ambleside towards Grasmere, a lane overhung with trees turns up to the right, and there, at some few hundred yards from the highway, stands the modest cottage of the poet, elevated on Rydal mount, so as to look out over the surrounding sea of foliage, and to take in a glorious view."[38] And so to the panorama. (But the epithet in the phrase "modest cottage" surely has more to do with the public image of the poet than with the character of the building.)

The original *Homes and Haunts* used wood engravings to illustrate the scenes it described, in line both with the conventions of travel books and with publishing trends of the time. Again, Wordsworth's poetry reaped an accidental advantage, one that would likely have been unwelcome to Wordsworth himself, from the changes in fashion and technology that made pictorial illustration increasingly common and important in the Victorian mass market; film, television, and the Internet continued the process through the twentieth century.[39] Poets work with images. Wordsworth evoked picturesque or sublime landscapes and rural scenes, but typically and deliberately in a generalized way: a rainbow, a lake, a common wildflower, a mountainside. "Natural, and therefore durable," as Johnson observed, such images served his overall purpose of writing for the future as well as for his own time. But it was the ideas that the images conveyed, not the external world itself, that Wordsworth supposed to be imperishable and universally accessible. When he expressed the desire to make verse "deal boldly with substantial things" in *The Prelude,* he meant exactly the opposite of concrete and material objects. Using "substance" in the philosophical sense, he meant spiritual realities that underlie appearances.[40] Though to a scholar the literal-minded representations of mountains, waterfalls, rainbows, and daffodils, everywhere reiterated, miss the point entirely, from the point of view of long-term reputation and commercial success, Wordsworth was fortunate in his decision to settle in the Lakes. School textbooks and the *Norton Anthology* may be able to do without them, but products that keep Wordsworth's name before the general public—coffee-table books, biographies, movies and television series, not to mention mugs and T-shirts—naturally exploit and reinforce this association.

Another important development of Victorian publishing, one that Wordsworth was better able to foresee and to attempt to forestall, was the coming of the freestanding literary biography. Posthumous editions of writers' works traditionally included prefaces introducing the author and disclosing something of his or her circumstances. But within Wordsworth's lifetime, literary biography became a major element in the book market and a key component in authorial fame. This development had been heralded by media attention that dated back at least to the 1770s, when daily newspapers reported the comings and goings of Johnson and Boswell.[41] In the great explosion of periodical literature that coincided with Wordsworth's youth, newspapers and magazines competed with one another for copy, and living writers were as vulnerable to their intrusive curiosity as other public figures. All the major Romantic poets were afflicted by this development; all reacted ambivalently to it. Coleridge composed his own eccentric autobiography partly as a form of self-defense against the image of him disseminated by hack writers— "anonymous critics in reviews, magazines, and news-journals of various name and rank," as he put it in the *Biographia,* and "satirists with or without a name, in verse or prose, or in verse-text aided by prose-comment" to whom, however, he believed that he owed "full two thirds of whatever reputation and publicity I happen to possess."[42]

Wordsworth hated the way in which readers were encouraged to confuse the life with the works; he spoke out most vehemently against this trend in his "Letter to a Friend of Robert Burns," published in 1816. But at the same time, he wrote habitually in the first person and often made a point of affirming personal experience as a source for the subjects of his poems, thus adding authenticity to his work. Not waiting for posthumous assessment, journalists and editors started quite early to tell his life story. The anonymous prefatory "memoir" in Galignani's affordable one-volume collection of Wordsworth's works of 1828, for instance, begins by observing "that Mr Wordsworth's writings are in their very nature and essence a species of auto-biography"— and what they reveal is that he is a worshipper of nature. Then it outlines his family background, education, and domestic circumstances.[43] Since it was obvious that when he died this kind of unwelcome attention would only increase, Wordsworth took steps to limit it. The first freestanding biography of him, the pious official *Memoirs* of 1851, written by his nephew Christopher— which referred to its subject throughout as "the Poet" and tied the events of the life to the composition of the poems—was an exercise in damage control. Yet by its very insistence on the integrity and coherence of Wordsworth's life and work ("the spirit of his poetry was embodied in the life of the Poet"), it may have fostered the personality cult it was intended to prevent.[44]

In biographies and editions, the authorial portrait had long been a desirable feature (think of the Shakespeare First Folio), and in the illustration-obsessed nineteenth century it became essential. Published portraits of Wordsworth are particularly revealing (figs. 3 and 4).[45] The 1851 *Memoirs* deliberately chose the portrait of a benevolent old man by Henry William Pickersgill, with the aim of diverting public attention away from Wordsworth's radical past. It dwells on the older Wordsworth, on his mature judgment, on his status as a Victorian sage. This conscious emphasis set the terms for later discussions even when, in 1916, another biography challenged the official view with the argument that "Wordsworth at his best, in his great years, when he was most truly himself, when he was animated by courage and hope, was a fervent Revolutionist," and provided a different portrait—William Shuter's picture (1798) of an unkempt, rather sardonic-looking young man—to reinforce this new image.[46] By transferring attention to the early years, this biographer, George McLean Harper, and Émile Legouis between them turned the course of Wordsworth's reputation in a new direction. Harper published the story of Annette Vallon and Wordsworth's illegitimate French daughter, Legouis fleshed it out, and both presented it in a way that rather than destroying his moral authority, the incident strengthened it. Wordsworth was thus remade for a youthful, modern, liberal readership. Legouis was chiefly responsible for promoting *The Prelude* as an autobiographical work (though Christopher Wordsworth had also drawn on it freely) and putting it at the center of Wordsworth's writings, the position that it holds in the academy to this day.

Fig. 3. Frontispiece portrait of William Wordsworth from Christopher Wordsworth's *Memoirs of William Wordsworth, Poet-Laureate, D.C.L.* (1851), vol. 1. Courtesy of Special Collections, University of Waterloo Library.

The shift of emphasis to Wordsworth's early years in twentieth-century biographies of the poet and his circle introduced more exciting events, but the controversy itself may have been the best part of the life story as far as his fame is concerned, since it gave everyone something new to talk about. The dispute between the biographers over their two Wordsworths, the young and the old man, extended into the academic studies of the twentieth century—literary history, criticism, and textual scholarship. Are the early versions of Wordsworth's poems better, or the late ones? Does his poetical development show progressive refinement or decline? Was it all downhill for life and works alike after 1805? If so, on what grounds does he keep his place in history?

The academic publications that debate such questions, numerous as they are, are only the tip of an educational iceberg. What was most distinctive about *Lyrical Ballads* when it first appeared was the relative simplicity of the language. Readers loved or hated it, critics commended or attacked it. The words "puerilities" and "childishness" were bandied about. Early on, some-one had the bright idea of giving some of the lyrical ballads to children. In 1801 Lindley Murray included one of Wordsworth's poems, "The Pet Lamb," in his *Introduction to the English Reader,* a selection offered to the youngest

Fig. 4. Frontispiece portrait of
William Wordsworth from
George McLean Harper's
William Wordsworth (1916).
Courtesy of University of
Toronto Libraries.

readers as part of a series that went into scores of editions, many of them printed in the United States. Another schoolbook, John Evans's *Parnassian Garland* of 1807, took up "The Wandering Jew." In 1810 Frederick Mylius's *Poetical Class-Book* used three, one of them "Nutting." By 1817 Coleridge was complaining, in print, that children were *playing at* "Goody Blake and Harry Gill" and "The Idiot Boy."[47] Wordsworth had always seen himself as a teacher (so did others: Leigh Hunt greeted *Peter Bell* in 1819 as "another little didactic horror of Mr. Wordsworth's").[48] In 1831 he gave permission for his work to be used in a classroom anthology produced by his own publisher, Moxon, though he was later vexed to find that Joseph Hine's collection consisted entirely of Wordsworth verses. As soon as his early work went out of copyright, illustrated editions for children began to multiply across the full spectrum from luxury to economy, and they are still being produced today.[49] This development—the presentation of Wordsworth as a wholesome influence on children through textbooks and gift books—anticipated the emphasis on his lyric poems in adult anthologies and selected editions later on.

In terms of its share of the book market, the adult audience for new poetry has now shrunk back so far as to be almost invisible, and it was shrinking already by the time of Wordsworth's death. For the last century or so, widespread recognition of the writings of any dead poet has depended on exposure in youth through the schools, where particular works become shared knowledge and thus a form of cultural capital. Wordsworth's reputation benefited greatly from the fact that his work, judged safe for children, was firmly rooted in the school systems of the English-speaking world by the time of the First World War, thanks in part to the active advocacy of Matthew Arnold.[50] The introductory essay from Arnold's selection of Wordsworth's poems in the "Golden Treasury" series, reprinted in the second series of his *Essays in Criticism,* has come down to us in editions of Arnold's work. In it he describes Wordsworth's high reputation at Cambridge in the 1830s, asserts that his greatest work was in the lyrics and not in the long poems, and declares him one of the "chief glories of English literature."[51] Wordsworth's influence on Arnold, and Arnold's influence in turn on the forming of the literary curriculum, are well known. Not satisfied with the presumption of indirect effect, though, Ian Reid has recently made a strong case for Wordsworth himself as the true progenitor of English studies, the "shaper of institutionalized cultural practices" and the framer of a set of "critical assumptions through which Shakespeare and all other writers are normally evaluated and interpreted."[52] Perhaps he goes too far; but Wordsworthian poetry and Wordsworthian ideas continue to be at least congenial to educators, for reasons that we tend to take for granted. The work is technically complex, it's serious, there's plenty to choose from, it raises interesting problems to discuss, it's generally improving but nonsectarian, it rewards reflection. At the postsecondary level, which includes the most dependable set of readers year after year, Wordsworth still dominates the widely used North American textbook anthology, the *Norton Anthology of English Literature,* now in its ninth edition, as well as Duncan Wu's comparable British anthology, *Romanticism.*

The undisputed prominence of Wordsworth—his work and his way of thinking—in educational circles may have arisen from inherent qualities of the verse, but it also has much to do with the way Wordsworth became cast as a leader in the literary history of his age, and that in turn has to do with the controversy surrounding him and his closest associates before 1820. The early, unwarranted, but memorable lumping together of the "Lakers" as a supposedly radical literary movement meant that when one name appeared the others went with it, as Coleridge complained in the *Biographia:* "my literary friends are never under the water-fall of criticism, but I must be wet through with the spray; yet how came the torrent to descend upon *them*?"[53] The three names— Coleridge, Wordsworth, Southey—thus closely linked helped for a time to keep one another afloat, as they echoed and reechoed through memoirs and reviews of the period, and they do so still through group biographies and documentary or pseudo-documentary films such as Julien Temple's *Pandaemonium* of 2001. Wordsworth was portrayed as the leader not only of this supposed rebel sect in literature but also, by extension, of what came to be called—much later, by a strange and convoluted process—Romanticism, or the Romantic movement. A late addition, really an afterthought to European theories of Romanticism, the label appeared as a tool of periodization in the literary histories of the late nineteenth century and thus found its way into the curricula of newly formed departments of English.[54] David Perkins explains that it was around or shortly before 1900 that a "decisive break" took place in the way the literature of the period was defined: "Before then there was a period when the movement might be seen . . . as inspired by the French Revolution or, with the Pre-Raphaelites, as essentially apolitical. The triumph of the latter view coincided with the bestowing of the name Romanticism."[55] But both before and after that moment of naming, when politics had been considered fundamental and when it came to be considered so again, as well as in the period of aestheticization, Wordsworth was seen as the leader. Throughout the twentieth century, as Andrew Franta observes, in criticism of the Romantics, "it is not too much to say that 'Wordsworth' and 'Romanticism' are interchangeable."[56]

To sum up, the fact that poems by Wordsworth continue to be read—they have endured, to use his own word—and that more than two centuries after the first publication of *Lyrical Ballads,* his name is as widely known as that of any of his literary contemporaries, is due to a concatenation of circumstances, most of which Wordsworth himself could not have foreseen, most of which he would have objected to if he had foreseen them, and most of which had little to do with the communication of eternal truths. Besides the serious study that he hoped for, his works derived accidental benefits from their variety and from the size of the corpus; from their visualizability, or susceptibility to pictorial illustration; from their supposed suitability for children; from discoveries about the author's early life that his descendants would have preferred to conceal; and from his association with the popular Lakes, the "Lakers," tourism, and the rise of literary tourism. Serious study alone, almost entirely confined to the universities, would never have been enough to achieve the cultural prominence that his works have maintained for at least a century.

Wordsworth's Theories

An overview of the history of the reception of Wordsworth's work offers little support for his theory of the autonomous isolated genius who generates works of overwhelming intrinsic merit and wins over readers one at a time until the enlightened audience achieves critical mass. On the contrary, it reveals a process of regular reinterpretation involving, at every turn, the vital initiative of other agents. Perhaps we are affected by Wordsworthian notions of the heroic author when we describe his works as being debated, reprinted, collected, edited, illustrated, excerpted, anthologized, adopted, canonized, and so forth. We use the passive voice, which seems to imply that they did it on their own or that some supernatural power watched over them. Actually these activities required human intervention that was not the author's and that was beyond his control. In their wars among themselves, hostile and friendly contemporary reviewers chose to make an issue of Wordsworth's poetic strengths and weaknesses, thus fostering debate and the formation of critical parties. Somebody at Longman, Moxon, Macmillan, and Oxford committed those firms to publishing many editions of his work and of related writings. William Howitt undertook the expeditions that he describes so engagingly in *Homes and Haunts*. Christopher Wordsworth wrote the official biography that came in due course to be challenged by Harper and Legouis. Francis Turner Palgrave and Arnold championed Wordsworth wherever they saw an opportunity— Palgrave, for instance, not only in *The Golden Treasury* but also in Moxon's Miniature Poets series and in his *Children's Treasury of Lyrical Poetry*, designed for children between the ages of about nine and sixteen, which contains more poems by Wordsworth than by anyone else. The tally of influential historians, scholarly editors, biographers, and commentators from the late nineteenth century to the recent past working on his behalf is impressive: leaders include William Angus Knight, George Saintsbury, Ernest De Selincourt, Helen Darbishire, Mary Moorman, Geoffrey Hartman, Robert Woof, Stephen Gill, Stephen Maxfield Parrish, and Jonathan Wordsworth. All of which is only to say, contradicting Wordsworth's opinion and stating what now seems obvious, that other people have played and must always have played a crucial role in creating the taste by which he is enjoyed. Mediators stand between the creative writer and the receptive reader.

The theory of audiences in the "Essay, Supplementary" stands up to the test of history better than the theory of authorship, although there too the outcome was not what Wordsworth predicted. With Horace and Milton, he planned to start from a small audience, fit though few. He seems to have expected that the number of "fit" readers would increase over time and the number of misguided ones diminish, though he held out no hope that "errors and prejudices" would ever be completely eliminated.[57] In analyzing sectors of his own readership, he astutely defined a normal state of affairs in the world of letters, that is, the existence not of a single cohesive audience but of disparate groups in occasional fluctuating alliance with one another.[58] How that mixed readership was ever to turn into a more "correct" consensus is not clear, and in any case, that is not what happened. In absolute numbers, Wordsworth's readership no doubt has vastly increased since 1815, as populations have grown and literacy spread, but the proportion of serious students, whom he identified as his ideal readers, to other groups is surely still about the same (and even they can hardly be said to have reached consensus). His cultural prominence depends less on them than on a plurality of what are now called niche markets, groups that are drawn to him and his works for different reasons and in different ways. "Nichification" is a new word for an old phenomenon.

One surprising consequence of considering Wordsworth's afterlife in these broad terms is that we find that it provides a stronger recommendation for Johnson's assisted model of authorship than for his own. Wordsworth repeatedly declared that he did not care about posthumous fame, but he seems to have meant fame for himself personally. He made great efforts to ensure that his works would continue to be read, and he could hardly have improved on the outcome had he purposely followed Johnson's advice from the start. Like Samuel Butler as Johnson described him in *The Lives of the Poets,* Wordsworth strove to be an original thinker relying on ideas "generated in his own mind" for his primary materials. From the negative example of Cowley, he could have learned not to be satisfied with writing in whatever the currently fashionable style was. Like Johnson's Shakespeare, he represented characters who were "natural, and therefore durable" in language that struck a middle way between the polite and the vulgar and that was not drawn from books. Like Johnson himself, he was not squeamish about saying that he wanted to earn money by writing. As Johnson would have predicted, most of the customary rewards of fame came to him in his lifetime: Johnson, like Horace, thought that the true poet was likely to have a following among his contemporaries even if he was not universally admired. And over time, the works of Wordsworth proved to please many—whether the many were critically astute or not, and whether they wanted to be instructed (to be students) or not. "Readers of every class, from the critic to the waiting-maid" found something to satisfy them. But Wordsworth did not operate in isolation in his lifetime, he did not lack recognition, and as Johnson had repeatedly pointed out in his accounts of Wordsworth's predecessors, after his death the works depended on other champions—biographers, critics, publishers, and fans of many kinds—to keep up the momentum of fame.

We know that more than five thousand writers published at least one volume of original (that is, new) poetry between 1770 and 1835, but from their ranks we recognize few names and are acquainted with the works of fewer still.[59] The number even of those few shrinks steadily as some are squeezed out to make room in the collective consciousness (and curriculum) for classics of later periods. Merit is only part of the reason—arguably a quite small part, since the proportion of survivors to nonsurvivors is vanishingly small and since we keep thinking that we have discovered authors who deserved to survive but did not, such as Blake, John Clare, and a small posse of women writers who were admired in their time but spurned by the gatekeeper critics of the late Victorian period. Most of them did not have enough backing, commercial or critical, to earn posthumous recognition. Those who had achieved a threshold level of renown in their own time, however, upon their deaths generally passed the preliminary hurdles of the collective edition, the new reviews, the retrospective appraisals, and the first proper biography. But the literary world is never stable, and some of them stumbled at the next hurdle or the one after that. The rewards of fame are also prognosticators. Was there a public monument? Did a society emerge to look after the writer's interests? (The first author so honored appears to have been Burns in 1801.)[60] Is there a museum or shrine? What about translations and adaptations? Was the work picked up by an important anthology or included in a prestigious publishers' series? Who celebrates the anniversaries, and how? Sharing similar literary environments and subject to the same rites of passage, authors of the Romantic period grew farther and farther apart in succeeding generations, in ways that seem disproportionate to the merits of their work.

When Wordsworth lamented that his work was not popular (as he did repeatedly), he appears to have meant that his sales fell far below those of Scott and Byron; in a letter of 1833 he corrected "popular" to "fashionable" and named those poets specifically.[61] But the success of first Scott and then Byron as poets was a publishing phenomenon of an unprecedented kind. To put the growth of Wordsworth's reputation (and sales) into perspective, and for a further test of contrasting models of writing and the desire for immortality, we can consider the more readily comparable cases of George Crabbe and Robert Southey.

Crabbe and Wordsworth

George Crabbe makes an instructive comparison precisely because his is not an extreme case. A notable success in his lifetime, he did not fall into oblivion and his works did not go out of print soon after his death. On the contrary, after a distinguished career marked by both critical esteem across party lines and better sales than Wordsworth's, his literary afterlife fell into a pattern that is like Wordsworth's on a smaller scale.[62] Wordsworth himself, who as a teenager had been impressed by Crabbe's poem *The Village,* predicted that Crabbe's writings would "last, from their combined merits as Poetry and Truth full as long as any thing that has been expressed in Verse since they first made their appearance"—and although he did so in a letter to the bereaved family, and the promise of survival through the work is the common currency of compliment in the writing fraternity, the wording is careful and there is no reason to doubt his sincerity.[63]

Crabbe's son George wrote an excellent life-and-letters biography to accompany the posthumous collected edition that Crabbe's publisher, Murray, brought out in eight volumes in 1834 and kept in print in one format or another until 1901, at which point Oxford took over responsibility for Crabbe's texts (fig. 5). Murray's editions generally included engraved scenes from the life or the works as a visual adornment, and there were at least two later illustrated editions, one in the luxury Classical Library series published by Charles Daly about 1845, the other by Blackwood in 1873: Crabbe had the visualizability that was so important in the Victorian marketplace. Eminent authors testified to Crabbe's impact, from Byron, Scott, Austen, and Wordsworth in their day to figures as diverse as Thomas Hardy, Ezra Pound, E. M. Forster, and Benjamin Britten later.[64] Once in a while, an eminent critic took him up as part of a larger project: F. R. Leavis championed him as a master of the short story in a few pages of *Revaluation* (1936), for example, and M. H. Abrams included him in the study he made of writers addicted to opium, *The Milk of Paradise* (1934). He had his Galignani edition in his lifetime and his French life-and-works biography (by René Louis Huchon, a student and follower of Legouis) early in the twentieth century. Like Wordsworth, Crabbe was associated with a particular region: his birthplace, Aldeburgh in Suffolk, treated him as a local hero and saw to the celebration of centenaries—ironically enough, since he had been miserable there.[65] His name appeared regularly in anthologies and literary histories, scholarly editions were periodically revised in the course of the twentieth century, and he maintains a place in university textbooks to this day, albeit in the scrum of minor authors subject to the pressures of time and the whims of instructors. But his standing overall declined even as Wordsworth's grew—almost, it seems, in inverse relation to Wordsworth's, and perhaps for good reason.

Wordsworth and Crabbe exercised a degree of reciprocal influence on one another and have always invited comparison. *The Village* (1783) staked Crabbe's claim much as *Lyrical Ballads* did Wordsworth's. Samuel Johnson approved it as "original, vigorous, and elegant," making some suggestions for revision but declaring that even without them "I do not doubt of Mr. Crabbe's success."[66] Crabbe's originality was both literary and ideological: he proposed to write about the lives of the working poor without pastoral

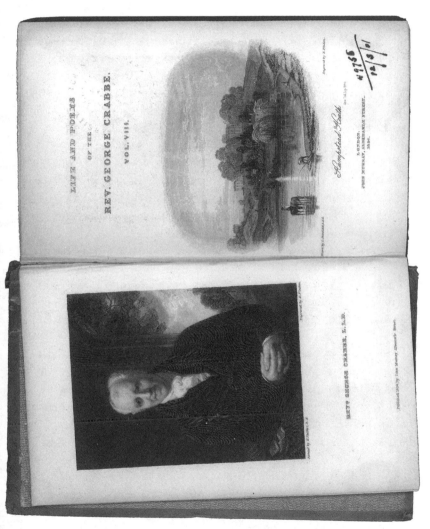

Fig. 5. Frontispiece portrait and engraved title page from Murray's 1834 edition of George Crabbe's *Poetical Works*, vol. 8, *Life and Poems of the Rev. George Crabbe*. Courtesy of University of Toronto Libraries.

embellishments, and to expose social evils that stemmed from poverty. "I paint the cot," he wrote, "as truth will paint it, and as bards will not."[67] He turned the same unflinching eye on the harsh coastal landscape that offered little support for human life, and concluded that village life was in reality "a life of pain."[68] But after a few professional false starts, Crabbe became a clergyman, and family life and other interests and responsibilities halted his poetic career for more than twenty years.

When he returned to it in 1807 with a volume of *Poems* that included the new "Parish Register," and still more so with *The Borough* in 1810 and *Tales* in 1812, he took up his original project with fresh vigor and with an engaging new narrative dimension. This work focused on the stories of strongly individualized characters—based, he said, on real-life figures—who at the same time stood for recognizable types: the rapacious lawyer, the separated lovers, the brutal master, and so on. Readers lapped them up. Walter Scott (who would quote from Crabbe frequently in the Waverley novels) told Crabbe that his poems were the Scott family's regular evening entertainment, their twelve-year-old daughter proving especially good at reading them aloud.[69] They must have been well suited to such occasions, for they are various, dramatic, thought-provoking, moving—and just about the right length, each work broken into bite-sized parts called "Letters" or "Tales" or sections of a parish register. The narrative voice is serious (though with mild humor sometimes), calm, and compassionate. Scott anonymously paid tribute to Crabbe as "our English Juvenal" in *Waverley*, but Crabbe's satire in this phase of his development was much gentler than Juvenal's, and he made it clear that his moral purpose was less to expose social follies or evils than to awaken sympathetic understanding by demonstrating that the same feelings operate in all classes. Readers who want a quick introduction to Crabbe's work or a reminder of his style may turn to the readings recommended in the appendix.

By this time Wordsworth was also writing seriously and empathetically (though also from a certain distance) about country people in inhospitable surroundings, so reviewers routinely contrasted them. Crabbe was perceived and publicized as the poet of "realism" as opposed to Wordsworth's "imagination"— realism in several senses, including a pragmatic attitude, everyday subjects with real-life originals, absence of grandeur, and masses of precise concrete details, especially ugly details. (William Hazlitt commented that Crabbe "describes the interior of a cottage like a person sent there to distrain for rent.")[70] In an 1808 issue of the *Edinburgh Review*, Jeffrey used a favorable review of Crabbe's *Poems* as part of his campaign against the Lakers, "the Wordsworths, and the Southeys, and Coleridges, and all that misguided fraternity," and he continued to offer support over the years—albeit sometimes qualified support, when he thought Crabbe's commitment to sordid details had gone too far.[71] Writing for the opposition, Hazlitt likewise persisted, brilliantly, in his attacks.[72] Which is only to say that the world of the reviews was highly partisan and that Wordsworth and Crabbe were controversial writers.

Both were gifted, both original, both controversial, both influential, but one became a famous name and the other did not. Why not? It is always impossible to give a simple answer to this question: there are too many variables. As one rueful writer has observed, "There is a randomness in the operation of the laws of fame that approaches the chaotic."[73] But they are not absolutely chaotic, and the framework established earlier for Wordsworth can bring out some patterns in the seemingly random.

The writers' names themselves might have something to do with it. There never has been an adjective for Crabbe. What would it be: Crabbish? Crabbist? Crabbean? The fact is not as trivial as it seems. It cannot mean that there is no set of features identified with Crabbe's name, for the combination of relaxed heroic couplets, minute descriptions of village life, and personal histories is distinctively his. It suggests rather that Crabbe was one of a kind, not the leader of any movement to which his name could be attached as Wordsworth's was (whether accurately or not); he was not part of a band that gathered strength from the union. His literary associations as the protégé of Edmund Burke and Johnson were, if anything, of the wrong kind and worked against him, since they cast him as a follower, not a leader. He was handicapped by his almost exclusive use of heroic couplets, a form that was already well past its heyday when he started out. Furthermore, while Crabbe had a mode of his own, he had only the one, unlike Wordsworth who experimented with new genres and built up a large and varied body of work that could be reconfigured in many ways. When the long poems that they both counted on began to lose ground to prose fiction, Crabbe could not be recast as a writer of lyrics. Though his work was represented by extracts in early Victorian anthologies designed for an adult audience, it seems never to have been thought suitable for young children—Scott's twelve-year-old daughter notwithstanding—and that important audience was closed to him. (It's understandable: *The Borough* deals matter-of-factly with such grown-up concerns as drunkenness, prostitution, wife beating, sexual sadism, and sibling incest.) For all these reasons, his work lost its wide appeal and became a historical curiosity among nonacademic readers or, at best, a specialized and eccentric taste—and fame does not flourish through isolated enthusiasts.

As far as the general public was concerned, Crabbe's reputation suffered from other, nonliterary disadvantages. His family gave up its stake in his works, his homes were demolished, and Suffolk was never as popular a tourist destination as the Lake District—though there is an entry for him in Howitt's *Homes and Haunts*. In spite of the fact that his life had great potential for a biographer (humble origins, vicissitudes, eminent friends, opium, a strange late-life engagement), no legend grew up around him, let alone a personality cult. Crabbe was elderly when he made his second start as a poet, and the existing portraits (such as the one in fig. 5) show him only as a man in his sixties. Though biographers periodically attempt to revive interest in him, they struggle with the image of an old man working in an outdated form, a holdover from another century, an anomaly in a revolutionary age.

The generation gap proved a serious problem also for canon makers and literary historians, and hence in due course for the university programs and academic publishing so crucial to the survival of older literature in the twentieth century—an environment in which Wordsworth flourished but Crabbe did not. The earliest collections, some published as preliminary assessments of living contemporaries, included writers on the basis of some degree of renown within a simple time frame. John Watkins and Frederic Shoberl's *Biographical Dictionary of the Living Authors of Great Britain and Ireland* (1816), for instance, listed Blake ("an eccentric but very ingenious artist"), Robert Bloomfield, the early Byron, Crabbe, Maria Edgeworth, Leigh Hunt, Southey, and Wordsworth (as leader of "a particular school of poetry, the characteristic of which is simplicity"), but not Austen, who published anonymously, and—presumably for the same reason—Scott only as a poet. Others added genre as a criterion. J. W. Lake's remarkable editions of British poets, published in Paris in the 1820s, presented Byron, Scott, and Thomas Moore in separate volumes as the greatest poets of the age, with a supplementary volume added in 1828 to accommodate the second string: "Crabbe, Wilson, Coleridge, Wordsworth, Rogers, Campbell, Miss Landon, Barton, Montgomery, Southey, Hogg, Barry Cornwall, and Others." These named poets are described in biographical-critical introductions and represented by generous selections from their works. Clare, Shelley, Keats, and Felicia Hemans are among the "Others" represented by a handful of poems each, without commentary.[74] Robert Chambers's *Cyclopaedia of English Literature* (1843–44) attempted rudimentary periodization, writers of "1780 to the present" being bundled together in groups by genre; but later revisions shifted the date boundaries and added "spirit of the age" labels to the separate periods, with the result that in the final revision of 1901–3, "the Nineteenth Century" was defined as the era of a "Renascence of Wonder in Poetry" and Crabbe was excluded. When the label "Romantic" finally took hold in histories and textbooks at the very end of the nineteenth century, whatever it was taken to mean— anticlassical, anti-Enlightenment, neomedieval, sublime, nature-worshipping, idealistic or individualistic—Crabbe did not fit in. He was not radical enough, not innovative enough, not complicated enough, not Wordsworthian enough.

Crabbe's Pragmatic Model of Authorship

Given all the strikes against him, it might seem that Crabbe's limited success in the long term was overdetermined; it may be surprising that his works have survived even to the extent that they have, maintaining their place in the histories and attracting advocates from time to time. His attitude toward fame, also, could hardly have been in greater contrast to Wordsworth's. Did that make a difference? What was the relationship between his expectations for his work and the actual fate of it? At a pivotal point in his life, Crabbe had been rescued from impending disaster by Burke and Johnson. It is not surprising that his notions about authorship and immortality were much the same as Johnson's, particularly in his awareness of the social role of mediators.

In his first successful work, *The Library*, published anonymously in 1781, Crabbe invoked the ideal of immortal fame only to reject it: though it might be commonplace to think of libraries as "the tombs of such as cannot die," the view of the speaker is that books are subject to fashion, the earnest works of earlier generations being for the most part completely disregarded in a more frivolous age, and the authors thus—though he does not put it quite this way—doubly dead. Books are, rather, "the lasting mansions of the dead," physical memorials but empty monuments.[75] Crabbe cared about his literary reputation but did not raise his sights much above his own time. From the start, he wrote frankly for money and aimed to please his contemporaries. (When he defined his goals, he wrote invariably in terms of pleasure, delight, or amusement, not instruction—though as with Johnson, it might be that he took it for granted that readers should learn something.) When *The Library* was well received, he ventured *The Village*. When he decided after a long absence to publish again because he had sons to send to university, he was sufficiently encouraged by the response of the public to carry on in the same vein. So he said in a private letter to Scott (who charmingly replied by confessing that he had written *The Lay of the Last Minstrel* to pay for a horse), and public statements in prefaces and dedications express the same practical approach to literary work.[76]

Even as a very young man, Crabbe believed that he could not succeed as a writer without enlisting the aid of more powerful sponsors. His son's biography quotes Crabbe's own account of the reasoning that led him to appeal to Burke, in a passage that shows that he had faith in himself and also in the contemporary readers who were to judge it. "He did not so far mistake as to believe that any name can give lasting reputation to an undeserving work; but he was fully persuaded, that it must be some very meritorious and extraordinary performance, such as he had not the vanity to suppose himself capable of producing, that would become popular, without the *probat* of some well-known and distinguished character."[77] For Crabbe, poetry was not a calling but a sideline; his ambitions were modest, and he accepted the prevailing order in the publishing world. Not for him the narrative of neglect or the extreme self-reliance that could either spurn public approval or secure it on the writer's own terms. He sought out powerful support and regularly submitted drafts to other writers for advice. In gestures of gratitude that doubled as publicity—celebrity endorsements, we might say—he used the dedications and prefaces of his later works, from the 1807 *Poems* onward, to thank his aristocratic patrons and literary advocates individually by name.[78] (This practice his sons continued when they dedicated the memoir of his life and the "Posthumous Tales," the two substantial sections of previously unpublished work in the collected edition of 1834, to William Lisle Bowles and Samuel Rogers, respectively.)

Looking beyond his small circle of friendly judges, he used the preface to the *Tales* of 1812 also to address his larger, unknown audience, expressing appreciation for its reception of his work and responding specifically to the advice of an anonymous reviewer, which he said he agreed with but could not accept. The tone is respectful and reasonable. In explaining at length why he could not raise the level of his writing and produce an epic poem, Crabbe put the case for his kind of poetry, that is, realistic narrative designed to appeal to "plain sense and sober judgment" in the traditions of Chaucer, Dryden, and Pope (not Spenser or Milton). Thus nailing his colors to the mast, he expressed the conviction that, at its best, such poetry could have the same kind of positive psychological effect upon readers as the pleasurable fictions of romance. Let the poem be properly conducted, he writes, and "the occurrences actually copied from life will have the same happy effect as the inventions of a creative fancy" that arouse sympathy without causing pain.[79]

On his death, Crabbe left a volume of unpublished tales for the benefit of his family (as Wordsworth left *The Prelude*), observing shrewdly but not unkindly that posthumous productions are often valued "partly as they are old acquaintances, and in part because there can be no more of them."[80] Crabbe understood audiences: his tales did well in one sector of the middle-class market, "a certain Set of Readers for the most part probably of a peculiar Turn and Habit," as he told Scott; he did not aspire to the universal appeal of Scott's verse romances.[81] He seems to have been pleasantly surprised and was certainly content with the level of popularity that he achieved in his lifetime;

long-term success was more than he hoped for. His limited ambitions do not appear to have constrained him or to have compromised his literary integrity. On the contrary, not having pinned his hopes on posterity might even have freed him to write as he did on topics of local urgency, such as the housing of the poor and the treatment of the insane.

Robert Southey

Southey, unlike Crabbe, *is* an extreme case, a byword for posthumous failure that seems all the more pathetic—or ironic, or ludicrous—in light of his aggressive pursuit of success. He wholeheartedly endorsed the heroic model of authorship, and from the point of view of his contemporaries was as likely a prospect for immortality as Wordsworth, his fellow Laker, whose name is permanently linked with his. Jeffrey's attacks on Wordsworth actually started with his review of Southey's *Thalaba* in 1802.[82] The public lives of Wordsworth and Southey followed a similar path, and their personal histories were intertwined both in the periodical reports of the time and in memoirs and biographies later. Their career paths, too, were similar. A favorable response to early works in the 1790s—Southey's *Joan of Arc* and Wordsworth's *Lyrical Ballads,* both with significant contributions from Coleridge— encouraged them to persevere as poets, but after that promising start they suffered mixed reviews and poor sales in a midcareer slump before achieving widespread recognition. Both were controversial figures, partly for political reasons as they turned their backs on the radicalism of their youth, and partly for literary ones as innovators in poetry. Wordsworth followed Southey as poet laureate. Southey's poems sold markedly better than Wordsworth's (at about the level of Crabbe's, nowhere near Scott's and Byron's), though neither of them ever enjoyed the degree of popularity or the financial rewards they hoped for.[83]

Practically all his life, Southey had his eye on eternal laurels. At the age of thirteen, according to his autobiographical memoirs (themselves a sign of sanguine expectations), he concluded a long poem with a dream vision of the poetic Elysium in which he was about to join "Homer, Virgil, Tasso, Spenser, Camoens, and Milton."[84] Before he was twenty he was advising a friend to take Pope as proof that it was perfectly possible to earn both financial independence and fame by writing: "Popes [*sic*] abilities were not above comparison. . . . Chuse either epic or a metrical romance, and in the intervals exercise yourself in the lower ranks for with us lyrics are very subordinate."[85] This was certainly his own program, as he dashed off short poems for newspapers and then later turned out reviews, editions, and translations for a livelihood but protected a block of time each day to work on the major original work that was meant to bring him lasting fame.

Southey's long, fantastical narrative poems were variously described on their title pages as epics, romances, and tragedies; we might classify some of them as historical fictions (*Joan of Arc, Roderick the Last of the Goths*) and others as adventure fantasies. Some reviewers declared him better than Milton (who "astonishes the head," whereas Southey "touches the heart") or Wordsworth (who seems remote from other human beings, whereas Southey excels "in the development of character, and in the expression of the tender affections.")[86] In the manner of the day, the poems were backed up by pages and pages of learned footnotes, but the stories themselves are full of action, lavish description, and extreme situations; they often include warrior women and sometimes wizards. In the nineteenth century they might have lent themselves to adaptation as melodramas or operas, and in the twentieth as action movies or role-playing games, but they never caught on in that way.[87] When they were new, they sold their two or three editions but then went dormant. For a time, when he found that poetry didn't pay and he could hardly afford to indulge in it, Southey thought of shifting his energies to writing history; eventually he juggled the two, so that toward the end of his life he said he felt confident that he had done enough to ensure his eternal reward for either.[88] An appropriate sample from *Roderick* is listed in the appendix.

In 1815–16, about when Wordsworth was writing the "Essay, Supplementary to the Preface," and when his own career as a writer of epics was effectively over, Southey was especially preoccupied with the difficulties of reconciling contemporary and future fame and the likelihood that they were inherently incompatible, as Wordsworth said, in which case the writer whose heart was set on longevity would have to give up on the present. "I am perfectly certain," Southey told his brother, "that great immediate popularity can only be obtained by those faults which fall in with the humour of the times, and which are, of course, ultimately fatal to the poems that contain them."[89] From another remark of about the same time, it is clear that for him as for Wordsworth—probably they spurred one another on—the rejection of contemporary society was not just a professional calculation about the instability of fashion, but had moral and spiritual significance. Literature and religion alike reward the unworldly, Southey wrote: "I have taken especial care to make it known, that a faith in hereafter is as necessary for the intellectual as for the moral character, and that to the man of letters (as well as the Christian) the *present* forms but the slightest portion of his existence. He who would leave any durable monument behind him, must live in the past and look to the future. The poets of old scrupled not to say this; and who is there who is not delighted with these passages, whenever time has set his seal upon the prophecy which they contain?"[90]

Thus the Horatian monument met Christian renunciation—though not complete renunciation, since Southey still aspired to fame in this world, albeit posthumously. In public pronouncements as well as in private letters that he foresaw would be published one day, Southey presented himself as alien in spirit to his own time. A melancholy lyric, still popular enough to be offered in greeting cards and often used to sum up his life, "My days among the dead are past" (meaning "passed"), ends thus, with a flourish of faith: "My hopes are with the dead; anon / My place with them will be, / And I with them shall travel on / Thro' all Futurity; / Yet leaving here a name, I trust, / That will not perish in the dust."[91]

Recognition and Rejection

No one could have done more than Southey did, in a practical way, to ensure that his name would not perish.[92] He picked a biographer when he was barely in his thirties. He worked sporadically on an autobiography, believing that "there can be no doubt I shall be sufficiently talked of when I am gone."[93] In his sixties he preemptively edited his poetic works in ten volumes, thus asserting control over the texts themselves, many of which were revised for the occasion, while at the same time defining the body of work and his preferred chronological arrangement. He reprinted everything he had published without omission, he said, partly to frustrate the pirates and partly because he had no regrets: he'd never written a line he now wished he'd blotted out "for any compunctious reason."[94]

This late-life edition had two further significant benefits. It established a new period of copyright, and it gave Southey an opportunity to forge or correct his public image through the prefaces that he wrote for every volume. (In the third volume, for instance, he carefully set out his version of the circumstances that led to his being offered the poet laureateship after Scott had declined it.) The first paragraph in the first preface is, like Wordsworth's "Essay, Supplementary," a proud declaration of authorial independence in which Southey claims to have already achieved a reputation "equal to my wishes," without ever having stooped to "accommodating myself to the taste or fashion of the times." He presents himself as an independent spirit, a man living a retired life, "communing with my own heart, and taking that course which upon mature consideration seemed best to myself."[95] His attitude throughout these prefaces is defiant, not defensive, and the tone dignified. He reprints his early radical verse although he no longer has a high opinion of its literary qualities: drawing a parallel between himself and a seventeenth-century predecessor, Sir William D'Avenant, he predicts that posterity will be interested even in his juvenilia because of his eminence ("characteristic memorials of one who held no inconsiderable place in the literature of his own times") and because of the light the early, slighter poems shed on his greater works.[96]

Southey's authorial confidence was a mixed blessing. On one hand, it presumably kept him going, protected his self-esteem when he came under attack, and drew others to him as a leader. The adjective "Southeyan" emerged in his lifetime as a word for a style or set of characteristics associated with him and his followers. His name inevitably appeared in contemporary lists of the top ten living poets in the competitive 1810s and 1820s—though not always among the top five, which tended to divide along party lines. William St. Clair includes him among the eight poets who represented "the consensus choice of a broad range of opinion for half a century."[97] There is some evidence that his work was considered suitable for children: Southey rejoiced in the publication of a selection of his work for schools, by Moxon, on the model of the editions for Wordsworth, and a resourceful children's publisher brought out a prose version of some of the stories from *Thalaba* and *Kehama* as *Stories of the Magicians* in 1887 (fig. 6), but in both cases there appears to have been only one edition before the era of print on demand.[98]

Southey earned some of the same forms of recognition as Scott and Byron enjoyed, though on a smaller scale: there were a few translations, offshore collections and reprints (including a Galignani), abridgments, and pictorial interpretations during his lifetime; some extracts or shorter poems found their way into anthologies. He did get his French biography, by Jean Raimond, but not until 1968. The two literary giants, Scott and Byron, are the contemporaries he is properly compared to, all three of them writers of strictly "Romantic" verse narratives according to the terminology of the time—unlike Wordsworth. Both Scott and Byron expressed great admiration for his poetry or rather, in Byron's case, for *some* of his poetry. Scott generously assured Southey that Southey was the better poet, while he (Scott) was only temporarily more popular. Byron told his fiancée, "I think Southey's Roderick as near perfection as poetry can be—which considering how I dislike that school I wonder at—however so it is—if he had never written anything else he might safely stake his fame on the last of the Goths."[99]

On the other hand, Southey's assurance irritated reviewers even more than Byron's flaunting of his peerage, and it positively invited hostility or ridicule, especially after he became poet laureate. Jeffrey's attack on *The Lay of the Laureate* in 1816, one of many, claimed that Southey wrote "rather worse than any Laureate before him," filling his public poems with "praises of the

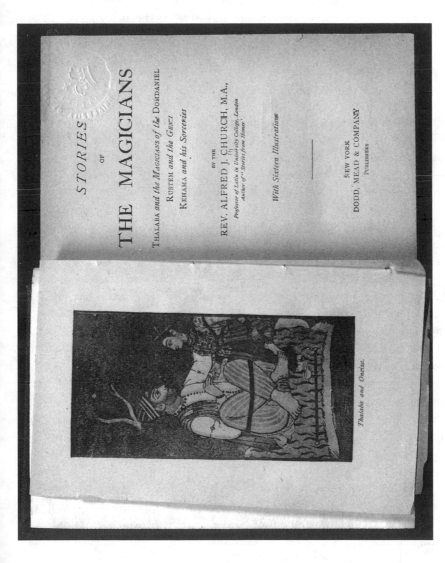

Fig. 6. Frontispiece and title page from Alfred J. Church's *Stories of the Magicians* (1887), which includes prose versions of Southey's *Thalaba the Destroyer* and *The Curse of Kehama*, for children. Courtesy of University of Toronto Libraries.

author himself, and his works, and his laurel; notices of his various virtues and studies; puffs of the productions he is preparing for the press, and anticipations of the fame which he is to reap by their means, from a less ungrateful age."[100] Southey made powerful enemies, Byron undoubtedly the most damaging among them, with both Jeffrey and Hazlitt (who had been on opposite sides where Crabbe was concerned) not far behind, in the highly partisan publishing world of their day. It's one thing to agree that there is no such thing as bad publicity and that controversy feeds fame, another to cope with the fact that after two centuries, Byron's jokes at Southey's expense—unremitting from *English Bards and Scotch Reviewers* in 1809 to the *Vision of Judgment* and *Don Juan* a decade and more later—are still remembered and quoted when Southey's poems are not. Byron's fame during his lifetime and for a long time after his death eclipsed that of all his rivals. His admirers easily adopted his antipathies, with the consequence that, as Southey's sympathetic biographer Geoffrey Carnall observes in the *Oxford Dictionary of National Biography*, Southey's reputation has never recovered from Byron's public ridicule.

Lukewarm support from his friends and fellow poets may have done almost as much as the direct attacks of enemies to undermine Southey's reputation. The only one who gave unstinting praise seems to have been Walter Savage Landor, and Landor was a notorious contrarian.[101] Coleridge and Wordsworth spoke up for Southey but glossed over his poetry. In the *Biographia*, Coleridge defended his personal and professional qualities. Wordsworth's letters more often than not express reservations about Southey's verse, while commending his prose and his good citizenship. Damning with faint praise, Wordsworth declared Southey a master of prose, and by the time he did so, it had become the common theme. Even Byron and Hazlitt gave him that.[102] Being a master of prose was hardly a threat to other poets. Chambers's *Cyclopaedia*, first published shortly after Southey's death, observed regretfully that "few authors have written so much and so well, with so little real popularity, as Mr. Southey." The pick of the prose, it said, was his little *Life of Nelson*; its general assessment of the major poems was that they were already outdated, "unsuited to the taste of the present generation."[103] This early overview would be echoed in reference books and literary histories ever after. The body of Southey's work was voluminous and various, the long poems good enough to have repaid continued attention—as Byron's tribute and as periodic efforts to revive them demonstrate. Southey had indeed been an influential figure in the literary world, and his closest associates came to dominate the textbooks of the twentieth century. But Southey was left behind.

Why did he fall so far short of the expectations held out for him? It is helpful to compare his afterlife with Crabbe's as well as Wordsworth's. The main cause for the decline of readership in the case of both Southey and Crabbe was their almost exclusive commitment to long poems, a form that lost ground to prose fiction steadily and seemingly irreversibly, during and after the Victorian period. Of the top thirty-seven long poems listed in order by volume of sales in the Romantic period in William St. Clair's *Reading Nation,* only five were reprinted in separate (solo) editions between 1900 and 1950.[104] Southey's were not among them. Of that small group only three, all poems by Scott and all standard school texts, were regularly reprinted after 1900, and even they ceased to appear after 1950. For authors thought to be important enough, such as Wordsworth and Byron and Crabbe, collected editions filled the need; but the stereotype plates of Longman's one-volume collected edition of Southey were melted down in 1895, and no publisher stepped in (as Oxford did in Crabbe's case) to take over.[105] The last printing of the collected American edition was in 1884. Like Crabbe but unlike Wordsworth, Southey could not be remade as a lyric poet; his body of work did not readily lend itself to anthologization; and so he lost his popular audience.

It is more surprising to find that there was no place for Southey in the academy either. Genre must always have been an issue, the fantastic tales not seeming serious enough for advanced study. Byron's popular "Oriental tales," which are closer in kind to Southey's epics than anything Wordsworth wrote, are also not found on university programs of study. But the main problem seems to have been the contrast with Wordsworth. Like Crabbe, Southey was nowhere near Wordsworthian enough for the founders of the curriculum, and editors have yet to be persuaded to include him on other grounds: the ninth edition of the *Norton Anthology,* which dominates the North American market, has no pages devoted to his work but 131 for Wordsworth and 135 for Byron (those figures covering both prose and verse); Wu's *Romanticism* gives him 13 compared to Wordsworth's 230 and Byron's 154. The association with Wordsworth and the Lakers, which began as a strength, appears eventually to have turned against Southey; his stature shrank in the shadow of Wordsworth. As Lynda Pratt, the latest and most successful of the academic writers who have gone to bat for Southey, has pointed out, literary partisanship did not end at Southey's death.[106]

The process of comparison, disparagement, and dismissal began early. William Howitt, for example, included Southey among the poets of his *Homes and Haunts* in 1847 but made it clear that for all his talents and virtues, Southey was no match for his neighbor Wordsworth. He could have been a great poet of liberty, Howitt declared, but he changed sides to become "the laudator of crime, tyranny, and carnage!" "The man who set out on a career that augured the life of a second Milton [ended] as the most thorough, though probably unconscious tool of tyranny and state corruption." Moreover—and this may have been the greatest sin in Howitt's scheme of things—although Southey certainly loved Cumberland, he never seemed really to settle in there. "Has he, like Wordsworth, woven his verse into almost every crevice of rock?" No, "there is scarcely a line in his poetry which localizes itself in the fairy region where he lived forty years."[107]

Southey was less fortunate even than Crabbe, let alone than Wordsworth, in his posthumous supporters. Neither the Lake District nor his home city of Bristol chose to make a local hero of Southey, as the Lakes did of Wordsworth and Suffolk of Crabbe. He had not written about them, and they did not strongly identify him as one of their own. (Bristol took up Chatterton instead.) His family split into hostile factions after his death. No Southey Society emerged to look after his interests and turn his home or his gravesite into a shrine. The word that Howitt used—like Chambers in the *Cyclopaedia* before him—to sum up Southey's career was "melancholy." Instead of pride and admiration, his name prompted pity in the earliest assessments, from a sense of the discrepancy between what he could have been and what he actually became. Howitt's concerns at the time when he used the word "melancholy" were political, Chambers's literary, but both may also have been affected by the sad end to Southey's life, when he had to care for his mentally incapacitated wife and then, after she died and he remarried, fell prey to dementia himself and lingered for several years, unable to work or to recognize anyone. When the official biography came out in 1850, there was no concealing the dreadful decline toward the end. Like Crabbe, Southey would be remembered as an old man—and worse, a broken one. Wordsworth's biographers could present him at first as a dignified sage and later as a young radical, to suit the temper of their own times; with Southey it was impossible to overlook the catastrophe of his old age.

Readers and commentators find themselves embarrassed by the gulf between what Southey desired and worked so hard for, and what became of him at last. His politics, the sales of his poetry, his state of health—all proved disappointing. His ambition conformed to the same pattern. Unlike Crabbe, Southey had trumpeted his hopes in prefaces and letters for all to see, so the discrepancy was obvious. Moreover, he protested too much, raising suspicions that his sense of destiny had always had a shadow side of doom.

Southey could be uncommonly gracious and generous to other poets, especially to younger ones but also to his peers and rivals. Crabbe, he declared, was an original and his work would endure.[108] Posterity would rank Wordsworth with Milton. (As he said so, Southey distanced himself from both by observing that his own poetry was of a different kind, more like that of Tasso, Virgil, or Homer.)[109] Sensitive to charges of writing too easily, he suggested to Scott, who had a similar facility, that there might be a direct correlation between volume and merit and that it would do Wordsworth no harm to produce more than he did.[110] He frequently put his own productivity to work for others. For example, he prepared an edition of Chatterton's poems for the benefit of the family in 1803. In 1807 he did the same for Henry Kirke White, a promising poet who had died a student at Cambridge at the age of twenty-one. This edition was one of the steady best sellers of the nineteenth century, in large part because of Southey's prefatory life, which was reprinted independently as a biographical classic. The story he told is so prominent in Southey's writings as to suggest, by proxy, an alternative personal myth—not neglected genius, but genius destroyed by overwork.

Southey's pathetic account of Kirke White paradoxically inspired another impoverished young poet, Herbert Knowles, to seek Southey's assistance; but then Knowles too died, before he was twenty, just after entering the university.[111] Another martyr on the Chatterton and Kirke White model—at least in Southey's view—was Lucretia Davidson, an American poet who died shortly before her seventeenth birthday; writing about her in the *London Review* in 1829, he attributed her death to "over-excitement."[112] Nor was the risk confined to youth. Southey attributed his wife's mental breakdown to many years of anxiety about their finances.[113] When Scott, dangerously ill in 1819, wrote warning him to beware of overwork, Southey commented, "I am afraid no person ever took that advice who stood in need of it. . . . I believe I manage myself well by frequent change of employment, frequent idling, and keeping my mind as free as I can from any strong excitement."[114] Scott recovered that time but drove himself harder than ever to dig himself out of bankruptcy after 1826, and died in 1832 after a series of strokes. Southey himself suffered the fate he had probably feared most of all, years of mental confusion and incapacity before he died. If his reputation, unlike Scott's (for Scott's end was also sad), has been "dogged by anecdotes of failure," it is in part because he counted so much and so publicly on success.[115] Otherwise the decline in his reputation would appear as just normal obsolescence. So it seems that both his intense desire for literary immortality and his program for achieving it—ambitious long poems, unremitting labor, and alienation from contemporary society in the name of self-reliance—proved in the long run to be counterproductive.

A New Theory of Literary Fame

The comparison of these three cases could lead to various conclusions. That the heroic model of authorship was misguided at best and might actually be destructive. That Johnson's concept of assisted authorship more accurately predicted the reality of the afterlives of authors of the Romantic period than the traditional Horatian model. That literary works can never break free of partisanship or the pressures of fashion to arrive at a judgment that is fixed for all time—what Kett referred to as "permanent approbation." That writers cede control of the interpretation of their works at the moment of publication and have diminishing opportunities to win it back as time passes: "Let no man dream of influence beyond his life."[116] But I want to return to Wordsworth's theory of audiences to make a less obvious and potentially more significant point.

In his reflections on audiences, Wordsworth described a state of affairs in which good readers were vastly outnumbered by bad ones; that is, serious, well-informed, attentive, studious readers represented only a fraction of the actual readership, most of which sought personal gratification in some way. His distinctions were not based on class or markets (mass versus elite), but on motivation and competence or, to put it more neutrally, different modes of reading—ones that might easily coexist in a single individual. He thought that if the writings themselves were worthy, the proportion of good to bad readers and good to bad readings should increase steadily over time, although he doubted that the bad ones would ever be eradicated altogether. When we consider the reputations and afterlives of Wordsworth, Crabbe, and Southey, however, what we see is that over the long term, literary works can really flourish *only if* they have multiple audiences. They and their authors are better off not aspiring to uniformity. Crabbe had his local audience and his literary descendants as well as scholarly interest; Wordsworth had those and more—children, tourists, connoisseurs, readers of biography, and so on. For more than a century now, only scholars—and those rarely—have attempted to champion Southey.

In principle, a single copy of a single work might keep alive a writer's chances of success—Blake is a case in point—but in practice, no dead author's work can be sustained without a convergence of audiences. Fame is a condition of being talked about. A small group or coterie sharing its enthusiasm is practically inaudible, whereas numerous groups, all discussing the same name (author or title), even if their ideas are at odds with one another, create reverberations—what today we call buzz. For authors who have been dead a long time, the studious audience of the academy—readers of the kind Wordsworth wanted—is a sine qua non. Though its direct effect is limited to scholarly debates, indirectly its influence may be gradually diffused through its graduates to audiences of quite different kinds; it in turn is capable of responding to popular pressure, as demonstrated by the canonization of

Frankenstein, a Gothic extravaganza and written by a female to boot. Wordsworth's appeal to a studious public was well founded, but a studious public alone would never have won him the vast following he has.

We are accustomed to think of audiences in terms of binary opposition: lower or upper class, mass or elite market, popular or critical success, financial or cultural rewards. But these exclusive categories make for a blunt analytical tool even in the hands of a critic of the caliber of Bourdieu, the best-known theorist of cultural status. Wordsworth's theory of audiences raises the possibility of something more flexible and dynamic, a theory of literary fame that traces different kinds of fame to different groups of readers with different systems of rewards. Such groups form and dissolve or evolve over time, so the number cannot be settled, but we might consider, to begin with, four general modes of reading corresponding roughly to Wordsworth's categories, and moving from larger to smaller circles of readers.

For Wordsworth's four ages we can substitute four modes of knowing associated with four kinds of audiences, four means of measurement, and four kinds of fame to which we could give names that are already in general use—though we'd have to agree to dedicate them to these meanings and to stop using them as virtual synonyms. Most of those who recognize the name of Wordsworth or any of his cohort do so from common knowledge of his life and personality, without firsthand acquaintance with any of the writing. This is the widest and shallowest form of fame; it brings the tribute of numbers. A smaller but still substantial group has a casual acquaintance with his poetry: they learn it or keep it by them, and turn to it occasionally as the need arises. They are the ones chiefly responsible for steady sales. A still smaller set of readers has studied the work methodically: they know it professionally, as critics or students. And the smallest group of all consists of other artists who absorb the work and use it, whether or not they are aware of doing so. These groups confer, respectively, celebrity, popularity, critical approval, and influence—different kinds of fame that may not be of equal value but that have, each of them, their peculiar merits. They must be measured by different yardsticks, not by sales or Google hits alone. Any one of them might be capable of generating, sustaining, or reviving an author's fame, given a large enough constituency, but the writer and the work stand a much better chance where more than one group is engaged.

Every reader knows some authors one way and others another, or knows the same author in different ways at various stages of his or her own life. In 1809, for instance, in *English Bards and Scotch Reviewers,* Byron invoked an image of Wordsworth that was all about his personality and way of life, not about the poems: he described him as a sort of wild man who lived alone in the Lakes and didn't cut his hair. A decade later, in *Don Juan,* exhibiting the second way of knowing, he made common cause with readers who had tried to read *The Excursion* and *Peter Bell* but been baffled or disappointed. Finally, as a writer himself, he both echoed and rebelled against Wordsworth's example; for influence, an unconscious and covert force, always cuts both ways.

To try out this new hypothesis—that for a writer's work to last, it must attract multiple audiences and bear diverse (even contradictory) meanings—and to add substance to the sketch of the afterlife of the Romantic author, the next chapter turns to prose fiction and to the aspirations and legacies of Scott, Brunton, and Austen.

3

The Stigma of Popularity

Around 1800, the highest prize that writers could aspire to was a form of immortality through their works. Old orthodoxies about what that would entail and how it might be achieved could be challenged or qualified by newer models (Johnson's pragmatic concept of assisted authorship, Wordsworth's idea of radical independence), but the goal itself was not in question—for poets, that is, since it was taken for granted that the highest prize was available only to the highest kinds of literature. Other indicators of success, such as large sales figures in one's lifetime, warm reviews, parody and imitation (both of which depend on and reflect general recognition), and wide dissemination were at best means to an end; at worst, judged by the strictest Wordsworthian principles, they might actually be impediments to future glory. For all inferior genres including prose fiction, however, these lesser prizes represented a glass ceiling, the best their authors could hope for. Yet the work of a handful of novelists of the period proved to be far more durable than that of any poet and far more likely to win new readers in later generations. Following the pattern of the previous chapter, this one considers the careers and afterlives of Walter Scott, Jane Austen, and Mary Brunton in conjunction with their ideas about literary fame.

Walter Scott

Like journalism (including reviews), plays, and translations, novels were typically published anonymously or pseudonymously in the early nineteenth century—a sign that they belonged to the category of potboilers and hack work. Being the author of a novel was not something to be proud of, rather the reverse. When Anna Letitia Barbauld wrote her introduction to a set of *British Novelists* published in fifty volumes in 1810, she struck an apologetic note, acknowledging at the outset that "A Collection of Novels has a better chance of giving pleasure than of commanding respect."[1] Peter Garside quotes an even more rueful remark from a preface of 1804: "An acknowledged Novel-writer is, perhaps, one of the most difficult names to support with credit and reputation." His statistical analysis of publishing trends bears out that writer's observation, for fewer than half the new novels published between 1800 and 1829 (970 out of 2,256) carried the names of their authors on their first appearance.[2] Custom, caution, shame, and the sense of participation in an ephemeral enterprise combined to produce among writers of prose fiction a pattern of behavior almost exactly the reverse of the epic poet's quest for glory, with the name of the author concealed, money represented as the prime motive, numbers courted, and the present taste of the public a constant point of reference.

But Walter Scott changed all that. Though responsible literary history must be wary of large claims for isolated individuals, it has to make an exception in this case and declare that by precept and example, Scott single-handedly (or as near as we ever get to single-handedly) opened Parnassus to the writer of prose fiction. A publishing phenomenon in both verse and prose, Scott used his prestige to raise the status of his fellow authors. In the 1820s, when he produced a set of *Lives of the Novelists* parallel to Johnson's *The Lives of the Poets,* he revealed his own standards and expectations as Johnson had done before him.

Scott's sensational career and the aftereffects of it always invite superlatives: he was "the most popular author of the romantic period and later, both in verse and in prose, not only in Great Britain but in English-speaking communities elsewhere"; "no other writer before him had been so well received by his contemporaries—*ever*"; "all British, American, and European novelists of the nineteenth century learned from his ways of writing"; and yet in the twenty-first century, "nobody cares much about Scott."[3] Only the last of these statements is a calculated exaggeration; the others have been repeated without a dissenting voice in histories and reference books for a century and a half. The most seemingly hyperbolical claims have solid support from an array of different kinds of evidence—sales figures, reviews, the personal correspondence and journals of readers generation after generation, and the tributes of painters and musicians, as well as of other writers. Scott appears to have swept everyone before him in a remarkably long run, so that practically the only matters of debate are when that run came to an end and whether it can be said to be finally over.[4] The outline of his rise to success is so well known that I shall just sketch it out, to spend a little more time on the less commonly discussed topic of the gradual decline of his reputation.

A lawyer who dabbled in antiquarian research and ballad hunting like many of his peers, Scott had his first notable success in 1805 with *The Lay of the Last Minstrel,* which he had modeled on medieval verse romances. This unusual blend of chivalric fiction and historical fact, accompanied by an apparatus of learned notes, generated such demand that six editions with ever-expanding print runs, to a total of about nine thousand copies, were called for in the first two years.[5] A set of illustrations "taken from designs on the spot" (fig. 7) followed in 1808, the year that proved that the *Lay* was not just a flash in the pan, since *Marmion: A Tale of Flodden Field,* based on the same formula, did even better: it had four editions for a total of eight thousand copies in 1808 alone. And that was outdone by the next, *The Lady of the Lake,* with eight editions and sales of twenty thousand copies in 1810. Though Scott never matched that record again, his new poetic works continued to sell extremely well by anyone else's standards.[6] Nevertheless, before 1815 Scott could sense that the tide had turned: after 1812 he had stiff competition from Byron, and literary fashion seemed to have shifted; perhaps he himself felt less confident in his powers. But he had a backup plan. While *The Lady of the Lake* was still work in progress, he had boldly declared, "If I fail it will be a sign I should never have succeeded, and I will write prose for life; you shall see no change in my temper, nor shall I eat a single meal the worse."[7] And that is essentially what happened. He had started work on his first, groundbreaking novel in 1808, even as he was finishing *Marmion.*[8] (It was also in 1808 that he wrote the first portion of his autobiographical memoirs in a preemptive bid, like Southey's, to control his public image; and that he and Murray first discussed the possibility of a set of reprinted novels, the origin of the project that led eventually to the *Lives of the Novelists.*)[9]

Scott attached his name proudly to all his big poems, and he could have capitalized on it when he shifted to prose fiction, but he chose instead to publish *Waverley* (1814) anonymously, in accordance with convention, and then to print subsequent works in the same genre as "by the Author of *Waverley.*" This routine procedure turned out in his case to be a very successful marketing device. Either because the style and content were so distinctively his, or

ILLUSTRATIONS

OF

WALTER SCOTT's

LAY OF THE LAST MINSTREL:

CONSISTING

OF TWELVE VIEWS

ON THE RIVERS

BOTHWICK, ETTRICK, YARROW, TIVIOT, AND TWEED.

ENGRAVED BY JAMES HEATH, R.A. FROM DESIGNS TAKEN ON THE SPOT

By JOHN C. SCHETKY, of Oxford.

WITH

ANECDOTES AND DESCRIPTIONS.

LONDON:

PRINTED FOR LONGMAN, HURST, REES, AND ORME, PATERNOSTER ROW.

1808.

Fig. 7. Title page of a set of illustrations to Scott's *Lay of the Last Minstrel*, by John Schetky (1808). © The British Library Board.

because word had got out, his authorship was an open secret from the start, while a degree of mystery, however slight, fueled discussion, which fuels fame. The formula "by the Author of" is a compromise between anonymity and proclaimed authorship: while withholding the name, it still affirms sole creative responsibility and guarantees the integrity of the series. In the language of modern advertising, it underwrites the brand. Scott did not formally acknowledge his authorship of the Waverley novels until 1827 and thus retained a provocative atmosphere of uncertainty around the products of his second spectacular writing career.

Though it appeared with no author's name on the title page, *Waverley* undoubtedly benefited from Scott's established reputation. The earliest reviews reported the widespread opinion that he was the author and reinforced that opinion with internal evidence. In September 1814, before she had even laid hands on a copy, Jane Austen playfully complained that it was "not fair" that Scott should have produced this novel: "He has Fame and Profit enough as a Poet, and should not be taking the bread out of other people's mouths."[10] Seven British editions, a total of 9,500 copies, were published between 1814 and 1817; given that novels were sold mainly to circulating libraries rather than to individuals, this was an extraordinary record. Richard Altick has calculated that throughout the nineteenth century, "the ordinary circulating-library novel seldom had an edition of more than a thousand or 1,250 copies"; but for *Waverley* he records, on the authority of J. G. Lockhart, six thousand sold in the first six months, for *The Antiquary* six thousand in the first six days, and for *Rob Roy* ten thousand in the first two weeks.[11]

Once launched as a novel writer, Scott had every incentive to continue. The shift of medium gave him more scope, greater profits, and access to a wider audience, and yet in essential ways (plots, characters, historical underpinnings) the novels followed the same congenial path as his other literary work. He himself drew attention to his consistency as a writer in the "Advertisement" to his edition of the *Somers Tracts* (1809–15) as he approached the turning point of his career. Anticipating doubts about his scholarly seriousness, since he was known as a writer of verse, he reminded his readers that his devotion to history came first and had never left him: "The Muse (to use the established language) found him [Scott] engaged in the pursuit of historical and traditional antiquities, and the excursions which he has made in her company, have been of a nature which increases his attachment to his original study."[12] And so he carried on as he had begun, multitasking as lawyer, antiquarian, editor ("the greatest editor of his age," according to the *Oxford Dictionary of National Biography* [*ODNB*]), poet, and novelist, maintaining such a stream of publications that it sometimes seemed that he could write faster than anyone else could read.

With his Edinburgh associates James Ballantyne, a printer in whose business Scott was a private partner, and the well-connected bookseller Archibald Constable, Scott commanded a formidable publishing machine, so that for twenty years he could operate on a scale unavailable to his contemporaries. (The *Oxford Companion to the Book* calls him "arguably the most influential figure in 19th-century European publishing.")[13] Besides the new titles regularly appearing, that machine repackaged older ones in the guise of selections, collections ("poetical works," "novels and romances," *The Poetry Contained in the Novels, Tales, and Romances,* and the like—collected editions in the author's lifetime), and spinoffs such as Westall's engraved illustrations for *The Lord of the Isles* (1815). When Constable and Ballantyne crashed along with much of the publishing industry in 1826, Scott only stepped up the pace, producing more fiction and histories to pay off his creditors even as he wrote prefaces and notes for the grandest scheme of all, the "magnum opus" edition of his novels, poetic works, and miscellaneous prose, finally complete in eighty-eight volumes in 1836, four years after his death. The forty-eight volumes of "Waverley novels" in this set include twenty-two separate titles. Whereas with Constable, Scott had been gradually increasing the format and price of the novels, after the crash, with his new publisher Robert Cadell, the magnum edition was an experiment in affordable mass publication. Sales of one small but nicely printed illustrated volume every month vastly exceeded expectations, "upwards of 30,000" copies at a time rather than the four or five thousand they had been aiming at.[14]

Afterlife and Afterdeath

For a very long time after his death, Scott's reputation flourished and his readership increased, just as Horace and Johnson predicted would happen to the best poets. By any measure, he was the leader of his generation. If, as Keats reported as early as 1818, there had been three literary kings in his time, "Scott—Byron—and then the scotch novels," Scott was two of them, and his or their supremacy continued unchallenged.[15] To judge by the criteria laid out earlier in connection with Wordsworth, for instance, Scott also had honors (a baronetcy; he declined the laureateship and recommended Southey for it), portraits, a giant biography that became a classic in itself, a massive public monument, an architectural shrine (Abbotsford), and Scott clubs and societies to foster interest in his work. His public image was admirable. Lockhart's life-and-letters biography presented his subject as a humane and lovable man; and though his end, like Southey's, was sad, it was at the same time honorable and even heroic, Scott being represented as having killed himself by overwork rather than endure the stain of bankruptcy. So the legend grew.

Like Wordsworth's, Scott's work was strongly identified with a particular place. Since the place was a country, he became a national hero—in some eyes a national villain for pandering to the English and inspiring purveyors of souvenirs, but in any case larger than life. (One attribute of success that Scott, like Crabbe, lacked, was an adjective, but that was for a special reason, which turned to his advantage; "Scottish" was already in use, serving to strengthen the association of the man with the land.) Like Wordsworth's and unlike Southey's and Crabbe's, his body of work was large and varied enough that if one old favorite began to pall, something else could take its place. (As Scott once pointed out, "Horace himself expected not to survive in all his works; I may hope to live in some of mine. *Non omnis moriar* [I shall not wholly die].")[16] Like all three of the poets considered in the last chapter, he did what he could to manage his literary estate in such a way as to ensure that it would provide for his family after he was gone: the magnum edition, in particular, effectively extended copyright in his works. Even so, his publishers struggled to keep ahead of the tide of reprints, selections, supplements, commentaries, imitations and adaptations generated by presses throughout the nineteenth century.

Scott's stories lent themselves readily to pictorial illustration—a quality that became increasingly important in the Victorian period, as previously mentioned. His publishers exploited this quality almost from the start by commissioning engravings that could be sold separately or incorporated in deluxe editions. At home and abroad, artists found inspiration and profit in taking familiar scenes from Scott's fictions (verse and prose) for their subjects, for they were able to count on their being familiar.[17] His writings were considered safe for children; indeed, one of the early signs of decline was their being demoted to the status of children's books, thus sharing the fate of the ancient works of chivalry that Scott himself had loved as a boy, after "the huge volumes, which were once the pastimes of nobles and princes, shorn of their ornaments and shrunk into abridgments, were banished to the kitchen or nursery, or, at best, to the hall-window of the old-fashioned country manor-house."[18] Toward the end of the nineteenth century, the major poems and a few of the novels were adopted as textbooks in schools, thus generating a secondary literature of cribs and criticism such as the Normal Tutorial Series, with its paraphrases and "Notes on English Classics." Such "enforced reading" might have contributed, as one major scholar has rather wickedly speculated, to the decline of his popularity; but it did no apparent harm to Austen, so there is room for doubt.[19] What seems to have happened is that these school editions of the novels, relatively abundant between about 1886 and 1913, ceased to be reprinted after the First World War.

In one respect at least, Scott's novels had a great advantage over Wordsworth's poetry: they were easy to translate. It is said that in 1830, "editions of Scott accounted for three-quarters of the British novels, and more than one-third of all the novels published in France."[20] And of course they benefited from—might even have led the way in—the general flight from long narrative poems to three-decker novels that took place in the first half of the nineteenth century. Their diffusion across the Continent and around the world was as prodigious as practically everything else about Scott in his golden years, and that meant, on one hand, that the signs of readers' devotion (such as pilgrimages to the places that Scott had written about) multiplied but, on the other hand, that responses varied in different cultural climates. British theaters, unconstrained by copyright, staged adaptations of the novels and plays, but on the Continent they produced operas.[21] If British imitators reflected Scott's conservative side, "the Scott who embodies above all the permanence and stability of property," those on the Continent tended to have read him "in politically radicalized terms," concocting their own politically radical, nationalist versions of Scott's historical narratives. In the twentieth century, Continental critics read his novels through the filters of Marxism.[22] What readers make of the works they read naturally differs from reader to reader and from group to group, depending on the interests and concerns of the moment. But the works of a writer such as Scott, whose reach was all but universal, are particularly subject to differing interpretations. Thus he is often credited or charged with having had an influence on public events through the sway that his works held over readers' imaginations—the most notorious instance being Mark Twain's assertion, in *Life on the Mississippi* (1883), that by establishing "reverence for rank and caste" (this is the nostalgic, conservative Scott of the English-speaking world) he was personally responsible for the American Civil War.[23] Cardinal Newman thought Scott had prepared a new wave of converts to Roman Catholicism.[24] In his family history *The Hare with Amber Eyes*, Edmund De Waal recently described having come across receipts of purchases made for a Jewish boys' charity school in Odessa in 1892, including "280 volumes by Beecher Stowe, Swift, Tolstoy, Cowper, Thackeray and Scott."[25] What can generations of boys at that school have made of their reading? The mind boggles.

"The author of *Waverley*" was "the first regular best-seller in the history of the novel."[26] But best sellers by their nature cannot carry on forever; no matter how successful they are, sooner or later their familiar features give way to fresh faces. If they're lucky they may be redefined as "classics," perhaps after a period of abandonment, and thrive again in that separate league that Jonathan Brody Kramnick describes as a zone of seclusion watched over by "a clerisy of experts."[27] All authorities agree that interest in Scott's work fell off at last, but different dates are offered and correspondingly different reasons are given. Walter Bagehot, in an interesting review that I shall come back to, observed as early as 1858 that new books and new interests had already deposed the Waverley novels. Audiences had changed, he wrote, and the new readers of the day mainly wanted love stories, not sweeping historical narratives, even if love stories were included along with the history.[28] Then there was the independent activity of budding writers coming out of Scott's shadow. Realists and fastidious stylists made his tales look old-fashioned and sloppily composed, with the result that in 1871, in the midst of the celebrations of the centenary of Scott's birth, Leslie Stephen heard intimations of mortality, whispers "that Scott is dull."[29] By that time it would seem, to adopt Johnson's phrase, that Scott had been lost "in his own lustre."

Historical scholarship locates the actual end somewhat later. In his survey of Scott's critical reception, John Hayden settles on 1885 as the date by which Scott's work "ceased to be popular with the reading public at large," citing the development of "newer techniques in novel writing."[30] In the *ODNB*, David Hewitt opts for the 1890s, when Scott's work was taken over by the schools. Other historians give him twenty or thirty years longer and trace the decline to the effect of the modernist movement after the First World War, which deliberately rejected nineteenth-century literary values and practices. The fact that after 1914 there were virtually no new printings of Lockhart's *Life* lends support to this theory.[31] (On the other hand, since the origins of modernism itself keep being shifted back into the 1880s, perhaps there is less distance between these rival theories than there appears to be.) One of the most recent analysts of Scott's career gives him until 1930, up to which time, he asserts, "the Waverley novels were omnipresent"—and after which they were given a fresh lease on life, if only in intellectual circles, by Lukács's *The Historical Novel*.[32]

There is no doubt that the works of Scott fared badly in the post-Victorian environment, as they did in the increasingly important realm of academic criticism for most of the twentieth century. Oliver Elton, whose multivolume *Survey of English Literature* reached Scott in 1928, is said to have been "one of the last critics of the twentieth century" to rank him anywhere near the top of the list of British writers.[33] On the centenary of his death, in 1932—the talismanic hundred years that Horace had mocked—it was clear that the spread of Scott's reputation had ceased and was fast receding. The tidal wave of mass-market reprints dried up and was not replaced by textbooks; *The Lady of the Lake* vanished from the curriculum about 1950; and of the novels only *Waverley,* thanks to its historical importance, clings to a spot on university syllabi, with one or other of the rest of the Waverley novels occasionally taking its place for the purposes of a particular instructor. Anthologies seldom include whole novels—certainly not on the Scott scale. The powerful schools of, successively, formalism, feminism, postcolonialism, and deconstruction showed no interest in Scott unless to disparage his work. When they ceased to be part of the realm of common knowledge, Scott's stories lost ground in the burgeoning marketplace of the cinema.[34] Still, he has always had his advocates, who detect signs of a renewal of interest in the present academic climate of globalization and internationalism, with the prominence of cultural studies and the history of the book—all areas in which the works of Scott could provide valuable evidence. In the academy his reputation may well be on the rise again.[35] Furthermore there has never yet been a time when it could seriously be said that "nobody cares much about Scott."

If caring is the issue, we need to shift from the quantifiable external criteria of honors, shrines, tourism, and sales figures and consider instead the theory of audiences that was introduced in chapter 2. Then a different pattern emerges, less like the linear rise and fall of stock markets, the swing of a pendulum, or the ebb and flow of tides than like musical polyphony. External criteria themselves rest on the internal motivation not of individuals but of groups, for fame is social recognition. Honors, tourism, sales, and so forth require collective action, which in turn implies common values—groups of people who care, and who care *alike*. In his "Essay, Supplementary" of 1815, Wordsworth sketched out a theory of audiences that divided the reading nation into four such groups. I have suggested extending his scheme to denominate groups associated, respectively, with celebrity, popularity, critical approval, and influence. In his heyday, Scott had them all, and though one or another of them might have faded for a time, and numbers have fluctuated, jointly they continue to sustain his reputation. The difference is a matter of degree and proportion: what looks like a fall into oblivion in comparison with Scott's earlier glory might be considered a respectable standing for almost anyone else.

The first and last groups are easily accounted for. Now as then, there are many who know something of Scott's achievements in the absence of firsthand acquaintance with his work, because he is historically important; he has that kind of widespread celebrity. History also accounts for his continuing and ineradicable, though increasingly indirect, impact on other writers. If "all British, American, and European writers of the nineteenth century learned from his ways of writing," no twentieth-century novelists in the West can have escaped his influence.

Among readers—the group crucial to literary fame—significant numbers must still be turning to his works for pleasure, not because they have to; otherwise there would not be so many of the trade paperbacks that continue to be produced on top of the existing second-hand stock. Not a single Scott novel or long poem is out of print today, and though a few of them might technically be in print only thanks to print on demand, others, even relatively obscure titles, are available in multiple editions, some of them from reputable presses such as Oxford. No doubt Scott's work has "ceased to be popular with the reading public at large," as Hayden observed, but it evidently continues to appeal to many nonacademic, recreational readers. In Google hits (though we have to allow for other people of the same name), without leading the pack, Scott easily holds his own with other Edinburgh writers past and present: Walter Scott, 2,720,000; James Hogg, 412,000; Mary Brunton, 13,800; Ian Rankin, 724,000; J. K. Rowling, 15,000,000.[36]

Walter Bagehot's essay of 1858 offers another, intriguing way of thinking about the category of the recreational reader. His version of the four-part model further subdivides readers belonging to this group, distributing them across time in four hypothetical generations, of which the first may be delighted but cannot be expected to be much changed by new writing, and the fourth is unlikely to be delighted at all. "Contemporaries bring to new books formed minds and stiffened creeds," he points out, but "posterity, if it regard them at all, looks at them as old subjects, worn-out topics, and hears a disputation on their merits with languid impartiality, like aged judges in a court of appeal."[37] If a writer's work is ever to have a formative effect, therefore, it must be on readers belonging to one of the two intermediate generations. Of these, the earlier "rising generation," overawed, is the less likely to respond to "papa's books" whose "fame is itself half an obstacle to their popularity." Only when the awe wears off is the time ripe for profound impact, in a context of serious debate: "The generation which is really most influenced by a work of genius is commonly that which is still young when the first controversy respecting its merits arises; with the eagerness of youth they read and re-read; their vanity is not unwilling to adjudicate: in the process their imagination is formed; the creations of the author range themselves in the memory; they become part of the substance of the very mind."

Bagehot does not develop the implications of this model, and he suggests that it is actually not a perfect fit for Scott, whose novels had been read with avidity in the second generation. But he proposes to initiate "a slight criticism of these celebrated fictions" after their long unchallenged run, as though to stimulate the current, third generation to its appropriate reaction and to rekindle waning excitement.[38] (If that was his intent, he failed.) Bagehot's variation on the four-part theory of audiences complicates the history of Scott's reputation without contributing much to the understanding of it, since he presents Scott as an exception to his own general rule. Nevertheless, it is a helpful reminder that audiences are not stable but change over time according to their distance from the moment of creation, and it might yet in future serve—with "generations" perhaps reconceived as phases—as an analytic tool, a way of thinking about the history of taste.

As to critical approval, from the reviewers of Scott's day to the critics of our own, students and literary professionals have never doubted that with the Waverley novels Scott achieved something new and distinctive, superior to the run-of-the-mill fiction of the period he lived in. They might consider the effect of his work ultimately pernicious—there were minority dissenting voices long before Mark Twain's—but debate is proverbially good for sales as well as for fame. In 1814 one of the earliest reviews of *Waverley* set the tone: "We are unwilling to consider this publication in the light of a common novel, whose fate it is to be devoured with rapidity for the day, and to be afterwards forgotten forever." The unknown writer described *Waverley* as "a vehicle of curious accurate information" on an important subject, the history and manners of a proud but ruined race.[39] Notable examples of respectful critical overviews even in Scott's lifetime that took the novels as well as the poetry into account are Robert Chambers's *Illustrations of the Author of Waverley* (1822, enlarged in 1825) and J. W. Lake's "Memoir" in the one-volume Galignani edition of the *Poetical Works* (1827).

The serious critical attention that the novels earned for themselves was bolstered by the introductions and prefaces that Scott wrote as they appeared (or wrote specifically for the magnum edition), in which he defended his prolificacy and described the successful author as "a productive labourer" and "a benefactor to the country."[40] In various ways, including anonymous reviews, he consistently acted as an advocate for prose fiction in general, not only for the kind he wrote himself. But his major contribution to the growing respectability of the novel was *Lives of the Novelists*, published originally as a set of sixteen prefatory essays in Ballantyne's Novelist's Library between 1821 and 1824 and then collected in two volumes by enterprising presses in Berlin, Paris, and Philadelphia in 1825. (There were to have been more, but these represent a substantial critical effort.) Other offshore editions and translations followed. Scott's estate was eventually able to reclaim the *Lives* for inclusion among his *Miscellaneous Prose Works* in 1834. Though he made light of the merits of the

Lives to a correspondent, Scott assured his son that the copyrights would one day be "valuable property," and in 1830 he told his publisher Cadell that he "had always a good opinion of these Lives of Novelists."[41]

Lives of the Novelists

Scott was, to say the least, experienced in the ways of the literary marketplace, and as a rule, like Johnson, he took a pragmatic approach to publication. He freely acknowledged that prose fiction was low-status work. Though success in that line was gratifying, he was not going to let it turn his head, for as he said, he was "far from thinking that the novelist or romance-writer stands high in the ranks of literature."[42] But that is not to say that things could not be or ought not to be otherwise. *Lives of the Novelists* reveals Scott's aspirations for the novel in the future through his critical comments on and ranking of novels of the past.

Like *The Lives of the Poets,* on which it was modeled, even in its incomplete state Scott's *Lives of the Novelists* presents a national literary history through biography. (Only one of the writers he discusses, Alain-René Le Sage, was not British.) Like Johnson's work, it establishes a canon by discriminating between writers and between the better and worse works of a given writer—usually by invoking the same critical criteria that Johnson used for poets, and anticipating the same rewards. Lesser writers might be popular for a time, in Scott's view, but theirs would be a bad form of popularity like that of Laurence Sterne, based on eccentricity (not on nature) and imitation (not originality).[43] Sooner or later, true merit would be revealed. Followers of fashion and topicality would produce only "ephemeral and forgotten effusions," but genius, originality, and imagination combined in the great writer would generate faithful representations of human nature and thereby leave an "imperishable monument" and an "immortal" name.[44]

In his opening essay, Scott describes Fielding as "immortal as a painter of national manners," and he names *Tom Jones,* "founded upon the plan of painting from nature," as "the first English novel."[45] Samuel Richardson's *Pamela* was already as good as forgotten, he observes, but *Joseph Andrews,* Fielding's parody, "continues to be read, for the admirable pictures of manners which it presents." (Three years later, when he came to write the essay on Richardson, Scott wavered: Richardson could also be described as a pioneer, "perhaps the first . . . in this line of composition" to throw aside the shackles of romance and found "a new style of writing" based on nature.)[46] Fielding's writings for the stage had not had the same staying power as his novels, Scott suggests, because dramatic texts depend on physical realization. They speak "to the eye and the ear," whereas fiction, though it too involves characters and plots, speaks to the imagination.[47] In this essay and throughout the *Lives,* Scott emphasizes the incorporeality of fiction, the wonderful illusions, especially of human character, that can be created through words alone. Fielding's Squire Western, he notes admiringly, was "imitated from no prototype."[48] In the case of Le Sage, too, the dramatic works, according to Scott, proved to be ephemeral but the fictions, particularly *Gil Blas,* "must afford delight and interest, so long as human nature retains its present constitution."[49] Scott brushes off charges of plagiarism that might call the originality of Le Sage into question (as Johnson did for Pope's *The Rape of the Lock*), by asserting that *Gil Blas* did not after all closely resemble its alleged sources and was original in every way that mattered—"that which constitutes the essence of a composition."[50] Like Johnson before him, Scott here and elsewhere takes advantage of the loose definition of the word "originality." Originality takes many forms, apparently. Sterne is condemned as an entertaining plagiarist; Henry Mackenzie, on the other hand, is raised to the top rank among novelists because "his works possess the rare and invaluable property of originality, to which all other qualities are as dust in the balance."[51]

Tobias Smollett presented a problem, for Scott admired his novels but was hard put to make a case for them on the grounds of either originality or truth to nature. Smollett, he admits, might not have been the first to write in a given mode; he might not have created unforgettable characters out of nothing; and the device of multiple points of view, so effectively employed in the letters of *Humphry Clinker,* might have been copied from Christopher Anstey's *The New Bath Guide.* But Smollett could still be considered original for having realized the potential of Anstey's comic device, besides earning credit as having made "the first candid attempt to do justice to a calumniated race," the Jews, in *Ferdinand Count Fathom.*[52] Scott attempts to make up for this obviously strained argument by changing his ground and introducing another standard. Smollett, he maintains, exhibited the powers of imagination to an extraordinary degree. (The parallel figure in Johnson's *Lives* is Milton.) He refers to him as a "poet" capable of sublime effects and compares him to Byron: "He was, like a pre-eminent poet of our own day, a searcher of dark bosoms, and loved to paint characters under the strong agitation of fierce and stormy passions."[53] Therefore Smollett deserves to be considered an equal first with Fielding as a man "whose genius has raised an imperishable monument to his fame."[54]

Not surprisingly, since many of his own novels played variations on this theme, Scott presents the history of the novel as a contest between the old ways that must pass and the new that must prevail, with admiration for the new but a deep attachment to the old. The historical trend that he traced in the *Lives of the Novelists,* broadly speaking, is a movement away from the traditions of romance to the establishment of a new form of fiction founded in human nature and relying on minute details to build up an "air of reality," "a reality even in fiction itself"; but his final essay, on Ann Radcliffe, celebrates an exception to the general rule as one of the pinnacles of prose fiction.[55] If poetry may exist without meter, Scott writes, Radcliffe, "this mighty enchantress," was a poet, "the first poetess of romantic fiction"—such were her powers of imagination and description.[56] While the terms that Scott chose to convey critical approval—genius, imagination, nature, originality—were conventional, bromides even, it was bold of him to apply them to writers of prose, and it does seem that in the course of a few years the experience of being "the Author of *Waverley*" had altered Scott's opinion of the novel. At first it had been a fallback choice: if the poetry failed, he would write fiction. But eventually he became convinced that the best fiction could rank with the best poetry, that some novels had stood the test of time, and that he might reasonably hope that some of his own work would one day belong to that category.

The *Lives,* moreover, were not entirely conventional. In some significant ways, Scott chose to challenge traditional wisdom. He did not just apply the rules of poetry to the realm of fiction; he changed the rules by expanding them to include new criteria. His stance was proud, though defensive. While his profiles of the great novel and the immortal novelist showcased the strengths of his own work (the exercise of the imagination, lifelike representations of manners built up with masses of detail, a pioneering example that others would follow), the *Lives* incidentally also raised issues that we know Scott was sensitive about: voluminous publication, mercenary motives, and popularity.

Profusion, Profit, and Popularity

Critical orthodoxy did not favor the ready writer; great works are not supposed to come easily. Yet one important advantage that Smollett had over Fielding, in Scott's view, was the "profusion" of his imagination, which expressed itself in many publications and meant that, in the end, he was not just a one-book man. If he wrote nothing as good as *Tom Jones,* still he had three novels better than either *Joseph Andrews* or *Amelia.*[57] Scott developed this idea further in other places, for example in his introduction to *The Monastery* in the magnum edition, where he represents himself as looking around his library and realizing "that, from the time of Chaucer to that of Byron, the most popular authors had been the most prolific."[58] It's worth noting that the examples he cites here are poets, some of them (or at least one, Chaucer) immortal as well as prolific and popular.

Money was a thornier issue: not many of the great poets had grown rich by writing, and the prevailing view was that they shouldn't. By the eighteenth century, as pointed out in chapter 1, the distinction between the fame motive and the money motive had grown into a contradiction. If they were not simply driven by necessity, if they had a choice, writers were supposed to choose sides. Without going as far as Johnson's "no man but a blockhead ever wrote, except for money" (and even that was taking sides), Scott rejected this standard position. In the *Lives of the Novelists* he quotes Sterne's assertion that he wrote "not to be fed, but to be famous," only to add that *Tristram Shandy* in fact brought Sterne "both fame and profit."[59] Sterne's fame might not be the lasting kind, but the point is that the dichotomy itself is false: fame and profit are not necessarily incompatible. Scott thought Radcliffe did deserve a lasting reputation, but she had profited from her work as well, with unprecedented sums paid for the copyrights of *Udolpho* and *The Italian* (£500 and £800, respectively).[60] Scott is frank and specific about the sums involved, and his own admirers followed suit: Lockhart's biography drew extensively on publishers' account books, and even before Lockhart, the figures were in circulation. Lake's 1827 "Memoir" included plenty of information about Scott's profits.

Scott knew that he was vulnerable to charges of mercenariness. The success of *Marmion* had elicited a scathing response from Byron in *English Bards and Scotch Reviewers* (1809), where Scott is described as "Apollo's venal son," a "hireling bard" with a "prostituted Muse":

> No! When the sons of song descend to trade,
> Their bays are sear [*sic*], their former laurels fade.
> Let such forego the poet's sacred name,
> Who rack their brains for lucre, not for fame.[61]

According to Jane Millgate, this public insult rankled with Scott for twenty years.[62] It rankles with scholars as well; they keep repeating the phrase and attempting to answer the question, which *did* he write for? One or the other, both, neither? Are the terms of the question themselves misleading? Millgate argues that Scott cultivated a "gentleman-poet persona" and that maintaining this image was a factor in his decision not to go into bankruptcy at the end. The gentleman poet presumably seeks neither fame nor money, only the satisfaction of exercising his talents in some quietly useful way; Scott referred to a "vocation" and an instinctive "love of composition."[63] His biographer Edgar Johnson, however, has a chapter entitled "For Lucre *and* for

Fame"—which is also the answer given by the bibliographers Todd and Bowden: "Like most men of letters it may be stated simply that Scott wrote first for fame, as he more than once conceded, and then, increasingly, for the money required to extend his estate and advance his position."[64] Fame and *then* lucre is their response. Scott himself spoke up for the dignity of the profession of authorship when he described the money motive as properly secondary: "no man of honour, genius, or spirit would make the mere love of gain the chief, far less the only, purpose of his labours," he affirmed, and "no work of imagination, proceeding from the mere consideration of a certain sum of copy-money, ever did, or ever will, succeed."[65] The great writer might make money, then, but would not write simply *for* money.

Popularity was the defining feature of Scott's career; even his spectacular wealth was only a by-product of it. The word seems to be permanently attached to his name: "Scott" and "popular" go together like horse and carriage, as many quotations in this chapter indicate. For an unprecedented period, both as poet and as novelist, he *embodied* literary popularity; in the end, popularity was what he lost. Though his works may still be read and in some circles admired, all parties appear to agree that those circles, smaller and different, are no longer "popular" circles. But like other terms of value, "popular" and "popularity" are bandied about with such a muddle of meanings that book historians have increasingly found it necessary to untangle them and in some cases to propose restricted definitions.[66] Without attempting to provide the "substantial work on the concept of 'the popular'" that Benjamin Colbert has called for, I hope to tease out some of the complexities involved in the way the term has been used, especially in accounts of Scott and the history of the novel. One thing that is clear is that whereas "popular" in these contexts always means "many readers," it may mean one or more of a number of other things as well, most of them negative.

Even before he emerged as a novelist, Scott began his memoirs in 1808 by marveling at the popularity he had already achieved, more than he had expected, he said, and frankly more than he wanted. It exceeded, he wrote, "not only my hopes, but my merits, and even my wishes."[67] This statement, rhetorically effective in the way that it establishes his modesty, could also well be true. In the contest for fame, popularity is a two-edged sword—or rather, single-edged, a straight razor of artistic suicide. One of the latent meanings of "popular" is "shallow." When he published his lecture on the "living poets" in 1818, Hazlitt readily acknowledged that "Walter Scott is the most popular of all the poets of the present day, and deservedly so."[68] But he argued that Wordsworth was the most original, and therefore the one most likely to be valued by future generations. Scott deserved his popularity, but Wordsworth deserved immortality. Hazlitt's lecture provides the clearest articulation in the period of the doctrine of the incompatibility of present and future fame, or lifetime success and long-term survival. Fame (that is, enduring fame) "is the recompense not of the living, but of the dead. . . . fame is not popularity, the shout of the multitude . . . but it is the spirit of a man surviving himself in the minds and thoughts of other men, undying and imperishable."[69] On one side are mortal life, the present, a multitude of readers, and popularity; on the other, death, the future, spiritual heirs, and eternal fame. Hazlitt's dichotomies are entrenched in our habits of thought. They appear in debates about literary fame at least as far back as Horace and Pliny and as far forward as Bourdieu's analysis of the inverse relationship between market value and cultural value. In these discussions, popularity nearly always carries an undertone of contempt. What's wrong with it?

Etymology provides a partial answer by highlighting social connotations, as noted in chapter 1. *Populus* designates "people" but people en masse and "the common people" specifically; a near synonym is *vulgus*. Wordsworth, with his democratic principles at stake, was careful to change "popular," as an attribute of Scott and Byron, to "fashionable" in a private letter and to introduce in print his distinction between the great abstractions of the People, whose voice over time is infallible—"that Vox Populi which the Deity inspires"—and the Public, which he felt free to despise: "that small though loud portion of the community, ever governed by factitious influence."[70] Everyday usage is less scrupulous and less sensitive to the implications of language than Wordsworth was, with the consequence that the label of "popular" in literature perennially arouses class prejudices. It evokes fears of mass behavior, mob frenzy, for the popular audience is generally conceived as large but low—if not actually lower-class in the sense of working-class, then uneducated or inadequately educated and at a relatively low level of literary competence, like the stereotyped young ladies who supposedly scoured the circulating libraries for the newest potboilers in the late eighteenth and early nineteenth centuries. This readership is presumed uniformly foolish and easily led, and thus Scott, a popular author, is represented as a kind of literary Pied Piper, "the Wizard of the North." Reviewing Lockhart's biography in 1838, Carlyle roundly declared that "no popularity, and open-mouthed wonder of all the world, continued even for a long series of years, can make a man great."[71] His sneer at gaping, open-mouthed wonder, like Wordsworth's "loud" and Hazlitt's "shout of the multitude," evokes the ignorant Roman rabble of *Coriolanus* and *Julius Caesar*, tellingly though probably inadvertently. We still see class values obviously at work in the area of "popular culture" and various "people's" initiatives today, as in the institution of "people's" prizes as opposed to critics' choices for film festivals and book prizes. (The phrase "popular culture," not yet available in the early nineteenth century, was itself, as Roger Chartier reminds us, an invention of the learned.)[72]

Popularity means pleasing many, and both "pleasing" and "many," innocuous as they seem, turn out to be problematic for authors. Even if pleasing many is separated from the stratifications of class and reconceived as broad appeal across literary and social class lines—the power of works to which Johnson gave his highest praise, as in his accounts of Gray's *Elegy* and Pope's *The Rape of the Lock*—the stigma remains, not entirely without reason. Here is Thomas Love Peacock in 1818 describing the typical response to a new novel by Walter Scott, "perhaps the most universally successful in his own day of any writer that ever lived": "He has the rare talent of pleasing all ranks and classes of men, from the peer to the peasant, and all orders and degrees of mind, from the philosopher to the man-milliner. . . . On the arrival of *Rob Roy,* as formerly that of *Marmion,* the scholar lays aside his Plato, the statesman suspends his calculations, the young lady deserts her hoop, the critic smiles as he trims his lamp, thanking God for his good fortune, and the weary artisan resigns his sleep for the refreshment of the magic page."[73]

Peacock describes Scott as the most successful of all writers "in his own day": that's part of the problem. The work that pleases intensely in its own day is apparently not, in the nature of things, a work for all time. Scott's novels eventually became "papa's books," as Bagehot put it. The calculation must be that such popularity cannot be sustained forever, because the popular writer has to conform to the tastes of the day (which are bound to change as time passes) and then compromise still further in order to find common ground among disparate classes of readers. Popularity normally, perhaps inevitably, entails dumbing down. Universal accessibility comes at a cost. That was the point made by J. W. Lake in 1827, when he observed, respectfully but regretfully, that the choice of "common topics, images, and expressions" which guaranteed Scott's popularity must put his reputation among more "discerning" readers at risk.[74]

Lake's observation brings another distinction to the fore. The "popular" audience, which confers popularity and which, however it may be composed, is large, is not the critical, expert, "discerning" audience, which is always comparatively small. By achieving wide appeal, the popular author sacrifices critical esteem, whether the "many" are found in one (large, inferior) social group or drawn from a range of different orders. By implication, the multitudinous audience, even if it is not socially uniform, must be uniformly undiscriminating to be so uniformly pleased. It is easy to please, it suspends judgment, it is uncritical. If we believe that, then we cannot conclude, with Johnson, that there may be good popularity (signaling timeless and universal appeal) or bad (tainted by the politics and special interests of the passing day); popularity in any form is a poisoned chalice.

But this is a patently unreasonable, as well as a patronizing, position. Large groups, just like small ones, are composed of separate individuals whose motives and responses are ultimately unknowable, perhaps even to themselves. The large group might arise from a convergence of fragmented small groups, as well as from a single coherent unit. The notion of the massiness and natural inferiority of the large audience has proved durable, however, even among members of it, so there may be other factors besides class difference and competence to take into account. Pleasure seems also to be part of the problem. The Horatian tradition decrees that a work that is to endure must please and instruct at the same time. But the popular author seeking a large audience aims above all to please, and is successful only as long as readers find "refreshment," as Peacock called it, in the writing. If popularity is founded on pleasure and refreshment, as distinguished from work and study, perhaps to be popular is necessarily to be easy, entertaining, unserious, simply delicious. That criterion takes us back to audience response.

The author seeking popularity aims to please, and the reader must be prepared to be pleased. If popularity depends on a particular attitude or frame of mind in the consumer, then perhaps only recreational reading (so perceived by the reader) is eligible to be popular, and popularity is a matter of function rather than design. That would seem to be the logical consequence of Chartier's proposal that the use of the word "popular" should be confined to a way of reading rather than be attached as a permanent attribute to this or that text. Then there could be a popular mode of apprehension (Chartier refers to "appropriation," adapting the term made fashionable by Michel de Certeau) of *The Odyssey* or *Moby Dick* alongside a learned one, and the same scholar who reads *The Odyssey* one way might read *Moby Dick* quite differently.[75] The novel in Scott's day was exclusively recreational reading, so the successful novelist was doubly blessed—or cursed—as a popular writer in a popular genre.

All of which is only to state the obvious: those who describe Scott as a popular author do not all mean the same thing by it. At times, "popular" connotes "frivolous." When Scott himself declared that the popularity of his verse exceeded his wishes, he was expressing uneasiness about the size of the readership, apparently for fear that his work would not be taken seriously. Compared to the editing of historical documents, as he acknowledged, the poems were "of a lighter and more popular nature."[76] At other times, "popular" means "having crowd appeal." Carlyle's fulminations about open-mouthed wonder attacked the ignorance of a mass market drawn to mediocrity and constitutionally incapable, in his view, of recognizing greatness when they saw it. Or "popular" can mean "ordinary," as opposed to "extraordinary." When Hazlitt called Scott deservedly the most popular among the living poets, that was a barely concealed sneer at the accessibility of his style and thought: "his sentiments, of which his style is an easy and natural medium, are common to him with his readers."[77] Wordsworth's correction of "popular" to "fashionable" and his distinction between the people and the public emphasize the transitoriness of lifetime renown as opposed to eternal fame—and incidentally point to another hazard of popularity, the possibility of being sought after for nonliterary reasons, as the object of a passing fad.

When modern scholars such as William St. Clair and Hayden write of Scott's extraordinary popularity and of his having ultimately "ceased to be popular with the reading public at large," they mean that a lot of books had been sold, but by using the word "popular" (as is conventionally done) and not just "profitable" or "best-selling," they are also interpreting the evidence to imply something about the ways the books were read. Ideally, we would use "popular" only when we could supplement the quantitative evidence of sales with evidence about audiences. Many a textbook has strong sales figures but it is not likely that anyone would call such a book popular. The Bible is a perennial best seller: is it therefore popular? Sales figures indicate how many new copies of a book have been purchased but cannot account for library users or the second-hand market.[78] Furthermore, they show what is being bought but not by whom, nor for what purpose, nor how it is read, nor even whether it is read at all. All that sales figures and library holdings of Scott's writings reliably indicate is that, relatively speaking, he was far more successful in his lifetime than his contemporary rivals; that his works dominated the market for fiction in English through most of the nineteenth century, outstripping those of far younger writers; but that since the early twentieth century he has lost ground significantly. All the same, in comparison with all but two novelists of his period, Jane Austen and Mary Shelley, he is still doing well as one of a handful whose works remain in print, and not only in textbook editions. We do not, however, know what exactly the numbers signify. We can speculate that, like Radcliffe, William Godwin, Edgeworth, and Hogg, he has become a niche author for specialist interests, and that a convergence of niche markets puts him, like Wordsworth, in a relatively strong position. (He has roles in the academy, in the Scottish diaspora, among collectors, and among historical fiction enthusiasts. He is said to be "a popular and highly regarded novelist and poet" in Japan—whatever "popular" can mean in that context.)[79] But we do not know who exactly is buying what, nor what they are getting out of it, let alone what the future holds for Scott and his works.

Like Johnson's and Wordsworth's, Scott's concept of authorship owed something to tradition and something to personal experience. He accepted the idea of inspired genius, with the concomitant of originality; he aspired to lasting fame in the form of generations of new readers continuing forever. But he resisted some of the trends of his own day. He insisted that neither riches nor popularity disqualified a writer for immortality. He defended quantity of publication as likely to be advantageous to reputation.[80] He often represented himself as working in conjunction with others or as indebted to others; the heroic isolation of the Wordsworthian model was not for him, any more than writing for posterity "instead" of for his own time. ("I do not think so ill of the present generation as to suppose that its present favour necessarily infers future condemnation," he wrote.)[81] But the support that he needed was not exactly like Johnson's assisted authorship either, with its reliance on the publishing industry and its apparatus of editors, reviewers, and tastemakers. Scott looked to other writers for ideas and to actual (not ideal) readers for judgment; the role of the press was simply instrumental as far as he was concerned. David Hewitt, in the *ODNB*, describes Scott's "repeated, irritatingly deferential, acknowledgement of the part played by [his] friends and coadjutors in the creative process" but concedes that the debts were real. Scott was "the great transformer of inherited materials" and therefore may be seen as "uniquely indebted to others, writers past and present as well as friends."

To sum up, Scott expected that the best writers in verse and prose alike would work within the taste of the time, would produce a substantial body of work, and would accept the judgment of the reading public. On this last point about audience, he aligned himself with Johnson and against both Horace's cadre of connoisseurs and Wordsworth's self-reliance. Indeed, he went further than Johnson, who often expressed reservations about the judgment of readers in the writer's lifetime, whereas Scott trusted or at least accepted it. He imagined someone objecting to his rate of production, "The world say you will run yourself out," and he responded, "The world say true; and what then? When they dance no longer, I will no longer pipe."[82] To Scott's concept of the writer's role, which involves reshaping preexisting materials to suit contemporary readerships, we might give the name of *responsive* authorship.

Mary Brunton

Three years before the publication of *Waverley,* an Edinburgh novelist, publishing anonymously with Manners and Miller in Edinburgh and Longman in London, enjoyed an unexpected, perhaps unprecedented success. The author's excitement is practically audible in a letter written at the time: "Mr. Miller states the sale to be unexampled here. In five days 240 went out of the hands of the publishers."[83] The novel was *Self-Control,* and the unnamed author was Mary Brunton, the wife of a Church of Scotland minister. According to a review in the *Scots Magazine,* there was a buzz about the book in Edinburgh "almost before there was time to form any judgment of its contents."[84] The buzz spread to London, where Jane Austen, who was seeing her first novel through the press and feared that she might have been scooped (for *Sense and Sensibility* also advocates self-control), was unable to get hold of a copy.[85] The publishers had underestimated demand but quickly made up for their mistake. Three editions appeared in 1811 and a fourth in 1812. The book was certainly fashionable as well as "popular," for we have a glimpse of the young Byron at Hopwood Hall in 1811 before the days of his own literary celebrity, oddly dressed in embroidered shirts and white linen trousers, with a long gold chain around his neck; one morning, while other house guests were being entertained by having *Self-Control* read out to them, Byron "came in very often and smiled at 'the cant of it all' as he termed all the serious parts."[86]

Self-Control was unusual in a number of ways. Byron's reaction indicates one of them, its explicitly religious program. The "Dedication," addressed to Joanna Baillie, spells out the purpose of the book: "The regulation of the passions is the province, it is the triumph of RELIGION. In the character of Laura Montreville the religious principle is exhibited as rejecting the bribes of ambition," etc. Following on the enormous success of Hannah More's didactic *Coelebs in Search of a Wife* (published in December 1808 with five more editions in 1809), Brunton likewise aimed to make the circulating libraries into sources of the antidote as well as of the poison that they were generally blamed for dishing out. The movement toward serious, improving fiction, begun by the Evangelicals, strongly divided readers and reviewers: the *Critical Review* damned Brunton's novel as "methodistical *palavering,*" but the detractors were apparently offset by warm supporters.[87] Garside describes Brunton as leading the way in a "chain" of "morally charged domestic fictions."[88]

Unlike *Coelebs,* Brunton's novel is spirited and exciting, the story of a fatal love affair. The irresistible Colonel Hargrave, possessed of a fortune and "the near prospect of a title," is in love with seventeen-year-old Laura Montreville, daughter of a recently widowed half-pay officer—and she is in love with him. In the opening chapter, he impulsively urges her to elope with him and become his mistress. But Laura, as pure as she is beautiful, not only rejects the idea with horror but also refuses his proposals of marriage the next morning with a sharp rebuff: "I fear, Sir, I shall not be suitably grateful for your generosity, while I recollect the alternative you would have preferred."[89] Matters go from bad to worse, and although she is increasingly impoverished, isolated, and defenseless, Laura holds out against Hargrave and manages to detach herself from him emotionally, until in the end he resorts to having her kidnapped and carried out of the country. At the last moment she makes her escape, but Hargrave, believing that he has driven her to her death, takes his own life. Having learned the hard way to distinguish between love and romantic delusion, Laura marries the worthy, steadfast, self-controlled Montague De Courcy instead, and lives happily ever after. The last sentence of the book makes the moral unambiguous: "The joys that spring from chastened affection, tempered desires, useful employment, and devout meditation, must be felt—they cannot be described."[90]

As this summary suggests, spiritual education accounted for only a small part of the appeal of *Self-Control*. Religious and moral principles sustain Laura Montreville: like Richardson's Clarissa before her, this heroine repeatedly invokes Christian values, quotes the Bible, and trusts to Providence. But the novel, never sententious for long, is full of adventure and incident. Laura is remarkably self-sufficient. At one point, fending off a suitor in a carriage, she takes the reins herself and stops the horses long enough for her to climb out and make her own way home; notoriously, in the final chapters she escapes from a log cabin somewhere near Quebec City by going over a waterfall in a birchbark canoe, an episode that excited universal derision. Yet for all the thrilling external events, the principal site of action is clearly within and between the minds of the characters, and the most momentous events occur there, as an epigraph from Cowper about "warfare . . . within" and spiritual triumphs announces on the title page. To convey the mental states of her characters and to illustrate the value of self-examination or "devout meditation," Brunton developed a sophisticated technique of interior monologue. We call this technique (her second departure from the novelistic run of the mill) free indirect discourse and the product of it, psychological realism. While reviewers of Brunton's time praised her knowledge of the human heart without attempting to explain how she achieved her effects, close-reading critics of our day now argue that she deserves some of the credit for innovations in the novel that often have been assigned to Austen.[91]

A third component in Brunton's surprise success was her Scottishness, a quality that may have contributed to the buzz in Edinburgh. What Edgeworth had done so successfully for the Irish, Brunton was now attempting to do, in a small way at first, for the Scots—no doubt with the approval of her Edinburgh publishers, who specialized in Scottish authors and subjects. The action of *Self-Control* begins and ends in Scotland, with extended descriptions of scenery and social behavior. Laura's first language, we are told, was Gaelic; she is found in her native village and passes through "romantic Edinburgh" on her way to London. Her servants speak in dialect. Even her English suitor De Courcy has enjoyed the benefit of a Scottish education because his wise widowed mother sent him to university at Edinburgh rather than expose him to the temptations of the English universities. And we have a glimpse of the diaspora: when Laura is alone and penniless in North America, it is an honest Scottish captain who trusts her for her fare home.

Encouraged by the responses of readers and reviewers, Brunton made much greater and more daring use of Scottish materials in her second novel. In it the protagonist Ellen Percy, once a great heiress and coquette in London, loses her fortune and slides down the social ladder, finding work as a governess in an Edinburgh household and then, as she slides further, witnessing life in the tenements before finding a haven with a prosperous Highland family. Brunton's carefully documented Highland scenes would have had a more spectacular effect if *Discipline* ("by the Author of 'Self-Control'") had been published a few months before *Waverley,* instead of a few months after it; as it was, Brunton thought she would have to remove them but was talked out of the idea by her husband, who argued that both works might benefit from a second, different treatment of the same subject.[92]

Discipline was another commercial success, with two more British editions in 1815 as well as an American one. As the interchangeability of the titles might suggest, it shares some of the same features as *Self-Control.* It is a religious novel in the Evangelical mode, with an exciting plot that ends, after much vicissitude, in the happy marriage of the heroine; and it has even more of the intense interiority that marked Brunton's first effort. But its heroine is almost the opposite of the first—not a paragon but a penitent, a spoiled child redeemed by great suffering. Structurally the book is almost evenly divided between the sinful, selfish, heedless stage that precedes her fall and conversion, and the long and arduous process of spiritual rehabilitation. (For the Evangelicals, a true change of heart could not be the work of a moment.) In another departure from the *Self-Control* model, Brunton chose to make the flawed protagonist the first-person narrator—a risky decision that paid off in greater suspense and readerly engagement with the character. Readers and reviewers had objected that Laura was too perfect, and Brunton heeded their views. As she once wrote to a correspondent, "Give me your advice, and, if I like it, I will take it."[93]

Brunton did not write to a formula; each work was an experiment. After *Discipline,* she wanted to break with melodrama and to attempt "a collection of short narratives, under the title of Domestic Tales."[94] But she died in December 1818 after the birth of a stillborn child. The only fictional work

that her husband published in a posthumous volume in 1819, along with letters and some other literary remains, was *Emmeline,* left incomplete but already 100 pages long and with a plan that showed how the story was to end.
Here the marriage of true lovers is not the end but the starting point of the
tale, with the further twist that the bride is a divorcée—a delicate subject
that Brunton handles without sensationalism or censoriousness. External action is humdrum to a degree; on the other hand, the psychological drama is
excruciating, thanks to the author's combination of sympathy and remorse-
lessness, and to the claustrophobic relationship of the lovers. For the most
part, Brunton exposes their unhappy circumstances without overt moralizing, in a powerful realistic narrative. The novel is written in the third person,
but the thoughts and feelings of the two central figures (also, very briefly, of
one other character) are revealed by a variety of devices, including dialogue
and free indirect discourse. Because they cannot bring themselves to talk
openly about their plight, Emmeline and her new husband misunderstand
and misinterpret one another. Their shared isolation has an increasingly
corrosive effect, until at the end, according to the draft of the plot outline,
love will be gone and Emmeline will be left completely alone.

In his introduction to the posthumous collection in which Mary Brunton
was officially named as an author for the first time, Alexander Brunton observed that the first two novels "rose very fast into celebrity, and their popularity seems to have as quickly sunk away."[95] He thought that if his wife had
lived and written more, she would have earned lasting esteem. *Emmeline,* a
mere fragment, did not enjoy the "popularity" of the earlier titles, but it did
receive positive reviews from *Blackwood's* (whose reviewer said it might be
just as well that it was left incomplete, because "the reader could scarcely
have borne a long story of such misery and such guilt") and from the
Monthly Review (which commended the moral and the serious treatment of
"secluded and domestic life," while acknowledging that the story was "pain-
ful"), and it was reprinted with the other titles in a complete edition of *The
Works of Mary Brunton* in seven volumes in 1820.[96]

For forty years after the death of the author, through roughly the first half
of the Victorian period, Brunton's works maintained a respectable place—
higher than Austen's—in the ranks of fiction, as indicated by publishing history and by coverage in reference books. *Discipline* appeared in a German
translation in 1822; *Self-Control* and *Emmeline* were translated into French
(with *Emmeline* completed by the French translator) in 1829 and 1830, respectively. *Self-Control* and *Discipline* were taken up by Richard Bentley in
1832 for his "Standard Novels" series, and both appeared in Routledge's
"Railway Library" series in 1852 (figs. 8 and 9). Anne Elwood's *Memoirs of*

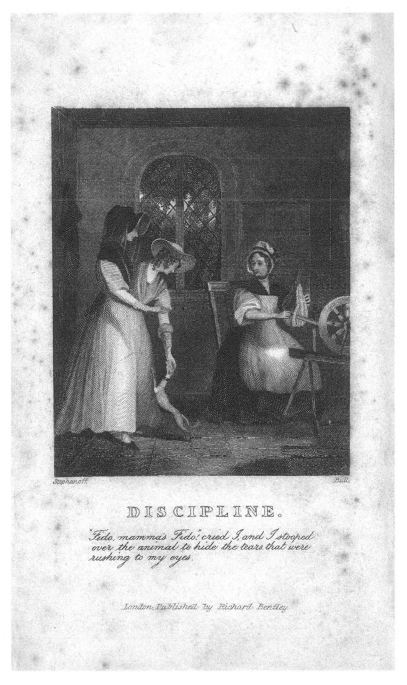

DISCIPLINE.

'Fido, mamma's Fido,' cried I, and I stooped over the animal to hide the tears that were rushing to my eyes.

London, Published by Richard Bentley.

Fig. 8. Frontispiece from Mary Brunton's *Discipline* in Bentley's "Standard Novels" edition (1849). © The British Library Board.

THE

STANDARD NOVELS AND ROMANCES.

WITH the view of placing this great collection within the reach of all classses of readers, Mr. BENTLEY has determined to publish

A NEW EDITION OF

The Standard Novels and Romances

at a price which will enable every family to possess a most entertaining Library of Fiction, consisting of the best Works which have issued from the press of late years.

The Publisher is induced to adopt this measure in the expectation that a very large number of copies will be sold in consequence of the increased number of readers. Thus, the STANDARD NOVELS AND ROMANCES, from their style of Printing, Embellishment, and Binding, will still be the

CHEAPEST COLLECTION OF NOVELS IN THE ENGLISH LANGUAGE.

List of the Works contained in this celebrated Collection:

VOL.		AUTHOR.
1	THE PILOT. 2s. 6d.	COOPER.
2	CALEB WILLIAMS. 2s. 6d.	GODWIN.
3	THE SPY. 2s. 6a....	COOPER.
4	THADDEUS OF WARSAW. 2s. 6d. ...	MISS JANE PORTER.
5	ST. LEON. 2s. 6d.	GODWIN
6	LAST OF THE MOHICANS. 2s. 6d....	COOPER.
7 & 8	THE SCOTTISH CHIEFS. 2s. 6d each	MISS JANE PORTER.
9	{FRANKENSTEIN	MRS. SHELLEY.
	{GHOST SEER, Vol. I. 2s. 6d.	SCHILLER.
10	{EDGAR HUNTLY	BROCKDEN BROWN.
	{CONCLUSION OF GHOST SEER. 2s. 6d.	SCHILLER.
11	HUNGARIAN BROTHERS. 2s. 6d. ...	MISS A. M. PORTER.
12 & 13	CANTERBURY TALES. 2s. 6d. each	THE MISSES LEE.
14	THE PIONEERS. 2s. 6d.	COOPER
15	SELF-CONTROL. 2s. 6d.	MRS. BRUNTON.
16	DISCIPLINE. 2s. 6d.	MRS. BRUNTON.
17	THE PRAIRIE. 2s. 6d.	COOPER.
18 & 19	THE PASTOR'S FIRE-SIDE. 2s. 6d. each	MISS J. PORTER.
20	LIONEL LINCOLN. 2s. 6d.	COOPER.
21	LAWRIE TODD. 2s. 6d.	GALT.
22	FLEETWOOD. 2s. 6d....	GODWIN.
23	SENSE AND SENSIBILITY. 2s. 6d.	MISS AUSTEN.

Fig. 9. List of Bentley's "Standard Novels and Romances" in 1849, from a copy of Mary Brunton's *Discipline* in the British Library, shelf mark 1578/2125. © The British Library Board.

the Literary Ladies of England of 1843 devoted sixteen pages to Brunton
compared with Austen's twelve, even though Brunton was Orkney born and
bred and could hardly be said to have been "of England" at all; less surprisingly, in the same year Robert Chambers's pioneering *Cyclopaedia of English
Literature,* published in Edinburgh, gave Brunton three pages and Austen only
one—though the difference can be accounted for by the inclusion of a long
extract from *Self-Control.* Ann Jones, who tracked the reputations of a substantial group of women writers through the nineteenth century, suggests that
the 1860 edition of Chambers, in which Brunton's entry was slightly shorter
than before but still longer than Austen's, marked the end of her viability as a
popular author.[97]

Jones's careful study *Ideas and Innovations: Best Sellers of Jane Austen's
Age* is a good example of the renewed attention given Brunton's work in the
late twentieth century, thanks to the feminist movement in literary scholarship. A hundred years after they had gone out of print, all three novels were
reprinted by specialist presses, and they are now also available through print
on demand and in digital versions on the Internet. Brunton is occasionally
the subject of academic articles and chapters in literary histories, especially
as a foil to Austen or as part of the literary history of Scotland. But as far as the
nonacademic audience is concerned, she remains a niche writer, unknown and
unread—as was only to be expected. That's the norm for all writers, especially
where, as in her case, the body of work is small. Moreover, since her novels
occupy a place halfway between her contemporaries Scott and Austen in a
system that has room for only a few stars, Brunton's achievement, real as it
was, was easily eclipsed by both of them. (Or, more accurately, by one after the
other: first by Scott while she held her own against Austen and other women
writers of their generation, and then by Austen when Austen displaced Scott
toward the end of the century.) I think of Brunton as a literary good loser—an
original and gifted writer who nevertheless fell by the wayside.

Comparison with the posthumous careers of Scott and Austen suggests
other reasons besides artistic inferiority and natural obsolescence for the decline of interest in Brunton's novels. Her husband died in 1854, about the time
that her works went out of copyright and therefore ceased to be of much
value to a publisher. The Bruntons had no children and, unlike Austen and
Scott, no extended family to take pride in the connection with her; thus they
had no homegrown champions. They were not associated with any particular picturesque spots. They did not command a publishing empire; Brunton's
works had to take their chances in the market without introductions or the
periodic renewal of illustrations and commentary (such as the prefaces Scott
wrote for his magnum edition). Alexander Brunton's memoir of Mary, like

the account of Jane Austen written on a like occasion by her brother in his "biographical notice" of 1818, stressed her Christian virtues and authorly modesty, omitting the more colorful or controversial aspects of her private life (the circumstances of their own courtship and elopement, for instance). But throughout the nineteenth century it was the only source of information about her, so biographically she is practically a cipher. Unlike the novels of Austen, which—as an influential textbook of 1836 observed—"may be placed in the hands of any reader," Brunton's novels were not considered suitable for children and never made their way into the classroom, let alone into the university curriculum.[98] While it's true that extramarital sex occurs in some of Austen's novels, it is so decorously veiled that it could easily be missed or misinterpreted, whereas Brunton's novels regularly and openly deal with adultery, illegitimacy, divorce, suicide, and violence in various forms. The hostile *Critical Review* remarked of *Self-Control* that parents would hardly wish to see their daughters "take up a *religious* novel and read of *rapes*."[99]

Mary Brunton's own expectations and aspirations may also have worked against her. Her letters, published in her husband's prefatory memoir, show that she carefully weighed her reasons for writing novels and knew what she was doing. There were strong deterrents. Brunton was even more retiring than Crabbe, perhaps for some of the same reasons. Like most women writing in the period, Austen among them, she dreaded public exposure and welcomed anonymity. She did not court popularity ("a mere lottery" as far as she could see, unrelated to merit) and seems to have been truly distressed when word got out that she was the author of *Self-Control*: she said she would have burned the manuscript if she'd known that was going to happen. She sounds sincere when she protests that she does not covet "fame," especially when she adds that she does fear censure and failure (by the latter, she appears to have meant neglect or indifference). Nor did she write to make money, "though I love money dearly." Nor did she cultivate the novel as an art form, though she was a warm defender of the genre and expressed keen appreciation of the best practitioners, Burney and Edgeworth for example. It might be conventional hyperbole, but she said of Scott's *Old Mortality* that "the description—the exquisite drawing of character—the humour—the unrivalled fertility of invention—or rather the boundless observation" shown in it "would immortalize the author, even if he had no further claim to immortality." (So she thought a novelist could deserve "immortality.") She did not overvalue her own work. The flaws of *Self-Control* troubled her conscience—she uses that word—and she was sufficiently sensitive to criticism to have kept a list of faults of which it was accused by other people, though she judged them wrong.[100] Still, she went on writing out of a conviction that it was the way in which she could be most useful, conveying "lofty" moral truths in a palatable form to readers who needed to hear them but would pay them no attention in any other guise.[101]

Brunton's personal model of authorship is unique in the group of writers on whom this study is focused, although she was not the only author of her time to adopt it. It could be called *missionary* or *vocational* authorship: something had to be done, she could do it, and she therefore felt called to do it. Awkward as it sounds to secular ears and for all its dreadful associations, "missionary" is perhaps the more accurate term. Brunton was quite defiant about the consequences of her convictions when she responded to friendly criticism in a letter of 1815. Well aware that an overt religious agenda was liable to injure both her art and her popularity, she would not muffle it or compromise an effort to do good to readers who could not be reached by tracts and sermons: "As for my *religion,* I allow that there is too much for amusement, perhaps for good taste; nevertheless I cannot bate you one iota. For the great purpose of the book [*Self-Control*] is to procure admission for the religion of a sound mind and of the Bible, where it cannot find access in any other form."[102]

We will never know what exactly it was that drew readers to *Self-Control*—by word of mouth, if the *Scots Magazine* is to be believed—even before there was time for opinions to have been formed about it. Probably it was the novelty of religious fiction, the prospect of instruction along with entertainment (or, more cynically, the prospect of *licensed* entertainment, entertainment with parental approval): Hannah More's much less engrossing *Coelebs* had also been an instant success. Whatever it was, Brunton's first novel caused a run on the bookstores, and her second seems to have been equally popular, even if they both "rose very fast into celebrity, and their popularity seems to have as quickly sunk away," as her husband put it. The charm gradually dissipated over time, as popularity based on novelty usually does.

Popularity itself may have been the nail in the coffin of Brunton's reputation. It provided the impetus needed to carry her novels into the publishers' series, but no more. To move beyond that point in the later nineteenth century, they needed support from another class of reader: the professional writer, critic, or publisher. As the earlier quotations from Peacock and Lake indicate, there was a widespread belief that a work that pleased many in its own day could not, almost by definition, be a work that would last for all time. Publishers sought out the new or the certified, and the specialists who provided certification, whether they were successful fellow writers or qualified scholars, depended for their cultural status on their distance from the crowd. Brunton failed their test, and even Scott may have been brought down at last by the weight of too much popularity. It put discerning readers off. Once works cease to be popular, the very reputation of having been popular operates against their ever becoming popular again. Jane Austen, however, suffered from no such disadvantage.

Jane Austen

Up to 1860, the career paths of Jane Austen and Mary Brunton were strikingly similar. If Brunton had an advantage in the reviews and reference books, Austen—who after all produced more novels—gradually took the lead in numbers of editions and reprints. Almost exact contemporaries, they both started publishing fiction for the circulating-library market in 1811 and achieved a measure of recognition before they were cut off by death, Austen in 1817 at the age of forty-two and Brunton in 1818 at forty. Within a year of their deaths, their families produced the customary posthumous tribute of a memoir with literary remains, in both cases publicly naming "the Author of" for the first time. Brunton's publisher brought out a collected edition of her works in seven volumes in 1820, but Austen had to wait until 1833, when Bentley, who had acquired the copyrights of her novels for his "Standard Novels" series from two separate owners, finally issued a set of "The Novels of Miss Austen" in five volumes.[103] Bentley kept the works of both authors in print through the 1840s and then, as individual titles began to come out of copyright, Routledge and other publishers moved in with cheaper editions—not many, but enough to suggest that the novels were still viable, and with the same target audience of "railway" readers and "parlour" readers.[104] Reference books of the time described them in similar terms as authors of morally improving domestic fiction—the one English, the other Scottish. The one early reader whom we know of who thought to compare the two—the actor William Macready, reading *Emma,* probably in Bentley's set, in 1834—expressed his preference for Brunton.[105]

When Brunton's name comes up in Austen's letters, Austen always makes a point of distancing herself from her rival's kind of fiction. She declares that *Self-Control* has nothing of "Nature or Probability" in it, though she concedes that it is well-intentioned and "elegantly-written"; on another occasion, she sportively proposes to write a novel as unlike her own and as much like Brunton's *Self-Control* as possible.[106] Following her lead, Austen specialists always stress the contrasts between them, particularly between Brunton's adopted vehicle of the "novel of incident," as Kathryn Sutherland legitimately labels it, and Austen's deliberately uneventful plots.[107] I do not deny the differences between Brunton's work and Austen's, nor the significance of those differences, but an exclusive concentration on what sets Austen apart from her contemporaries does both parties a disservice. Austen was neither a freak nor a pioneer hacking out a fresh path. Like Scott and Brunton, she had learned from her predecessors and wrote gratefully about them. She appears even to have learned lessons about the representation of interiority from Brunton.[108] (And Brunton may have learned from her. Though her letters do not refer directly to Austen's work, the plan to write more "domestic" fiction after *Discipline* and the marked absence of exciting incidents in *Emmeline* at least show her moving in Austen's direction. "Domestic" was a label that reviewers typically attached to Austen's novels.)[109] Austen's work was conventionally mainstream enough to thrive in a market dominated by circulating libraries, and good enough of its kind to earn the Prince Regent's request for a dedication (which she reluctantly provided, in *Emma*). Brunton and Austen both wrote improving novels with abstract titles, featuring likable and essentially good young women with flawed parents and sketchy suitors. They reliably include familiar conversation, comical minor characters, country houses, wise but unobtrusive narrators, hard cases of conscience, and happy endings. When I first read Brunton's books, it was the likeness between the style and settings of her novels and Austen's that struck me most. There is also some evidence that contemporary readers could not tell them apart: after Queen Charlotte died in 1818, the sale catalogue of her library attributed Brunton's two novels to Austen.[110]

What happened to Brunton—the gradual fading and extinction of her name—could easily have happened to Austen. From the vantage point of the 1860s, it might have seemed inevitable that it should. But as we all know, exactly the opposite happened: far from declining, the reputation of Jane Austen began an upward climb that looks, a century and a half later, as though it will never end.[111] Austen rapidly accumulated most of the tributes that the nineteenth century had paid to Scott (translations, adaptations, illustrations, pilgrimages) and garnered others unimagined by the Victorians, such as reenactments, academic conferences, the heritage industry, websites, and *Pride and Prejudice and Zombies*. Scott's reputation barely carried his works into the era of movies, but Austen triumphed in it. She is routinely described, with awe, as a classic equally successful in the academy and with the general public, "a major writer as popular and accessible to the public as any contemporary," in the words of Marilyn Butler, "a popular author as well as a great one, with a considerable cult," according to Brian Southam in his second volume of collected reviews and opinions.[112] There is no need for me to document this phenomenon, both because that has been well done already and because the proof is all around us.[113] What I can do is consider it in relation to the process of writing for immortality and in comparison with Austen's counterparts Scott and Brunton. I shall begin by considering Austen and her posthumous career in the years leading up to what is widely accepted as a transformative event, the publication of James Austen-Leigh's *Memoir* in 1870.

Jane Austen did not write for immortality—that is to say, there is no record of her declaring that ambition.[114] Of course she might have harbored hopes but been restrained by convention from expressing them: like Brunton, she was part of the respectable family of a clergyman and did not put her name to her books. Both women expressed horror at the idea of being publicly exposed as writers. Brunton said she would feel like a ropedancer, Austen that she would be like a wild beast on exhibition.[115] On the other hand, both spoke up for the novel and gave thanks for fellow artists, Austen notably in the extravagant defense of the novel ("work in which the greatest powers of the mind are displayed," etc.) given to the narrator in chapter 5 of *Northanger Abbey*, Brunton in the letters that were published with her husband's memoir in 1819. They seem to have believed that the best novelists deserved "immortality." But they forswore lasting fame for themselves, and I believe they meant it. That position would have been not only traditionally modest but also realistic under the circumstances: in the circulating libraries, novels circulated only until they were displaced by something newer. Austen and Brunton also rejected "popularity," though they both welcomed the prospect of riches that even a temporary popularity could provide. Austen's rare comments about her work invariably say that what she hoped for was not fame but money— though she did admit that she enjoyed praise, which is to say the approval of her own circle. Greed and vanity, she cheerfully declared, were the forces that drove her.[116] (Claire Harman admiringly calls her attitude toward publishing "hard-nosed.")[117] She did not further differentiate between these two favorite sins, but it's worth pointing out that while the commercial motive might have led her to write fiction in the first place, it was the desire for praise from the readers whose praise she valued, the people she wanted to please, that would motivate her to write as well as she could and then to rewrite and polish as much as she did. Hers was not a model of missionary authorship but not purely mercenary, either, as her casual comments in letters suggest. She was proud of writing well. I don't want to use "hard-nosed" or "selfish." Can we call it "self-motivated" authorship?

Until 1860 or so, Brunton and Austen held their places in the field of popular fiction more or less lockstep, as I have indicated, with Brunton enjoying perhaps a small advantage. In the 1860s, with hindsight, we can see that Austen's works began to outpace those of her rival, thanks in part to multiple American reprints of all her novels in the 1840s and 1850s, which had circulated along with English editions and laid the foundation of an overseas following. (The afterlife of Keats followed a similar pattern: American audiences led the way.) American reviewers of the 1840s and 1850s praised and recommended her work; we hear of an American fan, Susan Quincy, who contacted the Austen family in 1852 hoping for an autograph and was sent one of Jane Austen's letters.[118] British reviewers also spoke up for her occasionally, citing the positive views of eminent critics such as Walter Scott and Richard Whately, archbishop of Dublin.[119] In a particularly notable *Blackwood's* article published in 1859, G. H. Lewes described Austen as a novelist who was widely read but unknown, which is to say that readers enjoyed the novels but did not attach her name to them. He noted that Scott, Whately, and Macaulay had expressed their admiration, "but beyond the literary circle," he wrote, "we find the name almost entirely unknown." (There's a distinction to be observed here. Lewes did not say that the novels were unread—on the contrary—only that the majority of the readers who liked them did not make the connection between works and writer.) He pointed out that there was no portrait of the author and that people knew nothing about her life; he called for a proper biography. The reason for public ignorance, he suggested, was that the excellence of her work is "excellence of an unobtrusive kind, shunning the glare of popularity."[120] It seems to have been a groundswell of pressure such as this from diverse sources that eventually led members of the Austen family to marshal their resources for the first freestanding biography, persuading Bentley to adopt it as a companion volume when he issued a new edition of the novels in his "Favourite Novels" series in 1870.[121]

It proved a good investment. The *Memoir* was quite widely reviewed. It sold well enough to justify an expanded second edition in 1871 that included previously unpublished literary remains—*Lady Susan, The Watsons,* extracts from *Sanditon,* and a canceled chapter from *Persuasion*—entailing a fresh round of reviews and increased demand leading to further editions (six altogether by 1886).[122] Initially sold alongside Bentley's collected edition of the novels, it was incorporated as part of it when it was renamed the Steventon Edition—the name itself inspired by details in the *Memoir*—in 1882.

The *Memoir* was very much a family affair. Austen-Leigh built on Henry Austen's "biographical notice" of 1818 and acknowledged the contributions of sisters and cousins whose recollections supplemented his own.[123] Family industry carried the project of documentation and memorialization well into the twentieth century, when it was taken over by professional scholars. Austens laid the groundwork, providing among other things the essential instruments of an edition of Austen's letters and a definitive life-and-letters biography.[124] In 1894 a leading academic critic, George Saintsbury, coined a word and declared himself a Janeite.[125] But the type had existed as early as 1876, when what Leslie Stephen referred to as "Austenolatry" was already in the air, thanks mainly to the efforts of Austen-Leigh.[126] Although on close inspection, as Annika Bautz has pointed out, publishing history shows that the number of editions of Austen's works was already growing, that the *Memoir* had no immediate effect on sales, and that therefore it could be considered as merely "part of an upward trend" (reflecting rather than producing the reversal of Austen's reputation after 1870), what the *Memoir* unquestionably did do was create an enduring image for Jane Austen. It put a face to the relatively unknown author and made her an object of idolization.[127]

The first substantial biography and the only one available for the next forty years, the *Memoir* was the founder of the mainstream critical tradition as well as the origin of the cult. (Southam suggests that 1870 also marked the start of the countertradition that emphasizes Austen's satire, irony, and malice, in the form of an iconoclastic essay by a Shakespearean scholar, Richard Simpson. But Simpson's essay had little or no impact at the time.)[128] Austen-Leigh's act of family piety brilliantly matched Austen's life to the interests and values of genteel mid-Victorian Britain, creating a myth of enduring authority: that of a ladylike "dear aunt Jane," who lived contentedly in a country village "in entire seclusion from the literary world," put family duties first, and was, in her own words, "the most unlearned and uninformed female who ever dared to be an authoress." She was a natural genius, and "whatever she produced was a genuine home-made article."[129] What seem to us now the transparent distortions of the *Memoir* had a number of unexpected consequences. By conflating Austen with her heroines, they created a rounded portrait of an author who had been imageless before. By dwelling upon her unpopularity, they made her popular. The *Memoir*'s romanticized descriptions of places gave her locatability and visualizability. And Austen-Leigh's nostalgic representation of the family background made Jane Austen, whose determined realism had led some readers of her own time to reject her novels as too tediously ordinary, into a romancer, a historical novelist in her own right, poised to displace even Walter Scott.

Austen-Leigh was not yet twenty when Jane Austen died, and he had never known her well. He was over seventy when he wrote the *Memoir*. These facts make it easy to account for the method and tone of his work. In the first place, it is clear that he felt he had come to "know" Austen through her novels. (Interestingly, in a move that supports Bautz's research and her conclusions, he seems to presume that his readers had also already read them.) Unlike his predecessor Henry Austen, he does not make a clear separation between Austen's life and her fictions; on the contrary, in the Victorian mode of biographical criticism, he blurs distinctions and is given to circular reasoning with inferences from one to the other. The Austens' house in Steventon, he tells us, had on its southern side "a terrace of the finest turf, which must have been in the writer's thoughts when she described Catherine Morland's childish delight in 'rolling down the green slope at the back of the house.'"[130] The actual life, then, "must have been" the basis of the imagined world. Correspondingly, the imagined world provides evidence about the actual life. "There can be no doubt that Jane herself enjoyed dancing," writes Austen-Leigh, "for she attributes this taste to her favourite heroines." But there was no need for inference: Henry Austen's notice of 1818 had already testified that "she was fond of dancing, and excelled in it."[131] Using the novels as evidence of the life and personality of the author in the absence of more trustworthy sources such as letters and contemporary reminiscences, Austen-Leigh constructed a character as satisfyingly complete as any in fiction because it *is* a fiction.

For this beloved character he also provided a rich material background, reinforcing the impression he wanted to give of a retired and devout but definitely genteel life, untainted by scandal. At one point he quotes Charlotte Brontë's rejection of the Austen model, summed up as "ladies and gentlemen, in their elegant but confined houses," and thus reveals both the image that he endorsed (elegant houses) and the one that he opposed, that of the controversial modern woman writer—Brontë as represented by Elizabeth Gaskell in her celebrated *Life*, which he cites in a footnote, and for that matter Gaskell herself.[132] When Austen-Leigh came to write about Austen's family background, he specified indicators of class such as income and connections, just as Austen had done in her novels, but as commentators have often observed, he selected for respectability, mentioning the cousin who married a French count but suppressing the aunt who was charged with shoplifting and the brother who went bankrupt. Austen's immediate family "had peculiar advantages beyond those of ordinary rectories," he observed complacently.[133] He took the time to explain many customs and attitudes no longer prevalent, thus making Austen and her work representatives of a vanished era. This part of his work is charming still, with its details about rural and domestic life, for example the clipping of horses and home spinning, but it cultivated nostalgia and encouraged readers to use Austen's novels as an escape route from everyday life. In some ways he antedates her: it is disturbing to find him glossing the novels with parallels from the *Spectator* of a hundred years earlier, as though they belonged to the same era.[134] This part of the work, however, provides the groundwork for his assessment of her achievement at the end, when he maintains that she was above all an accurate portraitist, her writings "like photographs" that bring back a vanished world, "the opinions and manners of the class of society in which the author lived early in this century."[135]

The final element in the myth is contemporary neglect. Austen-Leigh added the name of Jane Austen to the growing catalogue of geniuses slighted by their own time—the model that Johnson had dismissed and Wordsworth promoted. He singled out for credit, however, the discerning few who had recognized her merit, strategically quoting a line from Horace that we have seen before, "satis est Equitem mihi plaudere" (It is enough if the Knights applaud me)—in Latin without translation, thus indicating that the people he was writing for were educated men like himself. He also names names and quotes testimonials or what we would call celebrity endorsements from respectable, serious men. "Archbishop Whately" and "Lord Macaulay" head the list, followed by other figures dear to the Establishment (at least at the safe distance of 1870), among them Robert Southey, S. T. Coleridge, Sir James Mackintosh, Lord Morpeth, Sir Henry Holland, William Whewell, Lord Lansdowne, Sydney Smith, and Sir Walter Scott.[136] "To the multitude" and to "readers of more ordinary intellect," on the other hand, according to Austen-Leigh, the novels still appear "tame and commonplace, poor in colouring, and sadly deficient in incident and interest."[137] Although the historical record clearly indicates otherwise—Austen always had numbers of readers, more than enough to keep up demand and keep her work in print—the effect of Austen-Leigh's survey in the *Memoir* was to endow her works with snob appeal, conveying the message that the novels were too subtle for common readers but that those who bought the complete edition with the *Memoir* attached belonged to a select, discriminating group. As Deidre Lynch points out in the introduction to *Janeites*, "Over the last century and a half much has been invested in the premise that the appreciation of Austen's excellence is a minority taste" or, in other words, "caviar for the deserving few." Thus "Austen's popularity is a function of her *not* being popular."[138]

The combination of image, nostalgic historical appeal, and caviar status contained in the 1870 *Memoir* and then reinforced in other projects of the Austen family lifted Austen's work over the next hurdles in the afterlife of a Romantic author—the rise of English literature as an academic subject, and the transfer to new media. Her works had already had a small role in education through Chambers's self-help series for young people and adults. Successive Elementary Education Acts between 1870 and 1893 ensured universal education for children in Britain; the Act of 1880 made schooling compulsory to the age of twelve. Unlike Brunton's novels, Austen's were judged suitable for children, and editors, abridgers, and publishers were quick to capitalize on the new market. In 1880, under the pseudonym "Sarah Tytler," Henrietta Keddie targeted young readers in *Jane Austen and Her Works,* a thick one-volume introduction that was successful enough to earn a public rebuke from Lord Brabourne in his edition of the *Letters* shortly after: he insisted that readers should not be content with Miss Tytler's summaries, but should read the books for themselves.[139] (In the long introduction to the letters, Brabourne revealed how he himself read the novels, reacting to the characters as though they had been personal acquaintances. "I frankly confess that I never could endure Mr. Knightley," he wrote. "I always wanted Emma to marry Frank Churchill, and so did Mr. and Mrs. Weston.")[140] Dramatizations of scenes from the novels began to appear about 1895, and abridgments about 1896.[141] Though the bibliographer David Gilson records no specially designed text-book editions of the novels before 1926, children were certainly being encouraged to read them, for instance Blackie's *Northanger Abbey* of 1895 in its "School and Home Library" series or Partridge's *Pride and Prejudice* of 1896, offered as "pure and healthy literature" for boys and girls in "these days of universal education"—along with Fry's chocolate, which was advertised on the back wrapper.[142]

In the same popularizing vein, in an increasingly competitive Austen market, publishers at the end of the nineteenth century raised the stakes with far more, and more creative, illustrations. Bentley's series had made do with frontispiece engravings of scenes from the novels. Some of the Routledge editions of the 1880s included attractive cover illustrations in color, and some of the serially published editions of the same decade included multiple woodcuts. An American edition of 1892 experimented with photographs. But the great phase of extensive illustration and named artists began in 1894 with Hugh Thomson's lively line drawings—kitschy, as Claire Harman complains, but almost as inseparable from the Austen image from then on as the illustrations of Phiz are from the works of Dickens (fig. 10). Drawings by C. E. Brock followed close on their heels, and today the list of artists associated with Austen illustrations runs to three tightly typeset columns in Gilson's index.[143] When the great age of illustration was succeeded by the great age of motion pictures, that in turn by video, and that in turn by the World Wide Web, Austen visualizers kept pace, and so it has come about that to some specialists today the majority of her fans seem scarcely literate: instead of rereading all the novels every year as their elders used to do, they watch "entire cycles of television and movie adaptations" over and over again.[144]

The Austen adaptation industry may have taken on a life of its own. Certainly the visual tradition has distinct conventions and its own line of descent, progressively more reliant on the cinematic kin and more independent of the texts that inspired them. But feature films are expensive to produce, and the

Looking on her with a face as pallid as her own.

Fig. 10. "Looking on her with a face as pallid as her own": an illustration by Hugh Thomson for Jane Austen's *Persuasion* (1913). Courtesy of University of Toronto Libraries.

triumphant sequence of Austen movies from the Olivier-Leigh *Pride and Prejudice* (1940) to the Bollywood *Bride and Prejudice* of 2004 and beyond, especially the boom from 1995 to the present day, would not have happened if readers had not been familiar with the novels since their school days, and *that* would not have happened if Austen's work had not been so universally approved of.

The contrast with Scott is telling. At the turn of the century, as Austen's star was rising, Scott's once universal popularity was waning, and complaints were more insistently leveled at the quality of his work. The mandarinate abandoned him. In 1896, when the self-proclaimed Janeite George Saintsbury, writing as a literary historian, described Scott and Austen as equally the parents of nineteenth-century fiction (he the father of the romance school, she the mother of the realistic novel), he expressed far warmer enthusiasm for Austen. She "set the clock," he said, for "pure novel-writing . . . to this present hour"—that is, she originated trends in the novel that came to dominate the nineteenth century and pointed the way forward, while Scott seemed always to be looking back. Saintsbury praised Austen's ability to extract "perennial and human" characteristics in her record of minute details in everyday life, thus achieving timelessness; but most of all he praised her irony as rare and subtle, and consequently inaccessible to duller readers.[145] (Scott, on the other hand, was and always had been notoriously accessible to readers of all kinds.) It was the backing of respected professionals such as Saintsbury, ones whose livelihood rested on their superior powers of discrimination, that saw Austen's novels onto university syllabi in Britain and North America even before the end of the nineteenth century.[146] Later significant academic landmarks were R. W. Chapman's edition of her works in 1923—the first scholarly edition of any British novelist, with full textual apparatus and historical annotation and illustration—and F. R. Leavis's co-opting of Austen in *The Great Tradition* (1948). Scott had historical importance that conferred one kind of lasting fame, but Austen's work appeared to be still relevant and still competitive with new writing—an extra level of distinction that belongs to real literary immortality.

Scott steadily lost both popular and critical support and was gradually relegated to the past, being no longer a household name, whereas Austen's readership continued to expand. Kramnick, citing Bourdieu, describes the way that popularity and prestige, or market values and aesthetic values, are perpetually at odds with one another, until those works that are identified as "artistic goods" are "released from the vulgar domination of commercial sales" and "the 'loser wins,'" but he does not discuss the further stage perfectly exemplified by Austen, whereby the supposedly unpopular author, having once gained canonical status, becomes commercially desirable as the source of a status-enhancing product.[147] When Virginia Woolf came to review an important new family biography in 1913, she could point out as a matter of fact that Austen's name would come at or very close to the top (first, second, or third) in anybody's list of the great English novelists.[148] And while Woolf herself may have felt some ambivalence toward Austen, other feminists adopted her—the mother of the novel, after all—wholeheartedly. Fellow writers—Kipling, James, Forster, and Wharton, for example—also expressed their admiration; she enjoyed high peer approval.

During the First World War and in its aftermath, while Scott might have been viewed, however unfairly, as a Scottish nationalist and even as a warmonger, Austen's novels came to symbolize core English peacetime values—though *which* values varied from time to time and from one sector to another.[149] Evidently Austen's works, like the Bible, contained something for almost everyone and could be selectively mined to support contradictory positions. The Jane Austen Society, founded in 1940 to see to the shrines and monuments, soon generated regional and international offshoots with their own evolving functions. Thus, by the middle of the twentieth century, Austen had attained the extraordinarily broad audience that we still see today: reader and nonreader, young and old, male and female, gay and straight. With its moviegoers, heritage tourists, quarreling academics, readers of popular romance, and historically minded reenactment buffs among others, her following remains unmatched for size, diversity, and loyalty by any of the poets. None of them comes close, not Wordsworth with his hillwalkers, Blake with his multimedia appeal, nor Byron with his international glamour. Much of her popularity she owes to her choice of genre, for everyone who can read can read novels, but for at least a century now not everyone has been capable of reading poetry, let alone of reading it for pleasure. But the process by which she outstripped other novelists of her age depended on less obvious factors, most of them extraneous to the works themselves, as the comparison with Scott and Brunton reveals.

Rising to Fame

In Scott, Brunton, and Austen, three writers of great gifts and great integrity, we find instructive examples of different attitudes to literary fame; different models of authorship; different career paths; and, of course, different outcomes. Brunton's success was shortest-lived and most conventional: after a flurry of public interest when her novels were new, they settled into a pattern of more or less respectable reliability. When they first appeared, the books benefited from some good reviews as well as from an element of controversy. They sold well enough in the early years to justify multiple editions, a collected edition, and some translations, and to be noticed in standard books of reference. But after fifty years they ceased to be viable and dropped out of sight. By the time they resurfaced, over a century later, as part of a feminist recovery project, they had become historical curiosities for specialists, mainly academics. It is hard, though not absolutely impossible, to imagine that Mary Brunton's novels will ever be read recreationally again. It *might* be done: anyone capable of reading Jane Austen would have no trouble with her prose. I like to think that one blockbuster movie or mainstream television series might do the trick. But in the absence of literary star power it does not seem likely, so she is left with a narrow readership and modest expectations.

Scott's success was of a different order of magnitude. Just as the initial sales of *Waverley* outstripped the other new fiction titles of its day, including Brunton's and Austen's, so Scott's productivity, his popularity, and the publishing juggernaut that he commanded swept the field to the end of his life and continued to grow for many years after his death. Translations, adaptations, and transfer into other media or what the analysts of cultural memory call "remediation" sustained his reputation and saw knowledge of his works diffused around the world during the nineteenth century.[150] Thereafter, without ever falling into oblivion like Brunton's, Scott's name and works ceased to be of current value—the books no longer read by everyone, fondly alluded to, taught in schools and devoured on holidays. Their status as classics gave them an extended but reduced shelf life in personal libraries. Their historical importance ensured a toehold in the world of learning, while changing frames of reference in the academy, from the Marxism of the mid-twentieth century through postcolonialism to today's variations on globalization, continued to guarantee them a place on the conference circuit if not—or barely—in the classroom. The recently completed first scholarly edition from the University of Edinburgh Press is certain to strengthen his presence in the universities, just as Chapman's landmark edition strengthened Austen's ninety years ago. Scott's fortunes have risen and fallen and could well rise again.

Mutatis mutandis, the rise to fame took much the same form for Austen as for Scott, despite her late start: once there were signs of renewed public interest (at his death, at her resurrection in 1870), the stakeholders set to work to supply the essential biography, the collected edition, and supplementary aids such as correspondence and reading guides. It proved to be an accidental advantage that her works were going out of copyright and Bentley no longer had sole control of them. Competitors added both cheaper and fancier editions to meet the needs of diverse markets, and thus Austen's sphere of influence spread just as Scott's had, generating more and more editions, biographies, adaptations, and offshoots. Unlike Scott and Brunton, who now rely on niche appeal (their Scottishness) and intellectual interest (the universities), Austen— "Austen" in this case comprising her personal image and the characters she created—is widely beloved. But so was Scott once. It seems more than likely that Austen will eventually lose her special status, brought down as he was

by overexposure and too much respectability, the price of unusually sustained popularity. Whether she does or not will be determined partly by circumstances that we cannot foresee, and partly by ones that we have repeatedly
seen in operation but that are beyond the control of the author: the energy
and effectiveness of agents acting on her behalf; the buzz generated by the
coexistence of multiple audiences; and successful remediation, or transfer into
the medium of the day, like the Scott operas of the nineteenth century and
the Austen movies of today.

Interlude

As the case studies in this book unfolded, I found patterns emerging from the growing mass of data and tried to gather them in the form of a checklist, a tool that I could use in the analysis of new cases. It would be a reminder of factors that had proved significant before, I thought, and a means of increasing consistency. Although the conditions of publication vary from time to time and from place to place, the general literary system in the English-speaking world has been fairly stable from the eighteenth century to the present day. As new works are composed and published, they are promoted—by their authors, the authors' allies, and the publishers—by whatever the current methods of publicity happen to be. They are reviewed, discussed, reprinted or not, and the author begins to build a reputation. When the author dies there may be a further flurry of activity with collected works, a biography, memorial tributes—all of them reviewed in turn, and so the process continues.

Writers of the Romantic period who had to make their posthumous way through the nineteenth and twentieth centuries faced a set of challenges they could not have foreseen, especially in the area of education, as English took a central place in the schools, recitation became a rite of passage, and books or works that had been fiercely argued over in their own day became modern classics that every cultivated person was expected to know and admire.[1] As classics they accrued new features: a secondary literature of interpretation and commentary, notice in reference books, allusions in new writing that referred to them as part of a common cultural code. Ann Rigney describes compellingly the way that Scott and the Waverley novels infiltrated "everyday remembrance" by "being repeated over again, in different media and different forums, which maximize their public presence"—that is, by a sort of buzz or constant hum of voices that keeps the name in circulation.[2] Something similar happens to every writer who achieves any degree of fame.

The following, then, is a list of categories that appear to have been necessary or desirable to produce lasting fame for the cohort of Romantic writers under investigation. In its original form, it followed a roughly chronological progression from publication to canonization in the academy. The separate steps or phases are not tied to specific dates; they might occur at different points in the afterlives of different writers, some of whom—Austen for example—were (historically speaking) late bloomers. But once the process started it usually involved many if not all of these phases in more or less this order. The list is far from comprehensive. Other categories could be added: I do not include evidence about the naming of streets and railways stations after fictional characters and places, for instance, as Rigney was able to do for Scott. Scores of towns and villages in America were named "Auburn" after the star home place in Oliver Goldsmith's popular poem *The Deserted Village* (1770), but that sort of evidence is beyond the scope of this study. Since the perspective adopted is that of book history, the emergence of bookish categories is natural and perhaps even circular. Forewarned is forearmed, however; though the evidence is certainly biased in favor of a published record, that record still includes many forms of cultural impact besides books, such as literary tourism and adaptation in other media. I found the list helpful as the work of analysis and comparison continued, and I offer it in the name of transparency, as well as in the hope that it might be useful to other scholars.

The Checklist

1. Authorial ambition
2. Threshold quality
3. Threshold quantity
4. Number of copies in circulation: (a) UK; (b) English overseas
5. Variety of corpus
6. Authorial adjective
7. Critical tradition (reviews > belles-lettres > academic criticism)
8. Controversy

9.   Associates
10.   Celebrity endorsements
11.   Collected edition
12.   Biography
13.   Reference books
14.   Translation/international dissemination
15.   Visualizability: illustration, photography, cinema, Internet
16.   Locatability: association with place; tourism; shrine
17.   Anthologies or publishers' series
18.   Variety of audience
19.   Adaptation: other media—music, painting, stage, cinema
20.   Champions (societies, descendants, keepers of the flame, individual advocates)
21.   Education system: suitable for children?
22.   Higher education: fit to canon?

Some of the headings in the list are more self-explanatory than others, so I append a few comments. Numbers 2 and 3 are fundamental, but at the same time debatable or at least subjective, for the darlings of one age may be the outcasts of the next, as Johnson disparaged "the Granvilles, Montagues, Stepneys, and Sheffields" of previous generations, and Wordsworth in turn poured scorn on some of the authors that Johnson's *Lives* were designed to introduce—"Roscommon, and Stepney, and Phillips, and Walsh." The point of the quality requirement (number 2) is simply to call into question the assumption that only the very best writers will be remembered and read for a long time after their deaths. The historical record suggests, rather, that there are many ways of earning fame, and that while a minimum standard of literary competence can be taken for granted, not all famous writers owe their fame to outstanding literary merit alone (I would argue that none of them does), and instances of outstanding literary merit do sometimes go unrecognized. By "threshold quality" of course I do not mean basic literacy or anything near it: longevity sets a high standard—just not stratospheric.[3] Though it is only by the belated recognition of merit that we can be sure that it had been overlooked for a long time—and by then it is so no longer—such recognition happens often enough that it is safe to assume that it will happen again, that other similar inglorious (not mute) Miltons are ripe for rehabilitation. When they appear, the canons of criticism may have to be adjusted a little to accommodate them; then, as the rules change, more candidates become eligible.

The third heading requires a body of work of some volume: is any writer in English famous for a single poem, play, or prose fiction? Among the

Romantics, the name that might come to mind is Mary Shelley: *Frankenstein* had a long run all on its own before feminists and scholars rediscovered her other work in fiction, travel writing, and other prose media. But then they did, and her niche role as the author of a pioneering horror story was rapidly complicated and expanded. All the English classic authors are *widely* known, in fact, for only a fraction of their work—Coleridge for three poems, Mary Shelley for one novel, and even Austen and Scott for only one or two novels each—but it is important that the rest of the iceberg should be there for the devoted.

The fourth heading is intended to cover rare cases like that of Blake, in which few copies physically survived the death of the author. Great names are not made out of nothing. Though Johnson identifies several classical authors whose works have vanished but whose names are celebrated, such names have only historical glory—the reputation of great achievements—without the second form of fame exclusive to literature and the arts: continuing renown in the present for work that continues to be experienced at first hand. In principle, a single copy, even a single manuscript copy, might form the basis of a great reputation, but in practice there are usually many copies in circulation and most major authors have had some works constantly in print. The question here might be, rather, is it possible to have too many copies in circulation; can saturation breed disgust?

The remaining headings require little or no comment, since they have been raised and discussed already, and previous chapters provide illustrations of them. Something that might not be obvious, however, is the way that some of the categories could backfire and have a negative effect. Authorial ambition or self-confidence could either win adherents or put people off, as seems to have happened with Southey. Controversy might be a good thing in general, as Johnson declared—and Boswell said he thought Johnson actually enjoyed being attacked in the press by "this perpetual shower of little hostile arrows" because it was proof of his renown.[4] But if the writer were defeated in the contest, that could be the end. For all his accomplishments and advantages, Southey definitively lost to Byron, with the result that some of his works are remembered only as the occasion of Byron's jeering verses. Celebrity endorsements certainly assisted Austen's cause, but the fact that Crabbe had been approved of by Johnson and Burke left him relegated to eighteenth-century studies in the long run. A good biography is often the way an audience is first attracted to a writer, as we have seen with Austen and will find again in later chapters; or it might consolidate a solid reputation based on the works themselves, as with Scott; but a bad or merely weak biography might do real damage. The same principle holds for other headings. Being taken into a successful publishers' series such as Bentley's "Standard Novels" was a lucky break for Austen and Brunton; being part of a series that went nowhere might be inconsequential, and it might even deter other publishers from making an investment and therefore be a disadvantage in the long run. Adaptation in itself is a positive sign, but a bad adaptation might mislead the public and drive people away from the original works, which would defeat the writers' purpose: Ken Russell's sensational orgiastic representation of the lives of the Byron-Shelley circle in Switzerland, the 1986 film *Gothic,* might be offered as an example. On the other hand, what is "bad" in such a context? Perhaps only public indifference. James Whale's 1931 version of *Frankenstein* was a travesty by literary standards, but it built on a theatrical tradition and brought Mary Shelley's work into the twentieth century with panache. The dissemination not of her name but of the name of the work has been phenomenal (genetically modified crops are popularly known as "Frankenstein" foods; on the drive to the airport, Torontonians pass a small business called "Frankenstein Fitness"), and it can nearly all be traced to Boris Karloff's Monster.

In the competition among "classic" works to stay in print through the nineteenth and twentieth centuries, the categories on the list can be shown to have played critical roles, and in all the most successful cases we find a convergence of categories operating simultaneously and dynamically in the author's favor (no single category being decisive). The categories themselves, however, ought ideally to be refined and calibrated for effectiveness. They might unintentionally have worked against the writer's interests, as I have explained. Less dramatically, since some advocates are manifestly more valuable than others, the advantages they confer may vary considerably. Association with Murray or Bentley gave writers access to resources and publishing experience they would never find with small presses such as that of John Taylor, who published Keats and Clare. The critical approval of a Macaulay, a Rossetti, or a Saintsbury counted for more, at crucial moments, than that of a Jeffrey or a Hazlitt, no matter how powerful Jeffrey and Hazlitt had been in their own day. I have not attempted any finer calibration of the checklist; it remains a blunt instrument, but I have tried to keep in mind the bluntness of it and the implicit presence of scales within scales.

A revised version of the list shifts from roughly chronological order to a ranking of categories by importance. The factors that appear to have been essential—what might be thought of, in the lingo of the questionnaire, as required fields—are marked with an asterisk in addition to being at the top of the list. On the suggestion of one of our smart graduate students, I renamed it a "scorecard" by analogy with sports and games, and played with systems of scoring that allowed for negative numbers (as in the case of disastrous defeat in controversy or seriously damaging revelations in a biography) so as to produce grand totals. It's still crude, it's far from scientific, but it produces some intriguing comparisons. It will serve as a point of reference in the chapters that follow.

The Scorecard

1. *Threshold quality
2. *Threshold quantity
3. *Champions (societies, descendants, keepers of the flame, individual advocates)
4. *Biography
5. Number of copies in circulation: (a) UK; (b) English overseas
6. Critical tradition (reviews > belles-lettres > academic criticism)
7. Visualizability: illustration, photography, cinema
8. Locatability: association with place; tourism; shrine
9. Adaptation: other media—music, painting, stage, cinema, Internet
10. Variety of audience
11. Anthologies or publishers' series
12. Reference books
13. Education system: suitable for children?
14. Higher education: fit to canon?
15. Translation/international dissemination
16. Controversy
17. Celebrity endorsements
18. Variety of corpus
19. Authorial ambition
20. Associates
21. Collected edition
22. Authorial adjective: positive/negative

4

What About Merit?

The commonsense answer to questions about why we (culturally, collectively, historically, and individually) admire Wordsworth and Austen more than Southey and Brunton is that they are immeasurably better writers, the authors of masterpieces. Though the checklists of the previous chapter give short shrift to merit, the concept of immortalization relies ultimately on the idea of the recognition of quality over the long term; the test of time was and is still supposed to be the guarantor of merit. Since I maintain, to the contrary, that many factors play a part and that no more than threshold competence—a relatively low standard of merit—has ever been necessary to keep a writer's works in favor, the present chapter aims to test and illustrate that argument by focusing on Keats and two contemporary poets who were regularly associated with him in his lifetime: Bryan Waller Procter (who published under the pseudonym "Barry Cornwall," which is the name I shall use here) and Leigh Hunt. Both Cornwall and Hunt, members of the same poetic circle as Keats, ranked much higher in public estimation than he did in their day, though both of them admired his work and spoke up for him when they had the chance. Their reputations faded even as that of Keats grew and blossomed, with the result that as poets, Hunt and Cornwall are all but forgotten today, though efforts are under way to bring them back to public consciousness. It may seem quixotic—even ungracious—to do it, but reopening this old rivalry is a concrete way of showing how small a part merit plays in the process of recognition and reward. The focus on literary quality means that, in contrast to other chapters, quotation and close reading will play a central role in this one.

Keats and Immortality

Keats is surely the acid test of merit. He may at present be the best-loved English poet of all time, with powerful appeal to every one of the broad categories of audience—fellow writers, literary professionals and academic specialists, the reading public and the nonreading public alike. He has become iconic, not so much "a writer" as "the writer," not just canonized but worshipped. The Canadian bookstore chain Indigo until recently gave out plastic bags printed with a quotation from his letters, calculated to warm the book buyer's heart: "Give me books, fruit, french wine, fine weather, and a little music . . ."[1] The thought itself is anodyne and has hardly anything to recommend it apart from the name of the author—which of course was also printed on the bag, with Keats's birth and death dates as a gesture to the educational establishment and, more humanly, as a reminder of the best-known fact about his life, that is, his early and poignant death.

The story of the evolution of Keats's reputation is relatively straightforward and has been told often, with few variations.[2] In the context of the tradition of writing for immortality, it is painfully but also triumphantly ironic. Keats is one of the best-documented cases of authorial ambition of his era, along with Wordsworth and Southey and (more ambivalently, though no less obsessively) Byron. In prefaces and published works as well as in private letters and impromptu verses, from the moment that he abandoned medicine and determined to make a career of literature up to the end of his life, Keats frankly and repeatedly expressed his desire for lasting fame.[3] In letters of October 1818, for example, meeting reports of poor sales and the hostility of critics with defiance, he wrote that he would "sooner fail than not be among the greatest," expressing confidence that "I shall be among the English Poets after my death."[4] But he also believed, in accordance with the conventional wisdom of the day, that the way to win that coveted status was by composing a great *long* poem. *Endymion* he knew was not good enough. (As an early American champion put it, he badly wanted fame, but more than that he wanted to deserve it.)[5] In his last and best writing year, from late 1818 through to the autumn of 1819, he abandoned several large-scale projects, including the two versions of *Hyperion*. At the time of his death he consequently believed that he had failed, and he left instructions for there to be no name on his gravestone, only the inscription—based on a line from one of the Jacobean plays that he admired—"Here lies one whose name was writ in water." As if a dreadful protracted illness and separation from the woman he loved were not enough, his unrealized dreams must themselves have blighted his end.[6] Keats was among other things a martyr to literary ambition.

No doubt the bold prediction of 1818 was sounder than the sense of despair that overtook him at the end. His potential had never been in question: all but the most transparently hostile reviewers gave him credit for that. And ultimately Keats, like Wordsworth, did come to be ranked among the greatest, though—also like Wordsworth—not in the way he would have imagined and not for the works he would have expected. Major factors contributing to the rise of his reputation in the decades immediately following his death included advocacy by influential friends; the general shift of taste away from the long poem to the lyric; some important publishing events with unforeseen consequences; and a landmark biography.

Keats's poetic output had been comparatively slight, three small volumes in four years, together with a few items published separately in newspapers and magazines. For at least two decades after his death, the work of dissemination was done mainly by way of collections and anthologies in which the stronger writers carried the weaker. As it turned out, the most influential of these collections were published outside Britain, part of the shadow trade of offshore publication.[7] In 1827 a group of booksellers in Paris, including Baudry and Galignani, issued an impressive two-volume set of *Living Poets of England . . . with Biographical and Critical Notices* (which in fact included a few poets recently dead), in which Hunt, Keats, and Cornwall were all included, with about twenty pages of selected poetry each, a respectable showing. Keats lost ground the following year, however, in a collection edited by J. W. Lake and published by Baudry. In *The British Poets of the Nineteenth Century. Including the Select Works of Crabbe, Wilson, Coleridge, Wordsworth, Rogers, Campbell, Miss Landon, Barton, Montgomery, Southey, Hogg, Barry Cornwall, and Others* (1828), which was intended to supplement Baudry's three single-author volumes devoted to Byron, Scott, and Moore, Keats counted only as one of the "Others" along with William Gifford, John Wolcot, Clare, Bowles, William Tennant, Shelley, Hunt, Lamb, George Croly, Baillie, Kirke White, Hemans, George Canning, Mary Ann Browne, and "Anonymous," each represented by a small number of poems (generally two or three) and without benefit of an introductory headnote. It was thus fortunate for him—and rather surprising—that Galignani, also in Paris, then grouped him with Shelley and Coleridge in a one-volume edition of their complete works in 1829, with an (anonymous) introductory "Memoir" by Cyrus Redding, another member of the Hunt circle.

That Galignani edition, reprinted in various configurations in the United States, secured him in America the following he lacked at home—even after Shelley and Coleridge had been replaced by Mary Howitt and Henry Hart Milman.[8] In 1842, well ahead of the official life-and-letters biography of 1848 by Richard Monckton Milnes that is usually seen as the watershed of Keats's reputation, James Russell Lowell declared Keats a rival to Milton; in 1854—drawing on Milnes's work but by no means slavishly repeating it—Lowell contributed a prefatory "life," frequently reprinted, to a Boston edition of Keats's works.[9] Milnes himself made a point of Keats's posthumous success in America, noting that though Keats was beginning to enjoy more recognition at home, his fame was brighter "in that other and wider England beyond the Atlantic, whose national youth is, perhaps, more keenly susceptible of poetic impressions and delights, than the mature and more conscious fatherland."[10] (This remark appears in the midst of a compliment to Lord Jeffrey, the dedicatee of Milnes's biography and one of the few who had reviewed Keats generously in 1820, but the compliment is double-edged. On one hand, Milnes implies that the American audience, like Jeffrey, had been able to judge fairly; on the other, he suggests that the best or at least the most appreciative readers for Keats are the young and unsophisticated.)

Besides the slow work of dissemination by way of anthologies and collections, during the relatively arid period from the 1820s to the early 1840s the memory of Keats was cherished and his poetry valued by a small number of fellow artists who shared their enthusiasm with one another. First were old friends from the Hunt circle, notably Shelley, Lamb, Hazlitt, Barry Cornwall, and Hunt himself, all of whom wrote about Keats's poetry with sincere appreciation—though not necessarily without reservations—and kept his name in circulation. Two early interventions proved particularly important in the long run. Shelley's tribute of *Adonais,* followed so soon by his own death and burial close by Keats in Rome, linked their posthumous fortunes inseparably. Hunt's account of Keats in his 1828 memoir of Byron and other contemporaries, a book that was widely condemned but also widely read, established key terms for the positive assessments of Keats that were to come.[11] Besides these personal friends there were a few admirers of the next generation who knew Keats only through his writings, such as Arthur Henry Hallam, Alfred Tennyson, and Richard Monckton Milnes, all of them aspiring poets. (Apostles at Cambridge together, as students they had arranged for the first English printing of *Adonais* in 1829. These influential Apostles, according to one commentator, "chose the unpopular for their heroes.")[12] Reviewers—one of them Hallam—were quick to comment, for good or ill, on the likeness between Keats's work and Tennyson's. Thus, as Tennyson's reputation grew, it too carried Keats's with it.[13] Considering the impact Keats made on the Pre-Raphaelites (Holman Hunt, the Rossettis, and John Everett Millais) later in the century, it seems that his reputation depended less on the efforts of particular individuals than on groups, overlapping networks of like-minded acquaintances starting up, on a small scale, the collective chatter that later becomes the buzz of fame.

To say of literary associates, whether they are of the same generation or not, that they "carry" one another—as the Shelleys carried one another, or Wordsworth and Coleridge, Byron and Moore, Boswell and Johnson—may be true in more than one way. With any pair or group, as with a family, the stronger member can keep the other going through periods of weakness. In the vicissitudes of literary fashion, analogously, there's a reciprocal advantage: the stronger partner may have periods of weakness and a need to lean on the other. For better or worse, in any case, the two are bound together. But there is another subtler way, more common between generations than within them, in which one writer may carry another, and that involves the rather sinister medical metaphor of infection or genetic inheritance, as when we talk about carriers of hemophilia. Tennyson so internalized Keats—as Keats had internalized Spenser and Shakespeare and Chatterton—that not only Keats's words but the deep structures of his way of using them came naturally to him. Thus the later writer can train readers to appreciate the earlier one—creating the taste by which his predecessor is to be appreciated, to adapt Wordsworth's formula. As George Ford puts it, "By the very nature of his poetry, Tennyson consciously or unconsciously prepared the way for the popularization of his predecessor."[14]

But the process of transmission through spiritual descendants is slow and unpredictable. Fortunately for Keats, a practical hero was also at hand. In the 1830s, when Tennyson's career was barely off the ground and the reputation of Keats still rested with the anthologists, Edward Moxon began to acquire literary property and to build up a business that specialized in poetry. He published several members of the Hunt circle—Hunt, Lamb, Barry Cornwall, Shelley—but he also introduced new names (he published Tennyson from 1832 onward) and gained the trust of seasoned writers such as Wordsworth and Southey. From 1846 to 1880, his company kept the market supplied with separate volumes of Keats's *Poetical Works,* which they brought up to date periodically with fresh introductions and illustrations, and which was included in the series of "Moxon's Popular Poets."[15] In 1848 Moxon did Keats at least as great a service by publishing *The Life, Letters, and Literary Remains of John Keats,* by—or as he scrupulously specified, "edited by"—Richard Monckton Milnes, later Lord Houghton.

Keats and Biography

Given the importance of the Keats legend in the history of the reception of his work, this seems a good place for a few general observations about literary biography—by which I mean not the actual facts of the life of the author as lived, or even the life story as conveyed informally one way or another, but the written account of the life of one author, composed by another.[16] It's a controversial subject. Some parties, particularly authors (who often cast themselves as the victims of biographers) and critics, emphatically deny that biography has or ought to have any part at all in the reception of creative work. (This was of course the position adopted by Wordsworth in his "Letter to a Friend of Robert Burns," an essay routinely quoted in the early days of the debate. It survives and thrives in recent theory, for instance in Foucault.)[17] Others—typically literary historians and single-author specialists, not to mention biographers themselves—may be inclined to give it too much credit. Because Keats, Austen, and Blake all had the benefit of impressive *belated* biographies that, being widely reviewed and reprinted, had the effect of drawing public attention again to authors who might have been in danger of fading from sight, those biographies are sometimes represented as the sole cause of their survival or revival. (Graham Robertson dramatically described Blake as having been rescued by Gilchrist "at a moment when the dark waters had nearly closed over him.")[18] But nineteenth-century publishers did not deliberately back losers, and in each case the writer's reputation was already "rising fast," as Matthews has observed of Keats, before the biography appeared.[19]

There can be no doubt, however, that Milnes's work appeared at a good moment and had a decisive positive effect on Keats's reputation. Early in the nineteenth century, following the recently established precedent of Boswell's *Johnson* (1791), a proper biography, which is to say a freestanding authored account of the writer's life as opposed to a mere prefatory memoir, became an essential step in the writer's posthumous progress. Simultaneously, biographical criticism—interpretation of the works in the light of known facts about the life—established itself as a dominant critical method.[20] Though he was not a Boswell and had never met his subject, Milnes was personally acquainted with several members of the Keats circle who lent their support to his project. The foundation of the biography had been laid by Keats's close friend Charles Brown, who handed over his materials when he emigrated to New Zealand. After the fashion of the times, Milnes's *Life* was a life-and-letters or life-in-letters biography, like Moore's celebrated life of Byron or Lockhart's of Scott, with the subject seeming to tell his own story. Also like many others, it was accompanied by a substantial quantity of previously unpublished or uncollected literary remains, which in this case occupied almost two hundred pages of the second volume.[21] So Milnes's work had the advantage of at least two features that we do not associate with the literary biographies of the present day: it significantly expanded the known body of Keats's poetry and it introduced Keats in prose, at his most thoughtful and engaging, by using many letters written to his family and friends to outline the events of the life.[22] The poetry made public by Milnes might not in itself have done much for Keats's reputation, since it consisted almost entirely of short pieces that Keats had not thought worth including in his published volumes, but in conjunction with a large number of eloquent letters in which he explained himself to a sympathetic audience—friends, family, and now the public at large—the effect was transformative.

However he chose to present himself, Milnes was not merely an editor. He had a story to tell and misconceptions to correct, for although his was the first full-scale life, it was not the first version of the life story. The legend that had already grown up around Keats—one that he himself had initiated and fostered, and of course believed—was of a young, sensitive, gifted, unworldly artist cruelly mistreated and eventually destroyed by the literary establishment. The legend drew strength from its close resemblance to mythical or ancient prototypes such as Adonis and Bion; literary counterparts such as Milton's *Lycidas*, Edward King; and tragic recent figures such as Thomas Chatterton and Henry Kirke White, both of whom were regularly invoked in contemporary notices of Keats after his death. (Keats identified himself with Chatterton from the start, dedicated *Endymion* to his memory, and expressed the singular view that Chatterton wrote the purest English of any poet.)[23] The rumor that Keats's death had been hastened if not directly caused by a cruel review was propagated by Shelley's provocative preface to *Adonais* and kept being repeated (as I am repeating it), even in the face of clear contradictory evidence.[24] Thus Keats acquired the reputation of hypersensitivity and hence unmanliness, both charges that gained credence from the lush imagery of his verse.

In the 1828 memoir, Hunt, for example, described Keats as having had "a young and sensitive nature" that left him vulnerable to criticism, and acknowledged that his characteristic weakness was "poetical effeminacy," though he declared him a man of genius and predicted fame for him in the future.[25]

Redding's similarly sympathetic "Memoir" in the important 1829 Galignani collection—a memoir based mainly on Hunt's chapter about Keats— emphasized his premature birth and death (he had been a seven-months child and was in delicate health all his life, according to Redding), his sensitivity and gentleness, and the role of the "unmerited abuse" from the *Quarterly Review* in hastening his death. Redding portrays Keats as an innocent victim of the hostility between rival parties, who "merited to be treated with indulgence, not wounded by the envenomed shafts of political animosity for literary errors." He ends his introductory essay by splashing out with a simile. As a poet Keats was, he says, "like a rich fruit-tree which the gardener has not pruned of its luxuriance: time, had it been allotted him by Heaven, would have seen it as trim and rich as any brother of the garden."[26] William Howitt's popular *Homes and Haunts of the Most Eminent British Poets* of 1847, which opened its entry on Keats with a fanciful woodcut illustration of the graves of Keats and Shelley in Rome under a full moon (fig. 11) and gushingly declared Keats "one of those sweet and glorious spirits who descend like the angel messengers of old, to discharge some divine command, not to dwell here," also emphasized how much Keats had made of the short time allotted to him. Howitt's account of the career and character of Keats, which he frankly acknowledged was indebted to personal communication from Hunt as well as published statements by him, describes Keats as having improved by leaps and bounds from the apprentice work of 1817 to the "vast, colossal, and dreamy" fragment of *Hyperion* in the 1820 volume.[27]

Like Howitt and Redding, who conceded faults in the poetry while also drawing attention to its scattered gems and to the general pattern of steady improvement, virtually all the early obituarists and biographers up to and including Milnes in 1848 praised Keats not for his achievements but for his potential. Robert Chambers's long-running *Cyclopaedia of English Literature,* first published in 1844 and revised regularly well into the twentieth century, affirmed that the *Quarterly*'s review of *Endymion* had "embittered his [Keats's] existence, and induced a fatal disease." While the *Cyclopaedia* with careful qualification paid tribute to Keats as "one of the greatest of the young self-taught poets"—great only among the young and the autodidacts—it also represented him as having had yet to learn discipline and self-restraint, which was a common theme of the late reviews and early posthumous assessments.[28] Milnes, for his part, began his work by proposing that in considering the life and death of Keats, "no one doubts that a true genius was suddenly arrested, and they who will not allow him to have won his place in the first ranks of English poets will not deny the promise of his candidature." As one of the proofs of his apprentice status, Milnes drew attention to the imitative character

JOHN KEATS.

"Where is the youth for deeds immortal born,
 Who loved to whisper to the embattled corn,
 And clustered woodbines, breathing o'er the stream,
 Endymion's beauteous passion for a dream !
 Why did he drop the harp from fingers cold,
 And sleep so soon with demigods of old !
 Oh, who so well could sing Love's joys and pains ?
 He lived in melody, as if his veins
 Poured music ; from his lips came words of fire,
 The voice of Greece, the tones of Homer's lyre."

Ebenezer Elliott.

WE come now to one whose home and haunts on the earth were
brief,—

"Who sparkled, was exhaled, and went to Heaven."

John Keats was one of those sweet and glorious spirits who
descend like the angel messengers of old, to discharge some
divine command, not to dwell here. Pure, ethereal, glowing
with the fervency of inward life, the bodily vehicle appears but
assumed for the occasion, and as a mist, as a shadow, is ready
to dissolve the instant that occasion is served. They speak and

Fig. 11. "John Keats" illustration from William Howitt, *Homes and Haunts of the Most
Eminent British Poets*, vol. 1 (1847). Courtesy of The Thomas Fisher Rare Book Library,
University of Toronto.

of most of Keats's verse: his first known composition was an "Imitation of Spenser," and the phases of his poetic career took him through a course of mimicry of other models from Chaucer to Wordsworth so that "you can always see reflected in the mirror of his intellect the great works he is studying at the time." All the same, Milnes declared his conviction that Keats possessed a truly "original genius."[29]

The early death of a writer lends itself naturally to a narrative of incomplete maturation. Along with the emphasis on youth and promise goes a presumption of improvement that leads in turn to a critical preference for the latest over the earliest works. Thus Milnes ends his biography by focusing on how much Keats had learned and his poetry changed in a very short time; on the evidence of his influence on Tennyson, the poet of the future; and on the moral lessons that might be learned from his "pure and lofty life," such as "the brave endurance of neglect and ridicule" and "the strange and cruel end of so much genius and so much virtue."[30] He struck the same note in the short "Memoir" that he wrote for Moxon's 1854 edition, which ends by alluding again to Wordsworth's lines on Chatterton. Even more amazing than the growing recognition for his work, he declares, is "the unaccomplished promise of this wonderful boy."[31]

Besides the crucial element of blighted youth, a second aspect of the Keats legend, one that had less mythic underpinning and was consequently easier to shake off as time passed, had to do with class politics, or class and politics together. From one point of view, Keats was collateral damage in the war between liberal and conservative parties in the public press, with Hunt, the editor of the *Examiner* and chief of the "Cockneys," on one side as the primary target, and the anonymous reviewers of *Blackwood's* and the *Quarterly* on the other. It was Lockhart in *Blackwood's* who coined the "Cockney" label in 1817 to suggest a low-class, undereducated, but presumptuous gang of Londoners, unsound in "versification, morality, and politics" alike.[32] Here the issue is not whether Keats was emotionally so sensitive that he could be "snuffed out by an article," as Byron facetiously put it in *Don Juan,* but to what extent he was poetically, philosophically, socially, and politically a disciple of Leigh Hunt.

Without doubt, Hunt's example, support, and mentorship were crucial to Keats's development as a poet. Before they ever met, Keats had written a sonnet to celebrate the release of Hunt (under the code name "Libertas") from prison, and had published his first poem, another sonnet, in Hunt's *Examiner.* Once they did meet, Keats had entrée not only to the Hunt house in Hampstead but to the whole circle that congregated there, artists and musicians as well as writers and radicals. In that stimulating environment, members of the group walked, ate, and discussed books together; held sonnet writing competitions; carried on dialogues in verse; reviewed one another; and attended one another's lectures and exhibitions.[33] In 1817 Keats dedicated his first volume of poems to Hunt. But much as he admired and learned from him, Keats was not Hunt. He grew increasingly irritated at being classed as a follower, as he repeatedly was in unfriendly reviews of *Endymion* in 1818. (The *British Critic* sarcastically called it a "delicious" poem in the Hunt manner and affirmed that Keats was "not one whit inferior to his mighty master.")[34] There were squabbles within the circle. Keats had always venerated Wordsworth as a writer; in 1818 he saw a good deal of Wordsworth and began to say more, in his letters, about the importance of independence to a great writer. Wordsworth, he observed, was not sociable (as Hunt was), in fact he gave offense by his "egotism, Vanity, and bigotry"—but he was a great writer all the same.[35] Without going so far as to break with Hunt (indeed he went back to Hunt's house in 1820 to be cared for before he left for Italy), Keats himself started the process of separation that critics have pursued on his behalf ever since, as the connection with Hunt proved increasingly embarrassing.[36] In Victorian literary society and afterward, being linked with Tennyson and the aesthetic movement was good for Keats's reputation, whereas being linked with Hunt and Huntian politics would have diminished it. By the end of the century, Saintsbury was declaring, as though it were simply a matter of fact, that Keats had "no political creed."[37]

Steeped in the Keats letters and privy to the views of several members of the former circle, Milnes strove to correct what he saw as damaging "misapprehensions" about Keats, two in particular: oversensitivity and Cockneyism.[38] Reacting against persistent images of Keats as weak, unmanly, and voluptuary, Milnes recast him as resolute and independent, nobody's disciple. He vigorously refuted the legend about death by review. He represented Keats as having had a fairly typical middle-class upbringing and a normal professional education (that is, he was not to be considered uneducated or self-educated, and not working-class). He noted that as a schoolboy Keats was good at sports and a formidable fighter. And he played down the role of Hunt, a man whom he describes—Hunt was still alive when the biography appeared, and about to publish his *Autobiography*—as "regarded by some with admiration, by others with ridicule, as the master of a school of poets, though in truth he was only their encourager, sympathizer, and friend." Any connection with Hunt was dangerous, Milnes pointed out, since Hunt's "liberal and cosmopolite politics" drew down "undiscriminating injustice" on all his associates.[39]

But of course one man's stigma may be another's badge of honor, and every biographer hopes to displace the one before. When he came to present Keats to an American readership, James Russell Lowell drew freely on the evidence in Milnes's biography, but he mocked his notions of gentility. To Lowell, Keats appeared as a working-class hero (just a surgeon's apprentice and the son of a groom who had married his master's daughter) whose natural poetic sensibility did leave him vulnerable to criticism, even if he was not literally killed by a bad review. As far as Lowell was concerned, it was to Keats's credit that he made so much of himself without the advantages of class or education—or mentorship, for Hunt plays no role at all in the story as Lowell tells it.

Later on, in further reversals of the image, the Pre-Raphaelites, Aesthetes, and Decadents admired a sickly, sensitive, depoliticized, aesthetic Keats before he was recuperated in other forms, even as a political radical again, in the twentieth century.[40] Which all goes to prove, once more, that controversy generally sustains fame; if writers are to be talked about, there has to be disagreement and debate. The case of Keats also highlights the way in which a strong early biography can come to dictate the terms of discussion for a long time after, perhaps forever. Was Keats manly or unmanly, imitator or original, damaged by the *Quarterly Review* or not, Cockney or not, steadily improving or not? Opinions vary, but the issues that may be discussed remain the same. No amount of corrective effort changes them, because for every serious, sustained, revisionary critical biography there are scores if not hundreds of casual, short, derivative, but memorable versions of the old story repeated in reference books and reinforced in fiction, journalism, and mass-market editions, not to mention bookstore bags, so that wherever the poems appear, the abridged life story comes attached. It cannot be unlearned.

Distinguishing Keats

Biography foregrounds individuality: the subject is set apart and is *conceived* as set apart from other people. Critical tradition likewise exaggerates differences: though it may define a writer's lineage, it must at the same time articulate his or her originality. It is therefore just as much in the interest of the critic as of the biographer to widen the gap between writers and their contemporaries or rivals. That process is clear to see in the second half of the nineteenth century, when Keats came to be defined as the quintessential poet and critical preference settled on a handful of poems from his final volume. The path was far from smooth, however.

In the aftermath of Milnes's *Life* and perhaps in response to Moxon's efforts at publicity, the poetry of Keats began to establish a larger presence in anthologies and collections, to such good effect that the *Encyclopaedia Bri-*

tannica of 1857 could describe him as being by that date among the top two or three most "popular" poets of his generation, referring to him as the one who had had the greatest influence on new poetry "of the last thirty years."[41] A significant coup was the inclusion of eleven poems in Palgrave's *The Golden Treasury* (1861) and its successors, some of which were put to use in the schools.[42] Keats was better represented in the *Treasury* than most of his contemporaries, on a par with Burns and far ahead of Chatterton (0) and Hunt (0), though falling well short of Shelley (22), and Wordsworth (34). (The *Treasury*, which excluded living poets, was dedicated to Tennyson.) Actual school editions of poems of manageable length—first the *Hyperion* fragment and later *The Eve of St. Agnes*—followed, from 1877 onward.[43] In a survey of nineteenth- and twentieth-century anthologies, Christopher Bode maintains that five of the Big Six poets of the Romantic period—Wordsworth, Coleridge, Byron, Shelley, and Keats—had already been established as canonical by about 1860. (The sixth at that time was still Southey; Blake replaced him later.)[44] The selection chosen to represent Keats stabilized early: from Ward's *English Poets* (1880) up to today's version of *The Oxford Book of English Verse* (1999) we find dependably the opening lines of *Endymion*, short extracts from *Hyperion*, two or three sonnets ("Chapman's Homer" and "Bright Star" invariably), *The Eve of St. Agnes*, usually "La Belle Dame sans Merci," and three or four of the great odes (always "Nightingale," "Grecian Urn," and "To Autumn").

Partly as a result of the wider exposure, Keats's works began also to be adapted in other media, particularly the visual arts. Some of his close friends, notably Benjamin Haydon and Joseph Severn, had been painters; both left portraits of him (besides Haydon's life mask) that served the biographical tradition well. But it was the poems themselves that attracted visual artists—or rather, it was a small subset of the narrative poems with descriptions of imagined places. Burne-Jones reported that when he and his friends travelled on the Continent as students in 1855, they took with them only one book, a volume of Keats.[45] The first painting publicly exhibited that was based on a subject from Keats, Holman Hunt's *The Eve of St. Agnes* (1848) brought Hunt and Dante Gabriel Rossetti together. Even as Moxon's illustrators exploited the visualizability of Keats's poems in successive editions, the Pre-Raphaelites and others put their own versions of selected narrative poems onto the walls of galleries and into the hands of collectors. Hunt's *The Eve of St. Agnes* was followed by Millais's *Lorenzo at the House of Isabella* (or *Isabella*, 1849), Rossetti's drawings after "La Belle Dame sans Merci" in the 1850s, Arthur Hughes's *The Eve of St. Agnes* (1856), and Hunt's *Isabella and the Pot of Basil* (1868).[46] These canvases both presumed and promoted acquaintance with the original works, for viewers needed to be able to recognize the episode being represented. Thanks to this development and to these influential tastemakers, the shorter narrative poems gained prominence and Keats himself was recruited into the Aesthetic Movement. The Rossettis, Morris, Wilde, and Swinburne all sang his praises in a far less guarded way than had been done before—partly, presumably, because they were using him to promote their own values.[47] Wilde called him a "Priest of Beauty."[48] Their advocacy and example in turn spurred the book makers to greater feats of illustration: not Moxon alone but numerous publishers in Britain and the United States from the 1870s right through the twentieth century undertook illustrated editions of poems by Keats, often in luxury formats and limited print runs for connoisseurs.[49]

Serious critical studies of Keats's work—which is to say, not reviews or appreciations but methodical analyses and evaluations by literary professionals—began to appear in the 1850s. They may have been prompted by Milnes's advocacy, but they soon took on a life of their own, each critic in turn striving to correct the one before. In 1851, for instance, D. M. Moir singled out *The Eve of St. Agnes* and the odes as outstanding poems in a new poetic movement that included Shelley and Hunt.[50] James Russell Lowell went far beyond Milnes in his 1854 Boston edition of Keats's poems, where he declared that "the poems of Keats mark an epoch in English poetry" because Keats, more than any of his contemporaries, reacted effectively against the pedestrian prosy mannerisms of the eighteenth century.[51] This idea—that Keats was somehow responsible for the literary revolution that we now refer to as "Romantic"—became increasingly common as time went on.

David Masson, who was professor of English literature successively at University College, London (1852) and at the University of Edinburgh (1865), described Keats as "constitutionally a poet" of the highest promise who could reasonably be compared with Shakespeare and Spenser and deserved to be ranked "very near indeed to our very best."[52] The quality that the language of Keats (in Masson's view) shared with that of Shakespeare and Spenser was its "abundant sensuousness," "universality of . . . sensuousness"—which he illustrated with masses of direct quotation.[53] I don't know when or by whom this familiar label of sensuousness was first attached to Keats's work (Moir for one had praised the "sensuous beauty" of *The Eve of St. Agnes*), but Masson made it the theme of his essay and thereby turned what had previously been considered a weakness into a virtue. By the great authority of Milton, poetry was inherently "simple, sensuous, and passionate." Keats and his work might have been criticized for being oversensitive, self-indulgent, and luxurious, but to be sensuous with Shakespeare and Spenser was a different matter.

In the 1870s and early 1880s, major authorities echoed the praise of Milnes, Moir, Lowell and Masson, but with some awkwardness. All seem to have struggled to reconcile the ideas of greatness and immaturity. Matthew Arnold, writing in 1880, ranked Keats on a par with Shakespeare in certain respects, but he concluded that Keats "was not ripe" and lacked the firm moral sense of Shakespeare.[54] In his eccentric entry on Keats for the 1882 *Encyclopaedia Britannica,* Swinburne in the same breath declared Keats to be "in the highest class of English poets" and accused him of having written "some of the most vulgar and fulsome doggrel [*sic*] ever whimpered by a vapid and effeminate rhymester in the sickly stage of whelphood."[55] William Michael Rossetti, who privately preferred Shelley, described Keats as "a brilliant original poet partially infected with some of Hunt's vices of style," which he had effectively labored to cast off.[56] But then in a strange phrase, he wrote about some of the oddities of Keats's use of language as not just faults but "a distinct misdoing," a sort of calculated perversity; and yet he declared that he could not wish that Keats had lived to refine and perfect his art, because then it would not be Keats, and "Keats, youthful and prodigal, the magician of unnumbered beauties . . . is the Keats of our affections."[57] In 1878, either on his own initiative or under the direction of his publisher, Rossetti used the Severn portrait of Keats as a frontispiece to his *Lives of Famous Poets,* a collection of the biographies he had written for the "Popular Poets" series (fig. 12). The choice itself seemed to confirm Keats's status as a well-known popular poet, the object of "our" affections.

The storm soon settled. By the end of the century, the critical tradition had regained its equilibrium, thanks in great part to a major critical biography by Sidney Colvin in the "English Men of Letters" series (1887). Colvin's thorough study of the life and works concluded that Keats had been born with "instincts and faculties more purely poetical" than those of Scott, Byron, or Wordsworth, and the task of his life was to aim for the realization of those innate gifts; if he had not reached the goal, still he had so distinguished himself that "every critic of modern English poetry is of necessity a critic of Keats."[58] For George Saintsbury likewise—Masson's successor at Edinburgh and the magisterial (not to say overbearing) literary historian of the turn of the century— Keats's place was secure. Shelley might have been a better writer, but Keats was more "germinal." Coleridge, Wordsworth and Scott might have been the originators of "the great Romantic movement" in English poetry, but Keats, their successor, heard the "new note" and so enriched and refashioned it that "it became his own" (as Lowell had said), and all the poets who came after were indebted directly to him (as Milnes had suggested). In his *A History of Nineteenth Century Literature,* first published in 1896, Saintsbury made it a

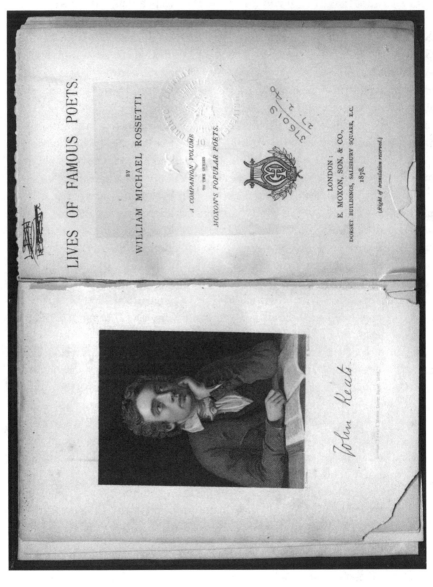

Fig. 12. Frontispiece and title page of William Michael Rossetti's *Lives of Famous Poets* (1878), featuring John Keats. Courtesy of University of Toronto Libraries.

matter of national pride that Keats, not a sybarite at all but "an honest, manly Englishman," was the "first leader" of the great enterprise, "the pouring of this English blood through the veins of old subjects—classical, mediaeval, foreign, modern." Like his predecessors, Saintsbury stressed the astonishing improvement in Keats's work over the short span of his writing career, but he parted company with them when he expressed the mildly provocative view that the poet might already have done his best and would have gone no further—after all, the "twin peaks" of his body of work, the "Ode on a Grecian Urn" and "La Belle Dame sans Merci," could hardly be improved on.[59]

The general drift of professional criticism in the critical second half of the nineteenth century was to define Keats's achievement in such a way as to make him eligible for the pantheon, so that he could indeed take his place as an original genius "among the English Poets." To be original meant to do something that had not been done before, or at least to be a pathfinder or trailblazer for a road that others would want to follow. It took some ingenuity, collectively, for the critics to present Keats as a leader, since none of his contemporaries seem to have thought of him in those terms and he manifestly was not the head of the Cockney School. Being the head of the set of poets who had died young would not have been good enough; nor would a prize for "most improved." There were, as previously discussed, some efforts to present him as a leader of the Romantic movement standing on the shoulders of Wordsworth and Coleridge—not the originator of the core beliefs but the one who somehow saw them through. (For the anthologists and critics who attempted to define the period by its revival of romance, he made a better fit than Wordsworth and Coleridge.) But a better solution was to cast Keats as the acknowledged leader of later generations, the progenitor of Tennyson and his successors. As Saintsbury, whose chapter on the period from Coleridge to Keats was called "The Triumph of Romance" and who labeled Keats "germinal," put it, "He begat Tennyson, and Tennyson begat all the rest."[60]

The question of a distinct style also caused problems. Keats had an unusual talent for mimicry: he could sound like Wordsworth or Milton or Spenser or whomever he pleased. But did he have a voice of his own, or could a high degree of skillful imitation finally amount to a distinctive voice? Milnes thought not, Lowell and others disagreed. The critics reached consensus, eventually, in the view of Keats as a "born" poet conforming to the ancient tag *nascitur non fit* ("he is born, not made"), a writer of such exceptional gifts that he was able in a short time to overcome such obstacles as the influence of Hunt and to make his own authentic voice heard in the best poems of his last volume (for there was little disagreement about which were best).[61] He did not, then, according to his advocates, *develop* a voice of his own; he found it. Possessed, all along, of the natural instincts of a poet, he had only to find his proper Keatsian mode of expression. But what was that, exactly?

All the vague and quasi-mystical references to Keats as "essentially" or "constitutionally" more poetical than any of his contemporaries struggled to put a name to a combination of desirable qualities that Keats seemed to have had and others lacked. Contexts provide some insight into what the critics might have had in mind. Masson, following Shakespeare's lines about "the lunatic, the lover and the poet" (as well as the theories of major Romantic critics), explained that the true poet is "one of those minds in whom . . . Imagination or Ideality is the sovereign faculty." Arnold pinpointed sensuousness and a "fascinating facility," on a par with Shakespeare's, in the use of words; Colvin cited an approach to composition that does not aim at technical correctness or high polish but at loading rifts with ore, striving for "a continual positive poetic richness and felicity of phrase."[62] Gradually, under such direction, the adjective "Keatsian," which had started as a slur, acquired positive associations with beauty, imagination, and technical wizardry. And so Keats became the poet par excellence.[63]

Audiences

By the early twentieth century, Keats was accepted as an established master with an established oeuvre, already recognizably the figure we study today. As Gladys and Kurt Lang pointed out in their detailed study of the reputations of graphic artists, "Once an artist has become a valuable property, greatness begins to feed on itself."[64] Institutional status and locatability came for Keats with the Keats–Shelley Association (founded in 1903 with support in both Britain and America) taking on responsibility for maintaining the house in which he had died in Rome, together with the pair of graves in the cemetery there. In 1921 successful fund-raising on both sides of the Atlantic by a memorial committee led to the acquisition and refurbishment of what is now known as Keats House in Hampstead, which was donated to the local borough council and opened to the public in 1925.

Between then and now, the conversation about Keats has continued along the lines I have described, through many fresh trade and textbook editions, anthologies, biographies, critical studies, and artistic or popular adaptations. I am obscurely ashamed to have to say that it is so. Little seems to have changed except that we are more consistently reverential in our attitude toward the man and his work than our counterparts of a hundred years or more ago were. The same few facts are rehearsed, the same few poems are cited, the same few lines are quoted, and the same few issues are debated in the standard reference sources and their web-based progeny. (The lowest common denominator consists of perhaps four elements: youth, death, the quest for beauty, and the mini-myth about the composition of the "Ode to a Nightingale," none of which requires actual contact with the poetry.) The critical tradition swings to and fro without much self-awareness; perhaps each new contributor honestly believes him- or herself to have discovered something that in fact goes back a long way. If Robert Gittings, in the closing pages of his valuable biography of 1968, reveals that in his view what makes Keats "different from any other poet" is his ability to evoke "the impression of the moment," there is no reason to doubt his sincerity. On reflection, however, the assertion is neither provable nor disprovable—it might even be considered nonsensical—and Saintsbury said the same thing in 1898, so Gittings's statement sounds suspiciously as though it comes from a deep well or a critical echo chamber.[65]

The positive side of the echo chamber effect is that it reinforces and thus consolidates a writer's image, which in Keats's case has something for everyone, allowing each sector of his audience to feel that it understands him and loves him in its own way. For nonreaders or those unacquainted with his work, he has an appealing personal history and a degree of historical importance—hence the shrines and the tourist traffic, together with commercial spin-offs from the *Keats Birthday Book* of 1895 to the T-shirts, coffee mugs, and plastic bags of the twenty-first century. The general reader is introduced to some of the poetry in school anthologies, and to the abridged version of the life story at the same time. Both verses and life story constitute a part of the common knowledge that we put to use in polite conversation and crossword puzzles. A few serious fans choose to dig deeper by reading more of the poetry and seeking out new biographical studies or imaginative reconstructions of Keats's life and personality. (Besides being known to readers of J. D. Salinger, the jingle "John Keats, John Keats, John / Please put your scarf on" has an independent presence as a favorite quotation on the Internet. Jane Campion's recent film *Bright Star* provided both an instance of and a focus for the constituency of nonprofessional enthusiasts.) In the academy, since Keats has been a major canonical author from the time that the basic curriculum was established at the end of the nineteenth century, scholarship and criticism continue on an industrial scale, not only by revisiting the key issues but also by applying new approaches and refining standard interpretations. Finally—arguably the most important of all, since they are the ones who can most effectively stimulate renewed interest—the peer group of other poets and creative artists has been consistently supportive to Keats. The label "poet's poet" is often applied to him, for good but complicated reasons that I wish to consider for a moment.

"From the time of Hood in the 1820's to the end of the century, he is the poet's poet": thus Ford sums up the impact of Keats upon the next and succeeding generations of poets who worked on his model, adopted certain themes and approaches from him, and buttressed his reputation with their own.[66] This is one way of using the phrase, to designate a professional role model, one whose work directly influences others, as that of Keats certainly did. But direct influence is only part of the story. Usually, more narrowly, it refers to someone who is not widely known and has little public recognition, but who is admired as a technician by fellow poets. Shelley was being consciously flattering when he wrote to Severn immediately after Keats's death to say that despite his transcendent genius, Keats—like himself—would never be a popular poet.[67] Only connoisseurs, those on the inside, could properly appreciate his work. By that standard, the phrase is harder to justify. Not only has Keats become common property as a cultural icon, but insiders do not always admire his work. Some of the fellow poets who labored most effectively on his behalf had reservations about it—Hunt, Shelley himself, Milnes, W. M. Rossetti, and Arnold, for example—but they championed him anyway, and without their efforts it is likely that he would have remained in the ranks of the insignificant along with Kirk White, Croly, Mary Anne Browne, and "Anonymous." (Bowles, from the same list, could also have been called a poet's poet—the young Coleridge adored his sonnets—but nobody actively took up his cause.) The unusual devotion that Keats attracted suggests that the reasons for it went beyond admiration for any technical achievement.

The process of idealization that can be traced back to early memoirs of Keats by his friends was rooted in his personality and in the pathos of his untimely death. Both his character, whether it was known directly or by report, or inferred from his writings, and the outlines of his story might have been specially designed to appeal to other writers. First there was the Chatterton effect: the cult of Chatterton paved the way for the cult of Keats. He was one of their own, and he died young. Tradition as well as personal affection dictate that poets speak up (usually, in verse) under those circumstances. Shelley's elegy looked back to the laments of Moschus for Bion and Milton for Edward King, and forward to Tennyson's *In Memoriam*. If Keats had in one way or another been the victim of the critics, the eternal enemies of art, then the story got better as time went on, for his growing success could be taken to prove the critics wrong. And so his suffering and death continue to be the themes of other writers' work (as Chatterton's were for the generation following him, though not for much longer than that). To take a tiny point by way of illustration, Galway Kinnell's charming poem "Oatmeal" is the latest in a line of porridge poems involving Keats that started with Browning's condemnation of the fame system in a poem entitled "Popularity" (thought to have been composed about 1848), the last line of which provided a memorable quotation and the title of another poem, George Sterling's "What Porridge Had John Keats?"[68]

Keats appealed to poets sometimes in spite of his poetic work, thanks in part to the power of his legend and in part to his service to literature. He dedicated his life to it: that fact could be inferred from his writings and became even more apparent upon the publication of his letters. Glorification of the poet, poetry, and imagination is the underlying theme of practically all his work from start to finish—certainly of all the work that won the approval of editors and anthologizers. (Endymion is a protopoet; Lycius dies when reality intervenes to save him; the realm of the nightingale is open to the viewless wings of poesy; the story of Hyperion is less about a war in heaven than about poetry wars.) Keats flaunts the literariness of his art, the way in which it finds its subjects in the work of other authors and adopts their modes of language, so that for a poetry enthusiast, reading Keats can be like opening a compendium of great works—Chapman's Homer, Shakespeare's sonnets, Spenser's Bower of Bliss all rolled into one. He seems to reincarnate them or, like the chameleon that he himself used as a figure for the poet, to take on their colors temporarily and thus to encapsulate literary tradition. This quality, which might escape or even repel less committed readers, excites the devotee. To one, it is bookishness; to the other, dialogue with the dead. Finally, Keats appeals to other poets by the ardor with which he expresses his ideas about poetry, and by the moments of insight that those ideas offer about writing in general, as well as about the motivations of his own work. The Keats letters are a rare body of informal but stimulating criticism by a working poet. Even T. S. Eliot, who opposed practically everything Keats represented as a poet, expressed unreserved admiration for the letters, "the most notable and the most important ever written by any English poet."[69]

The most striking thing about the appeal of Keats to all four of the major constituencies is the extent to which it depends on his life. And not just or not so much on his life as on the fact of his death and the charm of his letters. Though it was customary at the time for the heirs or publishers, if it were feasible, to mark a death with a collected edition, literary remains, and a biography, it is doubtful that any set of letters ever presented as attractive a character in as unguarded a way as the letters of Keats. Within a few years of Milnes's epistolary biography of Keats, similar biographies appeared for Coleridge (1838), Southey (1849), and Wordsworth (1851)—none of them with anything like the impact on the writer's posthumous reputation that Milnes's *Keats* had. Audiences learned to admire and pity Keats as a person and thereafter expressed their feelings in the ways that came naturally to them, whether it was learning his words by heart, writing poetry themselves, or engaging in critical debate to declare and rationalize their love. Leigh Hunt, who had loved him well, worked hard and effectively on his behalf, but when his own turn came there was no one to do the same for him.

Leigh Hunt

Keats and Hunt met in October 1816, the month in which Keats turned twenty-one and Hunt thirty-two. It was from the first a warm but unequal friendship, more unequal than even the gap in their ages might suggest. Hunt, like Keats, had begun publishing poetry in his teens. He had a string of successes recently behind him: *The Feast of the Poets* (1814), a literary satire like Byron's *English Bards and Scotch Reviewers*; *The Descent of Liberty: A Mask* (1815), which was occasioned by the defeat of Napoleon and which formally anticipated Shelley's *Prometheus Unbound*; and *The Story of Rimini* (1816), a long narrative poem based on the Paolo and Francesca story from Dante, written in loose heroic couplets like Keats's later *Lamia*. (Since they are not well known, samples from these works are listed in the appendix and available on the accompanying website.) Poetry was not Hunt's primary occupation, and yet at this moment he seemed poised for success as a poet. Indeed, for the next few years he was on a roll, with a collection of original poems and translations, *Foliage*, in 1818; "Hero and Leander" and "Bacchus and Ariadne" and a composite reprinting of his *Poetical Works*, both in 1819; and a translation from Tasso (*Amyntas, a Tale of the Woods*, dedicated to Keats) in 1820. None of these titles was a best seller on anything like the scale of Scott and Byron, but most of them went into two or more editions in those years, including separate printings in America, which was not the case for any of Keats's work—so their initial reception was more than creditable.

Hunt earned his living by his pen—precariously, as in so many cases—but not by his poetry. When Keats knew him, he was also already a seasoned journalist, having founded the liberal periodical *The Examiner* with his brother John, a printer, in 1808; the two of them were heroes of the left for having served prison terms in 1813–15 for libeling the Prince Regent (fig. 13). Hunt wrote *The Descent of Liberty* and worked on *The Story of Rimini* in prison; he and his brother carried on *Examiner* business as usual from their cells. The *Examiner* gave him a vehicle for the expression of his opinions about the arts as well as about politics, and so it was that in December 1816 he wrote

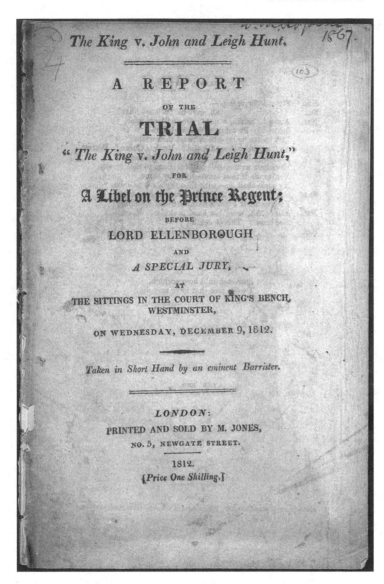

The King v. John and Leigh Hunt.

A REPORT

OF THE

TRIAL

"The King v. John and Leigh Hunt,"

FOR

A Libel on the Prince Regent;

BEFORE

LORD ELLENBOROUGH

AND

A SPECIAL JURY,

AT

THE SITTINGS IN THE COURT OF KING'S BENCH, WESTMINSTER,

ON WEDNESDAY, DECEMBER 9, 1812.

Taken in Short Hand by an eminent Barrister.

LONDON:

PRINTED AND SOLD BY M. JONES,

NO. 5, NEWGATE STREET.

1812.

[Price One Shilling.]

Fig. 13. Title page of *The King v. John and Leigh Hunt* trial report (1812). Courtesy of The Thomas Fisher Rare Book Library, University of Toronto.

and published one of many manifestos about a new movement in poetry, the "Young Poets" essay, in which he introduced Shelley, John Hamilton Reynolds, and Keats to readers of the paper, printing the whole of Keats's sonnet "On First Looking into Chapman's Homer" as an example of his work. The following summer he produced a long, generous review of Keats's first volume (the one dedicated to Hunt), reiterating and elaborating his theory about the new school.[70]

Hunt encouraged Keats and other friends to treat the *Examiner* and his later solo venture, the *Indicator* of 1819–21, as natural outlets for the ideas that they were informally sharing and shaping together. The circle was most active between about 1816 and 1822, and of course its members also used other means—anonymous or signed reviews, essays, anthologies, prefaces, and lectures—to declare their common values and their common opposition to what they saw as the old guard in society and literature.[71] Given that the group included Lamb and Hazlitt and (up to a point) Byron, they were bound to make their mark one way or another. But by virtue of his control of the *Examiner* and *Indicator,* as well as by his sociability, Hunt was their acknowledged leader and spokesman. An astute critic, in preface after preface and review after review he laid out the literary principles for the school that its enemies called "Cockney."[72] He was also a tireless anthologizer and literary hack who promoted the work of his friends at seemingly every opportunity, perhaps without consulting them: Keats, for example, deplored as "sickening stuff" Hunt's *Literary Pocket-Book,* a small diary or datebook for the year with a few pages of original verse at the end, in which some of his own poems were first published.[73]

Broadly speaking, Hunt believed that poetry could change the world for the better, but that it had to do so in its own way, through pleasure, not by hectoring or moralizing. His work aimed to oppose the influence of the "French school" of artifice and closed couplets by reverting to earlier English models such as Chaucer and Spenser and to the great masters of other countries or earlier times, especially to writers of romance such as Ariosto; and to develop a "natural" style with freer diction and versification than the polished manner associated with the eighteenth century. Reviewers attacked Hunt and his friends for straining or breaking the rules of language—making words up, for instance, or inventing clumsy compound epithets such as "weed-hidden" and "sigh-warm"—out of ignorance, but they were doing it on purpose.[74] The poet, Hunt declared in the preface to *The Story of Rimini,* "should do as Chaucer or Shakspeare [*sic*] did,—not copy what is obsolete or peculiar in either, any more than they copied from their predecessors,—but use as much as possible an actual, existing language,—omitting of course *mere* vulgarisms and fugitive phrases, which are the cant of ordinary discourse."[75] *Rimini* itself is the best example of his principles in practice, though a line about Francesca's having "strong notions on the marrying score" might be thought to strain his theory about "actual" language free of cant. Working on the hint of a few lines in Dante, Hunt retells the story of Paolo and Francesca with a well-constructed plot that begins and ends with public spectacles (a wedding procession and a funeral cortège, respectively) framing private anguish of various kinds. With notable subtlety, the point of view shifts from the populace to one major figure after another, while a sympathetic narrator comments on the unfolding tragedy. Description is lavish, but the psychological and physical action never flag; supple run-on couplets keep up the pace. William Howitt, writing thirty years later, recalled how three young men, himself and two friends, read the newly published poem during a ramble in Sherwood Forest and found themselves transported from "sombre heaths and wastes . . . to the sunshine of Italy—to gay cavalcades and sad palaces." At the end of the day, "up rose the three friends, drunk with beauty, and with the sentiment of a great sorrow, and strode homewards with the proud and happy feeling that England was enriched with a new poet."[76] In his hostile "Cockney School" article of 1818, Lockhart, by contrast, referred to "the odious and incestuous *Story of Rimini.*"[77]

At the time of the death of Keats, Hunt was a pillar of the left; an effective advocate for liberal values in church, state, and society; the author of several very good volumes of poetry; and the articulate leader of a literary movement threatening to the establishment. He was also gravely ill himself. At the end of 1821 he gave up the *Examiner* and set out for Italy on the invitation of Shelley and Byron, planning to start up a new periodical, the *Liberal,* with them, and hoping to recover his health. The periodical was not a success, however, and when he returned to England in 1825 after the deaths of Shelley and Byron, he resumed his career as a man of letters, turning his hand to whatever seemed likely to make money. His early memoir, *Lord Byron and Some of His Contemporaries* (1828) caused offense, but it did go into a second edition (for which Hunt wrote a semiapologetic preface) and was recycled in his lively *Autobiography* two decades later. He wrote many more essays and reviews; occasional poems, including a harsh, masterful antiwar poem, *Captain Sword and Captain Pen* (1835); a successful play; and a novel that went into three editions and was adopted by Bentley for the "Standard Novels" series along with Austen and Brunton. He regularly issued editions of his selected poetic works—in 1832, 1844, 1846, 1849, and 1855—and he left instructions for the authoritative posthumous collection of 1860. His journalistic and editorial work was prodigious, almost on the scale of Scott and Southey. Thus his name became associated with popularization and bookmaking for a mass audience, from *Classic Tales, Serious and Lively* (1806–7) through editions of eighteenth-century plays, to *A Book for a Corner* and *Readings for Railways* (1849).[78]

After his death, collections of his verse continued in print, in Britain and America, until the 1930s, with an authoritative edition by Humphrey Sumner Milford in 1923; but then they dried up. The essays did better, Symonds's edition of 1887 being reprinted many times, along with rival selections, well into the twentieth century. Scholarly editions of selected essays began to appear in the otherwise lean years (for Hunt) of the 1950s. Victorian editions of his correspondence were followed, in the usual way, by a respectful biography (by Edmund Blunden, 1930) and a French academic biography (by Louis Landré, 1936). Hunt's occasional supporters (there was no Hunt Society) kept urging his merits, but publishers and the general public showed little interest, and so his name faded from sight for half a century. With the turn to politics and historicism in the 1990s, there began to be clear signs of a surge of interest in Hunt's work in university circles, and although that has more to do with his historical importance than with his literary efforts, the recent major scholarly edition may yet bring about the long-overdue reappraisal of his poetry. The best of Hunt's work is original, entertaining, and accomplished; it excited his poetical peers (Byron and Shelley, for instance) in a way that Keats's did not. His theories and his example were certainly influential. If historical impact had been a criterion for lasting fame, or if the success of associates and followers invariably reflected glory on their mentors (as with Tennyson and Keats), Hunt by rights should have been remembered; but he was not. Where, when, and how did things go wrong?

The categories of the checklist and a comparison with Keats provide more than adequate answers to these questions, and I shall briefly outline the most significant of them. The first has to do with age and image. The cynic would say that Hunt lived too long and wrote too much, and though that response is glib, there is truth to it.

Keats died at twenty-five, Hunt at seventy-four. Hunt himself predicted in 1828 that Keats would "be known hereafter in English literature, emphatically, as *the young Poet.*"[79] His prediction was correct: as W. M. Rossetti observed, though Keats, had he lived, might well have come to write better poems, we love him as he is, forever young, with all his faults and partly *for* his faults. Hunt, on the other hand, lived on to disappoint his admirers. So biography, in the sense of the path his life took, worked against him; death in harness at a ripe age is not the stuff of legend. The achievement of *Rimini* was not repeated; the early work appeared to be his best; the trajectory of his career was not consistently upward. Indeed, it might be argued that Hunt's career as a poet ended about the same time as that of Keats, for apart from a satire on William Gifford and the anomalous *Captain Sword and Captain Pen,* he published no new volumes of original verse after 1820, though he lived for almost forty years longer and continued to produce translations, adaptations, and verse for magazines and annuals, some of which he admitted to his collected volumes.[80] His public image in the meantime was damaged not only by overexposure but also by the negative publicity of what was seen as ingratitude toward Byron in his memoir and by Dickens's notorious caricature of him as Harold Skimpole in *Bleak House* in 1853.

Besides all the usual hazards associated with long life, growing old has significant practical disadvantages for a writer. In the course of time, Hunt lost all four of his major constituencies or audiences. Fellow poets did not rally round. Hunt buried some of his closest friends and alienated others, so there were few to reminisce fondly about him when he was gone, or to promote his work as Hunt and others had done for Keats. Literary professionals did not promote him either: the stigma of popularity affected him. Because he had time to write his own biography and to see to the publication of all his own writings, there was no occasion for a champion such as Milnes or a visionary publisher such as Moxon. There were no lavish illustrated editions, and the Pre-Raphaelites did not paint from Huntian subjects, though his work would certainly have lent itself to visual representation.[81] The public that had sustained his collections, anthologies, and essay collections constantly sought new work, not old, and once the days of his great notoriety and popularity were past, there was little incentive for editors or scholars to take up his cause. Besides, a long life of writing generates a great quantity of material, and even if there is only the normal proportion of dross to gold (Keats himself produced a good deal of dross, both early and late in his short career), the amount of paper that has to be sifted through can be daunting.[82] Since Hunt had written mainly for money—which meant that to some extent he followed public taste rather than leading it, and that he was always writing in haste, under pressure from publishers' deadlines—the proportion of dross to gold is higher than normal, and the task of reading it through is all the more discouraging. Finally, since Hunt was not a specialist but would turn his hand to almost any kind of writing, his energies were diffused and his audience fragmented. His versatility and prolificacy told against him. He was never identified with one kind of writing nor even with one publishing house: in modern terms, he never developed a brand of his own. The examples of Wordsworth and Crabbe prove that longevity does not necessarily lead to diffuseness, but diffuseness is more likely to emerge in a long life than in a short one.

While growing old was arguably a bad career move for Hunt, it was of course not the only reason for the lack of interest in his poetry after his death. His work suffered like that of Crabbe and Southey from the shift of popular taste away from long narrative poems in favor of prose fiction. *The Story of*

Rimini could not sustain its success. Some of the rest of his best work ("The Nymphs," for instance, which led off *Foliage;* or *Captain Sword and Captain Pen,* which still has its admirers) were also too long to be reprinted in full in the anthologies. As for shorter poems, the earliest anthologies served Hunt better than later ones. In the Paris publications of 1827 and 1828, *Living Poets* and *British Poets,* he had about the same size of sample as Keats, with extracts from *Rimini* along with various short poems to illustrate his range. Chambers's *Cyclopaedia* gave him a respectable showing from the first edition of 1844 to the third in 1876. But he never had the platform of one of Galignani's volumes of collected works as Byron, Keats, and Shelley did, and his role in the anthologies shrank in the second half of the century (no poems in *The Golden Treasury,* for instance) until only two or three poems were widely known, and those were among his slightest—the "Rondeau" ("Jenny Kissed Me"), "Abou ben Adhem," and the sonnet "To the Grasshopper and the Cricket."[83] Hence Jack Stillinger's offhand remark about Keats's "Isabella," that twentieth-century criticism tended to condemn "its sentimentality, mawkishness, and vulgarity (all the qualities we call Huntian)"—as though nothing written by Hunt had ever been considered edgy, provocative, and exciting to read.[84] The adjective "Huntian" has never shed its negative connotations.

The want of a substantial presence in the anthologies must have been one of the reasons that Hunt was passed over by the makers of school readers and university curricula toward the end of the century. There was also the shadow of the hostile criticism that had resisted his unorthodox values and labeled his work "Cockney" and "vulgar." With the exception of the small handful of sentimental favorites just cited, his poems were not considered suitable for children, but they were not considered suitable for adult students either— too grown-up (polemical and sensual, even lubricious) for one group, and too juvenile (enjoyable, accessible) for the other. Furthermore, by the time modern English literature was finding its way into the universities, Hunt had been cast as the man who led Keats astray. The triumph of Keats involved the crushing of Hunt. In the view of Saintsbury, for example, Hunt was the one who had "taught [Keats] the fluent, gushing, slipshod style that brought not merely upon him, but upon his mighty successor Tennyson, the harsh but not in this respect wholly unjust lash of conservative and academic criticism."[85]

Finally, Hunt's own attitude toward his writings worked against him. He did not—at least, not openly—yearn for distinction and strive for immortality as Wordsworth, Southey, and Keats did. Poetry was not his vocation; he did not dedicate his life to it. Like Crabbe and Scott he professed to write mainly for money and to have no confident expectation of lasting fame. (He did admit the possibility, however: in the preface to *The Story of Rimini* he said

that he had published the poem without historical notes but that future generations, if they continued to read it, could write their own commentaries.)[86]
He did not claim divine inspiration: he wrote to please himself and his contemporary audience. In an engaging poem of 1823, "The 'Choice,'" in which
he allows himself to daydream about an ideal existence—the perfect house,
furnishings, friends, women, habits, and so forth—he includes writing verses,
in summer, "in the open air, / Stretched on the grass, under the yellow trees, /
With a few books about me, and the bees," but he adds, "I'd write, because I
could not help it," possibly meaning that writing was his livelihood (though
surely in an ideal world, it wouldn't be) but also acknowledging that writing
itself is habit-forming, a source of complex pleasures.[87] Like Scott, who re-
fused to be made to choose between motives of fame and lucre, he included
the compulsive pleasure of literary creation among his reasons for writing.
His model of authorship might be called "hedonistic."

Hunt's attitude may have had as much to do with the afterlife of his work
as the critical attacks of his old enemies, for he routinely disparaged his own
writing and promoted that of others instead, Keats and Shelley in particular.
He was a better advocate for the work of others than for his own; he seemed
content to stay in shadow. Whether from realism or genuine modesty or for
the rhetorical advantage of disarming criticism, he consistently presented his
efforts as inferior to theirs, and the goal of his poetry as being simply to interest the contemporary audience. In his preface to *Foliage* he suggested that
poetry, rather than being severely didactic, should serve the ends of "cheerful
leisure."[88] In a long introduction to the selected *Poetical Works* of 1832, in a
passage that deserves to be quoted at length, he frankly excluded himself
from the ranks of great poets but at the same time, like Crabbe, made a plea
for diversity of standards. He begins by explaining why this collection is selected and not complete:

> I do not believe that other generations will take the trouble to search for jew-
> els in much nobler dust than mine. Posterity is too rich and idle. The only
> hope I can have of coming into any one's hands, and exciting his attention
> beyond the moment, is by putting my workmanship, such as it is, into its
> best and compactest state. The truth is, I have such a reverence for poetry,
> pre-eminently so called (by which I mean that which posterity and the great-
> est poets agree to call such), that I should not dare to apply the term to
> anything written by me in verse, were I not fortunate enough to be of opin-
> ion, that poetry, like the trees and flowers, is not of one class only; but that
> if the plant comes out of Nature's hands, and not the gauze-maker's, it is
> still a plant, and has ground for it. All houses are not palaces, nor every
> shrine a cathedral.[89]

Hunt goes on to spell out his criteria. The merit of poetry in the highest and narrowest sense belongs, he writes, only to towering figures such as Shakespeare and Spenser, "but poetry, in the most comprehensive application of the term, I take to be the flower of any kind of experience, rooted in truth, and issuing forth into beauty."[90] (The repeated organic, vegetative imagery is highly characteristic.) He offers some possible categories: poetry of thought and passion, of scholarship, of courtliness, of gallantry, of wit and satire, of heartiness, and so on. And he proposes names to go with the categories: Shakespeare, Milton, Waller, Suckling, Pope, Burns. To illustrate poetic imagination, he quotes lines from Shakespeare, Milton, Shelley, and Keats. For his own part, he says, he does not pretend to belong in such company. He honestly doubts that his own verses deserve to last even "a dozen days longer": "I have witnessed so much self-delusion in my time, and partaken of so much, and the older I grow, my veneration so increases for poetry not to be questioned, that all I can be sure of, is my admiration of genius in others."[91] But this is an expression of uncertainty, not a judgment of worthlessness. It's not for him to say.

Public criticism, however, seems to have been happy to take him at his word and concur in the judgment that Hunt as a poet was second-rate, lightweight, not to be compared with his illustrious friends. The 1911 *Britannica* carefully defined him as an author of the second rank (though decidedly not "minor"), an "essayist and miscellaneous writer" notable for "mere exquisiteness of taste in the absence of high creative power."[92] In comparison with Wordsworth, who had come to set the standard for Romantic poetry, Hunt was manifestly *not serious*, which was to say, not grave and dignified in manner, but also not a great artist. Even the editors promoting his works have until recently tempered their advocacy with large doses of concession. For J. H. Lobban in 1909, Hunt was unquestionably a better prose writer than poet, and his fame rested on his journalism, his criticism, and his formative influence on better poets—though Keats had to get over "Hunt's namby-pamby voluptuousness of diction" before he could realize his full potential.[93] The devoted Milford in 1923 was also sparing with praise. "I do not claim greatness for Leigh Hunt," he wrote, "but it seems to me clear that he has been unduly neglected, and his genuine qualities obscured by adventitious criticism of his personality, and even more by concentration on his weak points, of which he has many."[94]

The risk, of course, in an altered critical climate, is that the twenty-first century will overstate the case for Hunt in order to prove its own higher wisdom. Perhaps Hunt's judgment really was greater than his powers of execution, and his work was as trivial and sentimental as literary history for a long time has told us it is. Entrenched opinion is not always wrong. Those short poems by which Hunt was remembered at the end of the nineteenth century do now seem trivial and sentimental, and many more like them could be found even in the selected editions produced by Hunt and later editors. But the same could be said of Keats from the earliest work to the latest ("The Cap and Bells," for instance, some of it written on the same sheet of paper as the much admired "This living hand, now warm and capable"), so the question should not be whether much of Hunt's work was drivel by our standards but rather whether there were gems in those editions too. Suppose the Victorian anthologists had selected for strength rather than for sentiment: would there not have been plenty to choose from?

Broader issues of criteria and relative merit can wait until after one more figure, Barry Cornwall, has been added for comparison with Keats and Hunt. At this point, since the judgment of the past has been so heavily weighted toward showing what was bad about Hunt's poetry, I shall simply try to explain what I think is good about it—intrinsically good, good in itself, setting aside special pleading on historical grounds. My basic contention is that Hunt produced a sufficient number of exceptionally good poems to have held his own with Coleridge, Keats, and Shelley—the Galignani trio—and that the aggregate of his poetry is much more interesting and impressive than we have been led to believe. When I use the name "Hunt" in the following paragraphs, it is to refer to qualities that are apparent in his writings, not to the historical person who produced them. Readers may test these frankly subjective views by consulting the substantial set of extracts from Hunt listed in the appendix and available on the website.

I think Hunt's copiousness is good in itself. The quantity of verse that he produced may be an asset, a sign of strength, as well as a handicap. It supplied a body of work of great variety—diverse in subject, mood, genre, and verse form—far from the reductive characterization of "sentimentality, mawkishness, and vulgarity." Consider the opulent descriptions and understated emotion of *The Story of Rimini;* the blunt challenge to readers about their complicity in war making in *Captain Sword and Captain Pen;* the cheery satire of *The Feast of the Poets,* where Apollo leaves Crabbe to be fed (and make notes) in the kitchen with the servants; the cozy confidences of "The 'Choice'"; and the elevated classicism of *The Descent of Liberty.* As with Wordsworth's corpus, if one mode palls, readers have their pick of others.

I admire his facility as well as his fertility. Keats also cultivated this gift: the Hunt circle, which we now call the Keats circle or the Shelley circle, encouraged displays of improvisation and rapid composition, as in their well-known sonnet competitions. (The two grasshopper poems cited in the appendix and available on the website were written in this sort of friendly contest.) Some of the poetry produced quickly in this way for periodical publication is as "slipshod" as Saintsbury suggested it all was, but much of it is not. Some of it was polished or revised for volume publication, and even where only the earliest versions are available, speed of execution sometimes supplies an appropriate sense of freshness and spontaneity. The three Hampstead sonnets cited in the appendix illustrate this talent: Hunt wrote them for the *Examiner* but did not include them in his midcareer collections. They render the impression of a moment, teased out into the split structure of the sonnet but still essentially simple and singular.

It seems to me a good thing that Hunt is a risk taker of a poet, ready to tackle practically any subject or form, and to try neologisms or combinations of words never seen before or since. The result is not always an unequivocal success, but at least the reader is kept on edge. (What further surprises might be in store?) He was famously prodigal with compound epithets of the kind the reviewers sniped at, which Coleridge, who was criticized for this fault himself, once described as the besetting sin of the youthful poet, citing Milton and Shakespeare in evidence.[95] For example, Hunt warns Byron, in an epistle, about the "rosy-cushioned mouths" of Italian girls; the Hampstead sonnets evoke "house-warm lips," "uptumbling" smoke, and "morn-elastic feet"; in a space of six lines "The Nymphs" includes a "grass-gliding breeze," a "grateful-breathing violet," and the "sheath-enfolded fans" of rosebuds. Sometimes, no doubt, Hunt did not know where to stop. But then he is seldom dull. And he is often funny; though it might not fit our notion of High Romanticism that that should be the case, contemporary readers had a great appetite for comic verse, and Hunt, like Byron, was adept at it. Also like Byron, he was capable of conveying serious emotions as well: witness the extracts cited from *The Story of Rimini* and *Captain Sword and Captain Pen*.

Hunt is strikingly empathetic. In the *Rimini* extract, the vantage point shifts from that of the citizens to Guido, the duke, and then to his daughter Francesca; the very horses that pull the carriage taking Francesca to Rimini have a few lines devoted to their feelings, as they "thrill, and curvet, and long to be at large" when they feel turf under their hoofs, but then "dip their warm mouths into the freshening grass" (lines 178–81). (Hunt also writes movingly and not sentimentally of the plight of horses on the battlefield, in *Captain Sword and Captain Pen*, lines 282–300.) For the twenty-first century, Hunt's sensitivity to plants and animals appears as a creditable protoenvironmentalism, though to the original readers it might have seemed kooky or even disturbing. The lines on fishing in "The Choice," for instance, make a moral argument by both direct and indirect means:

Fishing I hate, because I think about it,
Which makes it right that I should do without it.
A dinner, or a death, might not be much:
But cruelty's a rod I dare not touch.
I own I cannot see my right to feel
For my own jaws, and tear a carp's with steel;
To troll him here and there, and spike, and strain,
And let him loose to jerk him back again.

The lesson is clear, and persuasion does not rest with the lesson alone. The very choice of a personal pronoun, "him" rather than "it," subtly conveys an attitude, while the succession of strong verbs at the end—"troll," "spike," "strain," "jerk"—creates a vivid kinetic image.

The focus on physical sensation that appears in these quotations is a key feature of Hunt's poetic style from first to last, and its chief effect is to express and create empathy, not only for human and animal subjects but even for supposedly inanimate elements of the landscape—smoke that rises with "whirling glee" (in one of the Hampstead sonnets), grapes that "throng / Their laughing cheeks together on our vines" (in *The Descent of Liberty*), and of course whole forestfuls of trees—"Wild pear, and oak, and dusky juniper, / With briony between in trails of white . . . And still the pine, long-haired, and dark, and tall, / In lordly right, predominant o'er all" (in *Rimini*). Wordsworth once hurt Keats by dismissing his "Hymn to Pan" from *Endymion* as "a pretty piece of Paganism." The charge could be laid against works of almost every member of the Hunt circle, Hunt especially, but from another point of view it's hardly a charge at all; on the contrary, the kind of pagan sensibility that Hunt expresses in many passages of natural description can be seen as a positive asset. (Keats may have been more wounded by "pretty" than by the idea of paganism. The context of the remark suggests in any case that Hunt was Wordsworth's real target.)[96] The best example of Hunt's pagan way of seeing is the long poem *The Nymphs*, which, on the model of the Rosicrucian machinery in Pope's *The Rape of the Lock*, describes an order of supernatural beings—Dryads, Hamadryads, Napeads, Limniads, Oreads, and so on—responsible for protecting the plants and animals of the woods and mountainsides. The Dryads, for instance, "screen the cuckoo when he sings; and teach / The mother blackbird how to lead astray / The unformed spirit of the foolish boy / From thick to thick, from hedge to layery beech, / When he would steal the huddled nest away / Of yellow bills, up-gaping for their food, / And spoil the song of the free solitude." With their interlocking rhyme and artfully calculated sound patterns, these lines are far removed from the "fluent, gushing, slipshod style" we have generally been told to expect;

they represent his polished, sophisticated style better than the standard anthology pieces do. In fact, I'm not sure where I would look among Hunt's poems for gushing and slipshod, though I concede fluent. Along with some of the other "isms" for which it was castigated by hostile critics in its time—liberalism, for instance—the paganism of Hunt's poetry could make it very attractive to a twenty-first-century readership. Leigh Hunt played an important part in fostering the poet in Keats and teaching English readers how to enjoy his work. Their styles and attitudes are close enough that now, in a reversal of roles, readers who have grown up on Keats ought to be able to develop a taste for Hunt.

Barry Cornwall

Keats was not the only small, boyish, pugilistic, sensitive young poet whose talent was fostered by Hunt and his circle in the last years of the Regency; who rejected the legacy of the eighteenth century and emulated classic English poets and the great writers of Greece and Italy instead; who wrote movingly about love and melancholy; but whose poetic career was cut short early in the 1820s before he had realized his full potential.[97] Barry Cornwall, a few years older than Keats and a few younger than Hunt, began his career as an author in much the same way as Keats did. Though qualified in a profession—in his case, the law—he became completely devoted to literature and aspired to make his living by writing. (The nom de plume that he adopted, made up from the letters of his real name and at best a thin disguise, was devised originally to separate his literary and professional identities.) Like Keats, he started by contributing poems to periodicals. Like him, he published three volumes of verse before 1821: *Dramatic Scenes and Other Poems* (1819), *A Sicilian Story, with Diego de Montilla, and Other Poems* (1820), and *Marcian Colonna, an Italian Tale, with Three Dramatic Scenes, and Other Poems* (1820). These books established a pattern. As the titles indicate, each began with a few substantial works but also included miscellaneous shorter poems such as sonnets, songs, and verse epistles. Cornwall's publisher at this stage was the firm of C. and J. Ollier, who also published Hunt, Lamb, and Shelley, but who had broken with Keats after his first volume. Later on, in 1829, Cornwall and Keats both enjoyed the advantage of a Galignani compendium volume (fig. 14), though Cornwall was linked with Milman, Bowles, and John Wilson rather than with Coleridge and Shelley, so the advantage would turn out to be a mixed blessing.

Keats and Cornwall had many interests and topics in common; both, for example, wrote poems on the seasons, the arts, and mythological subjects.

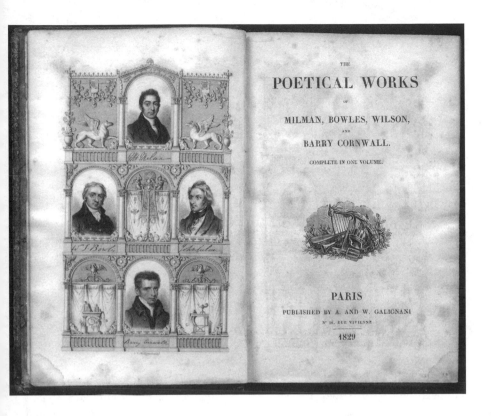

THE

POETICAL WORKS

OF

MILMAN, BOWLES, WILSON,

AND

BARRY CORNWALL.

COMPLETE IN ONE VOLUME.

PARIS

PUBLISHED BY A. AND W. GALIGNANI

N° 18, RUE VIVIENNE

1829

Fig. 14. Frontispiece, title page, and detail (depicting Barry
Cornwall) from *The Poetical Works of Milman, Bowles,
Wilson, and Barry Cornwall* (1829). Courtesy of John W.
Graham Library, Trinity College, Toronto.

Both looked to books for inspiration, especially to English writers of the Elizabethan age, though both also admired and imitated some of the great names of the generation just before their own, particularly Wordsworth and Coleridge. They were published side by side in *Annals of the Fine Arts* in 1820: Keats's "Ode on a Grecian Urn" with Cornwall's sonnet to Michelangelo. Cornwall's *A Sicilian Story,* its title echoing Hunt's *The Story of Rimini,* was his version of the tale from Boccaccio that Keats also reworked and published as "Isabella and the Pot of Basil" some months later. They knew one another, though they were not close friends; it seems that Cornwall thought more highly of Keats's work than Keats did of his.[98] But that might have had something to do with the fact that the reviewers and the public took an opposite view. At the time that Keats left for Italy, Cornwall was a rising star. His books had sold out and been reprinted—by 1821 there were already three London editions of the *Dramatic Scenes* and *A Sicilian Story,* two of *Marcian Colonna*—and the reviewers were trumpeting his "original genius" and "exquisite tact and original power."[99] Subsequent American editions generated a faithful American following.

As a representative of what may well have been a largely female readership—like Byron's, on a smaller scale—on both sides of the Atlantic, Mary Russell Mitford wrote to a correspondent in 1820 about the young attorney who published under a pseudonym, saying, "By whatever appellation he chooses to be called, he is a great poet."[100] (She went on to publish her own *Dramatic Scenes, Sonnets, and Other Poems* in 1827.) In 1829—the year of the Galignani edition—Anna Jameson noted that he was thought of as "the 'Poet of woman,' *par excellence.*"[101] Cornwall's appeal to women must have been multifaceted. His poems typically dealt with intense relationships between men and women; many of his protagonists are women; he portrays himself, as a narrator, as a passionate servant of love (in the opening of the extract from *Marcian Colonna* cited in the appendix, for example). Furthermore, as Richard Marggraf Turley demonstrates, Cornwall's verse is erotic without overt indecency: it skirts or flirts with the forbidden, it "is suffused with an atmosphere of casual sexuality."[102] The voyeur scene in *Gyges* (also listed in the appendix), comparable to the undressing of Madeline in Keats's *The Eve of St. Agnes,* is an obvious example, but Cornwall's very landscapes and settings can be sexually suggestive. Marggraf Turley quotes aptly, by way of illustration, the following lines describing a summer night in the outskirts of Rome, from *Marcian Colonna:*

> The red rose was in blossom, and the fair
> And bending lily to the wanton air
> Bared her white breast, and the voluptuous lime

Cast out his perfumes, and the wilding thyme
Mingled his mountain sweets, transplanted low
'Midst all the flowers that in those regions grow.

Lines such as these, which bear obvious comparison with the botanical imagery favored by Hunt and Keats, look back to Shakespeare's Cleopatra and
Titania and (closer to home) Erasmus Darwin's notorious *Loves of the Plants,*
and forward to Tennyson and Swinburne. In due course, Swinburne would
write Cornwall's funeral elegy, hailing him as one of "the singers whose names
are deathless."[103]

The almost immediate success of Cornwall's poetry, by contrast with the
indifference or hostility that first greeted Keats—something that Marggraf
Turley aptly describes as "an inverse graph" on the popularity charts—is not
easy for readers today to understand.[104] Although some of Cornwall's narrative and lyric poems are close enough in subject and style to work by Keats
that they could be mistaken for his (and even experts have been known to
make that mistake), the poems with which Cornwall initially made his name
have no counterparts in the Keats canon.[105] Cornwall was known mainly for
his "dramatic scenes," an innovation that brought him contemporary renown. This experimental genre never became established, however (though
it was not uninfluential), and we now hardly know what to make of it. The
same might be said of Byron's "Turkish tales," which were wildly popular at
the time but proved to be a short-lived poetry fad and are now next to incomprehensible.

For Cornwall and his readers, imaginative literature was not a means of
coming to terms with the world we know but rather a way of temporarily es-
caping from it. That is not to say that it was an escape into a better and brighter
place; on the contrary. Cornwall had before him the model of his friend Charles
Lamb's *Specimens of English Dramatic Poets* (1808), an anthology of extracts
from plays by Shakespeare's predecessors and contemporaries. What he did
was write new verse that *looked* like extracts from plays and functioned like
minidramas. In one or more scenes, with dialogue and monologues in character and often with an introductory note to explain how the characters came
to the point where they're discovered, he was able to distill a complete dramatic action into the reading space of seven or eight pages. The time was
right. People were not just going to the theater, they were consuming play
texts. Closet drama and private reading parties were in fashion. Byron's *Man-
fred: A Dramatic Poem* (1817) represents the merest tip of an iceberg, the
bulk of which is unread today.[106] Popularizers like Lamb—and like Hazlitt,
who delivered and published sets of lectures on early English poets and on

Elizabethan drama in 1818–20—primed potential purchasers for Cornwall's modern, original equivalent of the most lurid and macabre moments of Jacobean drama. Cornwall and Keats attended some of those lectures.

Byron liked the *Dramatic Scenes* but expressed reservations about Cornwall's later attempts to imitate his own jaunty ottava rima poems and Hunt's couplet narratives. Still, he assured Murray that Cornwall had it in him to "do a World's wonder" with a great tragedy, provided he adhered to his declared policy of "natural" language and did not follow the example of the old dramatists too closely.[107] As someone who at first found most of the "scenes" as well as the ottava rima poems positively embarrassing to read, I was puzzled by Byron's confidence in Cornwall and by his praise for Cornwall's "natural style," because "natural" is the last word I would have used to describe the scenes and most of the other poems in Cornwall's collections. I would have chosen something like "feverish," "hectic," or "overheated." Marggraf Turley describes them as a combination of "impassioned dialogue, fruity badinage and gothic schlock."[108] Yet Cornwall's discriminating contemporaries lapped them up and called them natural.

The simple distinction that Cornwall's contemporaries observed but that I had failed to make was between Cornwall's subjects and his language. In the short preface to *Dramatic Scenes,* Cornwall made it clear that he saw himself as participating in the same program of reform of poetic diction that Wordsworth had announced in *Lyrical Ballads* and Hunt in *Rimini,* with the goal of extending it to writing for the stage. He was aiming, he said, at "a more natural style than that which has for a long time prevailed in our dramatic literature"; and he would if necessary sacrifice "poetical imagery" to the higher goal of "expressions of natural emotion."[109] As far as language was concerned, he stuck to his program, as the samples listed in the appendix show (for instance, "The Two Dreams," the opening poem in *Dramatic Scenes*): the diction generally falls within the range of common usage, and the syntax is almost too pedestrian.[110] Though Cornwall occasionally admits a Huntian flourish, as in "the waving wood and the evanishing sky" (in *A Sicilian Story*) or the use of "vermillioned" as a verb, for the most part his language is deliberately plain. Even the emotions that he depicts could be considered natural, given the situations of the dramatis personae. But the situations themselves are extreme. In "The Two Dreams," we know from the outset that the husband is going to drop dead. In *A Sicilian Story* Isabel tends a basil plant under which she has buried a portion of the body of her slaughtered lover (by an unusual scruple, Cornwall changed the original head for the heart, explaining that a head was too "ghastly" to contemplate). Other poems, too, conform to type. Werner, a Faustian figure who has achieved immortality, realizes he has cut himself off from humanity, tears himself from his daughter's arms as she tries to restrain him, and at last resolves to live alone in the mountains with the wolves. A young man comes home after two years at university to find that his beloved has married someone else, having been led to believe that he had abandoned her; he makes his way into her bedroom and dies there as she wrings her hands and her husband sleeps. A woman poisons her second husband in revenge when she discovers that he had poisoned the first in order to win her. In one of the rare happy endings, a rich woman finally accepts her poor suitor after he denies her request for his prized falcon, which he has just killed and cooked for her. The stories are seldom original; introductory plot summaries (as in "The Two Dreams") minimize suspense; thus the poet's skill is exercised in the expression and interplay of strong feelings, and since the action is concentrated in a scene or two, the emotional pitch is consistently high.

Cornwall's pathetic and thrilling dramatic scenes were designed to arouse the kind of excitement that an audience might experience at the climax of a play in the theater, not the meditative mood that we associate with Wordsworth's lyrics and Keats's odes. Hence the staples of the Cornwall diet: beauty, love, madness, and death. *Marcian Colonna*, a narrative poem with long passages of dialogue, is a good example of his art at its best. Marcian believes himself fated to become a murderer, and is subject to episodes of madness. But he loves Julia, who loves him back, and after she is widowed they are able to marry. The supposedly dead husband reappears, however, and Marcian first of all drags Julia into exile (which involves a terrific shipwreck; Cornwall liked writing about the sea), then hides her in a cave, and at last, rather than part from her, administers poison, which she appears to take willingly. Her spirit is thought to haunt the area around the cave. This poem is psychologically powerful: because the point of view is predominantly that of the unstable Marcian himself, it is not clear whether the husband really was still alive, or Marcian only imagined seeing him; nor whether Julia knowingly accepted the poison. Ambiguity complicates and deepens what might otherwise be a conventional melodrama.

Cornwall's reputation was at first not much damaged by the Cockney wars. Some of the encouraging reviewers linked him with Hunt and complained about the telltale signs of his discipleship ("bad epithets," irregular meters, vulgarity, etc.), only to assure the young poet of success if he could shake off Hunt's "misguiding influence."[111] Cornwall explicitly abjured politics, he was not as closely identified with Hunt as Keats was, and he had friends across party lines. His personal circumstances were in every way more fortunate than those of either Hunt or Keats. (He had been a schoolmate of Byron's at Harrow; in 1816 he came into an inheritance of £500 a year, which meant that he would never have to rely on income from writing.) In 1821 his play *Mirandola* had a respectable run of sixteen nights at Covent Garden, and three editions of it appeared in the same year.[112] In 1822–23 the Ollier firm went bankrupt, but Henry Colburn took Cornwall over and brought out his *Poetical Works* in three volumes (1822), followed by another collection of new work, *The Flood of Thessaly, The Girl of Provence, and Other Poems* (1823). But then the bubble burst. *Blackwood's*, which had previously supported him, panned the new book as an egregious example of Cockney Greekishness with nothing novel, powerful, interesting, or intelligent about it. Though not all reviews were quite as hostile, and Richard Willard Armour notes one that was actually laudatory, the net effect must have been seriously discouraging.[113] In any case, the market for poetry was beginning to dry up, making way for prose fiction.[114]

Cornwall's career as a poet effectively came to an end in 1823. When he had an enquiry from a reader in Newcastle for his collected works in 1856, he said they were not worth collecting (and there is to this day no complete collection). By 1870 he declared that he himself hardly recognized lines quoted from the verses of "a poor forgotten man who once imposed on the reading public under the name of Cornwall."[115] There was no second edition of *The Flood of Thessaly*, and no American edition at all. In 1824, with Hunt in Italy and Keats, Shelley, and Byron all dead, Cornwall married and returned to the law. He became a barrister, raised children, and in 1832—in a fitting gesture made apparently without reference to his writings—was appointed a Metropolitan Commissioner of Lunacy, a position that he retained for almost thirty years, which involved inspections of asylums throughout the country. He did not give up writing but he became, in his own word, a literary "amateur."[116] He continued to contribute occasionally to periodicals, including the modish annuals of the late 1820s and 1830s, and he took on occasional editorial and biographical projects. His one attempt at a fresh start (*English Songs*, published by Moxon in 1832) was of limited success; like the moderately successful tragedy of *Mirandola*, the *Songs* did not lead anywhere, though some were popular and the collection was reprinted a few times before his death.[117] Cornwall did not sustain the effort or repeat the experiment. In the long term, the *Songs* may have undermined his reputation by displacing the more original dramatic scenes in the anthologies.

If the first part of Cornwall's career resembled that of Keats, the second was more like the later years of Hunt, with a lot of hard work, responsibility, and tedious illness to endure. Fortunately Cornwall, like Hunt, was a generous host and a good friend who took pleasure in encouraging and supporting younger writers; they for their part enjoyed his hospitality and drew him out.

Two notable successes among them were his own daughter Adelaide Procter, whose popularity eclipsed that of her father but who died before she was forty; and Robert Browning, whose *Dramatic Lyrics* and *Dramatic Romances* (published by Moxon in 1842 and 1845) were, like Mitford's poems of 1827, in the tradition of Cornwall's *Dramatic Scenes*. Browning dedicated *Columbe's Birthday* to Cornwall in 1844; in collaboration with their mutual friend John Forster, Cornwall edited a volume of *Selections* from Browning's work in 1863. Elizabeth Barrett Browning also admired Cornwall's works and adopted techniques from them.[118] Cornwall's influence on women writers would be worth exploring.

After his virtual poetic death in 1823, Cornwall's earlier, popular work was carried for a time, like that of Keats, by collections and anthologies. It was comparatively well represented, as I have mentioned, in the important Paris collections of 1827 and 1828, *Living Poets of England* and *British Poets of the Nineteenth Century,* and in the Galignani volume of 1829. After that, it faded from sight, as was only to be expected. The introductory memoir in the Galignani volume characterized Cornwall's verse as having a "gentle chaste beauty" in spite of its morbid and eccentric subjects; remarked on its typically somber tone; and described him in person as having "an amiable though somewhat of a feeble, rather than masculine, character."[119] (Want of strong masculinity emerged as an issue for Keats as well, of course.) Most of the slight commentary on Cornwall in the 1830s and 1840s referred to his unrealized potential, generally with a polite hope that he might even yet live up to it. Unrealized potential may be a positive asset for a dead poet, but not for one who lives to be eighty-six and is socially respectable. Chambers's *Cyclopaedia* of 1844 gave Hunt, Keats, and Cornwall about the same number of pages but noted that "Mr. Procter's later productions have not met the promise of his early efforts."[120] William Howitt included Cornwall in *Homes and Haunts* (1847), though with a relatively short entry and no accompanying image. For Howitt, the past triumphs of Barry Cornwall belonged strictly to the past, and he "has never yet fairly and fully developed his whole power," but he was still intellectually vigorous and might yet prove himself a "true tragic poet."[121] Cornwall by that time was in his sixtieth year, and he never did produce the major tragedy that his supporters had hoped for.

In the 1850s and later, by the logic of the "inverse graph," as Keats's reputation soared, Cornwall's sank, despite an early effort made on his behalf in 1851 (in the wake of Milnes's biography of Keats) by David Moir, who put the case for Procter's distinctive blend "of gentle but passionate earnestness, of refined sentiment, of picturesque situation, and exquisite harmony of style"; offered lavish quotations; and observed that "of late years" there seemed to be a tendency to underrate his work "for the sake of the glorification of others, unquestionably not more deserving."[122] So far as I know, there was only one illustrated edition of Cornwall's work, the *Dramatic Scenes* of 1857, and it never went into a second British edition.[123] Palgrave did not include Cornwall in *The Golden Treasury*: Cornwall would have been disqualified in any case because he was still living, but Palgrave also excluded Hunt and may have thought of Cornwall as a follower—a "bantling" of Hunt's, as a scornful reviewer once said of Keats.[124] Furthermore, Cornwall's best work was not in the lyric but in dramatic and narrative modes. As recollection of the dramatic scenes and poems of that period faded, the more recent songs took their place in those anthologies that included Cornwall at all. Ward's *English Poets* (1880) gave him just four pages, all of them for slight, sentimental songs (in this too, his fate matches Hunt's). Finally, Cornwall's successful memoir of Charles Lamb (1866), together with J. T. Fields's anecdotal, sycophantic *Old Acquaintance* (1876) and the collection of reminiscences of his distinguished friends that appeared along with other literary remains in Cornwall's posthumously published *Autobiographical Fragment* (1877), marked him as a memoirist, a man of the past. When literature of the Romantic period began to make its way into the educational system, there was no place for him. The dramatic scenes were not suitable for children and could not be considered for schoolbooks, but they did not match the profile of Wordsworthian Romanticism either, so they never formed part of the university curriculum. At the end of the century, Saintsbury just sneered: Barry Cornwall had been "the friend of many good men but not a very good poet."[125]

After he died there was no landmark biography, no call for a collected edition, no shrine for literary pilgrims, no Cornwallian Society.[126] There was little support to be found in the publishing market. Professional scholarship, the last hope of dead poets, also turned its back on him. Saintsbury's judgment set the tone for the literary histories and criticism of the twentieth century, and Cornwall was written off. For him as for Keats, originality was an issue, with opposite results. Whereas some of the early positive reviews had made a virtue of Cornwall's powers of imitation, maintaining that he imitated the spirit rather than the language of his models, and that he did have a distinctive voice, a century later he was dismissed as derivative—not "entirely mimetic," according to the 1911 *Encyclopedia Britannica,* but largely so. The results of his fusion of Elizabethan and modern sources, according to the unnamed contributor, "are somewhat heterogeneous, and lack the impress of a pervading and dominant personality to give them unity, but they abound in pleasant touches, with here and there the flash of a higher, though casual, inspiration." Even Cornwall's first real biographer and champion,

R. W. Armour, was quick to concede that his subject had been a small man and a small poet.[127] Donald Reiman's introduction to a facsimile reprint of two volumes of Cornwall's poems in 1978 describes his work as possibly "the best example we possess of the futility of a poet with neither philosophic depth nor extraordinary command of poetic language trying to follow in the footsteps of great poets."[128]

Cornwall himself anticipated and even invited neglect. He was by nature quiet and diffident—qualities that might seem hard to reconcile with the sensationalism of his early poetry, but that actually help to explain it. Like the pseudonym, dramatic form (or, in the later years, songs composed in the character of a beggar woman, convict, or murderer) gave Cornwall a mask to wear when he had to face the public. His personal model of authorship was unusually self-effacing. As he wrote in the introduction to *English Songs,* "where a writer speaks in his own person, he expends all his egotism upon his lyrics," whereas an opposite "power of forgetting himself, and imagining and fashioning characters different from his own . . . constitutes the dramatic quality."[129] Thus it seems likely that instinctive shyness played a part in Cornwall's habit of disparaging his own work. So did its corollary, admiration for the achievements of others. Like Hunt, he thought more highly of the work of certain other writers than of his own and would far rather work to promote theirs. Finally, Cornwall must have considered himself something of a traitor to literature and therefore unworthy: after all, he had not died in 1824 but simply walked away from poetry, and he had never produced the major tragedy that everyone hoped for. As with Hunt and others before him, Cornwall's own idealism about literature could have contributed to his failure: he believed in eternal fame, but he had long since given up hope of winning it for himself. When he took leave of the public for the third or fourth time in the 1857 edition of *Dramatic Scenes,* he remarked, rather sadly, that time had quelled the aspirations of his youth and that he would now "leave to more active and heroic spirits, the glory of the struggle, and the crown that awaits success."[130]

In the twenty-first century, Cornwall has just begun to attract serious scholarly attention as a figure of historical interest and as a foil for Keats. This is the interesting point: practically every objection that was ever made to the work of Keats (Cockney, unmanly, derivative, over the top, carnal, promising but immature) could be applied to that of Cornwall, but so could practically every argument that has been made in its favor (innovative, sensuous, imaginative, an influence on major figures to follow). As far as reputation is concerned, the differences between them are largely personal and accidental. Keats died young, and his bereaved friends built a legend around him; a skillful biographer told his tragic story and introduced his extraordinary letters; midcentury artists gave his writings new life in visual form; and so the process of immortalization got under way. Cornwall did not inspire the same devotion. But if their personal situations had been reversed, couldn't the same case have been made for Cornwall? Suppose Keats had recovered in Italy and come home to claim his inheritance and marry Fanny Brawne, while Cornwall—who was in fact in poor health at the time, as he was for most of his life—was carried off by an infection. Keats might have composed obituary tributes for Cornwall, as Cornwall in fact did for him. Cornwall's friends might have blamed *Blackwood's* for striking a death blow to his sensitive spirit with the harsh review of *The Flood of Thessaly*. Someone would have written his biography and published his remaining works; an enterprising publisher (Moxon most likely) would have collected his poems. We might now be sharing our admiration for the stanzas on the death of the pauper (at the end of *Gyges*) and quoting "O power of love so fearful and so fair" (from *Marcian Colonna*) instead of "A thing of beauty is a joy forever"—which is not in itself an obviously better line or more profound sentiment.

I do not argue that Keats and Cornwall are interchangeable, nor that we ought to start teaching Cornwall as well as Keats. Even the recent surge of interest in Hunt and the Cockney School has largely ignored Cornwall, possibly because his role was underdocumented, or because he followed Shakespeare and the dramatists rather than Spenser and the romances, so that his characteristic style was not as obviously Huntian as that of some other members of the circle. I would not even say that Cornwall did not deserve to fall into oblivion. It is in the nature of things for writers to be superseded. Time passes and perspectives change. Cornwall's main innovation—his one area of undoubted leadership—was the dramatic scene, but the dramatic scene as a genre fizzled out. Popularity, short-lived or not, presents problems later on, so both the popularity of Cornwall's poetry in its day and its long history of subsequent neglect have tended to lend support to the negative judgments expressed by literary historians. Cornwall's plain-language policy means that his lines are less "poetical," less striking in themselves and therefore less memorable and less quotable, than those of Keats or Hunt. I do not personally find Cornwall's body of work as engaging as Hunt's. All the same, it would be possible to make a case for Cornwall on strictly aesthetic (as opposed to historical) grounds, along the same lines as the defense of Hunt above. In his early career, Cornwall produced enough original poems to hold his own with contemporaries such as Coleridge, Keats, and Shelley; his poetry in the aggregate is much more impressive than we have been led to believe. It warrants a second look. With Cornwall and Hunt alike, however,

in order to take a second look we have to deal with an uneven and unmediated mass of writing. Keats we have sifted; over the course of many generations we have settled on a relatively small number of poems still considered
worthy of attention, and for the most part we agree to disregard the rest. If
we had done the same for Cornwall, what might we have discovered? (When
he came to present a volume of his own favorite poems, Emerson gave thanks
for the sifting process: "What a signal convenience is fame! Do we read all
authors to grope our way to the best? No; but the world selects for us the
best, and we select from these our best.")[131]

With some misgivings because, as I have said, Cornwall's poems do not
really appeal to me, I propose six characteristic qualities that even a twenty-
first-century reader might find intrinsically attractive or at least interesting in
Cornwall's work, and I again refer readers to the presifted extracts listed in
the appendix to test my claims. Some of these qualities are common to Cornwall, Hunt, and Keats. They are easier to recognize because we are already
familiar with them through Keats. One is the conscious reference to literary
tradition: the author's frank admiration of his predecessors and his earnest
effort to build upon their achievements. Most if not all of Cornwall's lon-
gest and most polished poems are mediated by epigraphs and headnotes
that set a tone, showcase lines from other writers, and invite comparisons.
"The Two Dreams," for example, quotes Shakespeare and Byron and cites
Boccaccio as a direct source: thus Cornwall identifies the important literary
theme to which he is about to make a fresh contribution. Each subsection of
Marcian Colonna has its own separate epigraphs; in the second part, which
deals with the lovers' reunion, the epigraphs are taken from living poets,
Coleridge and Wilson. The verses that follow often echo other poets' lines
(this is true of Keats as well) in a way that is part tribute and part renewal—
Coleridge's "Quietly shining to the quiet moon" from "Frost at Midnight,"
for example, morphing into "Sent up in homage to the quiet moon." This is
neither theft nor allusion, but an enhancement of the literary experience for
a certain kind of reader (Keats's kind, Cornwall's, T. S. Eliot's).

Another quality that Cornwall shared with Keats and Hunt is his paganism—
what *Blackwood's* eventually condemned as Cockney Greekishness—though
in his case evocations of mythic figures are not usually occasions of happiness and celebration as they are with Hunt (whose Hampstead Dryads help
out mother blackbirds), but rather of regret for a spiritual richness lost to the
modern world. Thus a glimpse of the moon at the end of the extract from
Marcian Colonna provokes not only the conventional thought of Diana but
also a little scene of Diana kissing and weeping over her shepherd boy, and
then the sorrowful reflection that "The pale queen is dethroned. Endymion /

Hath vanished; and the worship of this earth / Is bowed to golden gods of vulgar birth." Likewise, a description of Derwent-Water in the aftermath of a storm briefly suggests fauns and naiads, gnomes and fairies, Oberon and Titania as well as Galatea, but then, having raised them, dismisses them as fancies no longer accessible to the modern imagination. While poems with ancient subjects such as Cornwall's mini-epic *The Flood of Thessaly* (retelling the story of Pyrrha and Deucalion) and "On the Statue of Theseus" provided him with natural opportunities to introduce classical mythology, he also brought in the old stories to enrich his new ones on much less obvious occasions. For instance, the following two stanzas about the "nymphs and deities" of the past appear as part of a digression in *Diego de Montilla: A Spanish Tale,* which is a weak imitation of Byron's manner in *Don Juan:*

> Oh! ye delicious fables, where the wave
>   And woods were peopled and the air with things
> So lovely, why, ah! why has science grave
>   Scatter'd afar your sweet imaginings?
> Why sear'd the delicate flow'rs that genius gave,
>   And dash'd the diamond drops from fancy's wings?
> Alas! the spirit languishes and lies
>   At mercy of life's dull realities.
>
> No more by well or bubbling fountain clear
>   The Naiad dries her tresses in the sun,
> Nor longer may we in the branches hear
>   The Dryad talk, nor see the Oread run
> Along the mountains, nor the Nereid steer
>   Her way amongst the waves when day is done.
> Shadow nor shape remains.—But I am prating
>   While th' reader and Diego, both, are waiting.[132]

The closest familiar parallel to these lines (and the comparison does not favor Cornwall) would be Keats's lines at the end of *Lamia* about philosophy unweaving the rainbow. Cornwall shared the nostalgia that Keats and Hunt also expressed for the imaginative world of pre-Christian Greece and Italy; like them, he celebrated it and aimed to revive it for a time through his own verse. But the emotional effect is different.

Among the qualities that differentiate Cornwall's poetry from that of Hunt and Keats is its striking consistency of tone. With few exceptions, he operated within a somber range that could accommodate sorrow, regret, grief, pathos, remorse, or tender sympathy in a dignified way, but not satisfaction or robust pleasure or unmitigated delight. When the lovers are ecstatically reunited in *Marcian Colonna,* their joy is both heightened and shadowed by the distresses of the past and the fatality that hangs over the future, so that the net effect is quite mournful. Cornwall's efforts at Byronic humor in ottava rima poems such as *Diego de Montilla* failed not only because the jokes were not very funny but because merriness is out of place in a Cornwall collection. Contemporary reviewers labeled his verse "melancholy." There is hardly any poem cited in the appendix that does not convey this characteristic mood to some degree or other, using a combination of situation, emotive language, and imagery—especially imagery of the Graveyard School kind. *A Sicilian Story* is the best example among the long poems: though the mood shifts, it is consistently sorrowful, even in the party scene at the beginning. The creepy poem "Marcelia" is a good short example: a desolate forest scene, shunned by animal life, with "funereal" trees sighing "like death," but where the speaker "love[s] to loiter." There is a story attached, a suicide just touched on—which is itself a reminder that Cornwall's poems stand apart from much of the first-person wallowing of the sentimental movement by the fact that their melancholy is a sadness felt for the lot of others. Compassion was a trademark of the Cornwall persona and a notable strength of Cornwall as a person, to judge by some of the observations in his letters; it extends to the unhappy of all classes, even the rich. Thus the pathetic lines about the funeral of a pauper at the end of *Gyges,* much admired, were written not on behalf of the pauper, or not only for him, but out of compassion for the foolish king Candaules, because nobody mourned his death. (That said, those stanzas, which veer in short order from voluptuousness through embarrassment to shock and pathos, only to end jokily with an outrageous comic rhyme, might not be the ideal illustration for my point about consistency, unless they serve to demonstrate that Cornwall did have range as well as tight control of his overall poetic effects. I believe he knew what he was doing. Contrast can heighten pathos.)

A related specialty of Cornwall's is his exploration of disordered mental states, both in his choice of mad subjects such as *Marcian Colonna* and *The Girl of Provence* (a poem based on the case history of a young woman who fell in love with a statue of Apollo), or in his treatment of the derangement of Isabel at the end of *A Sicilian Story,* and in his frequent—I am tempted to say obsessive—representation of dreams, which goes beyond the traditional literary use of dreams as plot devices or portals to other worlds. In Cornwall the dream, usually a nightmare, has an interest in and of itself. The hint for the story in "The Two Dreams" may have come from Boccaccio, but the horrific details and vivid representation of the experience of nightmare were Cornwall's distinctive contribution. Many other poems include dreams or "visions" of similar intensity. (One, simply entitled "A Vision," is described in the headnote as "little more than the recollection of an actual dream.")[133]

There may be a biographical foundation for this strong theme in Cornwall's work. Looking back on his school days from the vantage point of age, he distinctly recalled a spare room in the house of an uncle, where he used to stay during the holidays. The wallpaper in that room, with a pattern of strange faces and objects "partaking at once of the bird and the beast" inspired both "wonderful thoughts" and "terrors," even during waking hours. When he was left there overnight to enjoy "quiet rest," he found quiet rest impossible. "My imagination had begun to move," Cornwall remembered, with the result that "some things which were beautiful and many things which were terrible, operated very sensibly upon me. My brain was disturbed. I began to dream, and to recollect my dreams, and to dwell upon them, and strove to discover their meanings and origin."[134] He tellingly associates his dreams mainly with terrors, conceiving of the imagination as a great but frightening power: it turns wallpaper into acute experiences of beauty and of fear. Speakers in his poems, for instance the doomed husband in "The Two Dreams" and the first-person voice in "Melancholy," sometimes reflect on the ultimate significances of such dreams and mental disturbance, but Cornwall, with a kind of agnosticism that a modern reader might appreciate, provides no easy answers. Among poets of the Romantic period, Cornwall by no means had a monopoly on the subject of mental disorder, but he had serious things to say about it; he was listened to; and he is still worth hearing.

Finally, Cornwall's poetry from first to last is distinguished by the subtle musical qualities that the Brownings and Swinburne admired. Like Coleridge in "Kubla Khan," which represents the Romantic gold standard for this highly prized technical quality, Cornwall knew how to deploy rhyme, meter, vowel patterns, alliteration, and other repetitive sounds to euphonious effect: see, for example, the voluptuous lines on flowers previously quoted; stanza 29 in *Gyges;* or stanza 18 in *A Sicilian Story.* The effects are subtle, not showy, in keeping with the general tone of Cornwall's work. He seems particularly to have favored a quiet close, as with the muted finish (and off rhyme) of *A Sicilian Story,* the truncated conclusion of "On the Statue of Theseus," or the understated ending of "Derwent-Water and Skiddaw." (That poem also has a quiet opening modeled, undoubtedly, on Wordsworth; as a whole, in particular lines and in the development of ideas, it looks in turn like a model for "Dover Beach.") Cornwall may have lacked the facility of Hunt and Keats or may just have preferred not to publish work he considered imperfect. Certainly he valued craft and polish and took special care with meter.[135] He practiced a variety of traditional measures and did not let them become predictable or monotonous; as Barrett Browning observed, he also experimented with stanza forms of his own invention. When Cornwall adopted the Huntian run-on couplets, he would complicate the rhyme scheme with some sections of alternate or interlocking rhyme, as at the end of the first stanza in the extract from *Marcian Colonna*. Many of his longer poems incorporate shorter ones, the songs in the extracts from *A Sicilian Story* and *Marcian Colonna*, for example.

Contemporary readers and reviewers and early anthologizers bore witness to Cornwall's outstanding achievement as a poet; though we no longer read as they did, it is still possible to find positive value in the body of his early work.

But What About Merit?

The conundrum of Barry Cornwall's success with the same audience that spurned Keats once led Donald Reiman to invoke the test of time and the consensus of experts. He pointed out that "as the whole of literary history teaches, a large segment of any contemporary audience for poetry cannot accurately judge between Horace and Cordus, between Shakespeare and Kyd, between Dryden and Shadwell, between Pope and Philips, or between Keats and 'Cornwall.'"[136] But that was in 1978, when it was easier for readers to accept the idea of a solidly established canon based on the cumulative judgment of literary professionals. In the wake of feminism, canon wars, multiculturalism, capital-T Theory, social constructionism, and revisionist historicism, we find our confidence eroded and are inclined to believe that such erosion may not be a bad thing. We have been reminded of some general truths and have been asked to reopen such specific issues as the supposedly unquestionable superiority of Keats to Hunt and Cornwall. The test of time proves durability, but not the reasons behind it. We acknowledge—what philosophical critics like Johnson were saying centuries ago—that aesthetic judgments are provisional, not absolute. They depend on the judges' vantage points and the criteria they apply, to say nothing of the system within which they air their views. There are no ultimate standards, only evolving (and revolving) ones.

The monolithic "literary history" cited by Reiman itself consists of successive accounts of the past by individual historians. Every one of those historians might have had axes to grind, but all were obliged by publishing convention and readerly expectation to work within a familiar framework of storytelling and ranking, and none of them appears to have quarreled with that framework or even to have noticed it. Their work by its nature involves much synthesis and little innovation: they have to depend on the framework and make what they can of the evidence supplied by their predecessors. On

the large scale they might seem to be moving progressively toward equilibrium (for instance, the consensus of 1978), but on a finer scale (for instance,
in the critical histories of Keats, Hunt, and Cornwall) they can clearly be seen
to take sides, to vacillate, and to jostle one another. There is no reason to expect that the process will stop as long as writers seek readers through the
medium of publishers, and no reason to expect that it will ever achieve perfect stability.

Is Keats not a far better poet than either Hunt or Cornwall, judged strictly
by the body of work left behind, and setting aside for the moment as distrac-
tions such matters as politics, personality, life story, and even historical impact? The answer has to be yes and no. Yes, because his work enjoys almost
universal approval and has done for a long time now; and no, because judg-
ments of quality depend on the criteria applied. Since it is possible to discover criteria of the past that produced a different ranking once, it is possible
to imagine a future in which the answer might be negative again. For now, the
four broad categories of audience concur—other writers, literary professionals, lay readers, the general public. Keats is the best known of the three, the
most loved, the most widely popular: no contest. His words are in our
thought streams, ineradicably it seems (still unravished bride; O what can ail
thee, knight-at-arms?; There was a naughty boy, / A naughty boy was he; the
murmurous haunt of flies on summer eves), though of course the same was
once true of the poetry of Walter Scott. Success reinforces and magnifies
merit. Over time, winners like Keats change the rules—that's what is meant
by canonical status. They become benchmarks. Their own work is sifted, and
the work of others is measured by reference to the qualities most highly prized
in the handful of poems that are thought to be their best. If we measure the
poetry of Keats, Hunt, and Cornwall by criteria that have evolved on the
strength of his long-term triumph, Keats will by definition come out on top
and Hunt ahead of Cornwall; the exercise is futile. By other criteria, however, the result would be different.

If by a thought experiment we were to obliterate the critical heritage of the
nineteenth century and begin again, what poems would we read and what
criteria would we apply? Horace's criteria of technical mastery, leadership,
the approval of connoisseurs, and the ability to make money for the booksellers might have led him to pick Cornwall. Johnson looked for originality, just
representations of human nature, and the ability to please many: perhaps he
would have thought Hunt stood the best chance. Judged according to their
own personal standards, the three poets would not fare well. Keats thought
his work superior to that of the others but falling far short of what he aimed
at and believed he was capable of, since he measured his work against that of

Chaucer, Shakespeare, Spenser, and Milton. He published a cringingly apologetic preface with *Endymion,* abandoned both attempts at *Hyperion,* and told Shelley that most of the poems in the *Lamia* volume were two or three years old and would never have been published if he had not badly needed the money.[137] Hunt was always quicker to promote the work of his poetical protégés than his own: on a single, uniform scale he would certainly have ranked Keats ahead of himself and probably himself ahead of Cornwall, but he preferred not to use a single scale and instead, like Crabbe, recommended diversity or catholicity of taste. Cornwall was an early supporter of Keats and came to consider him exceptional (but that was late in Cornwall's life, in the third quarter of the nineteenth century, when much of the cultural work had been done for Keats). As a general rule Cornwall seems to have been willing to accept the verdict of the public, for himself as for others. Still, we know better than to accept writers' own assessments of their merit. Besides, in all these cases including that of Keats they were judging by potential or what they might have thought of as innate poetic ability, not strictly by a body of work. Under such circumstances, Keats's confidence (his determination to write for immortality) could have tipped the balance in his favor.

If we were to put ourselves in the place of their contemporaries and judge by the implicit standards of the public circa 1820, Keats would trail far behind Cornwall, and Hunt would lead the group. (They thought there was not much to choose among the three, but that Hunt was the ringleader and master; Cornwall adept and original; Keats a young man to watch, who might some day be as good as Hunt.) If we accepted the standards of professional critics of the time, Cornwall would outrank Hunt, and Keats would be in third place. If we looked to their peers, fellow poets, for comparative assessment, we would find that their opinions were strong but divided. Casual remarks by Wordsworth, Coleridge, and Byron suggest that they all thought more highly of the work of Cornwall than of Hunt or Keats. Shelley abominated Cornwall's work but had no very positive opinion of Hunt or Keats as artists either: he would surely have ranked Hunt highest of the three.[138] While these are only the poets who appear to us now to have been the best (the winners), their views, divided as they were, are probably representative of their kind. Keats did not begin to appear to stand out until twenty years or more after his death. By then, assessments of the work were already being distorted by the growing personal myth.

If we adopt the Johnsonian view that all contemporary readers are unavoidably partial, influenced by partisanship and swayed by the passing concerns of the day, and that enough time has to pass for passions to have cooled and comparisons to have been made and tested before a sound judgment can be made—in short, to let posterity decide—at what point do we stop the clock? Posterity has parties and passing concerns of its own that fluctuate from one generation to the next. It has been noted before that when Jane Tompkins investigated the reputation of Nathaniel Hawthorne, she discovered that "the grounds of critical approval are always shifting."[139] The Keats canon may not have changed much, but the same words were read differently in 1820 from the ways that they would be read in 1920 and 2010, on account of current critical assumptions as well as current concerns and interests.

And then who counts as a qualified judge? Johnson would have been ready to accept the evidence of sales figures, but Wordsworth believed that most readers (the ones who would produce the numbers for the sales figures) in any period are liable to be untrustworthy and that the best a writer could hope for was a gradual improvement in the proportion of good readers to bad. Reiman put his faith in literary history and the academic specialists who produce it (in the twentieth century, only specialists would have recognized the names of Cordus, Kyd, Shadwell, Philips, and Cornwall), but if the case histories of the reception of Keats, Hunt, and Cornwall prove anything, it is that literary history (or rather, historians) can be grossly misleading. In short, the accurate judgment that Reiman called for was and remains elusive. Anyone can judge, but no one can be sure of judging "accurately." There is no Olympian view of literary merit. There never will be.

These studies support several conclusions, some more tentative than others. First of all, if "merit" refers purely to literary quality, "merit" is not enough to bring about "immortality." All three authors, writing at their best, were gifted artists, meritorious in distinctive ways. Their worst, rightly, does not matter. All three produced a large enough body of outstanding verse to earn the recognition that they sooner or later enjoyed. All three had a positive influence on the next generation of writers after their own: Hunt, notably, on Keats, Keats on Tennyson, Cornwall on the Brownings. All three fulfilled the two criteria identified by the Langs as critical to the durability of artists' reputations, in that they left behind "both a sizable, accessible, and identifiable oeuvre and persons with a stake in its preservation and promotion."[140] But more was needed, or to put it another way, merit would have to be redefined to account for the victory of Keats and the rejection of the others. Keats had some secondary, unforeseen advantages over Hunt and Cornwall: more of his good poems were of anthologizable length; he expressed confidence about his own abilities (other things being equal, that encourages potential advocates); separated from his nearest and dearest, he put his thoughts and feelings into letters that they kept. But ultimately he outshone his similarly meritorious contemporaries by acquiring symbolic value as *"the young Poet"* (in Hunt's phrase) full of passion and imagination and promise, tragically thwarted by forces hostile to all that he stood for. The Keats legend arose directly from the circumstances of his death; the mechanisms by which it gained strength included peripheral writings (the letters that revealed his ideas and aspirations) and the efforts of multiple champions—biographers, editors, artists, fellow poets, publishers, reviewers, teachers, performers—who took up his cause and succeeded in spreading the word. Thus whatever intrinsic literary merit Keats and his writings possessed was supplemented by the symbolic value that can only be conferred by social groups, and Keats outpaced his rivals. Merit of this order is not a simple or single quality; it is complex, a bundle or package of valuable qualities.[141]

The same can be said of the author. With due deference to Wordsworth, the spokesman for all writers who call for the separation of the person and the works, and to critics such as Lake in the period or Foucault in recent years who have deplored the use of the same word (the name of the author) to refer to author and writings indiscriminately, the author too is a package, a compound entity.[142] Since classical times, encounters with written work have involved prior knowledge of the author, whether in the form of common knowledge (you don't need to have read anything by Gibbon or Tolstoy to know roughly who they were, when they lived, what they are renowned for) or in the form of prefaces and headnotes. Even anthologies normally include author profiles, and have done so for centuries. The name and the writings are mutually supportive: if readers encounter one without the other they will go looking for the missing piece, as writers who adopt pseudonyms or anonyms well know. In practical terms, in the English-speaking world, the names of authors are inseparable from the work known to be theirs, with the natural and necessary consequence that the evaluation of the work is affected by the associations of the name. The editors who mistook lines by Barry Cornwall for lines by Keats admired them as Keatsian. The writer "Keats," a composite made up of the historical person, the works, the legend, and the legacy, is a symbol, albeit a symbol in flux.[143]

As Tyler Cowen points out in his analysis of the fame economy, "the most famous figures usually represent more than one focal quality at a time—often to different audiences—thus broadening their appeal."[144] The multiplicity of audiences has been a recurrent theme in these chapters as a factor, especially important over the long haul, that both rewards and sustains success. There could hardly be better illustrations of this principle than the cases of Austen and Keats.

From the perspective of the present, "Keats" appears to have far more merit than "Hunt" and "Cornwall," though it is not inherent merit and does not reside in the poetry alone. Most of it was acquired over time, reflecting the collective investment of attention and devotion by readers over many years. It's a reality.[145] By reopening the question of the relative merits of Hunt and Cornwall, I do not aim to diminish Keats or to turn back the clock, only to shed light on the process by which he gained the huge advantage he now has, and to suggest that rather than ask which of the three is the best poet, we might indulge in counterfactuals and ask whether another outcome could have been possible: whether what was done for Keats could not just as well have been done for Hunt or Cornwall. As things stand, I doubt that "Hunt" and "Cornwall" will ever have more than historical value or be of interest to audiences beyond the academy, though it is not absolutely inconceivable that they should. In the next chapter I consider the so-called "recovery project" approach that did the trick for Blake in the nineteenth century and Clare in the twentieth, and that seems to be growing in strength now in the twenty-first.

5

Raising the Unread

In the literary world at present, "recovery projects" are so much the rage that a groundswell of rebellion is beginning to express itself. The phrase appears to have been introduced toward the end of the twentieth century to describe efforts made on behalf of writers who had been unjustly excluded, as their supporters argued, from public attention—specifically from the literary canon of academic study but also from general circulation.[1] Age-old prejudices about sex, class, and geography were generally held to blame, though idealism was not the only driving force behind the movement. Hungry publishers seeking new markets, graduate students looking for fresh subjects, politically committed activists within and outside the universities: all alike stood to gain from what was sometimes referred to as "opening up the canon."[2] Among writers of the Romantic period, women were the big winners. In fiction, which is easier to introduce to a trade market, scores if not hundreds more titles have been published over the past forty years than were available before, and in poetry, besides the specialized collections that had always existed in the shadows, all the major anthologies have now made space for substantial quantities of poetry by women, usually at the expense of "minor" male poets and essayists as well as of the Big Six. These are not trivial changes. However, no single author can be said to have emerged yet who comes anywhere close to rivaling those who have been the acknowledged leaders for a century. One of the questions I shall attempt to address in this chapter is why it should be so difficult to promote a deserving but neglected author. In order to do that, I want first of all to point out that with or without the label, recovery projects are nothing new; also that given time enough, they can be spectacularly successful. My subjects in this chapter are three working-class poets who died in poverty and whose names for a time seemed destined to be forgotten: William Blake, Robert Bloomfield, and John Clare. By far the most highly regarded of these three in his own day was Robert Bloomfield; in ours, William Blake.

Blake's Obscurity

Blake's may be the most extreme case of rescue from oblivion in literary history, and for that reason it is especially instructive. In terms of reputation, today he is more like Austen than any other Romantic writer in that his works are widely loved, read, and recognized. I once saw a hoarding a block long around a building site in central London that was decorated with a line from *The Marriage of Heaven and Hell*: "The tigers of wrath are wiser than the horses of instruction." (The graffiti were the product of a specific historical moment, to be discussed later.) The first object encountered by tourists visiting the British Library today—ironically, in more ways than one—is a huge bronze statue of Newton based on one of Blake's designs. Blake's lyric "Jerusalem," chosen for its patriotism and set to music by Hubert Parry in 1916, became first of all a defining hymn in the Church of England, then a defining anthem for both the Labour and Conservative parties, and then the favored chant of British sports leagues; it still holds those positions. The flagship nightclub in a chain called "Tiger Tiger" was the site—or perilously close to the site—of an unsuccessful car bombing in London in 2007.

Yet Blake's words were almost unknown to his contemporaries. Insofar as he had any reputation at all among them, it was as an engraver. As biographers and editors have always said, marveling, his poetry—the poetry of the most accessible lyrics, never mind the prophetic books—was known to barely a handful of readers in his own time. Blake's own publishing decisions played a part in the neglect he suffered—and he did suffer, for he wanted recognition. Since the Blakes had no children, they left no family to look after his interests after they both died. More than thirty years passed before his name was again brought to public attention by a biographical study, significantly subtitled "Pictor Ignotus" (the Unknown Painter). Even that crucial work almost failed to appear: the author, Alexander Gilchrist, died before he had finished it, and the work was only completed, in a somewhat different form from that which he had intended, by the concerted action of his wife Anne and the two Rossetti brothers. But once the first step had been taken, further progress was easier. In the afterlife of William Blake, successive recovery projects transformed his status from the unknown to the greatly popular by way of transformations in his public image from madman to proto-Wordsworthian, then aesthete, symbolist, visionary, and finally champion of radical reform. I doubt we are done reinventing him.

As a writer, Blake could be said to have been complicit in his own neglect and even to have courted it, though he undoubtedly believed he deserved recognition.[3] He earned his living as an engraver and artist. It was threats to his livelihood that drew out of him bitter remarks about having been overlooked and exploited. For example, speaking of himself in the third person in the *Descriptive Catalogue* of his exhibition of 1809, he wrote, "This has hitherto been his lot—to get patronage for others and then to be left and neglected, and his work, which gained that patronage, cried down as eccentricity and madness; as unfinished and neglected by the artist's violent temper."[4] Here he is lashing out, unwisely perhaps but understandably, against people who had cheated and misrepresented him, specifically the producers of the 1808 edition of Robert Blair's *The Grave* based on his designs (fig. 15). In a related notice, he likens himself to his idols Raphael and Michelangelo and warns the British public that if they ignore his exhibition, they risk overlooking a national treasure.[5] But his attitude toward his writings was rather different. As it is impossible to separate "Poet & Painter" in Blake himself ("I know myself both Poet & Painter"), so it is impossible to disentangle those strands in his reputation.[6] In the long run, each strengthened the other. Insofar as Blake's statements about authorship can be isolated from his views about the arts in general, however, the model he worked to was distinctive—on one hand highly independent (unlike Johnson's) and on the other hand completely self-effacing (unlike Wordsworth's).

Blake consistently represented himself, in both private letters and explicit statements in his literary works, as a vehicle or medium for truths emanating from the spiritual world. He scorned pressures from supposed experts, from fashion, and from the public—in short, he scorned worldliness. Toward the end of his life, when he was shown Wordsworth's 1815 prefaces and had a chance to leave comments in writing upon the heroic model presented there, he declared, "I do not know who wrote these Prefaces they are very mischievous & direct contrary to Wordsworths own Practise."[7] For his own part, he experienced the process of composition as practically involuntary, a sort of inspiration or dictation "without Premeditation & even against my Will"; he described himself as merely "the Secretary the Authors are in Eternity." He

Fig. 15. Frontispiece portrait of William Blake and title page of the edition of Robert Blair's poem *The Grave* (1808) with designs by Blake. Courtesy of Victoria University Library (Toronto).

said of the works he produced, "tho I call them Mine I know they are not Mine."[8] His insistence on his direct contact with the realm of spirits contributed to the reputation for madness that he complained about, although from a literary point of view such statements as these belong to a venerable tradition. Blake himself more than once cited the precedents of Milton and the prophets of the Old Testament: in the letter of 1799 from which the two last quotations are taken, for example, he continues, "being of the same opinion with Milton when he says That the Muse visits his Slumbers & awakes & governs his Song when Morn purples The East. and being also in the predicament of that prophet who says I cannot go beyond the command of the Lord to speak good or bad." The notion that Milton's work had been suppressed or unappreciated in his day, though contested by Johnson, was a cornerstone of Wordsworth's argument about the inevitable neglect of genius. The prophet is almost by definition destined to cry in the wilderness, disregarded. But the prophet performs his duty and fulfils his role by the mere utterance of his prophecy. The responsibility of the oracle extends only to the delivery of the message. Blake's was an oracular model of authorship.

Along with his uncompromising concept of authorship, the method that Blake used to propagate his work was, to say the least, impractical, although it was not so intended. Only two of his poetic works were printed in conventional typographical form in his own day, and Blake showed no concern about the fate of either of them. His first collection, *Poetical Sketches* (1783), was printed on the initiative and at the expense of two friends, John Flaxman and Anthony Stephen Mathew, but in an extremely small print run. Only twenty-two copies are known to have survived; apparently all copies were given to the author to distribute. Then later, although Joseph Johnson is named as publisher in the sole extant copy of *The French Revolution,* that unique exemplar appears to be a proof copy of a work that went no further.[9] Technically speaking, both works, though printed, could be said not to have been published at all—which is what Gilchrist first observed about all the original works that Blake produced in "illuminated printing": "these were in the most literal sense *never published* at all . . . simply engraved by his own laborious hand."[10] None was reviewed.[11] Thus Blake's works failed to meet one of the prime criteria of the checklist, being kept in print, not only because the poems were not conventionally printed in the first place, but also because until 1863 so few copies were in circulation at any time.

Among the "illuminated" writings of which no original copy apparently survives is a one-page prose prospectus "To the Public," issued by Blake in 1793. Fortunately, at least one existed before 1863, when it was described and published in Gilchrist's biography. It is a particularly revealing document as far as Blake's goals and the rationale for his method of production are concerned; it also contains a useful list of prices for the engravings and illuminated books he had on hand at that time. The opening paragraph shows that he accepted the narrative of neglect, but not for the reasons that Wordsworth gave later (bad readers), and certainly not with Wordsworth's conclusion that the truly original writer must write for posterity.[12] On the contrary, according to Blake, all the original writer needed was direct access to the public:

> The Labours of the Artist, the Poet, the Musician, have been proverbially attended by poverty and obscurity; this was never the fault of the Public, but owing to a neglect of means to propagate such works as have wholly absorbed the Man of Genius. Even Milton and Shakespeare could not publish their own works.
>
> This difficulty has been obviated by the Author of the following productions now presented to the Public; who has invented a method of Printing both Letter-press and Engraving in a style more ornamental, uniform, and grand, than any before discovered, while it produces works at less than one fourth of the expense.
>
> If a method of Printing which combines the Painter and the Poet is a phenomenon worthy of public attention, provided that it exceeds in elegance all former methods, the Author is sure of his reward.[13]

Blake evidently thought that his method of illuminated printing would be cheaper than conventional methods of publishing, and believed that public recognition and reward must follow from this invention. He did hope for recognition in his own time—he did not give up on the contemporary public—but he failed to achieve it. Though a commercial flop, the new method was nevertheless a breakthrough for himself as "Poet & Painter" (or as we would say now, a multimedia artist), and the next decade was his most productive. But by the time he died, few copies of his works had been sold, and very few people even knew they existed. Advised and protected by their friends, his wife disposed of some additional copies. When she died in 1831, the remaining stock of prints, copperplates, and manuscripts was left to one of Blake's followers, Frederick Tatham, who unfortunately destroyed many of the papers and claimed later that most of the plates had been stolen and melted down as scrap.[14]

Though the prospects of survival for Blake's works were at that point about as tenuous as they could possibly be, Blake himself would perhaps not have minded. He believed in a real afterlife, in comparison with which worldly "immortality" through art was insignificant: "The Grave is Heaven's golden Gate, / And rich and poor around it wait."[15] His oracular model of authorship meant that his only responsibility was to the world of spirits, where he could confidently expect the reward of his faithful service. As for recognition from other human beings, he must have been resigned to the idea that if it were to happen, it would have to wait for the millennium. In the polemical preface to *Milton,* he declares that although in the fallen state of the world people admire the wrong writers for the wrong reasons, "when the New Age is at leisure to Pronounce; all will be set right; & those Grand Works of the more ancient & consciously & professedly Inspired Men will hold their proper rank."[16]

It is not impossible, but it seems most unlikely that Blake's literary works would ever have found an audience if he had not first had an established reputation as an artist—part of it due to his originality and part to the debate about his alleged madness. Hardly any tribute to Blake by those who knew him or were close to him in age appears without some reference to mental instability, whether to affirm or to deny it. Henry Crabb Robinson, a close friend of Lamb and the Lakers, became interested in Blake at the time of the exhibition in 1809 and eventually met him in 1825 at the London home of the wealthy German merchant Carl Aders. Both Aders and Robinson collected Blake prints, and Robinson wrote a perceptive essay about him for a German magazine.[17] Robinson sincerely admired him and did a lot to spread the word about his poetry, but he took it for granted that Blake was not in his right mind: "this insane man of genius," he called him, and that was the theme of most of the positive criticism of the period. (Gilchrist, who thought otherwise, said that Robinson was the only one "of all I have met who actually knew anything of him" to have taken this view.)[18] Mad or not, Blake had a following among collectors and bibliophiles in his lifetime thanks to his involvement in two deluxe works produced for connoisseurs, the abortive folio edition of Young's *Night Thoughts* (1797), for which he was both designer and engraver, and R. H. Cromek's contentious edition of Blair's *The Grave* (1808) featuring Blake's designs, with its dedication to royalty and its subscription list of over five hundred names. About the time that Robinson met Blake, near the end of Blake's life, T. F. Dibdin's influential *Library Companion* (1824) expressed great enthusiasm for Blake's book illustrations and vividly evoked the kind of gathering at which Blake was already being celebrated, an evening party at the home of Isaac D'Israeli, who, according to Dibdin, owned a large collection of Blake drawings "and he loves his classical friends to disport with them, beneath the lighted Argand lamp of his drawing room, while soft music is heard upon the several corridores [*sic*] and recesses of his enchanted staircase."[19] Dibdin added, without elaborating, "Mr. Blake is himself no ordinary poet." But his slight and guarded reference to the poetry is, as usual, an afterthought.

With the exception of one small letterpress edition of the *Songs of Innocence and of Experience* (1839), the only significant publications concerned with Blake between 1827 and 1863—significant in that they had a chance of attracting an audience—were short anecdotal accounts of him (his visions, his poverty, his ecstatic death) in J. T. Smith's study of another artist, *Nollekens and His Times* (1828), and in Allan Cunningham's *Lives of the Most Eminent British Painters, Sculptors, and Architects* (1829). Perpetuating the image of the madman of genius, these helped to keep his name alive in the art world, especially among collectors: Smith's brief biography ends with an appeal for purchasers to assist Blake's widow.[20] By gradual additions the circle of admirers and collectors in the know was extended beyond the small set of friends and friends of friends such as Flaxman, Thomas Butts, and John Linnell, and came to include younger aesthetes such as Monckton Milnes, Ruskin, William Bell Scott, F. T. Palgrave, and Dante Gabriel Rossetti.[21] Gilchrist describes copies of Blake's works that he had seen in Milnes's collection, and as far back as 1838, a decade before he produced his biography of Keats, Milnes had thought of publishing selections from Blake.[22] Palgrave, interestingly, collected Blake prints but did not include any of his poems in *The Golden Treasury.*

As Gilchrist repeatedly pointed out, prints and drawings by Blake gained in both monetary and cultural value from the very fact that they were "rare" and "very rare."[23] The Print Room at the British Museum appears to have acquired its first Blake print in 1843 and its first important Blake drawing in 1847, with many more to follow, including a large set of prints and books of designs catalogued in 1856.[24] In 1847, coincidentally, Rossetti paid one of the keepers at the museum ten shillings for a battered notebook full of sketches and draft poems, "the most famous purchase of his life (besides his wombat)" as Deborah Dorfman says.[25] Blake's work appeared occasionally in public exhibitions such as the International Exhibition of 1862, which Gilchrist mentions.[26] Thus the value attached to Blake's drawings and engravings saw his writings through a long period of almost total neglect and prepared the ground for the biography of an "unknown painter"—never entirely "unknown," or there would surely have been no market for the biography—that eventually brought them to light.

Gilchrist's Biography

To call it a biography hardly does justice to Gilchrist's groundbreaking work, though it is a superb biography, sympathetic but not uncritical in its approach, thorough and meticulous in its research, and beautifully written. The title page might alert the modern reader to some of its exceptional features, most of which are absent from reprints and editions of the twentieth and twenty-first centuries. First of all, although it is the "life" of an artist by an author who displays his credentials as a biographer of artists, the title contains an allusion (followed up, inside, by an epigraph) to the recently published but hardly popular poem "Pictor Ignotus" by Robert Browning; and the contents are promised to include selections from the artist's hitherto truly "unknown" writings. The unexpected emphasis on literature is offset, however, by special treats for the connoisseur: facsimile reproductions, prints from Blake's original plates, and images produced by the very new technology of photolithography. Instead of being gathered in a section of plates, the "facsimiles" are integrated with the text in joyous profusion—a fitting tribute to Blake's own methods of production. The photolithographs, which *are* gathered in one section at the end of volume 2, consist of reproductions of the complete series based on the Book of Job, Blake's masterpiece as an engraver; they are followed by sixteen plates from *Innocence and Experience* made from copies of Blake's copperplates. It is visually an exciting book, a collector's item in itself.

The unusual design of the book is reinforced in the text by Gilchrist's glowing descriptions of Blake's graphic work: he gently teaches readers how to look. Conveying the qualities of works that most readers would never have seen, not even in reproduction and almost certainly not in color, was an age-old problem for the biographers of artists. An experienced art critic, Gilchrist adopted a traditional solution and devoted many long paragraphs to appreciative evocations of Blake's works—commissioned illustrations, original designs, illuminated books, watercolors, and works in what Blake called "fresco"—one by one. Here the warmth and precision of his writing operate wonderfully well, as the following illustration (fig. 16) may suggest, when he remarks that "it is sometimes like an increase of daylight on the retina, so fair and open is the effect of particular pages. The skies of sapphire, or gold, rayed with hues of sunset . . ." and so forth.

What he could confidently do for Blake's graphic art, Gilchrist attempted to do also for his writings, for Gilchrist was himself a writer and in this case the texts were even rarer than the pictures. He provided plenty of samples, with extensive quotations from every stage of Blake's career, accompanied by informed commentary. Although by modern standards his criticism has serious limitations—specifically, he struggled with the prophetic books and considered them by and large incomprehensible—it was sophisticated for its time. Gilchrist saw Blake as "singular," independent and out of touch with his time, saintly, an eternal child; and he saw Blake's art, both visual and

Milnes's superb copy. Turning over the leaves, it is sometimes like an increase of daylight on the retina, so fair

and open is the effect of particular pages. The skies of sapphire, or
gold, rayed with hues of sunset, against which stand out leaf or blossom,
or pendant branch, gay with bright plumaged birds; the
strips of emerald sward below, gemmed with flower and
lizard and enamelled snake, refresh the eye continually.
Some of the illustrations are of a more sombre kind.
There is one in which a little corpse, white as snow, lies
gleaming on the floor of a green overarching cave, which close
inspection proves to be a field of wheat, whose slender inter-
lacing stalks, bowed by the full ear and by a gentle breeze,

Fig. 16. From Alexander Gilchrist's *Life of William Blake*, *"Pictor Ignotus"* (1863), vol. 1.
Courtesy of The Thomas Fisher Rare Book Library, University of Toronto.

verbal, as a throwback to the styles of earlier ages. So he harps on the theme of the misfit, making the most of the popular myth of unappreciated genius. (A chapter title halfway through, "Years of Deepening Neglect," reveals the trajectory of the plot.) To Gilchrist, Blake appeared as a proto–Pre-Raphaelite in painting and a neo-Elizabethan in poetry.[27]

Gilchrist chose to begin with the fate of Blake's writings as deepest sunk in obscurity. Here is his opening sentence: "From nearly all collections or beauties of 'The English Poets,' catholic to demerit as these are, tender of the expired and expiring reputations, one name has been perseveringly exiled." The art establishment, he then observes, had also been hostile. To be "perseveringly exiled" sounds less like a consequence of indifference or ignorance than a deliberate persecution, an injustice, and so Gilchrist is at pains to prove not only that Blake's work had discerning admirers with well-established reputations (he cites Wordsworth, Flaxman, and Henry Fuseli in the second paragraph) but also that their admiration was well founded. Hence his plentiful images, generous extracts, and judicious commentary. Biographies as a rule celebrate well-known heroes or villains, but Gilchrist's was, like its subject, anomalous. *The Life of William Blake, "Pictor Ignotus"* is overtly a work of advocacy: Blake was not known, but Gilchrist thought he ought to be.

With all its strengths, Gilchrist's biography might not have been enough on its own to turn the tide for Blake and give him a second chance to earn the recognition that Gilchrist believed he deserved. (Gilchrist himself had had his doubts about the project—it was reported in 1859 that he had given it up because he feared "the subject would not be sufficiently popular.")[28] It could not have been completed without the encouragement and significant contributions of a number of members of the Pre-Raphaelite circle: Dante Gabriel Rossetti, William Michael Rossetti, William Haines, and also, behind the scenes, Swinburne. They were responsible for the whole of the second volume, and it is the second volume that really sets Gilchrist's *Life* apart from other Victorian biographies (including Gilchrist's life of William Etty). The second volume—that which was not "Gilchrist"—is excluded from modern editions of the biography for good reasons, but it was arguably this volume, precisely because of its flaws, that laid the foundations for Blake's subsequent popularity.

Gilchrist provided substantial summaries of and extracts from Blake's writings (ten pages, for instance, for *The Marriage of Heaven and Hell*), but there was still no edition of Blake's poetical works. He laid out a story of Blake's life, but the chronology and even the complete list of his works both literary and graphic remained to be established—a complex task because they were so various, in many cases so rare, and so scattered. Blake's situation was not like that of Austen or of Keats, where copies of the work had been in circulation all along, and where readers had something concrete to compare notes on. The only letterpress edition that readers might have had access to in 1863 was Garth Wilkinson's 1839 edition of *Songs of Innocence and of Experience,* published jointly by the firms of Pickering and Newbery, with its daunting Swedenborgian preface.[29] But the Rossettis and Haines made up the difference. Dante Gabriel put together a selected edition 176 pages long that included, besides the *Songs* and *Poetical Sketches, Thel,* previously unpublished poems from the notebook that Rossetti owned, the angry *Descriptive Catalogue,* and some shorter prose pieces. William Michael added an annotated list of drawings, writings, and original designs. Haines catalogued the engravings. A handful of letters appeared in an appendix. Thus one work in two volumes supplied a standard biography, bibliography, catalogue raisonné, and edition. The embossed covers of the revised edition of 1880 (though not the title page) renamed it "Life and Works of Wm. [*sic*] Blake."

Gilchrist's *Life* with the appended materials was in one sense a perfect package. It had everything a reader of the time could have been expected to want: a frontispiece portrait; a satisfying biography based on firsthand evidence and testimony from eyewitnesses; solid topographical information (Blake had not been included in Howitt, but Gilchrist was particularly good at identifying and evoking the places where Blake lived and worked); an extensive selection of Blake's writings; excellent critical commentary; a full list of works; masses of illustrations. What could and perhaps should have happened is that Gilchrist's would become the definitive "Blake" and would be kept in print for as long as demand lasted. It was pioneering. It established the terms of Blake studies to come and provided a starting point for diverse aspects of the future Blake industry—the editions, the textbooks, the critical and biographical debates, the facsimiles, the songs, the shrines, the legend. But it turned out to be no more than a starting point. Though it was widely reviewed, sales were relatively modest and there was no second edition for almost twenty years. Instead of its being established as a classic, what seems to have happened is that Gilchrist's *Life* was so effective in arousing interest in Blake and at the same time so inadequate to the demands of new readers that it stimulated fresh waves of publishers, biographers, bibliographers, editors, critics, and popularizers to supplant it. Most of its deficiencies can be traced to the second volume.

Anne Gilchrist acknowledged at least one major shortcoming even before publication and apologized for it in her preface. It had been intended to include better commentary on the prophetic books (that would have been Swinburne's part), but the idea had to be abandoned. After some delays, in 1868

Swinburne produced his complementary monograph, the first freestanding critical account of Blake's poetry and the first to attempt to explain the prophetic books. He expressed rhapsodic admiration for a Blake who was not mad but decidedly Swinburnian. He portrayed Blake as from start to finish a maverick, a heretic, a moral rebel, a prophet "like the Moses of tradition . . . 'drunken with the kisses of the lips of God.'"[30] *The Marriage of Heaven and Hell,* Swinburne wrote approvingly, "swarms with heresies and eccentricities" and is "the greatest of all his books."[31] But the prophetic books remained a great puzzle; moreover, only extracts of them were available in print, for Rossetti's selection in Gilchrist did not include the *Marriage,* nor any of the long "illuminated" poems engraved after 1794. And even the texts that had been made available proved controversial.

Blake's writings had seemed obscure to his contemporaries; obscurity only increases over time. Furthermore, whenever the self-educated poet encounters the conventionally educated editor, disagreements arise. Rossetti had a name for taking up the cause of neglected artistic merit. One reviewer, generally admiring, said that he was "amazed" to see how many "great unknowns . . . Mr. Dante Rossetti has discovered," sarcastically adding, with an allusion to Gray's "Elegy," that the list "fills us with a sense of living in a world that is choke full of inglorious Miltons and guiltless Cromwells."[32] On behalf of his protégés, Rossetti spared no effort. In Blake's case, he found it necessary to improve the poetry even to the extent of rewriting it, but his well-meant intervention did not go unpunished. Rossetti's selection sparked an editing war that hardly slowed until John Sampson's scholarly edition of the lyrics appeared from the Clarendon Press in 1905, and that clearly is not over yet.

The first challenge to Rossetti's edition came quickly; the battle for ownership of Blake was on. Basil Montagu Pickering, successor to Pickering, produced a new edition of its 1839 *Innocence and Experience* "with Other Poems" in 1866 (reprinted 1868, along with a new *Poetical Sketches,* and then again in a combined volume in 1874, later reprinted). In its waspish preface, the editor, Richard Herne Shepherd, declared that "the poems of William Blake are here for the first time printed in their integrity" and pointed out what was wrong with the versions of Wilkinson and Rossetti: the poems "rather appear as these gentlemen considered they should have been written, than as they actually were written."[33] Shepherd had access to a rival manuscript collection just acquired by the publisher and was able to include two previously unpublished poems along with the more authentic text for the others. His contribution to the emerging critical debate was the suggestion that Blake had anticipated the "return to simplicity and nature" generally associated with Wordsworth, indeed that Blake's poems would not have been out of place in *Lyrical Ballads*.[34] The Rossetti response came with William Michael Rossetti's "Aldine" edition of Blake's *Poetical Works . . . Lyrical and Miscellaneous* in 1874, which restored many of the readings altered by Dante Gabriel, offered a slightly expanded canon, and in a long prefatory essay reaffirmed the Pre-Raphaelite view of Blake as a "mystic and visionary." But this edition too steered clear of the prophetic books. Like Swinburne, William Michael Rossetti expressed admiration for *The Marriage of Heaven and Hell* as Blake's "greatest monument," but he did not print it and he declared regretfully that the prophetic books were in his opinion "neither readable nor entirely sane." In fact he seems to have thought that Blake's best work was his earliest, and that his poetry declined steadily after the astonishing *Poetical Sketches*.[35]

Once it became apparent that Blake was worth looking into and that Gilchrist's *Life* (or life and works) was not the last word, publishers and critics moved to fill the gap. But it did not happen overnight. Even if Blake's writings were no longer unknown, they were still decidedly a minority taste, far from popular. (Deborah Dorfman suggests that Blake's reputation even suffered a backlash in the 1870s, as appreciation of his work became associated with cliquishness.)[36] The seeds of popularity may have been sown overseas. Through Wilkinson's edition, *Songs of Innocence and of Experience* had been building up an audience in America. The *Songs of Innocence* had been addressed to children in the first place, and some of them were included in anthologies for children there.[37] Emerson was made aware of Blake's poetry before 1850, probably in conversations with Crabb Robinson, and an American reference book took note of Blake as a poet after his death ahead of any British one.[38] *"Pictor Ignotus"* galvanized a latent American readership as well as the domestic market, and Anne Gilchrist's revised edition of 1880 acknowledges assistance from some of those readers.

In Britain, in the meantime, Blake's literary reputation was now in the hands of professional writers and scholars for whom disputed texts, problematic dating and provenance, and obscure meanings were meat and drink. More documents came to light (letters most significantly), which called for fresh assessments. But the obvious gap remained the prophetic books, and the next major development was the monumental three-volume Yeats-Ellis edition of 1893, published by Quaritch, which at last made available full texts of nearly all Blake's works, even if it did recast the prophetic books as "symbolic" books allegedly referring to an incredibly complicated esoteric system (fig. 17), and also, notoriously, recast Blake himself as an Irishman.[39] Here again the obvious deficiencies of the enterprise spurred other editors and analysts to do better. From 1893 onward, the number of selected editions that included *The Marriage of Heaven and Hell* and some samples from the longer prophetic books proliferated and became steadily more affordable. The early years of the twentieth century saw the production of a sound scholarly edition of the lyric poetry (Sampson, 1905, with more material from the prophetic books included in 1913) as well as a previously unpublished biographical memoir and letters (Blake, 1906); a revised updated edition of Gilchrist in a mass-market format (1907); Arthur Symons's popular biography that treated Blake as a philosophical poet and compared him to Nietzsche (1907); and a scholarly commentary on the Job engravings (Wicksteed, 1910) that set new standards for Blake studies in the art world. The first Blake Society was formed in 1913.[40] Blake also began to be given star treatment in literary histories and to be anthologized for schools and universities. His early poems were considered suitable for children; his later ones fascinated older students. Saintsbury, who had declared himself a Janeite in 1894, wrote in 1910 that he had been "a Blakite" from childhood and defied Blake's other admirers to prove themselves "Blakitior" (more Blakite) than himself.[41]

To summarize the state of the recovery of Blake about the turn of the century, it is clear that Gilchrist's biography, with its accompanying edition and apparatus, contained all the elements of a revival and that it set in motion a process that is still unfolding as different aspects of Blake's work are taken up, improved, and refined. That body of work had potentially, in the terms of the checklist, all the properties important to long-lasting success: quality, quantity, variety, visualizability, adaptability, a personal myth. What it lacked was recognition in the form of accessible publications, champions, controversy, critical tradition, and a presence in anthologies and reference books. All these followed from the biography. Since Geoffrey Keynes established the pattern in the 1920s with his groundbreaking bibliographical work, a succession of enterprising scholars ready to devote their careers to Blake has reshaped the canon: it is as though each generation needs to undertake the whole Gilchrist project over again in its own way, by the highest standards available. Thus the photolithographs of 1863 gave way to better and better methods of reproduction: for a time it seemed that the fabulously expensive Trianon Press facsimiles would never be improved on, but now we have the digital Blake Archive, free to all. The incoherent enthusiasm of Swinburne and the frankly crackpot ideas of Ellis and Yeats led to—and then had to give way to—better informed and more rigorous criticism. The image of Blake as a neo-Elizabethan or a proto-Wordsworthian, which was based on knowledge of only a limited portion of his poetic output (the early lyrics), was succeeded by more complex ways of understanding his art and its place in literary tradition. The poignant

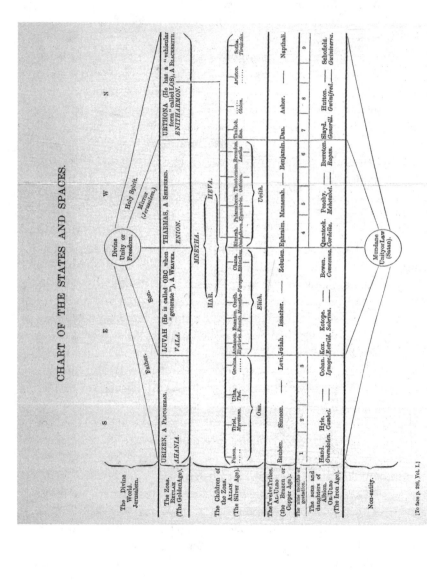

Fig. 17. "Chart of the States and Spaces" from *The Works of William Blake: Poetic, Symbolic, and Critical,* ed. W. B. Yeats and Edwin Ellis (1893), vol. 1. Courtesy of The Thomas Fisher Rare Book Library, University of Toronto.

myth of the neglected genius was contested by biographers who saw Blake as an active participant in the social circles and intellectual movements of his time. Trade editions became cheaper and more plentiful. All this was progress, not just change, and it originated with Gilchrist.

Gilchrist and his collaborators, however, were committed to the "unknown" Blake. The appeal of his work—as with early supporters of Keats and Austen too—was enhanced for them by its unpopularity.[42] This is a common feature of recovery projects: they require such a large investment of energy and persistence that the advocates bond with one another as a select band of initiates opposed to hordes of philistines. The counterpart to the stigma of popularity is the cachet of neglect. Dorfman makes the point that Blake's midcentury advocates recruited and used Blake "to reinforce the solidarity of a coterie position," although by doing so they effectively "cut him off from the mainstream of thought and letters."[43] The Blakite Saintsbury of 1910 noted rather smugly that Blake was still disregarded, "vastly as appreciation of him has increased in the last thirty or forty years," because he was too innovative and progressive for the mass of readers.[44] Just such antipopulist sentiment, coupled with Blake's reputation for eccentricity and difficulty, surely eased his way into the education system; though being taught in schools and studied in colleges could not be guaranteed to make his works beloved, at least it made his name familiar. Love came later.

Blake's Fame

The history of Blake's reception from 1863 up until about the time of the First World War has been well documented by Dorfman and others: it is "a history of reclamation" of his literary output, starting from almost nothing (no texts, no audience) but growing to wide accessibility.[45] Its twentieth-century evolution followed fairly predictable paths in the separate worlds of art, literature, music, and education, and these too have been the subject of some specialist studies.[46] Often mentioned in passing but so far not much explored, however, is the second most important "recovery" of Blake, which happened in the course of the 1940s and 1950s and came to a head in 1968, the year in which the tigers of wrath began to appear in graffiti around the world. At that time, like the subject in the print to which Gilchrist gave the name "Glad Day" (now known as "Albion Rose"), Blake was resurrected as an icon of youthful radicalism. This rather surprising development, which came about through a happy convergence of audiences, established Blake as the figure of cross-party, cross-class, cross-cultural importance that he remains to this day with only slightly diminished glory.

The first component of this new Blake (or to put it another way, the first distinct audience or constituency) was his reputation in America, where his works had begun to make their way and have an impact even before the publication of Gillman's *Life*. With ready access to new editions—by import, by local reprint, or by simultaneous publication (as with Yeats's important Muses' Library selection of 1893, with both New York and London imprints on the title page)—but with different systems of circulation and interpretation, American readers came to see Blake in distinctive ways. Children's literature aside, the American Blake from the start was more actively rebellious than his British counterpart. Americans unambiguously welcomed Blake's celebrations of liberty and assimilated his works to their own burgeoning national tradition—reading them in the light of Whitman's, for instance.[47] His Old Testament models and his religious fervor struck a familiar chord in the States. In this society, Blake's antiestablishment value was more political and religious than aesthetic, and more raucous than refined.

In the universities, where Blake was a fixture in the curriculum through most of the twentieth century, scholars concentrated on what seemed to them the most difficult and pressing tasks: correcting the records of Blake's life by securing reliable information and separating fact from legend; maintaining and updating bibliographies; producing editions and selections according to the latest notions of good editorial practice; integrating the products of new research into improved textbooks and biographies; and, above all, coming to terms with the prophetic books. North American scholars made major breakthroughs in criticism, notably S. Foster Damon with *William Blake: His Philosophy and Symbols* (1924) and *A Blake Dictionary* (1965); Mark Schorer with *William Blake: The Politics of Vision* (1946), and David Erdman with *Blake: Prophet against Empire* (1954), both of whom, in books over five hundred pages long, approached Blake historically as a man deeply engaged with the political debates of his time; and, above all, Northrop Frye, whose *Fearful Symmetry* (1947) delivered what Frye himself called "a square deal" for Blake by interpreting the whole body of his writings within the context of worldwide traditions of visionary thinking.[48] In academic circles, political Blake is a product of the historical approach represented by Schorer and Erdman, and intelligibly mystical Blake a product of *Fearful Symmetry*. Though none of these scholars can be considered directly responsible for the youthful revolutionary Blake of the late 1960s, they certainly contributed to the rehabilitation of his image.

On both sides of the Atlantic, beyond the confines of schools and colleges, creative writers at once reflected and built up a public idea of Blake. This came about not so much as a result of his influence on fellow poets such as Rossetti,

Swinburne, and Yeats or, later, Ginsberg, Roethke, Adrian Mitchell, and Patti Smith as from the way Blake was evoked or made use of in popular fiction and drama. Allusions to poets and poetry in other media depend on the poet's already being part of general knowledge, for without a measure of prior knowledge, the allusions would be irritatingly arcane, but *with* it they strengthen the bond between writer and reader. Working with a preexisting but perhaps vague familiarity, novelists and dramatists are able to highlight one aspect of the image or another, or to turn the reader's thoughts in new directions, imposing their own concept of Blake on the common image and thus extending and enriching it. But the writer has to have been talked about for a while before this can happen. The name needs to have become recognizable. Because of the time lag between the moment of reintroduction and the stage of general recognition, the earliest references of this kind to Blake appear to belong to the 1930s, and a few examples may serve to illustrate the chronological range and variety of this form of friendly appropriation and adaptation. Blake was quoted as a sage in J. B. Priestley's *Time and the Conways* (1937); served as inspiration to an amoral artist who cares for nothing but his painterly visions in Joyce Cary's hilarious novel *The Horse's Mouth* (1944); was made the subject of Adrian Mitchell's *Tyger!* (1971), a musical drama staged by the National Theatre in London; pandered for the pseudo-intellectual protagonist in Martin Amis's *The Rachel Papers* (1973); and appeared as a central character in Tracy Chevalier's historical fiction *Burning Bright* (2007). (The most inventive and daring of these, for it quotes great swaths of *Jerusalem* as well as of Blake's better-known works, is *The Horse's Mouth*.) In most if not all cases where Blake provides a theme or motif for other genres or media, it is not his work alone that is invoked but "Blake" the author-package, like "Keats" in the previous chapter—a compound of works, life, personality, and symbolic value. The persistence of this kind of reference, in fiction especially, is proof that Blake's name and reputation continue to have currency with nonspecialist audiences.

Then there is the opposite of general knowledge and mainstream culture, what social conservatives consider the lunatic fringe, those who seek esoteric knowledge or transcendence through unorthodox systems of belief, or who at least try to keep an open mind about such things. An artist of conspicuous integrity considered a madman by some of his contemporaries, Blake was available to be adopted as a personal role model or guru, whether the adopters understood his system of mythology or not. Understanding, indeed, was not the point: obscurity is inherently sublime, and in Blake's visions they might think they have caught glimpses of other worlds and higher truths than those available from conventional wisdom. As Coleridge said of Jacob

Boehme, they would feel that "there came more Light and precious Light thro' the cranny of [his] Madness than ever passed thro' all the doors and windows of . . . sober Sense, & acute penetration."[49] Often their expressions of acknowledgment to Blake take the form of connections to non-Western systems of belief, with the tacit presumption that there must be some truth to the same ideas independently articulated by different cultures—as with Yeats and Ellis in 1893. Their analysis of "The Symbolic System" begins thus: "The Hindu, in the sculptured caves of Elephanta; the gipsy, in the markings of the sea shell he carries to bring him good fortune; the Rosicrucian student, in the geometric symbols of medieval magic; the true reader of Blake in the entangled histories of Urizen and his children, alike discover a profound answer to the riddle of the world."[50]

Yeats and Ellis were by no means alone. All the commentators working to explain Blake's verbal and visual symbols relied more or less on arcana. Frye himself invoked comparative mythology in Blake's support, describing the "effort of vision" that led Blake to a "conception of art as creation designed to destroy *the* Creation," and comparing his effort to that of "Zen Buddhism, which with its paradoxical humor and its intimate relationship to the arts is startlingly close to Blake."[51] These commentaries, however, were directed to specialists. For a more popular version of this mystical Blake we have to look elsewhere.

In Hollywood in 1953, the ex-pat British novelist Aldous Huxley—a graduate in English language and literature and a convert to Hinduism—offered himself as a guinea pig in a supervised trial of mescaline. He wrote rapturously about the experiment in *The Doors of Perception* (1954), taking his title and epigraph from a slightly revised version of one of Blake's "Proverbs of Hell": "If the doors of perception were cleansed, every thing will appear to man as it is, infinite."[52] Attempting to convey the state of heightened sensation and spirituality that he experienced, he described it as being akin to being born again: "How can we ever visit the worlds which, to Blake, to Swedenborg, to Johann Sebastian Bach, were home?" The answer was, through psychotropic drugs: "by taking the appropriate drug, I might so change my ordinary mode of consciousness as to be able to know, from the inside, what the visionary, the medium, even the mystic were talking about."[53] Two years later Huxley enlarged on the theories introduced in *The Doors of Perception,* taking a title again from Blake, in *Heaven and Hell* (1956). These two books played a prominent part in the emerging drug culture.

Allen Ginsberg—Beat, Buddhist, and Blake-inspired—read *Howl* aloud to an audience for the first time in San Francisco in 1955.[54] In 1964 Timothy Leary and his coauthors dedicated *The Psychedelic Experience* to Huxley; in

1965 Jim Morrison took the name for his newly formed rock band, the Doors, from Huxley and thus indirectly from Blake. In 1968 Huxley's was one of the faces on the cover of the Beatles' *Sergeant Pepper's Lonely Hearts Club Band.*[55] Ginsberg started setting Blake's *Songs* to music and performing them in 1968, which was also the year of student unrest in Europe and America. But it does not appear to have been on account of Ginsberg or among students—in Chicago in April, at the Columbia University sit-ins of April and May, or in Paris in May—that Blake emerged as a source of slogans for revolutionaries. Improbably, it was in New York, in December, at the annual convention of the Modern Language Association (MLA).

Blake in America, Blake in the academy, Blake among theatergoers and bohemians and hippies produced the conditions under which a revolutionary Blake could miraculously materialize, but a catalyst was needed to bring them all together, something that explicitly identified him as a rebel and activist. I believe that catalyst was the scientist and polymath Jacob Bronowski.

At the turbulent December 1968 meeting of the MLA, after a year in which calls for radical reforms had divided university faculty and administrators and in which relations between student protestors and the police could hardly have been worse, three English professors were arrested for defacing private property by sticking up posters at the conference hotel. The only offending poster that I have ever seen quoted was the one with the line from Blake, "The tigers of wrath are wiser than the horses of instruction"—words that were immediately carried around the English-speaking world.[56] What led the professors to adopt that line out of all the lines available to them? The "Proverbs of Hell" had been in print since 1863 (in the biographical volume of Gilchrist, not in the second volume), and *The Marriage of Heaven and Hell* as a whole had been readily available, and often reprinted, since 1893. That particular line might have been in their minds just then thanks to a recent campus satire with an opening scene set at an earlier MLA meeting: *The Horses of Instruction* (1968) by a Blake scholar, Hazard Adams.[57] The novel, however, has no more of Blake in it than the title and an epigraph quoting the line in full—and why did its author fix on that "proverb" anyway? Ultimately the trail leads back to Bronowski and to his book *William Blake, 1757–1827: A Man without a Mask* (1944). Before Schorer and Erdman, Bronowski defined Blake in political terms and interpreted his works as political allegories, not parts of a coherent mythological system but rather ad hoc responses to the world around him. "William Blake lived in the most violent age of English history," Bronowski observed, adding that Blake had written the prophetic books in deliberately opaque language by necessity, because what he had to say was dangerous to say. ("The Seditious Writings" is one of the chapter titles.)

Blake's "prophetic manner" was just that, a manner, a rhetorical device, a mask or disguise that he put on when he needed it.[58]

Bronowski's representation of Blake differs from that of Schorer or Erdman not only because it precedes them but also because it is not narrowly historical. It treats Blake as the universal representative of a discontented people, especially of working-class people fighting back against the society that tries to silence them. Bronowski describes the energy of *The Marriage of Heaven and Hell* positively as "anarchism"; he invokes Marx repeatedly.[59] He was the only commentator since Symons early in the century to single out the "tigers of wrath" line as a key to Blake's meaning.[60] Finally, his work is unlike the others in being short (it was published under wartime paper restrictions) and racily written for a trade press, Secker and Warburg. Bronowski's book was original and stirring. It had a powerful effect on Blake's reputation, as the new publishers noted when they issued a revised, updated paperback edition in 1954. (A third edition, much expanded, appeared in 1965 under a different title and imprint as *William Blake and the Age of Revolution*.) Bronowski also had the opportunity to reiterate his view of Blake—"simply, innocently, and completely, he was a rebel . . . a man against authority"—in the introduction to his edited *Selection of Poems and Letters* in 1958. His Blake is a man for all times, whose depiction of "war and repression, poverty and fear and injustice . . . [is] still vivid to our generation, the generation of Belsen."[61]

Bronowski's little book was, I believe, the single most important factor in the creation of the compelling new image of Blake that emerged in the middle of the twentieth century and peaked about 1968. But behind Bronowski was perhaps the only force capable of bringing all the different audiences for Blake at that time together. Penguin Books, with its worldwide reach, published the first paperback edition of Bronowski's *William Blake* in 1954 and then commissioned his selection of poems and letters (1958) for the "Penguin Poets" series. In the same series came Michael Horovitz's landmark anthology *Children of Albion: Poetry of the Underground in Britain* (1969), inspired by Blake as the title suggests, and dedicated to Ginsberg; and in the related "Modern Poets" series, a joint volume for Corso, Ferlinghetti, and Ginsberg (1963). Penguin had been quick to pick up Huxley: *"The Doors of Perception" and "Heaven and Hell"* appeared in 1959. They had also brought out *The Horse's Mouth* in paperback in 1948 and kept it in print in the following decades. If you were reading Blake or reading about Blake in the 1960s, odds are you were reading Penguins and, since one Penguin leads to another—the readership was loyal—odds are you were reading about a Blake that had not been known before, an antiestablishment Blake for the People. The new Blake illustrated the power of Penguin.

These two critical moments in the posthumous reputation of William Blake represent very different kinds of recovery projects and yet they have some shared features. The first was a deliberate effort initiated by one man, though it required a team, in the end, to see it through; the second was a diffuse and largely accidental process. The first appealed to an exclusive group, the second to the broadest possible audience. The first took nothing for granted but Blake's status as an unknown; the second had to overcome a lot of preconceptions. Dorfman points out, commenting on the final stage in the reception of Blake in the late nineteenth century, that "like critics before him, Edwin Ellis created a Blake in his own image," and of course that is what critics and biographers usually do: whatever the constraints of the given materials, they take what they want and make of it what they will.[62] The years 1863 and 1968 had that much in common. They also shared reforming zeal: as far as the advocates were concerned, the distance was not great between an unknown Blake and a misunderstood one. For them the work of recovery was not like breathing life into a dying patient. It was like bringing to view something that was always there but that other people could not see; if they could be helped to a clear sight of it, as with a microscope slide brought into focus, it would appear to them as a revelation, completely new. Perhaps what we term "revival" or "recovery" would be better called "uncovering" or "discovery."

John Clare

Blake's case is exceptional among recovery stories for the degree of his original obscurity and hence the extreme contrast between his status as a writer in his lifetime and his status many generations later. The public career of John Clare followed the much more common pattern of a brief, heady success followed by years of disappointment and decline. He lived for almost thirty years after the publication of his last collection of poems, practically unregarded. But his history has much in common with that of Blake, not least in that more than once it took strenuous action by those who admired his writing to keep it from total oblivion and give it a fresh chance at fame.

Advance publicity for Clare's first and most popular volume set a tone for reception that was followed almost without exception until very recently, which is the condescending view that Clare's achievement was extraordinary *under the circumstances*.[63] Estimates of the value of his poetry seemingly cannot be separated from the conditions of its production. In January 1820, the first issue of the *London Magazine* ventured to introduce a name "hitherto altogether unknown to literature" with samples of short poems by "an agricultural labourer" who showed signs of genius but stood "in need of popular encouragement, and even protection." The anonymous contributor praised the poems for their "minute observation of nature, delicacy of feeling, and fidelity of description," and offered the opinion that "poetry affords few trifles of greater promise composed at so early an age and composed under equal difficulties."[64]

Launched in the same month by Keats's publisher, John Taylor, Clare's *Poems Descriptive of Rural Life and Scenery, by a Northamptonshire Peasant* went through three editions in 1820, with a fourth in 1821; *The Village Minstrel, and Other Poems,* in two volumes, followed in 1821 with a second edition (so called) in 1823 (fig. 18).[65] Clare was claiming a place—or his publisher was claiming it for him—within a tradition of poet laborers that had started with Stephen Duck, the "Thresher Poet" famous in the 1730s, and that included, in the Romantic period, the "Ayrshire Ploughman," the "Ettrick Shepherd," the "Nithsdale Mason," the "Sherwood Forester," the "Journeyman Wool-Comber," and many, many others. Most of them left no mark; the more fortunate among them repeated the experience of Duck, enjoying a brief celebrity as literary novelties or freaks, attracting wealthy patrons and sponsors, but soon fizzling out, never to be heard of again. Duck committed suicide. In his introductions to Clare's first two books, Taylor gave readers generous amounts of biographical information about the author, stressing his poverty, his virtue, and his humility. He went well beyond the standard disclaimers and excuses (Blake as an "untutor'd youth" for instance, in the preface written by his patrons for *Poetical Sketches*), for he presented Clare as a deserving object of charity. *The Village Minstrel* even includes a list of names of the subscribers to the trust set up for Clare the year before, with the amounts they had contributed. Part of the appeal of Clare's volumes for purchasers appears to have been the opportunity of donation: Taylor was able to report that thanks to the "benevolence of the higher ranks," Clare would have an annual income of £45 to sustain himself and his growing family when the period of celebrity came to an end.[66]

The contents of Clare's volumes were better than the "Northamptonshire Peasant" label and the appeals to charity might have led readers to expect. While the subjects for the most part came from rural life—birds, flowers, trees, rivers, the seasons, "a Lost Greyhound Lying on the Snow"—and Clare's occasional use of dialect meant that a glossary had to be provided, both in form and content the poems in these collections offer great variety. There are sonnets and ballads and love songs, descriptive verse and narrative, humor (the reviewers, generally encouraging, suggested that was not a strength) and plenty of pathos. Most of the poems are presented from the point of view of the peasant poet, but a few adopt a different persona, even that of a seduced

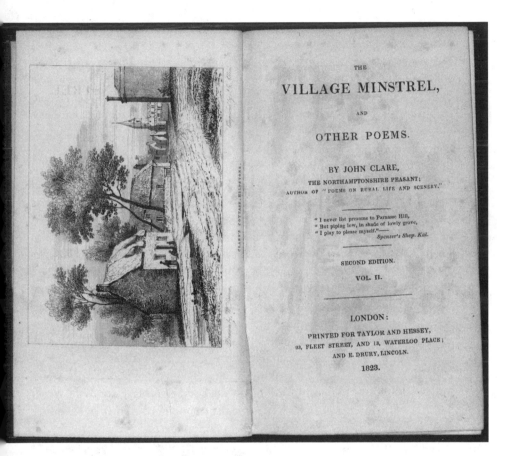

Fig. 18. Frontispiece and title page of the second edition of John Clare, *The Village Minstrel, and Other Poems* (1823), vol. 2. National Art Library, shelf mark Dyce L 12mo 2225. © Victoria and Albert Museum, London. The frontispiece reinforces the message about an authentic "peasant" writing about "rural life" by showing not just a generic village scene but "Clare's Cottage at Helpston."

and abandoned woman (as in "Dolly's Mistake"), or speak for a part of the landscape ("The Lamentations of Round-Oak Waters"). In the nostalgic spirit of Gray's Eton College ode or Goldsmith's much-loved *Deserted Village* (1770), Clare typically celebrates, with a mild melancholy, a way of life that has passed or is passing away, the sights and customs of his youth. The combination of celebration and melancholy is significant: there is regret but not anger or complaint or resistance, and the overall effect is positive appreciation of the small pleasures of rustic life.

Though he describes himself as a "lowly clown" in "An Effusion to Poetry," it would have been plain to every reader that the author was not untutored. Both by imitation and by direct tribute he shows his awareness of major figures of the past and present, from Spenser through James Thomson and Burns to Keats and Wordsworth. (The last two poems in the second collection, which appeared shortly after the death of Keats, are sonnets to Keats and to Autumn.) Clare can be seen to have grown in confidence, making bolder use of unconventional diction in his second collection (what other poet ever ventured "squish-squash"?) and relying less on trite circumlocutions such as "the shepherd's woolly charge," but both collections are uneven in quality, so that part of the pleasure for a sympathetic reader comes from the odd unexpected turn of thought or phrase that seems to mark the poem as especially Clareish. Two sonnets, "Hereafter" and "The Ants" from *The Village Minstrel*, are listed in the appendix, together with one of his later snapshot verses, "Grasshoppers." Neither the best nor the worst of Clare's works, they epitomize his development away from vague pieties toward sharply detailed, morally neutral though not unfeeling observation of the natural world. At the same time they illustrate the inconsistent quality of his writings. Clare is not identified with two or three especially striking poems as Coleridge is, but with a distinctive sensibility and craft exhibited in the course of a large body of work.

We now know that during his lifetime the character of Clare's publications was controlled by his publisher, John Taylor, and to a lesser extent by his patrons, Lord Radstock and Eliza Emmerson: they suggested topics, helped to make a selection from Clare's voluminous mass of manuscripts, put the poems in order, and turned them into readable texts by correcting spelling and meter, adding punctuation, revising diction, changing the order of stanzas, proposing titles, and occasionally censoring what they considered inappropriate sexual or political content. Clare understood that he needed their help; for the most part he accepted it gratefully. He could not have reached contemporary or later readers without them, and in the early years their guidance contributed to the creation of new work. (To this day it is impossible to read Clare except through an editorial filter, with the inevitable historical and ideological baggage that that entails: while this is more or less true of all writers, it is dramatically and flagrantly so of him.[67] Astute recent commentators describe the relationship between Clare and his contemporary editors and publishers as calculated choice, a "mutual investment in each other's fortunes" in "an unpredictable literary marketplace.")[68] But their combined efforts were not enough to sustain Clare's reputation once the novelty had worn off. In any case, 1820 was about the crest of the wave of public enthusiasm for any kind of poetry in Britain, and Clare's later titles *The Shepherd's Calendar* (1827) and *The Rural Muse* (1835) saw only one edition in the nineteenth century. That is a pity because both are, in different ways, more ambitious than the earlier titles, and *The Rural Muse,* selected by Eliza Emmerson from Clare's much larger manuscript "The Midsummer Cushion" and published by Whittaker, is varied, sophisticated, and innovative, with a number of dramatized nature walks ("The Nightingale's Nest," for instance), serious reflections on death and literary immortality, and many splendid sonnets. In spite of favorable reviews, sales were disappointing.

Clare's health, physical and mental, had been precarious for years, and about this time it worsened. He spent most of the rest of his life, from 1837 to 1864, as an "inoffensive lunatic" in asylums, where he was treated kindly and encouraged to write; one of the keepers at the Northampton asylum, his final home, transcribed many of the poems he composed there, and that transcription remains the only record of those works.[69] Once in a while he had visitors who recalled his former glory and wrote sadly about him. He made brief appearances in memoirs and journalism of the 1840s and 1850s, notably in articles by Cyrus Redding in the *English Journal* (1841) and a chapter by Edwin Paxton Hood in his book *The Literature of Labour* (1851).[70] A few of his poems found their way into anthologies, most usefully into Chambers's popular *Cyclopaedia of English Literature* (1844), which continued to be reprinted on both sides of the Atlantic into the twentieth century.[71] But his name did not appear in Howitt's *Homes and Haunts* in 1844, and he was not eligible for *The Golden Treasury* because he was still living when it appeared in 1861.[72] In 1854 kindly John Taylor, who had continued to look after Clare's welfare, made an effort to gather in his copyrights so as to produce a collected edition of his work, but the attempt failed.[73] Even if Taylor had been successful, the outcome would presumably have been merely the sum of Clare's existing publications. As far as the public was concerned, even if the man was still living, the poet was already dead and gone.

Clare, however, never ceased to write verses, some of which he gave to his visitors at the asylum, spurred on by force of habit as well as by an unaccustomed freedom from labor and perhaps by a lingering hope of recognition.

For he had clearly formed ideas about authorship and literary immortality—
conventional for the most part, but interestingly inflected by his experience
of celebrity. In poems, letters, and one particularly astute essay he laid out his
views quite plainly. For himself, writing was a pleasure and a compulsion: "I
wrote because it pleased me in sorrow—and when I am happy it makes me
more happy and so I go on," he told a correspondent; and again, "in spite of
myself I rhyme on."[74] (Money, when it came, was a by-product, a further incentive that never became a primary motive.) Beyond that private need was
the higher aim of celebrating the life of his own locality and thereby staking
its claim to rank with other parts of the country—which would also have
the effect of linking his name with regional writers such as Burns and Cowper who had similarly been visited by "the rural muse."[75] His alter ego Lu-
bin in "The Village Minstrel" is a lout like other boys in the village, but he
is set apart from them as "nature's child"; instead of joining in their games,
he seeks out hidden places and "hum[s] o'er his simple song." In the poem
"To the Rural Muse" that opens his final collection, Clare in his own person
reflects, not for the first time, on how it has turned out to be impossible for
him to part company with her and leave it to "abler hands to wake an abler
song."

> Not with the mighty to thy shrine I come,
>   In anxious sighs, or self applauding mirth,
> On Mount Parnassus as thine heir to roam:
>   I dare not credit that immortal birth;
>   But mingling with the lesser ones on earth—
> Like as the little lark from off its nest,
>   Beside the mossy hill awakes in glee,
> To seek the morning's throne a merry guest—
>   So do I seek thy shrine, if that may be,
>   To win by new attempts another smile from thee.

This stanza conveys the attitude typical of Clare in public pronouncements,
namely that while he believed in the possibility of a form of immortality
through literature, he did not aspire to it himself. He was a humble bard
serving a modest muse, not in the same league as Spenser, Milton, and Shakespeare, nor even the equal of his near contemporaries Keats and Bloomfield,
for whom he did predict eternal fame.[76] Privately, however, he entertained
hopes of survival for his works: a diary entry of 1824 about the design of his
tombstone, for example, for which he likely had Keats in mind, specifies that
there should be no date on it, "as I wish it [his name] to live or die with my
poems and other writings, which if it have merit with posterity it will, and if
they have not it is not worth preserving."[77]

Clare may have had vague hopes of posterity, but one thing he was quite certain about was the false counterpart to literary immortality: popularity or temporary fashion. His poems time and again expound, along standard lines, the vanity of the desire for "fame" or popular acclaim. The most direct and original expression of his views appears in an "Essay on Popularity" published in the *European Magazine* in 1825—the only essay he published in his life-time.[78] "Popularity is a busy talker," he begins, outlining the classic contrast between the "trumpeting clamour of public praise" and the quiet assurance of lasting fame: "popularity is not the omen of true fame" and again, "popularity is not the forerunner of fame's eternity." Much of the essay is taken up with Clare's admiring but ambivalent response to the career of Byron, who might seem an exception to the rule. Byron had been fantastically fashionable but might also have been a great poet whose work would endure. Clare's imagery in this section of the essay is itself highly Byronic. He declares that Byron "took fame by storm"; "he gained the heights of popularity by a single stride, and looked down as a freebooter on the world below"; "like Napoleon crossing the Alps," he brushed off the petty objections of critics and tastemakers; and so forth. His conclusion is that Byron "is no doubt one of the eternals, but he is one of those of the 19th century"—that is, not really eternal. Clare thought it might take three centuries for the dust to clear and a sound judgment to be established, but "Eternity" (by which he seems to mean a suitably remote future time on earth, not in heaven) "will estimate things at their proper value, and no other."

In an unusual move, Clare proposes an intermediate state between the two poles of popularity and fame, giving it the name of "common fame," which he defines as "names that are familiar among the common people." Like Wordsworth before him though in slightly different terms, Clare separates the public (slaves of fashion) from the people; unlike Wordsworth, he does not rate the kind of fame that can be found among the people as much higher than popular celebrity. Celebrity lasts for a day at the whim of fashion; common fame might last for a season, Clare says, but not as long as eternal fame and not on the same solid basis. Common fame is not hard to come by because the common people cannot tell the difference between "paltry balladmongers" and true poets. If they know the names of the poets at all, it may not be from firsthand acquaintance with any of their works: they know the name of Chatterton "as an unfortunate poet, because they saw his history printed on a pocket handkerchief," and if they have heard of Shakespeare it may be because they have seen his name on the notices posted by strolling players. Clare points out that some modern poets had courted common fame by cultivating simplicity, though in his opinion most such "naturals" display nothing but affectation, and the results are ultimately "unnatural." Nevertheless, in a few cases they are successful—his examples are Wordsworth and Robert Tannahill ("the Weaver Poet")—and Clare does not rule out the possibility that Wordsworth, who "has had little share of popularity," would achieve true fame in the end, "gaining ground by gentle degrees in the world's esteem." This seems to have been the hope that he held out for his own work in the 1820s: that since it was genuinely rustic and unaffectedly simple, it would win lasting fame by the route of common fame, being known and passed down among the common people from generation to generation. He unequivocally did not want what he had once had: popular celebrity. Given his hostility to artifice, his conviction that he wrote because it was in him and he could not help himself, and his choice of subjects from his own life and the life of the villagers and farm workers around him, Clare's model of authorship might be called "natural" authorship—with the caveats and ironies that unavoidably attend that overused word—but since he so readily handed over his compositions for reworking by his editors, "cooperative" seems to me more accurate.

Clare's Afterlife

Clare did earn posthumous fame, but not as he expected. After his death two publishing interests emerged, each in possession of a large quantity of Clare manuscripts—correspondence, journals, and poems—and both aspiring to produce the customary biography and retrospective edition. Only a fraction of his body of work (over three thousand poems) had been published, but the unpublished manuscripts were divided and disordered, for Clare had been accustomed to use whatever scraps of paper were available. Joseph Whitaker planned and advertised an illustrated edition that never appeared, apparently for want of a capable editor.[79] He did succeed in commissioning the first biography, Frederick Martin's *Life of John Clare* (1865), but that work is an embarrassment, full of fanciful anecdotes and hyperbolic claims. It did not reach a second edition until 1964. The final sentence is, to my mind, characteristic in its flagrant sentimentality, myth making, and narrow nationalism: "There now lies, under the shade of a sycamore-tree, with nothing above but the green grass and the eternal vault of heaven, all that earth has to keep of John Clare, one of the sweetest singers of nature ever born within the fair realm of dear old England—of dear old England, so proud of its galaxy of noble poets, and so wasteful of their lives."[80]

John Taylor of Northampton (a different John Taylor), on the other hand, though not so quick off the mark, found J. L. Cherry, who had visited Clare in his last years and who in 1873 produced a one-volume *Life and Remains:* a thoughtful biography, a selection of letters, and almost two hundred pages of previously unpublished or uncollected writings, including a hundred pages of what were defined for the first time as "asylum poems." The book, with illustrations by the popular Birket Foster, was widely reviewed and—more important—as part of the "Chandos Classics" series was stereotyped, easily reprinted, and thus widely read.[81] Cherry was thus Clare's Gilchrist. Though he had to rely on Martin for factual details, not having access to all the documents Martin had used, and though he confirmed the general outlines of the story Martin had developed (a pale, runty child with a passion for literature who, against the odds, enjoys triumphant success and then pays the price for it), Cherry told a more nuanced, complicated, and interesting tale.[82] He published for the first time some of the evidence upon which the story had been based and upon which a fresh assessment of Clare's achievement might be made. Furthermore, the *Life and Remains* made it quite clear that there was more work to be done: hundreds and hundreds of poems remained unpublished. Cherry's work was the foundation of all future Clare scholarship and criticism.

The foundation had been laid, the challenge was there, but there was no one to take it up. In terms of the checklist, by 1873 Clare could be seen to have produced work of high quality and considerable variety in sufficient, if not surplus quantity (as we have seen with Hunt and Scott, prolificacy can be a problem); he had a compelling personal myth and a capable biographer; he had locatability and visualizability; he had some presence in anthologies. What Blake and Keats had in their afterlives, however, that Clare lacked in his was a band of well-connected champions such as the Pre-Raphaelites, with their associates and their access to print outlets, to provoke rival editions and interpretations and keep the name of the author in circulation. Although there was plenty of scope for editorial warfare in the still unsifted mass of Clare manuscripts, pitched battles had to wait for the rehabilitation of his reputation in the twentieth century. In the meantime, he missed the crucial stage of adoption by professional critics in the late nineteenth. The founders of the academic curriculum passed him by. Like Crabbe, he could be seen as an imitator (in his case, of Thomson, Cowper, Burns, and Bloomfield) rather than an original. Also like Crabbe's, his work was too realistic to fit the emerging period criteria. Intellectually and aesthetically, it appeared lightweight and uncomplicated alongside comparable works by Burns, Wordsworth, or Keats. Finally, it was tainted by its temporary, long-past popularity. In 1887 Leslie Stephen's article about Clare in the original *Dictionary of National Biography* saw little merit in Clare's work and attributed his initial success to public curiosity: later works did less well, Stephen observed, once "curiosity was satisfied." In 1898 the Janeite–Blakite George Saintsbury wrote Clare off in a couple of sentences, saying that his only role in literary history was as a "farmer poet."[83] A short entry in the 1911 *Encyclopaedia Britannica* dismissed him as a poet who had once had a brief vogue "no doubt largely due to the interest aroused by his humble position in life."

In the long term, Clare would have to shake off the "Northamptonshire Peasant Poet" label that had long defined his public image. In the short term, it may have been the saving of him. For the centenary of his birth, a local history association, the Peterborough Natural History, Scientific, and Archaeological Society, made an active effort to collect manuscripts and memorabilia related to Clare for the Peterborough Museum. To that end, they first purchased Whitaker's large collection of manuscripts. Other gifts, bequests, purchases, and loans followed to ensure an impressive exhibition and catalogue. After 1893—coincidentally the year of the Yeats-Ellis edition of Blake—the bulk of the Clare manuscripts was available in one public space, had there been anyone with the will and the means to explore them.

The recovery of John Clare from a long period of neglect is often attributed to the poet Edmund Blunden, but it should really be traced back a decade before Blunden's campaign for Clare began, to the work of another poet and man of letters, Arthur Symons. His earlier edition of Clare not only introduced another batch of previously unpublished poems but also rejected the "peasant poet" label, observed the damage done by previous editors, and proposed a new way of thinking about Clare and his work.

Symons was one of the links between Clare and Blake, via Yeats. He dedicated his major critical work, *The Symbolist Movement in Literature* (1899), to Yeats; in *The Romantic Movement in Literature* (1909), he represented both Blake and Clare as having found themselves as poets when they retreated from reality.[84] In the intervening decade, Symons published his biography of Blake (1907) and his edition of Clare (1908) and then suffered a mental breakdown so severe that he had to be institutionalized for almost two years. The edition, *Poems by John Clare,* was included in the "Oxford Miscellany" series. It is a neat pocket-sized book with a brave introduction. Symons speaks up for Clare, pointing out that Burns for all his strengths "had no such minute local lore as Clare, nor, indeed, so deep a love of the earth." The fact that Clare was a peasant he shrugs off as almost irrelevant to his writing: "The difference between Clare and Bloomfield is the difference between what is poetry and what is not, and neither is nearer to or farther from being a poet because he was also a peasant." Symons replaces the peasant poet with another stereotype, the mad poet (like Blake), by affirming the superiority of the poetry written in the asylum years. According to him, "what killed him [Clare] as a human mind exalted him as a poetic consciousness."[85] The poems Clare wrote as a mature man, uninhibited by editors and publishers, seemed to Symons astonishing in their power and variety. And so they are. They exhibit a range of strong emotions, such as anger, lust, and scorn, that had seldom been exposed in Clare's published work; they offer revealing self-analysis; and they greatly extend the range of his adopted personas. (Two long works unsuitable for anthologies, *Don Juan* and *Childe Harold,* are to the Clare canon what Blake's epic poems are to his: major puzzles irresistible to the serious scholar.) Symons praises the work of Cherry, who had introduced him to the asylum poems in the first place, and reflects on the discrepancies between the manuscripts in Clare's own hand and the versions available in his published works ("what Clare actually wrote was better than what his editors made him write"—exactly the point made in Shepherd's edition of Blake in 1866); though for the asylum poems, unfortunately, as he acknowledged, he had had to make do with the keeper's transcriptions and could not get behind them to a Clare original.

Symons's provocative expression of preference for the asylum poems and his insistence on Clare's artistry injected life-giving controversy into the reading of Clare's work. Besides creating a new vogue for Clare as part of a different tradition from that which had previously defined him, Symons started a discussion of Clare on aesthetic grounds and invited further investigation into the texts of the poems. His shift of interest to the late verse also had biographical implications, since both early biographers, Martin and Cherry, had devoted only a few pages to the years following Clare's final publication, and those years needed to be reconsidered. Symons's little edition effectively laid out a program for scholarship in the twentieth century.

Edmund Blunden led the way. In 1920, with Alan Porter as fellow editor, he brought out Clare's *Poems Chiefly from Manuscript,* with a long biographical chapter and ninety poems published for the first time. What Blunden and Porter call their "introduction," though it consists of just a few lines of Shakespeare and looks like an epigraph, says it all: it is Polonius's account of Hamlet's decline into madness after his rejection by Ophelia. Their Clare is no longer a clown, then, but a melancholy prince. In their view, Clare's poetry and madness had a single source, imagination: "Imagination overpowered him, until his perception of realities failed him."[86] (Imagination was a quality that might admit Clare as readily as Keats into the Romantic canon.) The asylum poems, as they point out, often allude to Clare's "love tragedy," but they treat of many other subjects as well, and achieve "subtler music" than the earlier work. The editors end by quoting a lyric "Adieu!" and comparing it favorably with the work of a more highly esteemed poet: "In this sort of pathos, so indefinable and intimate, William Blake and only he can be said to resemble him."[87]

The advocacy of Blunden and Porter proved compelling; fresh interpretations began to appear, and the next thirty years marked a steady, though not uncontested, rise in Clare's reputation. His work became part (though typically an optional part) of the academic curriculum. In 1940 the magisterial *Cambridge Bibliography of English Literature* quietly reclassified Clare by relocating the entry for him to accompany the entries for the "major" poets of the period.[88] In 1949 Geoffrey Grigson brought out another edition, *Poems of John Clare's Madness,* with over a hundred previously unpublished items in it, and then in 1950 a broader selected edition. The close-reading New Critics also took him up in the 1950s, when three of his poems were introduced for discussion in the second edition of the influential, much-reprinted American university anthology, *Understanding Poetry.* Until it eventually tailed off, the vogue for the asylum poems among literary historians and critics threatened to eclipse the nature poet—a development that struck some later editors as so perverse that they rather snidely suggested that it could have happened only because "it seemed easier to editors to establish a text for them," since they didn't have to struggle with Clare's holograph manuscripts but could work with the keeper's transcriptions.[89]

Meanwhile, after 1920, Blunden went on to fulfill some of the other aspects of Symons's program. In 1929 he published *Nature in English Literature* in a Hogarth Press series, offering a critical context for Clare with appreciative readings of some of his "favourite master-pieces of English nature-poetry." As far as Blunden was concerned, Clare was "in some lights the best poet of Nature that this country and for all I know any other country ever produced."[90] In 1931 he published a group of biographical and autobiographical materials from manuscript under the title *Sketches in the Life of John Clare, Written by Himself;* in 1936 he published a memoir of Clare's friend and publisher, John Taylor. Blunden, himself inspired by Symons, inspired a generation with his 1920 edition, the first proof of his influence being a landmark biography by J. W. Tibble and Anne Tibble in 1932. He also set the pattern for the future by example, for it took successive waves of scholars to establish Clare's reputation in the twentieth century and beyond, and each wave appears to have found it necessary to start over—to rewrite the biography, issue new editions, and set everybody straight on the correct interpretation of the poems—just as they did for Blake.[91] That process continues in the twenty-first century. The final volume of nine in the now standard Clarendon Press edition of Clare's poetry appeared in 2003, but there is still no consensus about the best way to present Clare's texts. Every new editor grumbles about the faults of the one before, and as publishing evolves, readers' expectations change. The public of 1820 would have considered ridiculous the underpunctuated texts that we now consider authentic. (The appendix cites five renditions of Clare's sonnet "Beans in Blossom," by way of example.) There can seldom have been a better candidate than Clare for the new principles of "versioning" and the new possibilities of digital imaging associated with electronic editions.

The efforts of Symons and Blunden, building on Cherry, brought about a "recovery" of Clare's reputation that, as in the case of Blake some decades earlier, might better be called a discovery. The Clare they presented was as good as new, just about as "altogether unknown to literature" as he had been in 1820 before the publication of his first collection—and that in two ways. First of all, Symons and Blunden drew attention to the huge cache of manuscripts awaiting attention; second, they criticized the interventions of Clare's well-meaning sponsors, which meant that even the published work needed to be revisited and reassessed, since it was not exactly what Clare had written and it might have been better in its unedited state.

The middle years of the twentieth century consolidated Clare's reputation with both academic and popular readerships. By then the "peasant poet" and the "mad poet" had been reconciled in fresh editions, biographies, reference books, and anthologies. On the academic side, Clare had become a spokesman for his class, invoked by social historians and literary critics at both ends of the political spectrum. (What Hood in 1851 had called "the literature of labour" was renamed "working-class" or "local" literature, and the class-conscious, Marxist-inflected intellectual environment of a century later focused discussion on Clare's response to agricultural enclosure practices.)[92] A wider public welcomed him as a loving observer of the countryside, and publishers promoted this aspect of Clare's work especially in illustrated editions and anthologies, typically with traditional-looking drawings or woodcuts.[93] It was increasingly a sign of distinction, not inferiority, to be a poet of "the people." Thus Clare finally had a safe berth among writers of the past. But his ship was moored, not going anywhere. If he could no longer be condescended to as a peasant poet, still he was seen as a niche writer of only minor importance.[94] It took a second effort of recovery to raise his profile and widen his readership in the late twentieth century; it remains to be seen how enduring that effort will be.

Like the second-wave recovery of Blake, the recent reassessment of Clare has come about by a diffuse process. Perhaps it is only part of a natural evolution of cultural attitudes, but it seems more deliberate than that; certainly it has depended on a small number of hard-working activists. The Clare of the 2010s—to begin at the endpoint—appears less and less as a niche writer. With the completion of the complex, comprehensive scholarly edition that is the tribute of the learned world to a mainstream writer; with conference sessions and whole conferences focusing on his work; with a dedicated academic journal publishing articles about him; and with John Clare societies on both sides of the Atlantic looking after his interests, Clare's reputation is higher than it has ever been. At the same time, and thanks partly to the work of those same societies, he is now truly popular in a way that eludes even Keats, Wordsworth, and Blake. His life story has something to do with it, as does the accessibility of his writing (what used to be called "simplicity"), but the Clare cause also has powerful symbolic value and thereby appeals to a coalition of democratizing, localizing, and especially environmental concerns. What the countercultural hippy movement did for Blake in the 1960s, led by Huxley, Ginsberg, and Bronowski, the Greens have aimed to do for Clare forty or fifty years later.

The John Clare Society, which unites educators, local historians, writers, artists, naturalists, and members of the general public through their common interest in Clare, was founded in 1981. It has been the center of the buzz around his name ever since, and its achievements are already impressive. It produces a newsletter and a journal, an annual festival, and a program for schoolchildren. Clare now has a website, a weblog (where he is described as "the most important poet of the natural world from Britain"), and a Facebook account. The society coordinated festivities for the Clare bicentenary in 1993. With the support of its offspring, the John Clare Trust and the John Clare Society of North America, it purchased Clare's cottage in Helpston in 2005 and restored it as a tourist site and education center; it later added the nearby pub where Clare's body had been laid out before burial.[95] In 1989 it was instrumental in arranging for a plaque in Clare's memory to be installed in Poets' Corner in Westminster Abbey; the unveiling was done by the poet laureate, Ted Hughes, in a ceremony at which several of Clare's poems were read and one of his hymns sung.[96] The Clareites have been busy making up for lost time.

And they have been doing it with a passion that sets them apart from some of the cozier older groups of their kind. The John Clare Society is an instrument in the hands of a dedicated group of people. Whether they came to Clare themselves by way of their engagement in broad environmental and social issues, or the reverse—starting with Clare and moving outward—the results are the same: love of nature leading to love of man in a way Wordsworth hardly anticipated. Jonathan Bate, who established his literary credentials as a Shakespearean and Romanticist, published his first book on ecology (*Romantic Ecology: Wordsworth and the Environmental Tradition*) in 1991. In *The Song of the Earth* (2000), he argued extravagantly that "poetry is the place where we save the earth."[97] (Ecocriticism was burgeoning at that point:

James McKusick, another Clareite, published *Green Writing: Romanticism and Ecology* in the same year.) In 2003 Bate published both an excellent new biography of Clare and a paperback edition of his selected poems. John Goodridge, a current (2014) vice president of the Clare Society, has been writing for many years about the poet in the context of what he has termed "the self-taught tradition"—an alternative literary tradition parallel to the established canon of great authors—and is the general editor of two series of volumes presenting the work of eighteenth-century and nineteenth-century English "labouring-class poets." Bridget Keegan combines ecocriticism and working-class authors in her study of a century of "British labouring-class nature poetry"—with a chapter, for instance, on Clare's "fen poetry." Through the society and through other networks of which they are part, these and other like-minded champions have spread the word about Clare far beyond the range it had fifty years ago. In terms of the checklist, Clare now has locatability, through the Clare Cottage; a way of reaching schoolchildren; an authoritative collected edition; international dissemination; and a well-developed critical tradition, including controversy. He has not yet caught up with Keats and Wordsworth, and though he seems to be well on his way, sustaining readership will depend on how successful this generation of followers is in breeding another, especially in the schools and universities; on how adaptable Clare's work proves to be to other media; and on how responsive it can be to broader social trends. It might be that for a writer such as Clare, who missed the early stage of canonization in the late nineteenth century, the effort of recovery will have to be renewed repeatedly just to hold the position earned so far.

Comparing the recovery projects that brought widespread recognition to Blake and Clare leads to some provisional conclusions. Neglect turned out to be a crucial positive factor for both elite and mass audiences. Apart from a few connoisseurs, virtually nobody had read Blake's poetry, so when Gilchrist included large amounts of it in his biography, the connoisseurs' taste was confirmed and the general public was introduced to something that was, as far as they were concerned, completely new. When Cherry attempted to do something similar for Clare only ten years later, it was on behalf of an author whose works were still in circulation and were considered outmoded; his *Life and Remains* did not cause the same stir as Gilchrist's biography. By the time Symons took up the cause a quarter of a century later, however, it was possible to present Clare, too, as an author who had never really been read, since the published volumes had been interfered with by other people and the best work had never been published at all. That drew supporters to the cause and—again—gave them something new to work with.

Both cases highlight the contingency of taste and the inescapability of what I earlier called the authorial package (works, life, personality, and symbolic value). Leslie Stephen and Arthur Symons, respectively the naysayer and the strong defender of Clare in the early days, at least agreed that what counted was the quality of the poetry. Stephen voiced the suspicion that Clare owed his popularity to his unusual class background, whereas Symons stoutly declared that the fact that the poet was a peasant was beside the point. One found no merit in the poetry, the other a great deal: both alike believed they were judging by strictly aesthetic criteria. We might wish to do the same or even believe we are doing the same, but the history of reputations, Blake's and Clare's specifically, gives proof that the perception of merit is and always has been complicated by other values and other considerations. Symons persuaded readers to share his high opinion of Clare's poetry in part by telling the story of his life differently—and dramatically: "what killed him [Clare] as a human mind exalted him as a poetic consciousness." For Symons the circumstances of the life were essential: Clare's real-life madness freed him as a poet. To those who hail Clare rather as a preeminent poet of nature, it is likewise an important guarantor of authenticity that he should have led the life he did as a farm laborer. And Clare himself, though quick to say how much he owed to reading, obviously believed he had been set apart and formed as a poet by firsthand experience of rural life, unlike the would-be "naturals" whose work he found so "unnatural." Whatever his failings, hands-on farming experience was the source of his strength. Thus it is not only next to impossible to separate the life from the works, it can be important not to.

Robert Bloomfield

A potential candidate for recovery from long-term neglect in the twenty-first century is Robert Bloomfield, Clare's precursor, author of *The Farmer's Boy* (1800), "the poem which sold most copies and which circulated most widely" in the Romantic period.[98] A Robert Bloomfield Society was founded in 2000, its leadership overlapping with that of the Clare Society and its goals and methods much the same. The society promotes Bloomfield as an "unjustly neglected poet."[99] It faces an uphill battle, however: Bloomfield is out of favor now, partly because he was all too well known in his own day. In the long term, where neglect is a selling point, contemporary popularity can be a serious problem.

Born in 1766 in a Suffolk village, Bloomfield earned his living as a shoemaker (and part-time maker of Aeolian harps) in London until about 1812, when financial difficulties obliged him to move his family to the small town of Shefford in Bedfordshire. But for three years, from the age of twelve, he had worked as a laborer on his uncle's farm. While he established himself in his own trade in the city, he drew on that agricultural experience to compose *The Farmer's Boy, a Rural Poem.* Inspired by Thomson's *Seasons,* this long poem in four books in heroic couplets describes farm life from the point of view of Giles, "meek, fatherless, and poor," "untaught and unrepining," who drags himself out of bed every day to join in the work of the farm—plowing, harrowing, herding sheep, milking cows and making cheese, and so on through the four seasons of the year. Bloomfield himself was not exactly "untaught," though he was fatherless and poor. His mother was a schoolmistress, and he had some instruction in writing from another teacher. Like Clare, however, once he had learned to read he was largely self-educated. He started *The Farmer's Boy* as a present for his mother and tried to have it published in London.[100] After three rejections, he gave the manuscript to his brother to pass on. The brother, George, proved resourceful, and *The Farmer's Boy* was lucky. George took it to a Suffolk landowner and man of letters, Capel Lofft, who edited the manuscript, wrote a substantial introduction, and arranged for publication by Vernor and Hood, a firm that specialized in nicely produced ("elegant") illustrated books for well-to-do readers—especially women, apparently. In the preface to a later collection, Bloomfield expressed his pleasure at the "female approbation" of his work.[101]

The Farmer's Boy first appeared in an expensive edition with woodcut engravings, then in smaller, cheaper formats (often still with illustrations).[102] Three editions were needed in the first year, two more in 1801, and there had been fourteen London editions altogether by 1820. By 1822 the London editions alone are estimated to have sold about 57,500 copies.[103] Besides those and the Dublin reprints there were multiple editions in America and Europe, and the poem was translated into French and Latin: it was an international sensation. Bloomfield, to his embarrassment, was feted by peers and baronets. A patron, the Duke of Grafton, whose family seat was in Suffolk and who had been mentioned in the poem as "noble Grafton," stepped forward with a gift of money and eventually a small pension. Two further technical but significant proofs of Bloomfield's success were that the well-established firm of Longman soon joined Vernor and Hood on the title pages as one of his publishers and that Bloomfield's works were among the earliest selected for stereotyping, since they were expected to be consistent best sellers.[104] Reviewers praised the author's poetical instincts and generally judged that his work held its own in comparison with Thomson's; the *Monthly* praised Bloomfield's "musical ear, flowing numbers, feeling, piety, poetic imagery and animation," and so on.[105] Bloomfield's fellow poets were divided—Byron sneered at "cobbler-laureats"—but the first impressions of Wordsworth and Coleridge were positive, and Southey became a solid ally.[106] Clare was inspired by Bloomfield's poetry as a teenaged farmer's boy and continued to admire it as an adult. There were copycat compositions, as poets and publishers sensed a trend.[107] In one interesting development, Coleridge wrote to Longman in 1801 with a proposal for a poem "more likely to be popular than any thing which I have hitherto written—. It is in length about the size of the Farmer's Boy, and I shall annex to it two Discourses, Concerning Metre, & Concerning the Marvellous in Poetry." He had already, he said, commissioned a friend to draw head- and tailpieces to illustrate the work, showing "the wildest & most romantic parts of this County," and he wondered whether Longman would be prepared to pay to have the drawings "engraved or cut in wood." Finally, he revealed the subject: "The title of the Poem is Christabel, a Legend, in Five Books."[108] Longman turned him down and *Christabel,* never completed, was not published until 1816.

How do we account for the craze for *The Farmer's Boy,* so extravagantly received in its day and so little regarded now? From the better-known examples of *Childe Harold's Pilgrimage* and *Waverley,* it is clear that the market for new writing in the early nineteenth century was volatile. Once word got out, it could produce instant best sellers, and some of them stuck. There was a vogue for laboring-class poets who could be taken up and endorsed by middle- or upper-class readers: Bloomfield benefited from that. His verse was easy to read and safe for all age groups, so it lent itself to family reading. (Bloomfield composed lines in his head while he was at work and wrote them down later—like Milton, one might say, but the effect was altogether different.) There was nothing difficult, threatening, or ironical about *The Farmer's Boy.* It belonged to a familiar tradition of pastoral and bucolic poetry, transmitting an idealized image of the countryside to an urban leisured class. Like Cowper, another acknowledged influence and another much-loved poet, Bloomfield drew moral lessons from country life, but with a light touch, not sermonizing much; and also like Cowper, he had an eye for minute, humble details, which he conveyed in vivid vignettes. Some of these—such as his account of Giles digging turnips out of the frozen ground to feed the cattle in winter, and of pigs rooting for acorns in the woods in autumn—became favorite set pieces. Here, for example, are lines from "Summer" about flies pestering the cart horse Ball:

> Yet by th' unclouded sun are hourly bred
> The bold assailants that surround thine head,
> Poor patient *Ball!* And with insulting wing

Roar in thine ears, and dart the piercing sting:
In thy behalf the crest-wav'd boughs avail
More than thy short-clipt remnant of a tail,
A moving mockery, a useless name,
A living proof of cruelty and shame.
Shame to the man, whatever fame he bore,
Who took from thee what man can ne'er restore,
Thy weapon of defence, thy chiefest good,
When swarming flies contending suck thy blood.[109]

A running head highlights the moral, "docking of horses condemned." In keeping with the sensibility of the age, Bloomfield treats his subjects empathetically, focusing on Giles's feelings about the seasons, the land, and his work, but also considering the feelings of farm animals—in this passage, for example, imagining the way the buzzing of flies must sound like roaring to the ears of the tormented horse. Generations of readers evidently enjoyed this experience and sympathized with Bloomfield (or with "Giles") in their turn. Sentimental as it seems to modern readers, it is not entirely saccharine: the lambs Giles plays with have to be butchered in the end.

Most of these features were comfortably conventional, not peculiar to Bloomfield. Other qualities in combination with them, however, set his work apart. His name alone was a gift to a rural poet, almost as good as "Wordsworth." His work had unusually strong visual appeal. The illustrations that accompanied it from the start catered to genteel interests in art and the picturesque; acknowledging and reinforcing these associations, Bloomfield himself in later works invoked Bewick, Gilpin, and Wilkie, and *The Banks of Wye* recommended the Wye scenes especially to artists.[110] (John Constable, born in Suffolk, was a prominent admirer, most conspicuously in paintings that he exhibited in 1814 and 1817 with accompanying lines from *The Farmer's Boy*.)[111] Vernor and Hood added a volume about Bloomfield to their series of literary topographical prints by James Storer and John Greig in 1806, following volumes dedicated to Cowper and Burns (fig. 19). They also saw to it that Bloomfield's later *Wild Flowers* (1806) and *The Banks of Wye* (1811) were well illustrated, as did a different publisher for *May Day with the Muses* (1822), after the bankruptcy of Vernor, Hood, and Sharpe in 1812. Visualizability and locatability thus came together in the way that Bloomfield's works—*The Farmer's Boy* especially—were presented. In the later nineteenth century, extracts from his works routinely appeared in drawing-room books, in which prints or photographs were accompanied by verse passages but the emphasis was on the images.[112] One unfriendly modern critic has even suggested that the key to Bloomfield's sustained popularity was precisely its appeal to amateur artists: his work "offers easily-illustrated vignettes of the romantic country scene, of the kind made popular by Westall and Birket Foster"—both of whom did publish illustrations of Bloomfield's poetry—with many passages "ideal for the water-colour brush, or the pencil."[113]

Visualizability was important, increasingly so, throughout the nineteenth century, but there was more to Bloomfield's appeal than that. His personal story was also a winner, as his editor was quick to realize. Readers naturally read *The Farmer's Boy* autobiographically, and the poet, who sometimes referred to himself in the third person as "Giles," did nothing to discourage them. Capel Lofft included a firsthand account of Bloomfield's history by George Bloomfield in the first edition, and this engaging narrative, built up through later revisions and additions, laid the foundation of the Bloomfield legend. Bloomfield himself described it winningly as a sort of letter of introduction that had eased his entry into the company of strangers: "The plain, candid memoir, which has hitherto preceded the Poem, as given by my Brother to Mr. Lofft, has interested thousands in my favour. . . . Wherever I have been introduced, almost without exception, my history has been previously known, even to the 'selling of my fiddle,' and I have immediately been permitted to take my seat, and to join the conversation."[114] Capel Lofft also undertook a preemptive critical analysis, promised in the first edition and published in an appendix to the third later in the same year—by which time he was able to cite and quote favorable reviews and commentary, including long extracts from an enthusiastic essay on the pastoral tradition by Nathan Drake that declared that "in true *pastoral* imagery and simplicity I do not think any production can be put in competition with it [*The Farmer's Boy*] since the days of Theocritus."[115] Bloomfield wisely left this hyperbolic material out, against Lofft's protests, when he prepared the stereotype edition of 1809.[116]

Launched with considerable momentum, Bloomfield nevertheless chose not to capitalize on the success of his first poem by producing more of the same, and his body of work shows considerable variety of topics, forms, and meters. He composed songs, ballads, and extended narrative poems for three separate collections—all of which sold reasonably well, with two or more London editions in his lifetime and multiple editions in America. *Good Tidings; or, News from the Farm* (1804) was written to support the campaign for vaccination against smallpox. *The Banks of Wye* (1811), four books mostly in octosyllabic couplets describing a holiday trip, is a versified guidebook with notes. He edited an anthology of extracts about the Aeolian harp, *Nature's Music* (1808); published a prose story for children, *The History of Little Davy's New Hat* (1814); and wrote a prose drama, *Hazelwood Hall* (1823). But his typical and most successful poems after *The Farmer's Boy* were sentimental tales

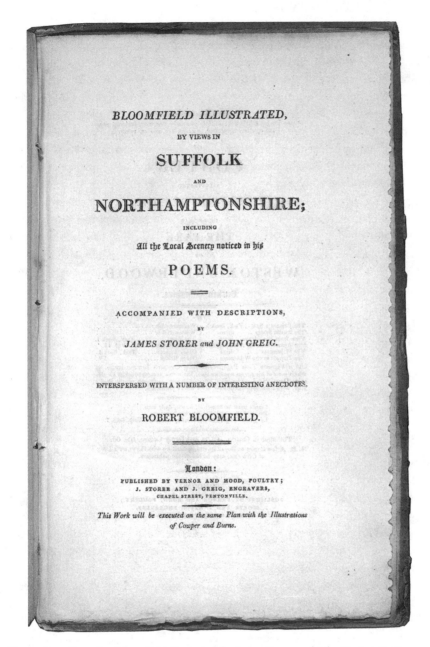

BLOOMFIELD ILLUSTRATED,

BY VIEWS IN

SUFFOLK

AND

NORTHAMPTONSHIRE;

INCLUDING

All the Local Scenery noticed in his

POEMS.

ACCOMPANIED WITH DESCRIPTIONS,

BY

JAMES STORER and JOHN GREIG.

INTERSPERSED WITH A NUMBER OF INTERESTING ANECDOTES,

BY

ROBERT BLOOMFIELD.

London:

PUBLISHED BY VERNOR AND HOOD, POULTRY;
J. STORER AND J. GREIG, ENGRAVERS,
CHAPEL STREET, PENTONVILLE.

*This Work will be executed on the same Plan with the Illustrations
of Cowper and Burns.*

Fig. 19. Prospectus for *Bloomfield Illustrated*, by James Storer and John Greig (1806).
© The British Library Board.

about country people, of a kind that Clare would also produce: "The Miller's Maid" (which was adapted as an opera and then as a drama), "Walter and Jane," "The Broken Crutch," "Alfred and Jennet." (The appendix cites what might be considered the best of the stories from *May Day with the Muses,* "Alfred and Jennet," so that readers may judge for themselves.) These tales typically treat of lovers overcoming adversity. For example, "Walter and Jane," from *Rural Tales, Ballads, and Songs* (1802), tells of a blacksmith and a servant girl who are first separated by having jobs in different places and then kept apart by his reluctance to propose marriage without financial security. Fortunately a squire appears with a legacy from Walter's uncle, and a benevolent patron sets them up in a new smithy. In "The Miller's Maid" the lovers seem to be forever parted by the discovery that they are brother and sister, but a passing soldier who turns out to be their long-lost father reveals that the boy, George, was actually his sister's illegitimate child, therefore the girl's cousin, and they are free to marry after all. As the plot summaries suggest, these tales are formulaic, with melodramatic emotions and more than a little implausibility.[117]

Though they seem to have continued to please some readers throughout the nineteenth century, Bloomfield's tales were completely passé by the twentieth. The audience for verse fiction disappeared (we do not read Clare's tales either, and seldom even Crabbe's much bolder ones), sentimentalism became suspect, and these poems were too long for anthologies and textbooks. Bloomfield's use of language is generally decorous and unadventurous (dialect is reserved for comic poems), and his vantage point as a working-class poet was compromised by his uncritical identification with the gentry in later works. In *The Banks of Wye* he observes reapers and gleaners from the comfort of a carriage like any other picturesque tourist following in the steps of Gilpin. Even in his last and best collection, *May Day with the Muses* (1822), in which a number of servants of the estate entertain their host and fellow workers with verse tales—for which reason the collection is sometimes seen as a demonstration of the intellectual potential of the working classes—the frame story tells of the benevolent squire who invited them to tell their stories in lieu of rent and who promises in the end to have the tales published.

Bloomfield was frankly taken aback by the success of *The Farmer's Boy.* It had been produced to please his family; it reached multitudes. Yet his attitude toward authorship remained modest and pragmatic, quite like Crabbe's. Like Crabbe, he realized that his work was unlikely to achieve recognition unaided, and so he sought out influential supporters. Like Crabbe, he wrote first of all for money. He wanted to earn enough to support his family, and so turned to popular genres such as tales and ballads; but he was exploited by his publishers and never received a fair share of the profits of his work. In 1816 his patrons organized a subscription to raise money on his behalf, and the family struggled on, but after he died in 1823 they were obliged to auction off his books along with other household goods. Insofar as Bloomfield hoped for a secure income through writing, he was disappointed.

A further motive that he shared with Crabbe was to do some good for the society of his time, hence the poem on vaccination and the moral lessons inculcated by his tales. In this context, it is clear that as his career developed, Bloomfield also hoped that his example would encourage other aspiring writers of his own class. He said so explicitly in the conclusion of his preface to the stereotype edition, which is dated June 1808:

> I have the gratification to know that this Poem [*The Farmer's Boy*] has given pleasure to thousands, and to make a contrary pretence would be something worse than affectation. Upon this conviction I rest my claim (with all due submission to the learned) of exhorting all persons of acknowledged taste and ability, when they receive a poor man's production, to read it with candour, and to judge of it with truth: so that, if it be found entitled to a share of public attention, the unlettered and the unfriended may not lose their chance of communicating instruction or entertainment to the world.[118]

This quiet and dignified assertion aims to affect the behavior of rich and poor alike. To the privileged classes it makes an appeal for justice and the overcoming of prejudice: they too could share in the gratification of having done good and given pleasure to thousands. To the poor it offers an example of success that might be within their grasp, not a hypothetical possibility but a well-publicized triumph. This unselfish ambition was surely fulfilled, were it only by the emergence of his best-known follower, John Clare. Bloomfield's might be called an "exemplary" model of authorship.

Bloomfield, like Crabbe, seems to have focused on the audiences of his own time and not to have looked to the future, but there is one piece of evidence to suggest that insofar as he did consider the prospect of posterity, it would have led him in the wrong direction. Capel Lofft and other supporters (Clare among them) predicted immortality for Bloomfield's work. This is a customary form of encouragement and Bloomfield did not take it too seriously, but no doubt it was an attractive idea. In a letter of 1804 to his sponsor, seeking assistance from him and his wife ("the sound judgment and true taste of Mrs Lofft"), and specifically trying to soften the blow of the cuts he was proposing to make to Lofft's preliminaries, Bloomfield considers his kind assurance "that 'the work will go down to posterity,'" proposing therefore that they should reduce the number of local and particular details in their apparatus. "How much local and momentary information, however good in itself, shall we be justified in attaching to it?" he asks.[119] He is concerned at this point about their prefaces, not about the poem itself, but it does appear that he thought his work would have a better chance of longevity if it were more universally applicable, and he does anticipate a time "when neither you nor I shall be here to arrange or correct." As time passed, however, it proved to be precisely the local and momentary that readers came to appreciate in regional and rural verse, and no good could come of attempting to universalize it.

When Bloomfield died in 1823 his publishers, friends, and family attempted to assemble, as an appropriate tribute, the collected edition, authorized biography, and volumes of correspondence that traditionally commemorated major artists (besides many insignificant ones whose estates could afford it). Clare would have written a biography, but the task was given to Joseph Weston, and Clare instead cooperated by sending some letters and three sonnets in Bloomfield's honor.[120] The *Remains,* published "for the exclusive benefit of the family of Mr. Bloomfield" and dedicated to the Duke of Grafton, was accompanied by three appeals for financial support: a call for donations to a subscription fund organized on behalf of the family by Samuel Rogers's bank in conjunction with Murray, Longman, and other prominent publishers; a proposal for the publication by subscription of Bloomfield's songs set to music; and an advertisement seeking a position for Bloomfield's daughter Hannah as a music teacher "in a respectable family."[121] The *Remains* represented an opportunity to revive Bloomfield's reputation, but it failed, and for good reasons. Weston's edition did contain some unpublished poetical "fragments" by Bloomfield, but not many, and nothing like the treasure trove of Clare's forty years later. For the most part, it was made up of prose pieces such as the journal of the tour on which *The Banks of Wye* had been based; some family correspondence; a few poems by Bloomfield's schoolmaster son, Charles; and tributes on the occasion of his death, mainly letters and elegiac poems. It was a ragbag, manifestly an attempt to raise money for the family and to stake a claim for the "Memoir and Correspondence" that were announced but still to come. In the event, the great loss to Bloomfield's cause was the absence of an authoritative biography. Even a long prefatory memoir such as Cherry's later profile of Clare might have made a great difference, but the promised memoir never materialized.

It must have been partly for lack of funding that neither the proposed life and letters nor the songs with musical settings ever appeared (the songs would have required a hundred subscribers), but lack of funding reflected a lack of public interest. By 1844 Robert Chambers could state as a matter of fact that not many people read Bloomfield anymore.[122] Actually, the period of neglect began long before then. No later publication by Bloomfield had approached the success of *The Farmer's Boy,* and though *Rural Tales, Ballads, and Songs* (1802) went through nine editions in the author's lifetime, none of the other titles did as well. Sales had been declining for at least a decade before he died. In 1820 Murray had rejected *May Day with the Muses.* There has never been a complete edition of Bloomfield's poetry, though some are called so; Longman simply added a volume to the stereotype *Works* in 1827 to incorporate the later poems.

After Bloomfield's works went out of copyright, they were picked up by some anthologies and deluxe collections, as I have indicated; a slim volume of selected letters was published in 1870; there was at least one school edition of an abridged version of *The Farmer's Boy,* in 1875; and reprints multiplied. His work was still finding new readers. But the critical consensus was that the poetry had been too derivative and too timid to leave a lasting mark. As early as 1818, Hazlitt's view that Bloomfield's work, while not bad, was seriously limited set the tone for critical appraisals of the future.[123] The fact that Bloomfield had once had a massive popular readership was also almost certain to count against him with the tastemakers and literary historians of the late nineteenth century, and so, like Clare, he missed the primary triage of authors destined for university students. In 1898 Saintsbury wrote him off along with Clare as "farmer poets," though he had slightly more to say in Clare's favor than in Bloomfield's, for "the *Farmer's Boy* of the latter is nothing but a not unpleasing versification of not uninteresting matter."[124] (He repeated this assessment in starker terms in his contribution to the *Cambridge History of English Literature* in 1932: "nature made him [Bloomfield] only a versifier; while she made Clare a poet.")[125] The inevitable comparison with Clare blighted his reputation among professional critics. A quip by E. V. Lucas in his life of Charles Lamb (1905), to wit that Clare had aimed at being a better Burns "but succeeded only in being a better Bloomfield," puts it in a nutshell.[126] In 1908 Symons firmly declared that the difference between Clare and Bloomfield was the difference between poetry and nonpoetry; even Blunden, Clare's great advocate, trying to put in a word for Bloomfield as well, had to concede that the best of his work was flawed by "an exaggerated respect for the literary model" which he (Blunden) did not find in Clare.[127] Thus as Clare's reputation grew, it completely overshadowed Bloomfield's; not even the Marxist critics of the 1950s and 1960s had a good word to say for Bloomfield.

It is hard to argue that this outcome was unfair. Clare might have been to Bloomfield as Keats was to Hunt, but Clare outlived his model and continued to grow as a writer, and Bloomfield had nothing like Hunt's impact on other poets. In terms of the checklist, though Bloomfield's work was kept in print through the nineteenth century and is back in print again now; though it had visualizability, locatability, variety, and adaptability, and was suitable for children; still it lacked some important features. There was no critical controversy about it, there were no interesting problems in text or interpretation for scholars to get their teeth into. There could hardly be said to be a critical heritage, for after the first reviews, critics were largely indifferent. There was no collected edition, no substantial collection of letters or private documents, and above all no biography, therefore no personal engagement with readers. The most characteristic poems were long—not lyrics—and therefore ill suited to anthologies. There was no Bloomfield in *The Golden Treasury.* Until the very end of the twentieth century, there were no effective champions to take up the cause, and when they emerged they grounded their defense on historical, social, and political arguments rather than on literary ones.[128] The twenty-first century has seen some foundational scholarly work in the form of bibliographies, collections of essays, edited selections from the poetry, and a good online edition of letters. The Bloomfield Society does what it can to encourage broader support, and the histories of Blake and Clare suggest that the movement they have started might gain strength over time. A good biography could yet turn the tide. But I find it hard to believe that Bloomfield will ever gain more than a coterie following—a niche market, as opposed to the multiple markets that sustain a really thriving reputation—because his work fails the fundamental test of threshold quality.

Bloomfield's inspiration came from eighteenth-century masters such as Thomson, Gray, and Cowper; his diction and verse forms were comfortably old school even in 1800. He composed in his head and revised very little; these techniques tend to generate verse that is easy to remember because it is both rhythmically and verbally predictable and uncomplicated. And the content is as predictable as the form—unexceptionable, but unsurprising. The seasons pass, winter evenings settle in, lovers are sorrowfully separated and joyfully reunited, the poet reflects on the virtues that sustained them. It is a greeting-card school of poetry. In order for it to find its way into the academic and popular anthologies or collections that nurture new audiences today, it would have to meet standards that have evolved in favor of complexity and unconventionality—as many works by Clare or the earlier examples of Crabbe, Cornwall, Hunt, and Southey could do—or else the standards would have to change.[129] At present, the case for Bloomfield can only be made on extraliterary grounds, highlighting his class, his regionality, his status as a self-educated writer, or his influence on one other rising star, John Clare. For a multitude of reasons, therefore, Bloomfield seems likely to remain no more than a local hero—a fate that would surely have satisfied him.

Conclusion

The three examples of recovery described in this chapter—one past, one in process, and one pending—illustrate some of the means by which writers of the Romantic period who lacked the necessary backing at the time of their deaths could begin to rebuild their reputations many years later. Successful recovery, it seems, is no more than deferred or delayed recognition. It can start from the smallest of foundations, so long as there is one surviving copy of the work and one reader to appreciate and share it. Word of mouth takes over, a few voices in conversation expanding to discussion with strangers through the social media of the day—books, newsprint, art, music, theater— until the author's name is widely known. In his work on canons and canon-icity, Wendell Harris observes that older works that had once missed the boat—"had not become part of, or had dropped out of, the diachronic canon"—could still enter it belatedly if they were "fortunate in their sponsorship . . . and sufficiently malleable to be linked to current cultural and critical interests."[130] Then the customary rewards or signs of recognition follow in essentially the customary sequence, only later: the collected edition, the biography, the scholarly attention, the translations and adaptations, the school textbooks, the societies, the anniversary celebrations, and so on, mutatis mutandis. If graffiti are the medium of the day, graffiti may be as eloquent a tribute as a major literary prize. They are at least proof of lay approval, which might be more important to the survival of recovered authors than to that of writers such as Byron and Scott who never underwent oblivion, for critical endorsement by the professional custodians of past literature is only part of the picture. Really successful recovery involves winning acceptance from multiple audiences as Blake and Clare have done—not literary scholars or connoisseurs only (influential though they may), but other kinds of readers as well, perhaps aspiring writers, artists, or musicians looking for fresh material, or kindred spirits making recommendations to their friends. A narrow niche and a coterie following, whether inside or outside the academy, are unsustainable: writers in that situation are like the unhappy figures in myth and folklore who are granted eternal life without having thought to ask for eternal youth as well.

All recovery is difficult, but revival of a once celebrated name is a harder sell than rediscovery of an unknown one, and the difficulty is not confined to the traditionally marginalized ranks of female, working-class, or foreign-born writers. Samuel Rogers, the wealthy banker who tried to help Bloomfield, was one of the most eminent poets of the day, a best seller, extravagantly praised and sincerely admired (at least for a time) by Byron, and I have no doubt that a case could be made for the merit of his work, but he is now "the deadest of the dead," and it seems almost inconceivable that future generations—or anyone, really—will be moved again by *Human Life* or *The Pleasures of Memory*.[131] It is difficult to promote long-lost writers, however deserving, because, as we have seen with Southey, Brunton, Hunt, and Cornwall in earlier chapters, their more successful counterparts were used to establish standards while they themselves had little or nothing to do with the shaping of taste over time. If they are judged by comparison with their more successful counterparts, they are inevitably found wanting, handicapped equally in the contest for two forms of posthumous fame: historical recognition and ongoing viability in the marketplace. So much time and emotional energy have been invested in the authors who have become classics that there is little left for those who have not. It is especially difficult to promote those who had once been popular. Prejudices about popularity work against them. They are subject, besides, to an intergenerational conflict that rejects the tastes of the elders—"papa's books," as Bagehot put it—as a matter of course. Neither Blake nor Clare had to contend with the stigma of popularity as Bloomfield did and still does.

On the other hand, given their resurrection (to varying degrees) out of quite deep obscurity and the freshness and vitality imparted especially to Blake's works by interpreters and artists of all kinds in the twentieth century, there seems to be no limit to what further efforts of recovery might achieve, and a great array of writers who might reward them. If Blake, if Clare, if possibly Bloomfield, then why not even Samuel Rogers, whose case Peter Murphy recommends by way of correcting the historical record, defamiliarizing the canonical set, and exposing our common critical assumptions. Serious attention to practically any lost but once admired author could do all that for us. My final short chapter has some practical recommendations to that end.

Conclusion

One of my fears when I embarked on this project was that the outcome was obvious, the conclusion foregone. Blake's warning haunted me: "the Man who pretends to be a modest enquirer into the truth of a self evident thing is a Knave."[1] This fear was compounded when a mischievous friend found a limerick that appeared to sum everything up in five lines.[2] But then I considered that when I started in I had not foreseen the histories and the complexities ahead; and that now, at the end, I think differently than I did before about the writing life, as well as about the literary history of the period I have been supposed to be a specialist in for decades. So to me the outcome had not been predictable. Perhaps other readers would have the same experience, surveying the same ground.

It is too late to counsel ambitious writers of the past, and even if we could time-travel and talk to them, the advice might not be palatable. There is no such thing as immortal fame in the arts. Put not thy faith in posterity. To authors active around 1810, we would say: If you're talented and you want your works to be read for the next two hundred years (we can't promise any farther), keep the poems short and make the novels all of a piece, though not formulaic. Be on good terms with your extended family, or find a surrogate family as Keats did with Hunt. Cultivate a personal myth. Choose a pretty place to live (or die) in; die young. Don't write too much, because your heirs and champions will have to sort through it all; but leave behind, unpublished, something—if only correspondence—that will bring your name freshly to the fore when you are gone. Preserve the decencies for the sake of schoolchildren.

Practical advice such as this would be pointless, however, if the message were instead: Don't worry about whether your works will be read forever or not. Once they are published they are out of your hands. Readers of different constituencies in your own time and later will love them, or not, in ways that you cannot foresee or control. Why torment yourself and perhaps write against the grain in order to second-guess the publics of the future? Better to maintain your integrity by writing to please yourself and satisfy a present publisher, than to drive yourself on as Keats and Southey did, aspiring to meet the imagined standards of an ideal audience.

In contrast to the common assumption that over time, the best writers come out on top, the reception histories selected and compared in this book show that for this cohort of writers—without denying the importance of exceptional abilities in the first place—long-term survival has depended more on external circumstances and accidental advantages than on inherent literary worth.[3] The concomitant casual assumption that the writers we no longer hear about are not worth reading (they are deservedly forgotten, as the members of the first group are deservedly remembered) is also unsound. That is where I feel most let down by my teachers and studies over the years. I had only the dimmest notion that the writers we all admire had come out of such an interesting literary environment; I was left unaware of the quality—of the very existence—of their contemporary rivals.

At the root of the whole system is the concept of writing for immortality, a resilient fantasy that profoundly affects the frame of mind in which authors compose, readers invest their time, critics pass judgment, and literary historians dispense what Byron called "the trophies of triumphant song."[4] At some levels no doubt it may be harmless. What sounds like self-aggrandizement ("I am writing for immortality") might be no more than a forceful way of saying, "I am trying my best." It can be a source of solace for a writer facing setbacks. It has become so entrenched as to seem a part of the natural order of things. But it has also had serious consequences over the long term. The following paragraphs sketch out some of those consequences and propose ways in which we might reduce the damage. Some offer only minor adjustments to received wisdom about literary fame and "Romanticism"; some are more radical; many are unabashedly technical, addressed to teachers and specialists. They are organized roughly according to the four general categories of audience introduced in the Wordsworth chapter.

Broadly speaking, though I like—and accept—Tyler Cowen's observation that "successful societies are full of false beliefs," the idea of literary immortality is not merely a metaphor and not innocuous, so I think it is time for this way of thinking to be replaced by more realistic ones such as those that book history supplies.[5] (The checklist introduced in the "Interlude" above does not claim to be a full-blown theory, but a theory could be developed from it.) A stable system in which a deity inspires the author, watchful providence ensures that the writings are recognized as works of genius, a priesthood interprets them, and the faithful worship would then come to be understood rather as a fluid process with no settled outcome but ever-changing cultural effects—a system still, but an unstable, dynamic one. In nineteenth-century Britain, new technologies including the methods for the reproduction of images; social measures such as the introduction of universal childhood education; major cultural phenomena like the craze for the Waverley novels—all brought about changes in the environment in which readers, writers, and publishers operated, and in which texts both new and old were received. The modern classics might be pillars of strength, but they could hardly be considered fixed points of reference in a changing world, for they were changing or being changed themselves. Artists illustrated them, publishers issued them in new formats, critics reinterpreted them, readers used them to meet their own needs. Pleasing many and pleasing long turned out not to be a matter of expressing eternal truths about human nature, as Johnson had proposed, but rather of adaptability.[6]

A theory of fame that allows for flux and variety and that recognizes the human effort required to make old works viable in changing conditions will require a flexible framework and new ways of thinking. For instance, if we give up the traditional metaphors from religion or biography (the ancestry, life and death, progeny, legacy, and immortality of books) we will want others to replace them. They might be based on evolutionary biology, fashion, warfare, elections, or competitive sport, but, since they are not yet ingrained, we would use them with a conscious awareness of their being metaphors. The one most often cited in book-history circles is Robert Darnton's "communications circuit," which is derived ultimately from physics.[7] For my part, I favor analogies that draw on human and social conventions over scientific ones that invoke natural laws, and would not reject even the metaphor of the stock market that Northrop Frye once scoffed at as "literary chit-chat."[8] Fame is the condition of being talked of; it needs chitchat.

Seen from a different perspective, authorship, readership, and the functions of criticism would all change too, to some extent, because they would be focused less on becoming or identifying the best so as to establish a permanent pantheon, and more on what best met the needs of the historical moment—which might themselves be quite various. "One law for the lion and ox is oppression," according to Blake.[9] Coleridge pleaded, "do not let us introduce an act of Uniformity against Poets."[10] Crabbe and Hunt, among the poets surveyed, spoke out for poetic variety partly, no doubt, because their own work did not fit the epic mould, but also because they were able to see merit in many forms of writing. The concept of a tiny cadre of immortals works against such catholicity of taste. But these days, when uniformity is out of fashion, when we endorse diversity and disparage monoculture in literature as well as in agriculture, it is appealing to think that we could make room for a greater range of realities and possibilities in our experience of the past than we have had for a long time. As specialists have been pointing out for some years, we would then acknowledge that there is not one uniform audience or market, there are discrete overlapping audiences; not one canon but multiple canons; not one model of Romantic authorship but almost as many different models as there are authors; and not one monolithic Romanticism but an array of Romanticisms.[11]

Nonreaders

This disrespectful-sounding name covers by far the largest group of persons who, in every generation, sustain the reputations of celebrity writers. They are not literally nonreaders, but readers who happen to know a particular author only by reputation, without having actually read any of the author's work. In this sense we are all nonreaders: for "they" in what follows, understand "we" as well. Since fame is a social construct and nonreaders have the strength of numbers, their role is important; but at the same time, because they are not in a position to judge for themselves, it is largely passive. They take in and respond to received wisdom as they find it in derivative reference sources, textbooks, and everyday media. They are unlikely to question or alter what they have found. But there are things they might do.

After carefully charting the reception of the Brontë sisters through the nineteenth and twentieth centuries and finding traces of their works and their personal histories more and more widely disseminated (and diluted), Lucasta Miller made a plea for a return to basics. She speaks for all writers and for most academic critics, and I endorse her conclusion: "We have to decide where the cultural value of these artists lies. It is time to turn the tables and put the writings first."[12] She does not say that the works have nothing to do with the cultural significance of the Brontës, only that as their names became increasingly widely known, adapted, and exploited, general knowledge no longer reflected shared experience of the novels themselves. The similar lament of Austen scholars to the effect that even card-carrying Janeites ritually watch the movies again instead of reading the books carries the same message: you may not legitimately claim to love *Jane Eyre* or *Pride and Prejudice* if you have not read the original works. And while it's obviously not reasonable to expect people who want to join in conversation to be well grounded in the works of all the authors they mention, there does come a point at which they will be disqualified if they are found to know nothing about them except at second hand.[13] So under some circumstances, the onus is on nonreaders to turn themselves into readers.

I would go further and encourage the nonreader who has developed an interest in the Romantic period through history or historical fiction or opera or cinema to do two things. First, to take note of what role the author's own words play in such remediations, for they are often absent or merely make up background music; and to seek out and support modern adaptations and updatings that incorporate and highlight the original writings, such as Steve Coogan's funny, surprising TV series *The Trip*. Second, to dabble in reading outside the conventional canons. Either one of these choices might lead to the other, and both would contribute to a better, more critical historical understanding of the era. The test of time is less like a separation of wheat from chaff than like clearing out the apartment of a dead relative, when you can't keep everything so you save the footstool but get rid of the clock, discard the nest of tables but reupholster the chaise longue because you can use it. The fact that the trendsetters and cataloguers or literary historians of the late nineteenth century favored Keats does not mean that Hunt, Cornwall, Brunton, and others might not be useful and pleasing to some of us now, as I hope my earlier chapters have demonstrated. With the noncanonical authors, there is less pressure to read studiously and more license to dislike them; there is also a stimulating freshness of contact where no prior expectations get in the way. Surf the anthologies, then the Net.

For nonreaders, the literature of the Romantic period comes so heavily mediated that approaching the works of major authors can be daunting in the way that visiting a great art gallery or museum is to novices. For that reason, sampling the less renowned might be easier than starting with heavyweights such as Scott or Wordsworth. Other authors come with less cultural baggage. The process of reception and reinterpretation is inevitably distorting: at every step, as Miller found with the Brontës, it layers on more of the concerns of the present and obscures those of the past. By way of illustration, consider the banner that directed visitors to a fine special exhibition of work by Romantic artists including Turner, Constable, and Blake that was on show at Tate Britain not long ago (fig. 20).[14] Struggling to reconcile the attributes generally

Fig. 20. The Tate's "Romantics" banner, based on a detail from *Chatterton* by Henry Wallis (1830–1916) in the Tate Britain collection. © Tate, London 2013.

associated with Romanticism with a collection of pictures from early nineteenth-century England, the curators chose as a representative emblem of Romanticism and the "Romantics" a detail from a painting of 1856 showing the last scene in the life of a poet who died in 1770. Why could they not find a typically "Romantic" image from among the paintings on exhibition? Because the concept of the typically Romantic was a product of the mid- to late nineteenth century. The curators' choice, though patently anachronistic, nevertheless was apt in its own way, for as we have seen, the fate of Chatterton hung heavy over the consciousness of the poets of the next generation or two. Fears of dying young, impoverished, and unappreciated affected their attitudes to the audiences of the day, even as Chatterton's posthumous celebrity—brief though it turned out to be—gave some of them hope for the future reception of their own work. The myth of neglected genius together with the cult of youth and death had enough power to carry Chatterton for a time and to shape the preferences of tastemakers right through the Victorian period. The artist who painted the picture, Henry Wallis, knew the Rossettis and had enrolled as a student at the Royal Academy in 1848, the year of Milnes's biography of Keats. This milieu, as we have seen, had a great, perhaps disproportionate influence on the afterlives of many Romantic writers.

I doubt that the Tate curators had British writers in mind when they sought an image that would match the stereotype for "Romantic" in the minds of viewers, but their choice shows, among other things, how much the mythologizing of the lives of writers had to do with defining the age. Their banner is also an effective reminder of the way that our understanding of the past has been mediated and filtered over time. But while mediation is unavoidable, it is not inescapable. One way of eluding it is by passing outside the boundaries of general knowledge, if only for as long as it takes to study one of the pictures actually produced in the period or to read one of the many poems, novels, and dramas that might not fit the standard mould.

Leisure Readers

The nonreader who becomes a reader joins the most powerful, though perhaps also the most dangerous, of reading constituencies: the one capable of bestowing or withholding popularity. That said, popularity signifies large numbers (not individual readers), and the supposed constituency of leisure readers is probably the most fragmented of all; a "group" might have only two members.[15] Readers who choose their reading to please themselves or to join in conversation with their peers come from different sectors of society and are subject to all sorts of different influences. But the present state

of low-cost digitization, social media, and book clubs is a climate exceptionally open to experiment and discussion. It is hard to imagine a reader finding
herself or himself alone in uncharted waters, as one unfortunate student of
mine did some years ago. He became obsessed with Wordsworth and read
everything; he made an ambitious class presentation on *The Excursion;* but
he believed it was all fruitless because there was "no one to talk to about it."
(*The Excursion* is hardly uncharted, but of course he meant no one his age.
Today there are ways of forming virtual fan clubs.) So I urge the leisure
reader, too, to read around and to spread the word. The aim would not be to
displace the great works but to understand them in context, and to feel free to
judge for yourself.[16] When you are reading because you want to, you can follow where the trail leads for as long as you like. It might be from one work to
another by the same writer, or to another by someone else, or away from the
writings to the author's life and circle—and there's no shame in that, for as
noted earlier, readers have always wanted to know about the person who
composed the work, and publishers have usually supplied something.

Why do some works "live" and others "die"—or to change the metaphor,
why do their stocks rise and fall, how do they stay in fashion? Not by merit or
the lack of it alone. Books are sustained by the interest of readers. Every reading is a sort of performance, a small act of revival, and no book is quite
"dead" until nobody ever reads it. Any reader or group of readers has potentially the ability, depending on their means of publicity, to renew public interest in a work that had been disregarded, as the Pre-Raphaelites did for
Blake. In the past, keeping a book in circulation depended upon material
formats and therefore upon publishers, but that is no longer the case. It is
only a matter of time before recoveries happen in cyberspace.

Literary Professionals

It may be quixotic to make a pitch for nonreaders and leisure readers to
engage with works that have been out of fashion for a long time, but literary
professionals—critics, publishers, educators—have a responsibility toward
the past, and I have more hope of them. They also have influence: they confer
esteem, often as a counterforce against popularity. It was a revelation to me as
I worked on these studies not only to see just how much influence certain men
and women of letters had in the nineteenth century (Jeffrey, Murray, Chambers, for instance), but also how high the standards of criticism on average
were then. We are inclined to think of the early days of the periodical reviews
in terms of partisan extremes, and of journalism in general as less rigorous
than academic criticism, but reading through the volumes in the "Critical

Heritage" series and the early critical and biographical essays and monographs much increased my respect for the army of educated, hardworking, underrewarded, often anonymous publishers' hacks such as J. W. Lake who kept the periodicals going. With more pages to fill than present-day reviewers and with different priorities from those of scholars, the periodical reviewers (with a few outrageous exceptions) tried to give balanced assessments and quoted large amounts of the work under review to buttress their opinions. They were conscientious guides. They too are worth a second look and make a useful check on current views: they can be unexpectedly astute, they reveal contemporary expectations, and they often set the terms that still define the subject (as with the debate about Keats and manliness—modern critics may disagree with their conclusions, but they are still discussing manliness in Keats's poems).

The process of canonization that began with the publishers and anthologizers of the period was, as Tricia Lootens has observed, a process of creation and, at the same time, of loss.[17] The number of authors and titles widely available shrank gradually—there is only so much room at the top alongside Homer, Virgil, Shakespeare, and Milton—and the reputations of the comparatively small number of still famous writers of the Romantic period were entrusted mainly to the universities and university presses, who became the custodians of immortality. Academics who wanted to get or to keep jobs, especially in North America, were advised to avoid backwaters and work on major authors so that they could effectively teach their students and participate in debate with their peers. But the consequence of this policy was that the chosen few of about 1920 have gone unchallenged for a century—except that fewer of their works are well known even in the universities, because some had to be dropped, toward the end of the twentieth century, to make room for works by women writers and living authors, and for world literature in English. When, upon investigation, the canon of 1920 appears to have been founded on sand but never made subject to comprehensive review by reformist literary historians, it would seem to be incumbent on the universities to undertake that review.[18] Instead of calling for wholesale change, however, I recommend small-scale local initiatives that ought to make people happier without great cost to their institutions or to the reputations of the great writers in whom we have, over time, invested so much. As Johnson said of Shakespeare, though "we owe every thing to him, he owes something to us"; whether we think of them as superhuman or not, we are committed to them.

As a general rule and apart from a few scraps of common knowledge, readers today have their first exposure to literature of the Romantic period in university courses. (That may be about to change in Britain with a new school curriculum that specifies Romantic poets, as noted earlier.) Some of those students go on to be artists or writers themselves—or editors or publishers or teachers—so the resources associated with that first systematic study can be the foundation of a lifelong connection. These days, up-to-date anthologies often have a web-based component that offers access to large quantities of supplementary material: works by the anthologized authors not already in the textbook, samples of writings by their contemporaries for context, and commentary. The anthologies of the future may well exist only in electronic form, which would make it easier to introduce more of the awkwardly long narrative poems that were so successful in the period and that writers such as Crabbe, Scott, Southey, and Hunt excelled in producing. Host websites such as Romantic Circles at present also link to other resources—bibliographies, databases, electronic editions. Thus the Internet makes it easier than it has ever been to range and explore a subject, but it presents difficulties too. There is a hierarchy of sites, some more accurate or more creative than others; how are students to differentiate among them? And where do they stop? Within the framework of a course of study, it is possible to allow and at the same time to direct anarchic searching—and that is what I encourage instructors to do. Give students a list of names or titles, with license to roam. Let them find an overlooked writer or poem or novel of the period that appeals to them, and set them to work, either singly or in groups. Make the history of reception a part of the exercise and make sure they look beyond the Net and have an opportunity to examine out-of-print editions to see how their work or author was presented at a given moment, preferably long before they were born. Google Books and other digital collections are wonderful, but a single contact with a physical copy of an edition from the nineteenth century or the early twentieth can expose their limitations dramatically.

From small details, larger pictures can be built up empirically either by the lone enthusiast over time or by networks gathering material to share, taking whatever approach looks promising. The traditional uses for such material would be personal anthologies, like the albums popular in the Romantic period, and selected editions (selected by author or theme) that could be assembled by a group; but readers should consult their own ways of using books and consider the technologies available to them. The reception history of a single poem or highlights of the history of a single poem are within the scope of a senior undergraduate, likewise the critical reception of a novel that is no longer famous, or the relationship between illustration and interpretation. For more advanced students and for experienced scholars, the "lost" writers, reviewers, and publishers of the period offer practically unlimited opportunities for new research and analysis, where the aim would not be full-scale "recovery" but piecemeal comparison and reassessment leading to a continually renewed understanding of the age.

Writers and Other Artists

Do the reception histories of writers who flourished two hundred years ago contain any practical guidance for writers of today? It's not really for me to say: writers who read these pages will surely have moments of recognition and fellow feeling, but whether they will find useful lessons to apply to their own work is uncertain. The imagined advice to the Romantic cohort about making sure they had families and settled in attractive parts of the country would not hold today, because the one thing we can be sure of is that the conditions of publication and the processes of acquiring fame will change at least as much in the twenty-first century as they did in the nineteenth. Developments that we cannot anticipate will determine the fate of literature—which is to say, all kinds of writing—in the future, as they have in the past.

Some of the general principles will continue to apply, however. In the twenty-first century, writers can still be heard in interviews and on talk shows declaring that they expect their works, or their dear friends' works, to live forever. The special kind of fame that is available in the arts—a name being known not only for historical achievements but for ongoing cultural impact—will continue to be a distinction worth aiming for but at the same time not one that writers can train for. It is also not one that they can achieve on their own: in their lifetimes they will depend on peers and predecessors, and afterward on advocates and champions. Other people will be responsible for creating the tastes by which the classics of the future are enjoyed. It might well be (as the cases of Blake, Austen, Keats, and even Wordsworth suggest) the taste of the tastemaker and not the taste of the originator. (As Mary Beard has said, "Reputation, inevitably, is in the hands of those who spread it, and those who have some stake in the spreading.")[19] Popularity is not incompatible with posthumous fame, but neither is the indifference of contemporary critics or long-term posthumous neglect. A writer cannot do without readers but does not need many, as witness Blake, Crabbe, and Clare. It might be that a writer's self-assurance would give him or her an edge, in that other people—the ones who are going to carry the name forward—would be influenced by it. Broadcasting your modesty as Hunt, Crabbe, and Cornwall did might deter potential champions. On the other hand, Austen wrote modestly about her two inches of ivory while Southey trumpeted his achievements, so perhaps not.

Thus the primary message that it is no use striving for immortality—there is nothing a writer, publisher, or publicist can do to guarantee it—would apply to writers today just as much as to those of the past. Writing for immortality is not a good idea. This is not a counsel of despair, however, but of liberation. Overtly addressing current (ephemeral) issues will not necessarily injure those writers' chances in the stock market of fame; seeking timeless subjects might, however, for most kinds of readers seek pleasure, not instruction, and imaginative literature is not the most natural vehicle for eternal truths. Writers who care about being read for generations to come should aim to please themselves first, their publishers next; and not attempt to restrict the way their work is to be understood. Instead of eternal truths, indeed, they would be well advised to be content with local, provisional, mutable ones, for flexibility of use (in the sense of adaptability or susceptibility to interpretation) means availability to more audiences in the long run, and great all-round success requires multiple audiences. And when they entertain dreams of their works' enduring forever, instead of dreaming of immortality, they can think in terms of building to last—a metaphor from architecture that allows for perpetual renovation—or, in the useful cant of this moment, of a metaphor from agriculture: sustainability.

Appendix: Recommended Supplementary Readings

The following selections are recommended as accompaniments for chapters 2, 4, and 5. They may be tracked down in libraries or online, and are also currently available as a group in PDF form on *T-Space,* the University of Toronto Research Repository (http://hdl.handle.net/1807/65448).

Chapter 2. A Heroic Model of Authorship

George Crabbe: *The Borough,* "Argument" and conclusion to Letter XVIII, "The Poor and Their Dwellings." Text from *Life and Poems of the Rev. George Crabbe* (London: Murray, 1834) 8:282, 292–97.

Chapter 4. What About Merit?

John Keats: Three sonnets on fame from the early, middle, and later phases of his career, "Written on the Day That Mr. Leigh Hunt Left Prison," "When I have fears that I may cease to be," and "On Fame." Texts from Keats, *Poems,* ed. Stillinger (1978).

Leigh Hunt: (a) From *The Feast of the Poets,* lines 75–110; (b) From *The Descent of Liberty,* lines 125–67, conclusion of scene 1; (c) From *The Story of Rimini:* canto 2, "The Bride's Journey to Rimini"; (d) From *The Story of Rimini:* lines 434–87 of canto 3, "The Fatal Passion," describing a pavilion in a garden; (e) From *Captain Sword and Captain Pen,* part 4, "On What Took Place on the Field of Battle the Night after the Victory," lines 194–266; (f) Three Hampstead sonnets from a series published in *The Examiner* in 1815: "Sonnet to Hampstead IV," "Sonnet to Hampstead VII," and "Hampstead VII. Description of the Village." All texts from Hunt, *Poetical Works,* ed. Milford (1923).

A timed sonnet competition between Hunt and Keats on the subject of the grasshopper and the cricket, 30 December 1816: Keats, "On the Grasshopper and the Cricket." Text from Keats, *Poems,* ed. Stillinger (1978). Hunt, "To the Grasshopper and the Cricket." Text from Hunt's *Poetical Works,* ed. Milford (1923).

Barry Cornwall: (a) A "dramatic scene" in full, "The Two Dreams" (1819); (b) From *Marcian Colonna* (1820), opening of part 2; (c) From *Gyges* (1820), the closing stanzas 29–39; (d) From *A Sicilian Story* (1820), the conclusion, stanzas 18–21; (e) "Marcelia" (1820); (f) "Melancholy" (1820). All texts from his *Poetical Works* in the Galignani (Paris) edition of 1829, with minor reformatting of stage directions.

Chapter 5. Raising the Unread

John Clare: "The Ants" and "Hereafter" from *The Village Minstrel* (1821) and "Grasshoppers" (composed in the Northborough Asylum between 1832 and 1837). Texts for the two sonnets are the versions published in 1821; "Grasshoppers" is from *Poems Chiefly from Manuscript,* ed. Blunden and Porter (1920).

John Clare, five versions of "Beans in Blossom": (a) From Clare, *The Rural Muse: Poems* (London: Whittaker, 1835) 130–31; (b) From *The Poems of John Clare,* ed. J. W. Tibble (London: Dent, 1935) 2:133; (c) From *Selected Poems and Prose of John Clare,* ed. Eric Robinson and Geoffrey Summerfield (London: Oxford UP, 1967) 159; (d) From Clare, *Poems of the Middle Period, 1822–1837,* ed. Robinson, Powell, and Dawson (1998) 4:191–92; (e) From *"I Am": The Selected Poetry of John Clare,* ed. Jonathan Bate (New York: Farrar, Straus and Giroux, 2003) 197.

Robert Bloomfield: "Alfred and Jennet" from *May Day with the Muses.* Text from Bloomfield, *Poetical Works* (1857) 214–23.

Notes

Titles of works and names of authors are generally given here in a short-
ened form; for the full entry, see under the name of the author in the bibliography.

Abbreviations

Bentley BR   *Blake Records*. Ed. G. E. Bentley, Jr. 2nd ed. New Haven: Yale
             UP, 2004. Print.
Bentley CH   *William Blake: The Critical Heritage*. Ed. G. E. Bentley,
             Jr. London: Routledge & Kegan Paul, 1975. Print.
BLJ   Byron. *Letters and Journals*. Ed. Leslie A. Marchand. 12 vols.
             Cambridge MA: Belknap P, 1973–82. Print.
CBEL3   *Cambridge Bibliography of English Literature. Volume 4:
             1800–1900*. Ed. Joanne Shattock. 3rd ed. Cambridge:
             Cambridge UP, 1999. Print.
CPP   *Complete Poetry and Prose of William Blake*. Ed. David V.
             Erdman. Rev. ed. Berkeley: U of California P, 2008. Print.
EY   *Letters of William and Dorothy Wordsworth: The Early
             Years, 1787–1805*. Ed. E. De Selincourt. Rev. Chester L.
             Shaver. Oxford: Clarendon P, 1967. Print.

Hunt *SW*	Leigh Hunt. *Selected Writings*. General eds. Robert Morrison and Michael Eberle-Sinatra. 6 vols. London: Pickering & Chatto, 2003. Print.
LY	*Letters of William and Dorothy Wordsworth: The Later Years, 1821–1853*. Ed. E. De Selincourt. Rev. Alan G. Hill. 4 vols. Oxford: Clarendon P, 1978–88. Print.
MY	*Letters of William and Dorothy Wordsworth: The Middle Years, 1806–1811*. Ed. E. De Selincourt. Rev. Mary Moorman. Oxford: Clarendon P, 1969. And *Letters of William and Dorothy Wordsworth: The Middle Years, 1812–1820*. Ed. E. De Selincourt. Rev. Mary Moorman and Alan G. Hill. Oxford: Clarendon P, 1970. (Distinguished by volume number.) Print.
ODNB	*Oxford Dictionary of National Biography*. Online.
OED	*Oxford English Dictionary*. Online.
SLC	*The Life and Correspondence of Robert Southey*. Ed Charles Cuthbert Southey. 6 vols. London: Longman, 1849. Facs. rpt. St. Clair Shores, MI: Scholarly P, n.d. Print.

Preface

1. As a rough gauge of name recognition, on 10 July 2013 Google reported 17,200,000 hits for "Jane Austen"; 14,600 for "Mary Brunton"; 2,620,000 for "John Keats"; 57,100 for "Barry Cornwall"; and 68,700,000 for "Brad Pitt."

2. "No coursework, more Shakespeare": *The Guardian* 12 June 2013.

3. Since Miller's book, *The Brontë Myth*, appeared in 2001, studies of this type have multiplied but Miller's was formative for me. On writers of the Romantic period, three excellent examples are Stephen Gill's *Wordsworth and the Victorians* (1998), earlier than Miller's book; Claire Harman's *Jane's Fame* (2009); and Ann Rigney's *The Afterlives of Walter Scott* (2012).

4. The concept of the perfectly autonomous author, derived almost entirely from Wordsworth's influential prefaces and the essay discussed in chapter 2, is still widely though not universally accepted as characterizing the age: see, for example, Woodmansee and Jaszi 16.

5. *BBC World News* 15 April 2010.

6. Sometimes, indeed, the idea of posterity is introduced in a practically meaningless cliché, for example when it (alliteratively but superfluously) reinforces the idea of preservation, as in the reference to "Dolly, the cloned sheep . . . now preserved for posterity by taxidermists" in a recent *New York Times* article (Susan Stellin, "Thirty-Six Hours in Edinburgh," *NYT* 14 July 2013).

7. Bennett 5. Bennett's approach is significantly different from mine. As he indicates in a note about William Blake (who was excluded from his study), "this book is more about the cultural production of the myth of the neglected genius than about the

actual obscurity of any individual poet" (203). His book is not concerned with empiri-
cal evidence about actual afterlives but with poets' ideas about their posthumous reputations.

8. Braudy 425.

9. Bennett, on the other hand, insists that "it is possible to discern a cultural shift
by the beginning of the nineteenth century," though he acknowledges that "the appeal
to posterity is a conventional poetic topos" (22–23).

Chapter 1. The Fame Tradition

1. Terry 65. In a revealing statement in an interview, the novelist Martin Amis, who
often shrugs off criticism by asserting that he is writing for posterity, was asked about
his father's opinion on that question. Kingsley Amis, according to his son, tended to say
no, he never thought about posterity—what good would it be to him when he was dead?
But Martin thought he was bluffing or deluded: he did care, because "all writers do"
(Toronto Public Library, 26 September 2012).

2. The opening chapter of Bennett's *Romantic Poets and the Culture of Posterity*
contains a useful collection of statements on the theme. Among the Romantics, Byron is
a particularly fertile—and witty—writer about fame, and the hardest of all to stay away
from.

3. *Aeneid* 4:173–95; *Metamorphoses* 12:39–63.

4. Xenophon 125, 123.

5. Pliny the Younger, *Letters* 3.7. All references to "Pliny" in this chapter are to
Pliny the Younger.

6. Braudy defines "celebrity" as "immediate fame" (14). Among many recent studies of celebrity culture of the present day and its origins, three stand out: Tyler Cowen's
economic analysis and two books by Tom Mole on the Romantics.

7. Phaedrus 3.9, 2.9.

8. According to Montaigne, "De la gloire," Chrysippus (280–207 BCE) and Dio-
genes (ca. 412–323 BCE) were the first to promote the contempt of fame.

9. Cicero, *Tusculan* 1.15.

10. Martial 1.25.

11. Cicero, *Letters* 5.12; Pliny, *Letters* 7.33.

12. Pliny, *Letters* 9.3.

13. See, for example, Lovejoy, Potkay, and Sabl. The tradition showed its strength
notably in eighteenth-century America, as indicated in the choice of title (derived from
Milton's *Lycidas*), *The Spur of Fame,* for a selection from the correspondence between
John Adams and Benjamin Rush.

14. Cicero, *De re publica* 6.23.

15. Cicero, *De re publica* 6.19, 6.23.

16. Braudy 425; Terry 73–74.

17. Marcus Aurelius 4.33.

18. Cicero, *De finibus* 5.69; Juvenal, Satire 10, lines 140–41; Pliny 1.8.

19. Homer, *Iliad* 7.90–91.

20. Homer, *Odyssey* 24:196–98; Ovid, *Tristia* 1.6.

21. Plutarch, *Moralia* 521. In his life of Cicero, included among the *Lives of the Noble Grecians and Romans,* Plutarch made a point of what he considered Cicero's excessive love of praise (319, 337).

22. Braudy's ambitious, exhilarating general study has surprisingly little to say about literary fame, which it appears to consider as being just like other kinds of fame, only involving distinction in a mental rather than a physical sphere.

23. Access to the work through replication is essential to the process—which must be part of the reason that even before the print era, writers had a great advantage over the plastic arts and music.

24. Horace, *Odes* 4.3.22, 4.6.41–44.

25. Suetonius, 2:467.

26. Horace, *Odes* 4.6, 4.8, 4.9.25–30.

27. Horace, *Odes* 2.20.9–20.

28. Horace, *Odes* 3.30.7–8.

29. Ovid, *Metamorphoses* 15.871–79.

30. Horace, *Ars poetica* 372–73.

31. Virgil, *Georgics* 3:7–8.

32. Horace, *Epistles* 1.19.22–23.

33. Horace, *Epistles* 2.1.63, 2.1.108, 1.19.37.

34. Horace, *Satires* 1.10.76–91. It's important to note that the allusion to "knights" creates a metaphor: Horace is not requiring social rank as a criterion of worth (though in practice, his connoisseurs *were* of high rank).

35. Pliny, *Letters* 7.7.

36. Horace, *Epistles* 2.1.48–49.

37. Surprisingly, considering how closely most of his successors followed his line of argument, the majority view later favored the hundred-year rule. For a serious philosophical defense of the test of time, see Savile.

38. Horace, *Ars poetica* 343–46.

39. *Spectator* 4:472.

40. Spenser, *Faerie Queene* 4.2.32–34.

41. *Spectator* 2:154.

42. Boswell, *Life* 1:208n.

43. Sterne, from a letter of 30 January 1760, quoted by Scott in *Lives of the Novelists,* perhaps from Sterne's *Works* (1808), 4:181–82.

44. Pope, "The First Epistle of the Second Book of Horace Imitated," lines 71–72; Samuel Johnson, *Johnson on Shakespeare* 7:91–92.

45. Boswell, *Life* 3:19–20.

46. Young 31.

47. The history and theory of canon formation for literature in English were much debated from the 1970s through the 1990s in light of the canon wars and culture wars in the universities. Harris and Kramnick are outstanding; other valuable contributions are Guillory, Lootens, Ross, Terry, and Walsh. It is Kramnick who makes the connection between the formation of the canon (defined as "a pantheon of high-cultural works from the past," 1) and the battle of the ancients and moderns, and sees the whole process as a dialectic between commercial and aesthetic forces; and Ross and

Terry who argue for dating the process back to the seventeenth or even the sixteenth century.

48. Johnson, *Rambler* 4:269, 5:16.

49. Johnson, *Rambler* 3:118.

50. Johnson, *Rambler* 4:200. Reputation seems to have been especially on Johnson's mind in August 1751 when he devoted several issues in a row to the topic. *Rambler* 145, a piece of advocacy for periodical writers—that is, writers whose work is by definition ephemeral—describes them collectively as a group who cannot afford to "indulge the chimerical ambition of immortality" (5:11), but it seems that he meant that it was so far out of reach that it was chimerical *for them,* not necessarily for all writers.

51. Johnson, *Rambler* 4:199–204. All quotations in this and the three following paragraphs are from this one paper, unless otherwise noted.

52. By contrast, William Godwin's *Enquirer* essay "Of Posthumous Fame" (1797) argued that the test of time could never be resolved, because human societies are inescapably partisan and disputation is never at an end: "the most which a successful author can pretend to, is to deliver up his works as a subject for eternal contention" (286).

53. Johnson, *Lives of the Poets* 2:119.

54. David Hume took this idea a step further a few years later, in his essay "Of the Standard of Taste," in which he observes that imaginative literature is much more likely to stand the test of time than philosophy is: "The case is not the same with the beauties of eloquence and poetry. Just expressions of passion and nature are sure, after a little time, to gain public applause, which they maintain for ever. ARISTOTLE, and PLATO, and DESCARTES, may successively yield to each other: But TERENCE and VIRGIL maintain an universal, undisputed empire over the minds of men. The abstract philosophy of CICERO has lost its credit: The vehemence of his oratory is still the object of our admiration" (1:279–80).

55. *Johnson on Shakespeare* 7:59.

56. *Johnson on Shakespeare* 7:60.

57. *Johnson on Shakespeare* 7:61.

58. For a summary of analysis and debate about the concept in Johnson's works, see the useful note in *Lives* 1:334–36.

59. *Johnson on Shakespeare* 7:61.

60. *Johnson on Shakespeare* 7:70, 65.

61. *Johnson on Shakespeare* 7:84.

62. The term "Matthew effect" sometimes applied to this phenomenon was coined by a sociologist, Robert K. Merton, in 1968 and is often cited (e.g., Cowen ch. 4). It alludes to Matt. 25:29, "For unto every one that hath shall be given, and he shall have abundance: but from him that hath not shall be taken away even that which he hath."

63. *Johnson on Shakespeare* 7:91.

64. I am using "theory" in the general sense of systematized thought, not in the narrower way that it came to stand for particular schools of Anglo-French criticism in the late twentieth century. For a longer version of this part of my study, see Jackson, "A General Theory of Fame."

65. Johnson, *Lives* 1:228.

66. He gives repeated examples of contemporary reputation that is maintained by the personal efforts of the writer or the writer's friends, apart from any special merit in the work, e.g., *Lives* 2:41, 3:107, 4:170.

67. Johnson, *Lives* 1:294.

68. *Johnson on Shakespeare* 7:84.

69. Johnson, *Lives* 1:294–95.

70. Johnson, *Lives* 2:7–8.

71. Johnson, *Lives* 4:70.

72. Johnson, *Lives* 3:113. He makes the same point when comparing rival translations of Virgil; he concludes "that Pitt pleases the criticks, and Dryden the people; that Pitt is quoted, and Dryden read" (4:95).

73. Johnson, *Lives* 4:67.

74. Johnson, *Lives* 4:184.

75. Johnson, *Lives* 2:41.

76. Johnson, *Lives* 3:85.

77. Quoted in Johnson, *Lives* 1:246.

78. Johnson, *Lives* 4:53.

79. Johnson, *Lives* 2:102.

80. Johnson, *Lives* 1:269–79. Modern criticism agrees with him: see, for instance, Walsh 53.

81. Johnson, *Lives* 3:37. Johnson's notorious ambivalence toward Milton can be detected here: Addison "made" *Paradise Lost* popular, and readers "think" they ought to be pleased by it; elsewhere, of course, he acknowledges its lack of human interest and thus casts doubt on its ability to please for long (1:290).

82. After having settled on this term, I was pleased to come across a remark by Johnson in his short life of the physician Morin: "mere unassisted merit advances slowly, if, what is not very common, it advances at all" ("Morin" 162).

Chapter 2. A Heroic Model of Authorship

1. Wordsworth, *Prose Works* 3:80.

2. For informed analysis of the cult of authorial genius, see Stillinger, Higgins, Levy, and Riede; for the failure to snuff it out, Haynes.

3. Woodmansee 16.

4. Boswell, *Life* 1:130; Beattie, *The Minstrel* 1.1–2.

5. Juvenal, *Satires* 3.164.

6. See Groom for a collection of essays that considers the Chatterton affair from various perspectives. Wordsworth's attitude toward Chatterton was ambivalent. Although his line about "Chatterton, the marvellous boy" in "Resolution and Independence," leading to the speaker's observation that "We poets in our youth begin in gladness / But thereof come in the end despondency and madness" is sometimes taken at face value as a tribute, by dramatizing and aggrandizing the speaker's self-pity the poem ultimately deflates and corrects it.

7. Braudy 425.

8. Kett 2:160.

9. Kett 2:162.

10. *MY* 3:284.

11. Wordsworth, *Prose Works* 1:120; *Prelude* 14.310 (1850 version).

12. Wordsworth, *Prose Works* 1:118; Woof 186. Modern scholarship confirms these subjective impressions of the time: see esp. Colbert.

13. On Wordsworth as a modern classic: Woof 756. Stephen Gill's excellent book *Wordsworth and the Victorians* tracks his reception and cultural impact into the twentieth century, ending with the establishment of the National Trust.

14. Wordsworth defines a spectrum of possibilities: "partial notice only, or neglect, perhaps long continued, or attention wholly inadequate to their merits—must have been the fate of most works in the higher departments of poetry" (*Prose Works* 3:67).

15. Wordsworth, *Prose Works* 3:80. Scholars are far from united in their understanding of Wordsworth's position. The contentious conclusion of the essay has been variously interpreted as Wordsworth's rejection of his actual contemporary readership in favor of an actual but unknown future one (e.g., Bennett); as an anticipation not of an actual future audience but an ideal "suprahistorical" one (Klancher 150); as a call for writers to create a taste for their work in their own lifetimes that would extend to future generations (Ferguson 101); and as a recognition of the mutual dependence of poet and posterity (Franta 60).

16. Wordsworth, *Prose Works* 3:80.

17. The phrase is Owen's, 229.

18. Wordsworth, *Prose Works* 3:70–71, 79.

19. Wordsworth, *Prose Works* 3:83.

20. Wordsworth, *Prose Works* 3:66.

21. Johnson had shifted the emphasis to pleasure—pleasing many and pleasing long—though it might have been because he took the didactic function of literature for granted.

22. Wordsworth, like Johnson, was a great admirer and advocate of Bacon's writings, and his reading of Bacon might have influenced the theory of fame here. (His 1809 *Convention of Cintra* pamphlet has two epigraphs, one from Horace's *Ars poetica* and the other from Bacon, and his *White Doe of Rylstone* of 1815 has one from Bacon and one from Wordsworth himself.) The opening paragraph of Bacon's essay "Of Praise" makes a distinction between the kind of praise that is worth having, which comes from "persons of quality and judgment," as opposed to the commendation of the "common people," which is more often bestowed on unworthy subjects (118). Another analogue and possible influence is Hume's essay "Of the Standard of Taste," with a paragraph that outlines the different tastes of different ages (love for the young, philosophical reflections for the old) and matches them with different authors: "At twenty, Ovid may be the favourite author; Horace at forty; and perhaps Tacitus at fifty" (1:281).

23. Wordsworth, *Prose Works* 3:62.

24. Wordsworth, *Prose Works* 3:82.

25. *OED*. Recently available online databases such as Google Books and searchable newspaper archives turn up many more early examples.

26. As in many titles between Herford (1897) and Johnston and Ruoff (1987).

27. Essential resources are Woof's volume on Wordsworth in the "Critical Heritage" series and Gill's *Wordsworth and the Victorians*. Other useful surveys are Bauer, Hanley, Healey, Jones and Kroeber, Peek, and Simpson.

28. Coleridge, *Biographia* 2:9. As an antecedent to the modern proverb about there being no such thing as bad publicity, see Johnson's metaphor for fame as a shuttlecock: controversy keeps it in the air (Boswell 5:400).

29. Jane Tompkins makes this point forcefully in her article about the reception of the work of Nathaniel Hawthorne: the critical frame of reference is always changing. As "the context changed, so did the work embedded in it," and thus "the 'true nature' of a literary work is a function of the critical perspective that is brought to bear upon it" (640, 627).

30. Gill, *Wordsworth and the Victorians* 30.

31. Brooke gave two series of Sunday afternoon public lectures on "theology in the English poets" in St. James's Chapel, directed to people who did not regularly attend church. The first was published: he delivered one lecture on Cowper, one on Coleridge, three on Burns, and nine on Wordsworth. He described Wordsworth as "the greatest of the English Poets of this century; greatest not only as a Poet, but as a philosopher" (93).

32. For examples of exercises in parsing and paraphrasing, see two textbooks: Wordsworth, *Selections* (1874) and Wordsworth, *The First Book of the Excursion* (1863).

33. In *The Classic,* Frank Kermode describes a modern vernacular "classic" as a work that continues to be read *because* it lends itself to reinterpretation (e.g., 133, 140).

34. Woof 761.

35. Atherton 30.

36. James 63. The figures for the sales of Palgrave's *The Golden Treasury* are included in the preface to the facsimile edition of 2000 (vii).

37. Wordsworth complained about tourists as locals usually do, but in conversation with Isabella Fenwick he expressed an indulgent attitude toward literary tourism as "a local tribute paid to intellect" and a credit to the feelings of the neighborhood even if it had nothing to do with the works (Curtis 73). I discuss some early promotion of literary tourism in connection with Burns, Cowper, and Bloomfield in chapter 5. The best and most comprehensive study of literary tourism in Britain is by Nicola Watson.

38. Howitt 2:328.

39. "It is a disgrace to the age," Wordsworth wrote to a correspondent in 1833, "that Poetry wont [*sic*] sell without prints—I am a little too proud to let my Ship sail in the wake of the Engravers and the drawing-mongers" (*LY* 2:617).

40. *Prelude* 13:235 (1850 version). Wordsworth said once that the poems of Scott could not last because they failed to address the spiritual part of human experience: "he has never in verse written anything addressed to the immortal part of man" (quoted from a dinner table conversation in 1844 in Christopher Wordsworth, *Memoirs* 2:445).

41. McGuffie provides a useful list.

42. Coleridge, *Biographia* 1:48.

43. Wordsworth, *Poetical Works* xiii. An important British publication, Chambers's *Cyclopaedia of English Literature* of 1843–44, adopts a similar line about him.

44. Christopher Wordsworth, *Memoirs* 2:437.

45. Wordsworth expressed his revulsion over author portraits forcefully in a letter to his publisher in 1830: "As to the Portrait to be prefixed according to the suggestion of the Booksellers—the notion to me is intolerable. These Vanities should be avoided by

living Authors—when a man is departed the world may do with him what it likes—but while he lives let him take some little care of himself" (*LY* 2:268).

46. Harper 1:15.

47. Coleridge, *Biographia* 2:159.

48. Woof 651.

49. Take, for example, a gift book of 1863, *Wordsworth's Poems for the Young*, with *Wordsworth's Poems* in the "Tit Bits Monster Penny Series" (ca. 1902) by way of contrast; and as a recent example, Alan Liu's *William Wordsworth* (2003) in the "Poetry for Young People" series, with illustrations by James Muir.

50. For Wordsworth's influence on educators in Victorian Britain from elementary to higher education, see Ward. A recent essay by Joel Pace, "Wordsworth and America," describes the impact of Wordsworth on American elementary education, notably in the founding of a girls' boarding school, the Rydal Mount Academy, by Sarah P. Green.

51. Arnold, "Wordsworth" 9:55.

52. Reid 8, 11.

53. Coleridge, *Biographia* 1:55.

54. The institutionalization of English as a legitimate subject in the British universities is usually dated to ca. 1900, with the establishment of independent Schools of English at Oxford in 1893 and at Cambridge in 1917. In comparison with studies of the theory and implications of canonization, there has been relatively little detailed historical study of the rise of English studies, but Baldick (1983) remains useful and Atherton (2005) combines a good survey of her predecessors with a fresh comparatist approach, adding to the standard accounts of the ancient universities evidence from three nineteenth-century institutions—Manchester, Nottingham, and King's College London.

55. Perkins 139.

56. Franta 55.

57. Wordsworth, *Prose Works* 3:67.

58. As Johnson's comments and quotations in the life of Pope indicate—*The Rape of the Lock* pleased "readers of every class, from the critic to the waiting-maid," and Pope's translation of Homer had "the mob" on its side, though not Addison and the wits—the publishing world already knew that there was no unified reading public. The theory of audiences has had considerable attention since Raymond Williams wrote about the shift from a patronage system to a mass market, but his influential formulation exaggerates the impact of a gradual shift that had begun long before the Romantic period. For innovative thinking about the way that writers shaped audiences, with the specific example of periodical literature, see Klancher; for audiences shaping writers, see Martin on Byron; for the commercial advantage of multiple niche markets, see Anderson.

59. Figures are derived from J. R. de J. Jackson, *Jackson Bibliography of Romantic Poetry*, http://jacksonbibliography.library.utoronto.ca/index.cfm.

60. *ODNB;* Watson.

61. *LY* 2:634, cited by St. Clair 663n. In 1820, as part of a defense of *Don Juan*, Byron composed a furious point-by-point rebuttal of Wordsworth's 1815 "Essay, Supplementary"; he had Murray print it, but in the end decided not to publish. He argued not only that it was possible for a poet to be both popular and immortal, but also that all the immortals had been popular in their time (*Complete Miscellaneous Prose* 88–119).

62. For a comparison of sales figures, see St. Clair, esp. 217.

63. *LY* 2:691–92. George Crabbe, Jr., quoted part of this letter in a footnote to *The Village* in the 1834 edition (*Poetical Works* 2:83n–84n).

64. For contemporary appreciation, see Pollard; for articles by later writers, see Bareham. On Hardy's relationship to Crabbe, see Michael Millgate, *Thomas Hardy* 404, and on Britten, Carpenter, esp. 155–57.

65. For the centenaries see Ganz (1905) and *George Crabbe . . . Bicentenary Celebrations* (1954). Thomas Hardy attended in 1905 and E. M. Forster in 1954.

66. Johnson, *Letters* 4:116–17.

67. *The Village* 1:53–54. Quotations are from Crabbe's *Complete Poetical Works* unless otherwise indicated.

68. *The Village* 2:2.

69. Crabbe, *Selected Letters and Journals* 378.

70. Pollard 213.

71. Pollard 54–60, 84–98, 163–71, 227–38.

72. Pollard 299–306. In his introduction, Pollard notes that "the Romantic reaction to Crabbe might well be summed up as Hazlitt v. Jeffrey" (20). As late as 1903, Ainger's volume on Crabbe in the "English Men of Letters" series began with a sustained contrast of the fates of the reputations of Crabbe and Wordsworth.

73. Justice 55.

74. Lake is an interesting figure, a poet himself and a hardworking ambassador for British writing in Paris in the 1820s and 1830s. Most of his work appeared anonymously, including the perceptive extended prefatory essays attached to his editions of Byron, Scott, and Moore, which were frequently reprinted and widely circulated in Europe and America. Byron commended his editing (*Letters and Journals* 10:204); Moore, who had helped him with small sums of money in Paris, described him in 1837 as "the only stationary representative, poor devil, of English literature in France" (Moore, *Letters* 2:812).

75. *The Library* (1781 version) lines 111–13.

76. Crabbe, *Selected Letters and Journals* 105–6, 110.

77. George Crabbe, Jr. 79.

78. This practice was sufficiently marked that some reviewers thought he was sycophantic, and Crabbe himself was aware that it might be interpreted that way, as he revealed in the preface of 1807: *Complete Poetical Works* 1:208–9.

79. Crabbe, *Complete Poetical Works* 2:8, 10–11.

80. Crabbe, *Selected Letters and Journals* 378.

81. Crabbe, *Selected Letters and Journals* 389.

82. Madden 68–90.

83. For comparative estimates of sales, see St. Clair, esp. 217.

84. *SLC* 1:120. Compare a letter of 1819 in which Southey indicates that he had deliberately sought to model himself on older poets "whose rank is now established beyond all controversy," specifically, Homer, Virgil, Dante, Ariosto, and Milton: *SLC* 4:335.

85. Southey, *New Letters* 1:39.

86. Madden 105, 214.

87. I have found just one adaptation for the theater, *Thalaba, the Destroyer,* adapted as a melodrama by Edward Ball (or Fitz-Ball), published about 1831 as part of *Cumberland's Minor Theatre* but with prefatory remarks that indicate that it was first performed at the Coburg Theatre on 13 August 1822.

88. *SLC* 5:22. (With the proviso, however, that he finish the ever-deferred *History of Portugal.*) Southey understood the special value of literary fame: the great writer, he said, would be better known than Napoleon (*SLC* 3:144).

89. *SLC* 4:105.

90. *SLC* 4:184.

91. Even in 1804, when he was only thirty, he described himself as living among the dead and liking them best (*SLC* 2:272). Text here quoted from Southey, *Later Poetical Works* 1:314.

92. For examples of the means employed by some later writers to control reception of their work—not quite the same as writing for immortality, but related to it—see Michael Millgate, *Testamentary Acts.*

93. *SLC* 3:47, 332. In the end it was not his designated friend, Grosvenor Bedford, but his son Charles Cuthbert Southey who completed the biography. The autobiographical memoirs to which Southey occasionally refers were published in the first volume of *SLC.*

94. Southey, *Poetical Works* (1837) 1:vii, 2:xv.

95. Southey, *Poetical Works* (1837) 1:v, xi. He later (5:xlii) contrasts his work with that of William Sotheby, who brought out his *Saul* about the same time as Southey's *Madoc:* Sotheby was following fashion, whereas Southey himself considered only "that Court of Record which sooner or later pronounces unerringly upon the merits of the case."

96. Southey, *Poetical Works* (1837) 2:xiv–xvi.

97. St. Clair 210. The eight were Byron, Campbell, Coleridge, Moore, Rogers, Scott, Southey, and Wordsworth.

98. *Beauties of the Poems of Robert Southey* (1833) and *Beauties of the Prose Works of Robert Southey* (1833), both "chiefly for the use of schools and young persons"; Southey refers to this project in *SLC* 6:161. *Stories of the Magicians,* in prose versions by the Rev. Alfred J. Church, who had published similar versions of stories from Homer, was published by Seeley in 1887. Though it appears to have been out of print for over a century, there are at least two new editions, 2008 and 2009, presumably as part of the Harry Potter phenomenon, so perhaps Southey's epics will find a new audience again after all.

99. Scott's letter is included in Madden 169; Byron's in *BLJ* 4:235.

100. Madden 217.

101. Chambers, *Cyclopaedia,* 2:351. For a strong public statement by Landor about Southey, see Madden 424–29.

102. Contemporary reactions, not limited to reviews, are helpfully collected in Madden. See, for example, Madden 45, 258, 331, 334, and 418 (these pages include comments by Byron, Coleridge, Hazlitt, and Wordsworth, respectively). Madden himself, in summary, discusses the "complex ambiguity of contemporary responses to his work" (1). For Lynda Pratt's summary of Wordsworth's "reservations" about Southey's poetry, see her "Family Misfortunes" 221; also Simmons 188–89.

103. Chambers, *Cyclopaedia* 2:350.

104. St. Clair 218. My rough tally of editions is based on *CBEL3* and WorldCat; it includes UK, US, and other overseas printings in English as they are recorded, whether they are denominated new editions or not.

105. St. Clair 655.

106. Pratt 220.

107. Howitt 2:264, 266.

108. *SLC* 4:355.

109. *SLC* 4:91, 105. He goes further in *SLC* 6:76: "A greater poet than Wordsworth there never has been, nor ever will be."

110. *SLC* 3:126. That was in 1807. Byron's taunt in 1809, in *English Bards and Scotch Reviewers,* takes the opposite point of view: "Oh Southey! Southey! cease thy varied song! / A bard may chant too often, and too long" (lines 225–26).

111. *SLC* 4:221–27; *ODNB.*

112. *SLC* 6:73. Some commentators, though sympathetic to Southey in most ways, have speculated that by deliberately avoiding "excitement" and cultivating a calm detachment, Southey deprived his poetry of the ability to move readers: Madden 3; Simmons 214.

113. *SLC* 6:262.

114. *SLC* 4:341.

115. Smith 342.

116. Johnson, *Lives* 4:53.

Chapter 3. The Stigma of Popularity

1. Barbauld 1:1.

2. Garside, "English Novel" 66.

3. St. Clair 632; Hayden 1; David Hewitt, "Scott, Sir Walter (1771–1832)," *ODNB;* Kelly 138.

4. For convenient collections of evidence, see St. Clair 632–44, 715–23 (sales figures); Hayden (significant reviews and readers' comments from 1805 to 1885); Pittock (Scott's influence on fiction, art, and opera on the Continent); and both works by Rigney (more elusive acts of cultural memory, especially "remediation"). Rigney, whose book on Scott is exceptional in taking as much interest in the decline of Scott's reputation as its rise, declares, "Once the Great Unknown, Scott has largely become the Great Forgotten" (*Afterlives* 10).

5. Todd and Bowden 42–49, 140–41. This meticulous bibliography is the principal source for production runs and sales figures below.

6. St. Clair (218) provides interesting comparative statistics for sales of "individual long romantic poems" throughout the period. Scott's first three poems are at the top of the list, and three others are in the top twenty. It is significant that Byron's *The Corsair* (1814) ranks fourth.

7. Quoted in Edgar Johnson 1:316.

8. *ODNB,* citing a definitive article of 1986 by Peter Garside. Edgar Johnson 1:316.

9. *Scott on Himself* 1; Edgar Johnson 1:308. One reason for not pursuing the project at that time might have been the rival fifty-volume set of *British Novelists,* with a prefatory essay by Barbauld, published by Rivington in 1810.

10. Both examples are from Hayden 67–68. The review is from the *British Critic* for August 1814, *Waverley* having been released on 7 July in Edinburgh and 30 July in London.

11. Altick, *English Common Reader* 263, 383.

12. Quoted in Todd and Bowden 146. In her study of the early years of the reception of the Waverley novels, Ina Ferris explains how Scott's success contributed to the shift of genre hierarchies in the nineteenth century, arguing that the validation of the series "depended crucially on their appropriation of the authority of history" (10).

13. Suarez and Woudhuysen 2:1137.

14. Jane Millgate, *Scott's Last Edition* 89–90, 98.

15. Keats, *Letters* 2:16.

16. Introductory epistle to *The Fortunes of Nigel* (1822), excerpted in Scott, *On Novelists* 460.

17. See, for example, Altick, *Paintings from Books,* and Noon, *Crossing the Channel.*

18. Scott, *Lives of the Novelists* 177.

19. Hewitt, "Scott," *ODNB.*

20. Wright in Pittock 296.

21. For dramatizations, see Bolton; for operas, two titles by Mitchell. There are also many musical settings of Scott songs, for which see Gooch and Thatcher.

22. Pittock 13, 8. Hayden (21) comments on the Marxist enthusiasm for Scott, citing in particular *The Historical Novel* by Lukács, first published in 1937 and translated into English in 1962.

23. Reprinted in Hayden 537–39. Kelly makes some interesting comments on this passage (152).

24. In an unsigned review of 1839, reprinted in Hayden 378–79.

25. De Waal 341.

26. Garside, "English Novel" 45.

27. Kramnick 6.

28. Hayden 395–96.

29. Hayden 440. In the same year, however, a retrospective essay in the *Athenaeum* speculated that a period of reaction against Scott had already passed, and his place in the pantheon was secure: "From the revival of letters to the present day it is questionable whether anything will, in the judgment of posterity, be found worthier to rank after Shakespeare's dramas and Milton's epics, than the Waverley novels" (Hayden 469).

30. Hayden 2. In an early survey of the critical reception of the novels, Hillhouse asserted that the novels maintained their "popularity with a broad reading public until nearly 1900" (331).

31. There had been a sharp decline after midcentury. The editor of a reprint of Lockhart's abridged version in 1871 observes that between 1837 and 1856 "there were sold, of all the editions, 38,900 copies. Between 1856 and 1871, only 1900" (Lockhart vi).

32. Maxwell 419.

33. Corman 181.

34. The IMDb (Internet Movie Database) shows that a wide range of Scott's fictions—prose and verse—were adapted as short movies in the silent era, but there are no listings at all for the 1930s and only one (a version of the opera *Lucia di Lammermoor*) in the 1940s. Four novels were adapted as movies in the early 1950s, followed by a succession of BBC TV serializations in the 1950s, 1960s, and 1970s, but the only big-screen versions of Scott since the early 1950s appear to have been opera productions. The dreadful 1995 film *Rob Roy* had nothing to do with Walter Scott.

35. A keyword search by decade in the *MLA International Bibliography* online—admittedly a crude measure—indicates that the total number of publications of all kinds (but all academic) in the 1970s almost doubled the number in the 1960s, going from 69 to 131, but that difference could be accounted for by the expansion of the universities at the time. Since then the figure has been fairly steady, dipping in the 1980s to 106 but rising again to 129 in the 1990s and 128 in the 2000s. The *MLA International Bibliography* is a tool with an inbuilt bias for writers of international reputation such as Scott, but even so, when his figures are compared with those for other writers (most of whom also show the early doubling), there does seem to have been a slight improvement over the last twenty years. The figures decade by decade for Byron are 331, 626, 623, 565, 661; for Austen, 124, 318, 352, 474, 652; for Wordsworth, 556, 1,110, 1,263, 1,067, 954; for Crabbe, 35, 38, 33, 20, 19; for Southey, 38, 71, 49, 81, 93; for Brunton, 0, 1, 1, 2, 3.

36. To put these numbers in perspective: Jane Austen, 12,800,000, and Barack Obama, 129,000,000, as of 29 July 2013.

37. Bagehot in the *National Review* of April 1858, reprinted in Hayden 394. The following quotations are from the same passage.

38. Bagehot in Hayden 395.

39. *British Critic,* review reprinted in Hayden 69.

40. Scott, *On Novelists* 258, from the introductory epistle to *The Fortunes of Nigel* (1822). Scott cites the job creation and diffusion of wealth associated with best-selling writings, as well as the absolute sum added to the economy.

41. Scott, *Letters* 10:95, 7:68, 11:324. Though the essays as they appeared in the *Novelist's Library* were technically anonymous, the publisher's "Advertisement" in the first volume anticipated that the "high source" from which they derived would "be at once recognized," and indeed the opening "Memoir" in that volume is dated from Abbotsford.

42. Scott, *On Novelists* 447.

43. Here is Scott's final judgment on Sterne in *Lives* 130: "All popularity thus founded carries in it the seeds of decay; for eccentricity in composition, like fantastic modes of dress, however attractive when first introduced, is sure to be caricatured by stupid imitators, to become soon unfashionable, and of course to be neglected." He echoes Johnson's verdict, not one of his best: "Nothing odd will do long. *Tristram Shandy* did not last" (Boswell 2:449).

44. Scott, *Lives* 81, 29, 17.

45. Scott, *Lives* 2, 11, 18.

46. Scott, *Lives* 249.

47. Scott, *Lives* 7.

48. Scott, *Lives* 19.

49. Scott, *Lives* 81.

50. Scott, *Lives* 90.

51. Scott, *Lives* 168.

52. Scott, *Lives* 59, 43.

53. Scott, *Lives* 69.

54. Scott, *Lives* 29.

55. "Air of reality" is a phrase he uses of Richardson (*Lives* 252); "reality even in fiction" comes from the essay on Le Sage (*Lives* 93).

56. Scott, *Lives* 308, 305. In his essay on Walpole, Scott refers to Radcliffe in passing as "a name not to be mentioned without the high respect due to genius" (*Lives* 190).

57. Scott, *Lives* 68. In 1822 Scott defended his own practice of churning out novels by citing the competitiveness of the market and the need to keep one's place by constantly producing new work. He also advanced some more surprising arguments, such as that a succession of titles over time levels out an author's reputation appropriately, and that (conversely, perhaps) weaker work serves as a foil to stronger: "Had I only written *Waverley*, I should have long since been, according to the established phrase, 'the ingenious author of a novel much admired at the time.' I believe, on my soul, that the reputation of *Waverley* is sustained very much by the praises of those who may be inclined to prefer that tale to its successors" (*On Novelists* 460).

58. Scott, *On Novelists* 447. There is an even more explicit statement in the 1822 introduction to *The Fortunes of Nigel*: "It is some consolation to reflect that the best authors in all countries have been the most voluminous" (460).

59. Scott, *Lives* 121.

60. Scott, *Lives* 310.

61. Lines 175–78, 182–83: Byron, *Complete Poetical Works* 1:234.

62. Jane Millgate, "For Lucre or for Fame" 196.

63. Scott, *On Novelists* 459, 460.

64. Jane Millgate, "For Lucre or for Fame" 198; Edgar Johnson 306–20, esp. 315–16; Todd and Bowden vii.

65. Scott, *On Novelists* 459.

66. Notably Chartier, "Popular Appropriations"; Colbert; Jacobs; and Sher.

67. Scott, *Scott on Himself* 1.

68. Hazlitt 5:154. In *The Spirit of the Age* (1825), Hazlitt went further, describing Scott as "undoubtedly the most popular writer of the age" (*Complete Works* 11:57) and the novels as vastly superior to the poems, "the same in matter, but in form, in power how different!" (11:61)

69. Hazlitt 5:143, 144.

70. The letter is cited in chapter 2 (from *LY* 2:634 via St. Clair 663n); the distinction appears at the end of the "Essay, Supplementary" (Wordsworth, *Prose Works* 3:84). In his "Essay on Popularity" (discussed at length in chapter 5), John Clare also adopts the standard metaphor of noisy mobs: "noise and bustle are the essence and soul of popularity" (Cherry 309).

71. Hayden 345.

72. Chartier, "Popular Appropriations" 83. Before book historians began to struggle with it, the meaning of "popular," especially in the phrase "popular culture," was widely debated by social scientists, almost exclusively in terms of Marxist theory and in connection with the idealization or demonization of working-class experience. Frow provides a helpful summary.

73. Hayden 144. This essay was composed in 1818 but not published until 1910.

74. Lake, "Memoir" x.

75. This is not Chartier's explicit conclusion but an extension of his argument.

76. Todd and Bowden 146.

77. Hazlitt 5:154. (The reference is to his "Lectures on the English Poets." A few years later, in his essay on Scott in *The Spirit of the Age*, Hazlitt wrote more frankly about the poetry but more generously about the novels: 11:57–68.)

78. Sher, whose subject is eighteenth-century Scottish authors, offers a "popularity rating" chart based on numbers of editions published in Scotland and England in a given period, adjusted for print runs, abridgments, and spurious editions. Jacobs tries to deal with the circulating-library readership by proposing a distinction between "canonical popularity," which is measured in the number of reprints and new editions, and "experiential popularity," which is measured by appearances in library catalogues.

79. That was according to the webpage of the Japanese Friends of Abbotsford on the Abbotsford website, http://www.scottsabbotsford.co.uk, accessed 12 July 2011.

80. This went for the age as well as for the individual. To complaints about the press groaning under the weight of its products, Scott responded by pointing out that such complaints were ancient, but also by suggesting that the productivity of his own period augured well for *its* future reputation: "Believe me, that even in the most neglected works of the present age the next may discover treasures" (Scott, *On Novelists* 461).

81. Scott, *On Novelists* 460.

82. Scott, *On Novelists* 460.

83. Alexander Brunton, "Memoir" xlvi.

84. *Scots Magazine* 73 (1811): 203. This early review gives some insight into the ways in which the novel must have been being talked about in Edinburgh. The reviewer affirms that the novel deserves the interest it had excited, because although the plotting is weak, it exhibits "vigour of thought and expression" along with "a knowledge of human nature" that raised it "far above the ordinary level" of new fiction.

85. Austen, *Letters* 278: "We have tried to get Self-controul, but in vain." Garside and Schöwerling 2:59n provides evidence from the Longman letter books of the shortage of copies in London, and of an increase over the usual print runs for the third and fourth editions.

86. Mary Loveday's journal, quoted in MacCarthy 144.

87. *Critical Review* 24 (1811): 161.

88. Garside and Schöwerling 2:59.

89. Brunton, *Self-Control* 1:33.

90. Brunton, *Self-Control* 2:296.

91. Ann Jones 79; Garside, "Politics" 70.

92. Alexander Brunton, "Memoir" lxiv–lxv. Though Scott and Brunton both lived in Edinburgh, and he was aware of her as the author of *Self-Control* (he revealed her

identity to a correspondent), it is not clear that they ever met and there is no record of his opinion of her novels.

93. Quoted in Alexander Brunton, "Memoir" lxxv.

94. Quoted in Alexander Brunton, "Memoir" xxxxiii.

95. Alexander Brunton, "Memoir" cv.

96. *Blackwood's* 5 (1819): 189; *Monthly Review* 91 (1820): 176.

97. Ann Jones 264. Her survey of reference books in this appendix dramatically demonstrates Austen's rise to fame after about 1880. The Chambers entry for Brunton included a long extract from *Self-Control*, ending with a paean to the Scottish homeland.

98. The quotation is from Robert Chambers's early foray into mass-market education, the *History of the English Language and Literature*, which was part of "Chambers's Educational Course," intended for the upper years of school and self-educating adults. Allan Cunningham's early overview of 1834 summed up Austen's work this way (157): "She is a prudent writer; there is good sense in all she says, a propriety in all her actions; and she sets her face zealously against romantic attachments and sentimental associations."

99. *Critical Review* 24 (1811): 169.

100. Quotations from her letters in Alexander Brunton, "Memoir" xxxvi, lxxi, xxxiv, xci, lxxxix, lxxviii.

101. She did express confidence in the originality of her approach. She had to have a "lofty" moral, whereas even the best English fiction, she observed, generally contented itself with moral lessons "of the humblest class. Even Miss Edgeworth's genius has stooped to inculcate mere worldly wisdom. 'Patience is a plaster for all sores'—'Honesty is the best policy'—'A penny saved is a penny got,'—seem the texts which she has embellished with her shrewd observation, and exquisite painting of character" (quoted in Alexander Brunton, "Memoir" lxxxii).

102. Alexander Brunton, "Memoir" lxxviii.

103. Gilson entry D6.

104. Sims [or Simms] and McIntyre of London published three Austen titles in their "Parlour Library" series between 1849 and 1851, and the two complete Brunton novels in 1852; Routledge adopted the Brunton titles in its "Railway Library" in 1852, adding two Austen volumes in 1857.

105. Extract in Southam (1986) 118.

106. Austen, *Letters* 244, 295.

107. Sutherland in Keymer and Mee, quotation from 250.

108. As indicated in n91.

109. Southam (1986) 47, 70, for instance, includes reviews from 1813 and 1816. The term might conceivably denote their exclusively English settings ("domestic" as opposed to "foreign") as well as their representation of home and family life, but the primary reference is to taking the household as a subject. As Kathryn Sutherland points out in Austen-Leigh 154, Bentley's office promoted Austen in the "Standard Novels" series as "emphatically, the novelist of home."

110. *Catalogue* (1819), Lot #2360.

111. On the day that I wrote this sentence, my Toronto newspaper *The Globe and Mail,* engaged in a special series about reforms in higher education, ran a huge headline

on the front page of its Focus section in which Austen's name was used as a symbol of literary culture as a whole: "Why Big Business Needs You to Read Jane Austen" (13 October 2012). In the week that I revised it, at the end of July 2013, we heard that Jane Austen's image is to appear on the British ten-pound banknote (beginning in 2017), with a line in praise of reading from one of her novels.

112. Marilyn Butler, "Austen, Jane (1775–1817)," *ODNB;* Southam (1987) ix.

113. Especially notable contributions are Gilson's wonderful bibliography (1982, rev. 1997), Southam (1968, 1987), Lynch (2000), Todd (2005), Sutherland (2005), Harman (2009), and Johnson (2012). The recent vogue for studies of afterlives that go beyond the critical heritage or traditional literary history and incorporate material culture has uncovered rich resources in connection with Austen.

114. Auden's witty, wicked "Letter to Lord Byron" is casually misleading on this point: reflecting on "How much her novels are beloved down here," he states, "She wrote them for posterity, she said; / 'Twas rash, but by posterity she's read" (*Letters from Iceland* 21).

115. Brunton clearly articulates her fear of "fame, however brilliant. To be pointed at—to be noticed and commented upon—to be suspected of literary airs—to be shunned, as literary women are, by the more unpretending of my own sex; and abhorred, as literary women are, by the more pretending of the other!—My dear, I would rather exhibit as a rope-dancer" (quoted in Alexander Brunton, "Memoir" xxxvi). Austen tried hard to keep the secret within the family and made the comment about being a wild beast when she heard that a Miss Burdett wanted to meet her; but once word did begin to get out, she said grimly that she would no longer lie about her authorship but would make people pay for the knowledge—unlike Scott, "I shall rather try to make all the Money than all the Mystery I can of it" (Austen, *Letters* 221, 241).

116. Austen, *Letters* 293.

117. Harman 46. Considering Austen in her role as writer, Jan Fergus concludes that by 1813 she had already defined herself as "a professional author who is acutely conscious of her sales and eager to increase her profits" (ix).

118. Southam (1986) 129, 143; Austen-Leigh 114–15.

119. Scott and Whately had both written extremely positive reviews of Austen for Murray's *Quarterly Review*—Murray being Austen's publisher by then—in 1815 and 1821, respectively, but of course those reviews were anonymous. Victorian readers most likely found out about their high estimate of Austen's novels from Lockhart's *Life of Scott* (1837), where Lockhart recorded Scott's opinion and at first erroneously attributed Whately's 1821 review to him as well but later (2nd ed., 1839) corrected the attribution. Whately's review was not published under his name until 1861 (Gilson 85). It is interesting that Austen-Leigh did not realize Scott had written the earlier review, and grumbled about it (107–8).

120. Southam (1986) 149.

121. Gilson entries D13, M125, M130. When Bentley's firm introduced the Austen-Leigh *Memoir,* it retired Henry Austen's "notice," which had hitherto served as preface to the novels.

122. For the reviews and editions, see Gilson entries M125 and M130.

123. Kathryn Sutherland's edition of the *Memoir* explains the role of other members of the family in it and includes the two preexisting manuscript memoirs that Austen-

Leigh was able to draw on, as well as the previously published "biographical notice" by Henry Austen.

124. *Letters of Jane Austen,* edited by her great-nephew, Lord Brabourne (1884); and *Jane Austen, Her Life and Letters: A Family Record* (1913), by a great-nephew and great-great nephew, W. and R. A. Austen-Leigh.

125. Lynch 13–14, 24 n24.

126. Southam (1987) 174.

127. Bautz 81. She contests the received wisdom, stemming from Southam's first volume of critical views (1968, rev. 1986), that the *Memoir* brought about a "sudden change" in the fortunes of Austen's name and works. It is only fair to point out that Southam's claim was always qualified by his following remarks that Austen-Leigh's book "fed a growing interest" in Austen's works and "encouraged" the development of a cult (1986, 1–2, unchanged from 1968).

128. Southam (1986) 2.

129. Austen-Leigh 9, 90, 95.

130. Austen-Leigh 23.

131. Austen-Leigh 32, 139.

132. Austen-Leigh 97.

133. Austen-Leigh 26.

134. Austen-Leigh 35, 37–38, 33.

135. Austen-Leigh 116.

136. Austen-Leigh 104–13.

137. Austen-Leigh 104, 114. Southam (1987) 7 drily observes that Austen-Leigh "struck the chord of cultural snobbery with unerring skill."

138. Lynch 11.

139. Brabourne 1:81. Keddie's potboiler was not after all a serious threat; it does not appear to have gone into a second edition. But it did offer a brief biography based on Austen-Leigh's, a critical defense of the novels, and leisurely individual summaries with extensive extracts, mostly of dialogue. It was addressed chiefly to girls, who were to learn from her example as well as from her works, for "The study of Jane Austen's novels is in some respects a liberal education" (41), and "Girls may well be proud of the girl who, strange to say, wrote two of her masterpieces, 'Pride and Prejudice' and 'Northanger Abbey,' before she had completed her twenty-third year" (2).

140. Brabourne 1:89. This edition is dedicated to Queen Victoria. Thinking of the characters this way was a part of the family tradition. We know that Austen herself used to entertain the family with speculations about the characters and anecdotes of their lives outside the novels. See Austen-Leigh 119.

141. Gilson H1, E85, E87.

142. Publishers' note, Austen *Pride and Prejudice* (1896) [4]. The "Marigold Series" of which this title was supposed to be a part appears to have gone no farther. This item is Gilson E84, and the Blackie's volume is Gilson E81. For textbook selections, see Gilson starting at E155.

143. Gilson E60–65, 68, 69, 76, 78, 79.

144. Claudia Johnson 184. For movie and TV adaptations, see Macdonald and Macdonald, also (slightly more up to date) the website created by Sue Perrill on the

Republic of Pemberley website, http://www.pemberley.com, and online databases such as IMDb. The interesting part of the contrast with Scott is that whereas there were film adaptations of Scott's works in the silent era, there were none of Austen's. Both were adapted for TV between 1950 and 1970, but almost all of Austen's works continued to be serialized in the 1980s and 1990s and on into the twenty-first century, whereas Scott's did not. Since 1995 big-screen movie versions dominate, and the pace of production seems to be increasing.

145. Saintsbury, *History of Nineteenth Century Literature* 128–30; he declared himself a Janeite ("Janite" in his spelling) in his introduction to *Pride and Prejudice* (1894), the edition that contained the first Hugh Thomson illustrations.

146. Southam (1987) 69.

147. Kramnick 34.

148. Southam (1987) 241.

149. The most recent study of contrasting images of Austen in the two world wars is Claudia Johnson 99–152.

150. For theories of remediation and their application to Scott, see both titles by Rigney.

Interlude

1. Bourdieu points out that success in "long-cycle production" depends on a few talent spotters and then "on the educational system, which alone is capable of offering, in time, a converted public"; and he describes a complete opposition between "bestsellers with no tomorrow" on one hand, and on the other "the classics, lasting bestsellers which owe to the education system their consecration, hence their extended and durable market" (*Rules of Art* 146–47).

2. Rigney, *Afterlives* 52, 18.

3. In a similar exercise, more tongue in cheek than this, W. H. Auden proposed a set of five criteria out of which a poet had to score "about three and half" to qualify as a "major" as opposed to a "minor" poet. A minor poet was defined as one "who wrote one good poem," but two of his five criteria for the "major" indicated a standard of quality, namely "must exhibit an unmistakable originality of vision and style" and "must be a master of verse technique" (*Nineteenth-Century British Minor Poets* 15–17).

4. Boswell 4:55.

Chapter 4. What About Merit?

1. The line is based on a sentence in a letter to his sister, Fanny: Keats, *Letters* 2:149.

2. Standard resources include MacGillivray, Matthews, Rollins, Colvin, and Ford.

3. Like Wordsworth—and very possibly under the direct influence of Wordsworth—Keats distinguished between transient popularity in one's lifetime and long-term fame. His letters from April 1818 onward vehemently express disdain for public opinion, "Mawkish Popularity," or "the poisonous suffrage of a public": Keats, *Letters* 1:267,

2:146. Three sonnets cited in the appendix, from the beginning, middle, and end of his short writing career, illustrate the persistence of the theme.

4. Keats, *Letters* 1:374, 394. Both these passages were published in Milnes's biography in 1848.

5. Lowell xvi.

6. In 1820 he wrote to Fanny Brawne about the two thoughts that preyed on his mind, one being his distress about losing her on account of his illness, and the other about his work: "'If I should die,' said I to myself, 'I have left no immortal work behind me—nothing to make my friends proud of my memory—but . . . if I had had time I would have made myself remember'd'": *Letters* 2:263. He then quotes *Lycidas* on "the last infirmity of noble minds," that is, the desire for fame.

7. Matthews usefully surveys thirty-three "representative anthologies containing nineteenth-century poetry" published in Britain between 1819 and 1859 and finds Keats notably underrepresented by modern standards: twenty-six ignored him altogether, and the two most generous had been compiled by Keats's personal friends Hazlitt and Hunt (10).

8. Keats's following in America was commented on as early as the 1840s and has been confirmed by modern scholarship—for instance, Matthews, MacGillivray, and Rollins.

9. Lowell published a dialogue about Keats in 1842, with a revised version in 1845 that is quoted in Matthews 300–301.

10. Milnes, *Life of Keats* 1:v.

11. Redding drew on Hunt for his memoir in the Galignani edition, as did Robert Chambers when he included Keats, Hunt, and Cornwall in two early educational, canonmaking series, *History of the English Language and Literature* (1836) and *Cyclopaedia of English Literature* (1844).

12. Elfenbein 172.

13. Ford 17–21; Matthews 25, 30–31, 264–72. Also Jump 36–37, 66, 73: the first reference is to Hallam's review, which placed Tennyson in the Cockney camp for his emphasis on beauty and sensation as opposed to the Wordsworthian emphasis on reflection, and the others are to Croker's deliberately wounding, heavily sarcastic review of Tennyson's *Poems* (1832) in the *Quarterly,* which is said to have deterred Tennyson from publishing again for a decade.

14. Ford 19.

15. Milnes himself was recruited for the 1854 edition, which also introduced illustrations by George Scharf; in 1872 and later, the introductory memoir was supplied by W. M. Rossetti and the illustrations were by Thomas Seccombe. The "Popular Poets" series appeared in twenty-one volumes in 1870–73, and Rossetti's introductions were collected as *Lives of Famous Poets* in 1878.

16. Boswell ingenuously describes the sort of literary fame by proxy that a biographer might enjoy: though his *Journal of a Tour to the Hebrides* had been attacked in the press, "yet it still sails unhurt along the stream of time" as an attendant on Johnson (*Life* 3:190).

17. Foucault, "What Is an Author?"

18. In the introduction to his edition of Gilchrist (1907) x.

19. Matthews 5.

20. For the conditions and conventions of literary biography in the period, see Altick, *Lives and Letters,* and Jackson, "What's Biography Got to Do with It?"

21. Though none of them would have wished them unwritten, later biographers and critics differed about the value of the poetical remains. Following hard on Milnes's heels, for instance, James Russell Lowell endorsed the image of Keats's career as progress toward the full expression of a great poetic gift, but he disparaged Milnes's judgment as an editor in publishing minor works that only showed "how ill his *biographee* could do any thing" (xxv).

22. He did not include the love letters to Fanny Brawne, which were not published until 1878, when they provoked a temporary backlash against Keats. Milnes did not name the woman Keats had been in love with; she had since married and was still living.

23. Keats, *Letters* 2:167. He was far from alone, however, in admiration of Chatterton's work: Southey edited Chatterton's works for the benefit of the family, and Coleridge contributed his "Monody on the Death of Chatterton" to that edition; Wordsworth's tribute to "the marvellous boy, / The sleepless soul that perished in his pride" (from "Resolution and Independence") has been routinely quoted in reference books and histories from that day to this. Milnes quotes these lines and draws the application to Keats early in his work (*Life of Keats* 1:12).

24. The story did not originate with Shelley, and he was not solely responsible for the way it spread, but under the circumstances it is probably just as well that he did not act on his idea of collecting Keats's literary remains and writing a critical biography of a fellow poet who, in his opinion, "in spite of his transcendant genius . . . never was nor ever will be a popular poet." Shelley, *Letters* 2:366.

25. Quoted in Matthews 252, 251, 255.

26. Redding in Keats et al., *Poetical Works* (1829) [v], vii.

27. Howitt (1847) 1:423, 431.

28. Chambers, *Cyclopaedia* 2:402, 404.

29. Milnes, *Life of Keats* 2:51–52. Milnes expressed the objection that he anticipated "against the originality of his genius" rather more strongly than his defense: "it is easy to refer almost every poem he wrote to some suggestion of style and manner derived from preceding writers." However, in Milnes's view, Keats copied the spirit and not just the form of his models and generally put in "some additional intuitive vigour" of his own. See also Milnes, *Life of Keats* 2:102–4.

30. Milnes, *Life of Keats* 1:3, 2:107–8.

31. Milnes, "Memoir" xl.

32. Lockhart used the Cockney label first in a review of Hunt's *The Story of Rimini* in the *Blackwood's* issue of October 1817; the second phrase is from his review of *Endymion* in August 1818—the latter reprinted in Matthews 101. Lockhart later tried to make amends in a review of Shelley's *Prometheus Unbound* in September 1820, saying that he had always thought Keats "might become a real poet of England" if he would only forswear Cockneyism and "the thin potations of Mr. Leigh Hunt." (quoted in Matthews 20).

33. The spirit of the group is captured in rich detail by Jeffrey Cox in *Poetry and Politics in the Cockney School.*

34. Matthews 91.

35. Keats, *Letters* 1:203, 237, 374, and 2:144.

36. As early as October 1817, when he was in the process of writing *Endymion,* Keats expressed anxiety about being claimed as a pupil by Hunt, whose writing Keats disparaged; in December 1818 he expressed revulsion over Hunt's manners and morals (Keats, *Letters* 1:169, 2:11). But the reviews that consistently identified Keats with the Hunt school must also have played a part in Keats's resolution to break free: it's in the letter of 9 October 1818, where he acknowledges that the critics were right and *Endymion* is "slipshod," that he declares his determination to write independently (*Letters* 1:374). So Duncan Wu is surely right to propose, in his essay "Keats and the 'Cockney School'"—paradoxically, given the amount of blame traditionally attached to the reviews—that Keats actually profited by the negative campaign against the Cockney School, insofar as it led him to reconsider his relationship to Hunt and the poetic style he stood for.

37. Saintsbury, *Short History* 672.

38. Milnes, *Life of Keats* 1:xvi.

39. Milnes, *Life of Keats* 1:20. According to annotations in Francis Palgrave's copy of 1848, which Palgrave was able to compare with the original manuscript, Milnes cut some passages to avoid offense to living persons, notably a long section about a falling out between Haydon and Hunt when Haydon asked for the return of a loan. This copy is in the British Library, shelf mark 10859.e.15.

40. Jack Stillinger catalogues some of his contradictory incarnations—aesthetic Keats, sensuous Keats, philosophical Keats, theoretical Keats, topographical Keats, theatrical Keats, intertextual Keats (with Spenserian, Huntian, Shakespearean, Miltonic, or Dantesque variations), political Keats, radical Keats, vulgar Keats, Cockney Keats, suburban Keats, effeminate Keats, macho Keats, and consumptive Keats—in *Romantic Complexity,* 101–2. Wootton also documents a "Multiple Keats" (2).

41. Matthews 367.

42. For an interesting educational spin-off, see *Poems of Wordsworth, Shelley, and Keats.*

43. MacGillivray 42, 46.

44. St. Clair maintains that the reputations of the eight poets widely recognized as the best of their generation around 1812 (as noted in chapter 2) "remained firm right through the century" (210, 414).

45. Ford 149.

46. Matthews 32; Wootton passim, esp. 44–51, 59–64.

47. Ford outlines the Pre-Raphaelite connections 93–169; see also Saintsbury, *History of Nineteenth Century Literature:* "It is to Keats that we must trace Tennyson, Rossetti, Mr. Swinburne, Mr. Morris" (89).

48. Quoted in Ford 172.

49. MacGillivray sections C and D; for broader context and analysis, see Wootton.

50. Quoted in Matthews 349, 352.

51. Lowell xxxi–xxxii, xxxv.

52. Matthews 357, 373, 383, in two essays from 1853 and 1860.

53. Quoted in Matthews 377, 380.

54. Arnold, "John Keats" 4:436.

55. Swinburne, "Keats," 22.

56. Rossetti xii.

57. Rossetti xxiii.

58. Colvin (1887) 1, ix.

59. Saintsbury, *History of Nineteenth Century Literature* 87, 90.

60. Saintsbury, *History of Nineteenth Century Literature* 89 and *Short History* 89.

61. Ironically, it may have been Hunt who first supplied this line of argument. The essay on Keats that he published in *Imagination and Fancy* in 1844 begins, "Keats was born a poet of the most poetical kind. All his feelings came to him through a poetical medium, or were speedily coloured by it." By way of illustration, he adds, "It might be said of him, that he never beheld an oak-tree without seeing the Dryad." *Imagination and Fancy,* 312.

62. Masson quoted in Matthews 373; Colvin (1887) 219; Arnold, "John Keats" 4:436.

63. The earliest use of the adjective "Keatsian" recorded in the *OED* is from a private letter written in 1845 ("the boneless Keatsian sort of poetry"). Two earlier, published uses (brought to my attention by Christopher Laxer) are also negative: a sneer at Cockneyism as "the Byronian, Keatsian, Barry Cornwallian school of poetry" in the *Gentleman's Magazine* in 1837 (161:632), and "the Keatsian whine" in the *Christian Remembrancer* in 1843 (6:261).

64. Lang and Lang 7.

65. Gittings 436; Saintsbury, *Short History* 673.

66. Ford 170.

67. Shelley, *Letters* 2:366.

68. Browning 1:722–24; http://www.george-sterling.org/poems.

69. Eliot 100.

70. Matthews 41–42, 55–63.

71. The dates are from Cox, *Poetry and Politics* 32.

72. Notable early statements appear in the original prefaces to *The Story of Rimini* (1816) and *Foliage* (1818); Cox ("Hunt's *Foliage*" 58–77) calls the latter a "Cockney Manifesto." The preface to Hunt's *Poetical Works* of 1832 and the essays in *Imagination and Fancy* (1844) provided important later opportunities for him to refine his views; these are included in Hunt *SW* 6:75–97, 4:1–124.

73. Keats, *Letters* 2:7.

74. These examples were cited in the *Quarterly* review of *Endymion:* Matthews 114.

75. Hunt, *Story of Rimini* xvi; Hunt *SW* 5:168.

76. Howitt 2:348.

77. Matthews 98. Hostile critics generally took the view that Hunt had let the lovers off lightly, given that they were not only adulterous (Francesca had been married by proxy, believing her husband would be like his brother Paolo) but also technically incestuous. Hunt revised the poem substantially for the 1844 edition, hoping to satisfy critics on the grounds of morality, but the critics were not mollified and the earlier version is better; Hunt himself restored it in 1855, then reverted to 1844 (or his heirs did)

for his final compilation in 1860. The current scholarly edition includes both versions: Hunt *SW* 5:161–206, 6:215–43.

78. *CBEL3* cols. 2159–2164 provides a convenient bibliographical summary of his anthologies and contributions to periodicals.

79. Hunt, *Lord Byron* 268.

80. *Bacchus in Tuscany* (1825) was a translation from Reni; *A Legend of Florence* (1840) was not a collection of poems but a verse play; and *The Palfrey* (1842) was based on Huon le Roi: only the last of these three is included in Hunt *SW.*

81. Moir's shrewd early assessment in the lectures of 1851 was that "the grand characteristic of Leigh Hunt's poetry is *word-painting;* and in this he is probably without a rival, save in the last and best productions of Keats, who contested, not vainly, with his master on that ground" (211).

82. Auden offers his opinion that "the chances are that, in the course of his lifetime, the major poet will write more bad poems than the minor" (*Nineteenth-Century British Minor Poets* 15).

83. J. H. Lobban, the editor of a rare school edition of Hunt's writings, *Selections in Prose and Verse* (1909), declared that only three of Hunt's poems were worth preserving (though he did in fact include a few more in his selection): "Mahmoud," "Abou ben Adhem," and "Jenny Kissed Me."

84. In Keats, *Complete Poems* 442. "Huntian" is not yet in the *OED*, but it was in use by the 1840s in a negative or, at best, neutral sense: Google Books searches reveal, for example, "Leigh Hunt-ian varnish" in 1845 and "Huntian flavor" in 1847.

85. Saintsbury, *History of Nineteenth Century Literature* 88. It is therefore remarkable that Saintsbury ranked Hunt highly as a technician: in his *History of English Prosody* he described Hunt as a second- or third-rate poet but a first-rate, innovative prosodist (3:94).

86. Hunt, *Story of Rimini* xii; *SW* 5:167. The revisions of 1844 were made partly to win over future audiences, for in the 1844 preface Hunt more boldly affirmed that the poem deserved to live "beyond the day" (quoted in Hunt *SW* 5:xxvii, 6:215).

87. "The 'Choice'" lines 119–21, 219, in Hunt *SW* 6:25, 28.

88. Hunt, *Foliage* 39. (Not reprinted in Hunt *SW.*)

89. Hunt *SW* 6:77.

90. Hunt *SW* 6:77.

91. Hunt *SW* 6:78–79.

92. Unattributed entry, "Hunt, James Henry Leigh," *Encyclopaedia Britannica* (1911).

93. Hunt, *Selections* x.

94. Hunt, *Poetical Works* xi–xii.

95. Coleridge, *Biographia* 1:6–7.

96. Haydon, Hunt, Clarke, and Severn all told versions of this story. Haydon's is the only eyewitness account, but Hunt published his version in 1828 and Milnes followed Hunt. See Walter Jackson Bate 265–66.

97. An excellent recent study of the literary as well as personal relationship between Keats and Cornwall, Richard Marggraf Turley's *Bright Stars,* comprehensively documents Cornwall's great popular success in the 1820s, drawing on reviews, memoirs, and

correspondence of the period. He also makes detailed comparisons of poems by Keats and Cornwall, whom he describes as a "stablemate" and treats as an illuminating foil or literary "double" of Keats (39, 6).

98. The extent and depth of their acquaintance has been a matter of debate among biographers and literary historians, as Marggraf Turley indicates (7–10) while making a subtler and more interesting case for their mutual effect on one another, poem by poem.

99. *Blackwood's* 5 (June 1819): 310, 315.

100. Quoted in Marggraf Turley 12.

101. Jameson, *Loves* 2:348.

102. Marggraf Turley 111.

103. The poem was published in the memorial volume of 1877, Procter *Autobiographical Fragment*, 117–18.

104. Marggraf Turley 29.

105. The notorious example of mistaken attribution is Cornwall's poem "A Voice," published first in Hunt's *Indicator* and then in the *Marcian Colonna* volume in 1820: Keats's Victorian editor Buxton Forman speculated that the lines had originally been part of *Endymion* and published them as Keats's; he was seconded by D. G. Rossetti (Armour 152–56).

106. J. R. de J. Jackson's *Bibliography of Romantic Poetry* (http://jacksonbibliography.library.utoronto.ca) shows that whereas the "dramatic poem" was well established, with plenty of examples from 1770 onward, along with occasional examples of the dramatic "piece" or "tale" or "romance" or "sketch," Cornwall introduced and for a time held a monopoly on the "dramatic scene." There is also just one "dramatic sermon."

107. *BLJ* 8:56; compare *BLJ* 9:83, where Byron compliments Cornwall directly, in the same vein but without the reservations. For his comic ottava rima poems without indecencies, Cornwall is introduced in *Don Juan* 11:59 under the name of "Euphues" as a promising writer who has been presented to the public "as a sort of *moral me*."

108. Marggraf Turley 40.

109. Procter, *Dramatic Scenes* [iii].

110. In a preface at the beginning of the volume, Cornwall indicated to readers that occasional deviations from ordinary language had been admitted for reasons of dramatic and historical propriety—by policy, then, and not inconsistently of out of ineptitude. "Let it be recollected, however, that the persons on whom these passages have been imposed, existed in ages more chivalrous than the present; and when men were apt to indulge in all the extravagances of romance" (*Dramatic Scenes* iii–iv). An example in the opening lines of "The Two Dreams" would be Shakespearean phrases such as "the piping winds of winter" and "cast out their sheeted fires."

111. Review of *Marcian Colonna, London Magazine* 2 (July–August 1820): 192. Reviewing *A Sicilian Story* in the *Edinburgh Review* in January 1820, the dreaded Jeffrey himself observed that while Cornwall was an able imitator of various writers from Shakespeare to Byron, the author he most closely resembled was Leigh Hunt—but he had "better taste, and better judgment" (146). In 1819 John Wilson of *Blackwood's* declared that Hunt and Keats had no right to consider themselves superior to Cornwall, since one of his dramatic scenes, "even the tamest . . . is worth both 'the two dead Eternities of the Cockneys'" (quoted in Marggraf Turley 33). St. Clair (574) quotes a letter

from the Blackwood papers indicating that at least the first positive *Blackwood's* review of Cornwall was solicited as a favor by William Jerdan, to whose review Cornwall was a regular contributor.

112. Wordsworth, who was inclined to be severe about other writers' work and who is known for his objections to sensationalism, the debasement of public taste, "sickly and stupid German Tragedies," and so forth, mildly remarked that although the action of *Mirandola* was rather improbable, it was rare to find "a good tragedy free from stale and mean contrivances and animated by new and suitable Characters. So that I am inclined to judge Cornwall gently, and sincerely rejoice in his success" (*LY* 3:44).

113. Armour 158–59 covers critical reception of the book in the year of publication.

114. Lee Erickson is one of many historians of publishing to make the point that "the industrialization of publishing quickly marginalized poetry in the 1820s" (13).

115. Both letters were first published by Armour: 250, 336.

116. Included in the posthumously published *Autobiographical Fragment* 126. In the introduction to *English Songs,* Cornwall (Procter) offers the new collection as "a farewell offering from a person who has met with much kindness from the Public, and is neither able—nor inclined—to forget it" (xvi), explaining that he has given up verse for "graver, and . . . more important occupations" [xxiv]. There were, however, further farewells.

117. The catalogue of musical settings of Romantic poetry by Gooch and Thatcher includes over two hundred entries for songs by Cornwall, by comparison with over three hundred for Keats, who did not deliberately write songs. Perhaps the most impressive items are two settings by Glinka for Russian versions by Pushkin, who admired Cornwall's work (entries 7329, 7340). The tallies are instructive: no entries for Hunt, just under two hundred for Coleridge, just over three hundred for Wordsworth, and roughly 1,300 each for Scott and Byron.

118. For recent analysis of the work of Adelaide Procter that highlights her relationship with her father and his poetry, see Gregory. The Brownings' personal friendship with the Procters is well documented but not their literary relationship, perhaps because it was taken for granted. Browning was never in any sense a disciple of Cornwall, but Cornwall's work was unquestionably an influence—an important one, I believe. (See, however, dismissive remarks by Jack: 64–65. The only widely acknowledged influence is the use of *Marcian Colonna* as a source for "Porphyria's Lover," for which see Browning, *Poems* [1991] 1:328–29, and Marggraf Turley 152–53.) There is more direct evidence of his influence on Elizabeth Barrett Browning (as she became): letters as early as 1829, long before she made his acquaintance, show her referring familiarly to lines by Cornwall (and assuming that her correspondent would recognize them) and adopting his experimental meters. For allusions by both Brownings, see Browning, *Correspondence* 2:223, 3:158, 3:322–23, 7:125. In a particularly interesting letter of 1844, Elizabeth offers a general assessment, writing that "I admire Barry Cornwall much" but also suggesting that the effect of his "genius" had been "to emasculate the poetry of the passing age" (*Correspondence* 9:13).

119. Procter, *Poetical Works* (1829) v.

120. Chambers (1844) 2:441. Surprisingly, the third edition of 1876 reduced the section devoted to Keats but increased Cornwall's, removing the critical remark just quoted and referring with approval (and more entries) to the *English Songs.*

121. Howitt (1847) 2:451.

122. Moir 231, 234.

123. There were, however, two American editions. This collection included a selection of previously unpublished poems and a preface signed with Procter's real name. The illustrators included Tenniel and Birket Foster.

124. Matthews 109.

125. Saintsbury, *Short History* 717.

126. I have come upon only one example of "Cornwallian" as an adjective—noted above in note 63.

127. Armour 125. Cornwall brushed aside proposals for a biography in his lifetime (Armour 308) but did begin putting together the reminiscences that were posthumously published under the title *An Autobiographical Fragment and Biographical Notes,* edited by Coventry Patmore at the request of the poet's widow.

128. Procter, *Dramatic Scenes* (1978) viii.

129. Procter, *English Songs* vi–vii.

130. Procter, *Dramatic Scenes* (1857) vi.

131. Emerson, v. His large and inclusive collection contains no Cornwall poems (though it does have many extracts from dramatic writers, plenty of Byron, and some Keats and Hunt): either Emerson didn't care for them or, more probably, they did not appear in the anthologies he was drawing on.

132. Procter, *A Sicilian Story* 138.

133. Procter, *Poetical Works* 18. (Headnote not included in the first edition, in *A Sicilian Story.*)

134. Procter, *Autobiographical Fragment* 18.

135. Though meter is only one of the elements that must combine to produce euphony, it is fundamental. Phelan's recent book on nineteenth-century (mainly Victorian) prosodic theory shows that there was active interest in the principles of it early in the century, focused on experiments by Southey and Coleridge. A key text in the subsequent theoretical debate was an essay of 1857 by Cornwall's friend Coventry Patmore. See Phelan 28–33.

136. Introduction to Procter, *Dramatic Scenes* viii.

137. Keats, *Letters* 2:323.

138. Some remarks by Wordsworth and Byron have been quoted already. Coleridge hailed Cornwall as a man of genius in a specially annotated copy of *Dramatic Scenes* (Coleridge, *Marginalia* 4:161–63). Shelley complained to Marianne Hunt that most of the poems in the *Sicilian Story* volume were "at once filthy and dull" (*Letters* 2:240); he seems to have been particularly exercised by the ottava rima imitations of Byron.

139. Tompkins 640. She continues, "*The Scarlet Letter* is a great novel in 1850, in 1876, in 1904, and in 1966, but each time it is great for different reasons."

140. Lang and Lang 331.

141. Harris, on canonicity, makes a similar point forcefully (120 n13): "The canonical status of a literary text—like the economic status of a rock musician, the reputation of a painter, the purity of the air and water, the desirability of consumer goods, or the majority positions on taxes, abortion, and nuclear power—can only be understood as the result of multiple causes."

142. Foucault, "What Is an Author?"; and Lake's remarks about the corrupting effect of readers' interest in the personalities of authors, in his prefatory biography of Thomas Moore, where he wishes people would stop "using the name of the poem and the poet indifferently" (xii).

143. Braudy also describes fame in general (not literary fame particularly) as consisting of four elements: "a person and an accomplishment, their immediate publicity, and what posterity has thought of them ever since" (15).

144. Cowen 19, where he has adopted the concept of "focal quality" from Thomas Schelling's game-theory analysis of conflict. He discusses the construction of merit in similar terms: "Just as fame increases in quantity with economic growth, so it develops in multiple and diverse directions, reflecting many different conceptions of merit" (112).

145. T. S. Eliot, sounding regretful, made a similar observation in 1933: "in estimating for ourselves the greatness of a poet we have to take into account also the *history* of his greatness. Wordsworth is an essential part of history; Landor only a magnificent by-product" (88).

Chapter 5. Raising the Unread

1. "Recovery project" has been used by extension to refer to other historical events and movements as well as to authors. For example, a *Times Literary Supplement* review of 15 June 2012 by James Phelan blames the peculiarities of a new three-volume *Encyclopedia of Romantic Literature* on "the results of 'recovery research' made possible by searchable electronic texts and databases," which introduce masses of undigested but "newly recovered" details (aquatic drama, say; Ann Batten Cristall) and avoid the familiar that is, by general agreement, tried and true and important (the Enlightenment; Goethe; Percy's *Reliques*).

2. See Fiedler and Baker.

3. In a letter of 1796, he congratulated his friend George Cumberland on a new book: "such works as yours Nature & Providence the Eternal Parents demand from their children how few produce them in such perfection how Nature smiles on them. how Providence rewards them. How all your Brethren say, The sound of his harp & his flute heard from his secret forest chears us to the labours of life. & we plow & reap forgetting our labour" (*CPP* 700).

4. *CPP* 537–38. This effort could be said to have backfired, given that it brought about the now notorious review in the Hunts' *Examiner* that described Blake as "an unfortunate lunatic, whose personal inoffensiveness secures him from confinement" (Bentley *CH* 66).

5. *CPP* 527.

6. *CPP* 730–31.

7. *CPP* 665.

8. *CPP* 729, 730, 701.

9. Bentley *BR* 56, 66, 473.

10. Gilchrist (1863) 1:2.

11. An exception on both counts—both conventionally published, and reviewed—is the single poem "To the Queen," the dedicatory poem in the edition of Blair's *The*

Grave (1808), of which a reviewer remarked, "Should he again essay to climb the Parnassian heights, his friends would do well to restrain his wanderings by the strait waistcoat. Whatever licence we may allow him as a painter, to tolerate him as a poet would be insufferable" (Bentley *CH* 131).

12. Blake's position on "posterity," as conveyed by Gilchrist, who had interviewed or corresponded with as many of Blake's acquaintances as he could, was that he "talked little about 'posterity,' an emptier vision far than those on which his abstracted gaze was oft-times fixed" (Gilchrist [1863] 1:245).

13. *CPP* 692.

14. Dorfman 53 n35.

15. Blake, "To the Queen" lines 7–8 (*CPP* 480).

16. *CPP* 95.

17. Bentley *BR* 573–603, 692–706. Aders's collection was dispersed through sales in the 1830s after business reverses.

18. Bentley *BR* 692; Gilchrist (1863) 1:338.

19. Bentley *CH* 91n. For the report of a similar party in 1861 involving Rossetti, Swinburne, Madox Brown, and Gilchrist, see Bentley *CH* 261.

20. Bentley *BR* 626.

21. Dorfman 52–53 n34 contains a useful list of nineteenth-century collectors.

22. Bentley *CH* 234–35; Robinson was still encouraging him to produce an edition in 1852 (Bentley *CH* 252). For Ruskin's mixed response to Blake—he drafted but ultimately suppressed a passage describing Blake and Turner as the two towering geniuses of the century for *The Seven Lamps of Architecture* (1849)—see Bentley *CH* index.

23. Gilchrist (1863) 1:2.

24. Paley, Eaves, and Bentley "Handlist."

25. Bentley *CH* 243 (the keeper was William Palmer, brother of Blake's disciple Samuel Palmer); Dorfman 59.

26. Bentley *CH* 262; Gilchrist (1863) 1:378.

27. The word "singular" is a favorite, e.g., Gilchrist (1863) 1:15. He does not use the terms "Pre-Raphaelite" or "Elizabethan" but compares Blake to Elizabethan poets and to artists of the Renaissance or earlier, using such terms as "Raphael or the Antique," "Gothic," or "old-fashioned" (1:98, 17, 201).

28. For Gilchrist's doubts, see Bentley *BR* 714.

29. Dorfman 48: "Wilkinson's edition and prefatory essay constitute the first effort to revive Blake and to do so specifically on the basis of his poetry." It was reprinted (under the imprint of the Swedenborgian New Church Press) in 1925.

30. Swinburne, *William Blake* 189.

31. Swinburne, *William Blake* 205, 204.

32. From an anonymous review in *Macmillan's Magazine* 11 (1865): 33.

33. Blake, *Songs of Innocence* vii.

34. Blake, *Songs of Innocence* ix.

35. Blake, *Poetical Works* lxxxvii, cxxl. Saintsbury adopted the same line and echoed some of Rossetti's words in his *History of Nineteenth Century Literature* 9–13.

36. Dorfman 170, 183, 187. On the other hand, it marks a high level of recognition in those sophisticated circles that Stopford Brooke, the queen's chaplain, delivered a

second series of lectures in 1873 on the topic of "theology in the English poets," covering Blake, Shelley, Keats, and Byron (the first series, which he published in 1874, included Cowper, Coleridge, Wordsworth, and Burns). See Brooke v.

37. Bentley *CH* 240, 242.

38. Bentley *CH* 246, 259.

39. Quaritch had been issuing facsimiles of some of the prophetic books in the 1880s; Yeats published an inexpensive one-volume selection in 1893 ("The Muses' Library" series) that included *Tiriel, The Marriage of Heaven and Hell,* and *Visions of the Daughters of Albion,* but only shorter poems from *Jerusalem* and *Milton.* For the claim that Blake was descended from an Irishman, see Blake, *Works* 1:2–4, and Blake, *Poems* xv; for the notoriety of the claim, Dorfman 196.

40. Dorfman 226n. Quaritch and Ellis had tried without success to form a society in the 1890s (Dorfman 194n). In 1949 Keynes was the prime mover in the establishment of a Blake Trust dedicated to the production of facsimiles of Blake's works (*ODNB*). In 1985 a new Blake Society was founded in London, especially devoted to Blake sites and specifically committed to lobbying for a grave marker and monument; see http://www.blakesociety.org.

41. Saintsbury, *History of English Prosody* 3:9 n2. (This volume, the third and last in a series, is tellingly subtitled "From Blake to Mr. Swinburne.") Saintsbury was born in 1845; thus he traces his infatuation with Blake to the pre-Gilchrist era. As proof of Blake's presence in the schools, see Elias; for the universities, see the chapter on Blake in a standard two-volume survey of 1912 by Oliver Elton, professor of English Literature in the University of Liverpool. Elton respectfully describes the whole of Blake's literary output, including *Vala* and *Jerusalem;* likens him to Byron and Shelley in the crusade for individual liberty ("in a manner more unaffected than Byron's, more masculine and humane than Shelley's and earlier than both"); points out affinities with Tolstoy and Nietzsche; praises Blake for having had "a deeper sense of beauty than any Englishman of his generation"; but concedes that "the lexicon of his symbolism is still to seek" (1:171, 149).

42. Referring primarily to Blake's visual art but implicitly also to his writing, Gilchrist (1863) said that in order to appreciate his style one had to be "almost *born* with a sympathy for it. He neither wrote nor drew for the many, hardly for work'y-day men at all, rather for children and angels; himself a 'divine child,' whose playthings were sun, moon, and stars, the heavens and the earth" (1:3).

43. Dorfman 168, 187.

44. Saintsbury, *History of English Prosody* 28–29.

45. Dorfman 228.

46. See, for example, Beer, esp. 206–20; Clark and Whittaker; Bertholf and Levitt.

47. Swinburne made the first notable public observations about the resemblance between Blake's works and Whitman's; Whitman was gratified but cagey (Ferguson-Wagstaffe). Swinburne was also, I believe, the first to develop the theme of rebellion, characterizing Blake as a "rebel" in his day, "born and baptized into the church of rebels" (3)—but he seems to have meant a maverick in art, religion, and morality, and to have been trying to avoid the word "dissenter."

48. The quotation is from Frye, *Fearful Symmetry* 5.

49. Coleridge, *Notebooks* 3:3975 (October 1810), cancellation omitted.

50. Blake, *Works* 1:235.

51. Frye, *Fearful Symmetry* 431.

52. Huxley title page. The original reading is "every thing would."

53. Huxley 14.

54. In New York in 1948, Ginsberg had a life-changing vision after reading *Songs of Innocence and Experience;* the incident—not drug-induced, according to Ginsberg—was made public in an interview with the *Paris Review* published in 1967 (Ostriker 111).

55. David King Dunaway, "Huxley, Aldous Leonard (1894–1963)," *ODNB.*

56. "Language Forum Hears Protests," *New York Times* 28 December 1968; "Radical Agitation among Scholars Grows," *New York Times* 29 December 1968; "Language Professors Oppose Draft Cooperation by Colleges," *New York Times* 30 December 1968; "Language Association Divided on Reform and Convention Site," *New York Times* 3 January 1969. Oddly, the writer of the first and fullest of the *New York Times* articles seemed to think that the "tigers" stood for the Chicago police, rather than seeing the quotation as an incitement to violence; perhaps that was a joke. See also Grumbach.

57. "Hazard Adams" is currently (in 2013) the name of a rock/Americana band based in Boston: it all coheres.

58. Bronowski (1944) 127, 9.

59. Bronowski (1944) 42, 133–34, 140, 142–43.

60. Bronowski (1944) 41. Yeats was the first to offer this line as a way of summing Blake up, though he used it to refer to Blake's attitude toward education rather than to revolutionary tendencies, remarking, "William Blake, as has been said, grew up with no formal schooling. He had early begun fulfilling his own aphorisms [*sic*], 'The tigers of wrath are wiser than the horses of instruction,' and living and thinking according to the imaginative impulse" ("Memoir," in Blake, *Works* 1:5, reiterated in the "Muses' Library" edition of Blake, *Poems* xiii). Yeats's friend Arthur Symons, a great promoter of the Aesthetic Movement, also invoked the tigers in his short study of Blake in 1907, in his case as part of a sustained comparison of Blake and Nietzsche, whose philosophies he thought had much in common: "Blake said, 'The tigers of wrath are wiser than the horses of instruction,' and it is partly in what they helped to destroy that Blake and Nietzsche are at one." (Symons 11).

61. Blake, *Selection* 9, 11–12.

62. Dorfman 193.

63. Precisely this phrase, summing up received wisdom, was used by Leslie Stephen in his article on Clare in 1887, in the original *Dictionary of National Biography.*

64. Storey 36, 37, 40. The writer was Clare's friend Octavius Gilchrist. Compare the wittier formulation of Edward Thomas a century later: "It is hard to imagine a combination with more possibilities for wretchedness than that of poet and agricultural labourer" (229).

65. "So called": Taylor had optimistically printed two thousand copies but left one thousand unbound; these unsold copies were bound with a new title page in 1823 (Storey 24).

66. Clare, *Village Minstrel* 1:vii–xxviii. Johnson had a pertinent comment on this phenomenon: "He spoke with much contempt of the notice taken of Woodhouse, the poetical shoemaker. He said, it [the poetry of Woodhouse] was all vanity and childishness: and that such subjects were, to those who patronised them, mere mirrours of their own superiority" (Boswell 2:127).

67. Modern editors are eloquent about the challenges of working with Clare's manuscripts. Bate sums up the "nightmare" of their situation in *John Clare* 309–10.

68. From Suarez and Zimmerman, who focus on "the *published* Clare" rather than on the unmediated Clare favored by Robinson and his colleagues in the current, controversial standard edition.

69. The quotation is from a poem published in the *London Magazine* in 1857 (quoted by Bate, *John Clare* 516).

70. Storey 247–67. See also Estermann entries 268–309.

71. Estermann includes a section on Clare's presence in anthologies from 1838 to 1983: it is useful, though not complete (no *Norton Anthology,* for instance, though Clare had a place in it from the start, in 1962). Only two entries (71–72) appear for the years before Clare's death. Some of his work had appeared, with an appreciative critical essay by Gifford, in *The Living Poets of England*—French publishers did not have to worry about copyright.

72. As Bate points out, however, Palgrave's preface names Clare and Tennyson as the two living poets whose work most deserved to survive (*John Clare* 548). The "second series" of *The Golden Treasury* (1897) did include three poems by Clare under Palgrave's idiosyncratic titles (for instance, "I Am" became "Lasciate ogni speranza").

73. Chilcott 195.

74. From letters to Thomas Pringle and to Henry Cary (quoted by Bate, *John Clare* 416, 418).

75. Compare, from a late fragment, "A charm is thrown oer Olney plains / By Cowper's rural muse / While sunshine gilds the river Ouse / In morning's meadow dews" (Clare, *Later Poems* 1:187).

76. Public statements of his admiration for Milton and Keats, respectively, include "To a Poet" ("Poet of mighty power!") in *The Rural Muse* and "To the Memory of John Keats," in *The Village Minstrel.* (In its first published form, in the *Sheffield Iris* in 1826, "To a Poet" was presented as supposed to have been addressed to Milton by Sir William Davenant, thus explaining its imposing style.) Besides memorial sonnets, Clare wrote confidently about Bloomfield as an "English Theocritus" in letters sent shortly after Bloomfield's death, describing him as having "dyed ripe for immortality" and with the assurance that "time will bring its own reward to the 'Farmers Boy'": Clare, *Selected Letters* 93.

77. Published in Cherry 89. Clare's sketches sometimes involved tombstones: a journal of 1824–25 includes one with the names Chatterton, Keats, and Bloomfield on it (*Catalogue* entry 100).

78. I cite the version published by Cherry in 1873 (Cherry 308–14), which reprints the magazine article.

79. Bate, *John Clare* 536–37.

80. Martin 295–96.

81. For reviews, see Storey 15–16, 289–91. Cherry, like all of Clare's editors, struggled with the texts. Many of the manuscripts, he observed, began well but deteriorated; others seemed to be nonsense. Of those he selected for publication, "scarcely one was found in a state in which it could be submitted to the public without more or less of revision and correction" (Cherry vii).

82. In the "Conclusion" to his biography, for instance, instead of wallowing in feeling Cherry offers reasoned reflection: "It may be that the publicity acquired by the Northamptonshire Peasant Poet simply brings to the surface the average life of the English agricultural labourer in the person of one who was more than usually sensitive to suffering" (130).

83. Saintsbury, *Short History* 717. He goes on to comment sarcastically that Clare, "like Christopher Smart, never acquired his full poetic power till madness seized him—as it had also seized Bloomfield, though with no such compensation"; even then, only a few of his works "are poems."

84. Symons 37–51, 288–92.

85. Symons, "Introduction," quoted in Storey 303. He recycled much of this introductory essay for his comments on Clare in *The Romantic Movement in Poetry*.

86. Clare (1920) 39.

87. Clare (1920) 45.

88. The next revision, 1969, does not use the word "major" but includes Clare along with Rogers, Wordsworth, Coleridge, Southey, Campbell, Moore, Hogg, Byron, Shelley, Keats, and Hood in the section for "Early nineteenth-century poetry" and significantly *not* in the section following, "Minor Poetry 1800–1835," which includes Bloomfield. Blake and Crabbe are covered in the earlier volume, 1660–1800.

89. Robinson and Powell xxv.

90. Blunden 38, 51.

91. The first to take on the challenge were J. W. Tibble and Anne Tibble, joint authors of the first scholarly biography (1932, published by Cobden-Sanderson, which had also produced Blunden's edition). In that book they declared that it had been "a new Clare that the enthusiasm and research of Mr. Edmund Blunden and Mr. Alan Porter revealed to the literary world of 1920, one hundred years after his first rise to fame" (12). In 1980, on the occasion of her edition of Clare's *Journal* and other prose works, Anne Tibble made the same point more forcefully: "As Monckton Milnes rescued Keats in 1848, as Sir Geoffrey Keynes did much the same for Blake in the 1950s, so Edmund Blunden rescued Clare in 1920" (Clare [1980], 28). The Tibbles went on to produce major editions of Clare's poems, of his letters, and of his prose. They were followed by the similarly multitasking Mark Storey, Eric Robinson, Jonathan Bate, and John Goodridge.

92. John Barrell's outstanding study of 1972 challenged current interpretations both of Clare and of the impact of enclosure generally, without putting an end to either controversy.

93. Examples include *The Wood Is Sweet* (1966), a selection of Clare's poems intended for children, with an introduction by Blunden and illustrations by John O'Connor; a series of private-press pamphlets with drawings by Rigby Graham (1959–76), and several titles published by Oxford UP (1964–70), edited by Robinson and Summerfield, with woodcuts by David Gentleman.

94. Major anthologies such as the *Norton Anthology of English Literature* (1962), David Perkins's *English Romantic Writers* (1967), and *The Penguin Book of English Romantic Verse* (1968) included some poems but not many: Clare's presence was minimal. In Ian Jack's *Oxford History of English Literature* (1963) and comparable histories, he is likewise noted but in a decidedly minor role.

95. The John Clare Trust operates within a national system of "educational and environmental" trusts of this kind.

96. In his recent biography of Clare (545–59), Jonathan Bate attributes Clare's rising literary stature to the support of fellow writers, describing him as a "poet's poet" and surveying modern British and North American poets influenced by Clare. I see them as part of a broader and looser coalition of supporters. Institutions are better at ensuring the kind of publicity that Lang and Lang describe as "the essential element not only in the survival of a reputation but in its 'rediscovery,' should it be lost" (315).

97. Bate, *Song of the Earth* 283.

98. St. Clair 219. Taking a longer view, B. C. Bloomfield finds that the London firm of Milner "sold 65,500 copies of Bloomfield between 1835 and 1895, and he was fifth in popularity, as measured by sales, during that period" for that company, when first to fourth were Burns, Byron, Milton, and Pope. Bloomfield suggests that his own calculation of more than 283,000 for sales of copies of *The Farmer's Boy* in all formats during the nineteenth century is probably an underestimate. B. C. Bloomfield, "Publication of *The Farmer's Boy*" 92–3.

99. Robert Bloomfield Society website (http://robertbloomfieldsociety.blogspot .co.uk), accessed 22 June 2013. Bridget Keegan points out that while "ecocritical approaches" had led to growing interest in the poetry of Clare, the poet to whom Clare acknowledged his indebtedness "has yet to receive adequate attention from most critics, environmental or otherwise" (10); and yet Bloomfield "deserves to be read as a key poet in the annals of environmental literature" (30).

100. Practically all biographical accounts of Bloomfield can be traced to the successive prefaces to his works, where his editor Capel Lofft, his brother George, and Bloomfield himself provided the drip feed of details and anecdotes that readers of the day required. I am treating such uncontested details as common knowledge, in the absence of a single authoritative biography. They will be found echoed in such standard reference works as the *ODNB* and Lawson.

101. Bloomfield, *Wild Flowers* viii. "Elegant" is the adjective used by the publishers in a set of advertisements for their other publications, included in a large-paper copy of the first edition of *The Farmer's Boy* in the British Library, shelf mark 11641.g.6.

102. There appear to have been three issues of the first edition at different prices, one expensive quarto on fine paper, one less expensive quarto, and one octavo. See B. C. Bloomfield, "Provisional Checklist" 290.

103. St. Clair 582. St. Clair estimates the overall number of copies of titles by Bloomfield produced during the Romantic period at 100,000, equal to Byron, only slightly behind Scott, and far ahead of any other poet (217).

104. On stereotyping, see St. Clair 182–85, 515. There were plans to stereotype Bloomfield's works as early as 1804, when John Taylor, who was then an assistant in the firm, reported in a letter that "'The Farmer's Boy' is now preparing to be transmit-

ted down to posterity with the greatest honours a Book can possibly receive—It will be the *second* work *stereotyped* in England" (quoted in Chilcott 10). But the stereotyped edition, which gave Bloomfield an opportunity to revise the text according to his own standards rather than to those of Capel Lofft, did not appear until 1809.

105. Quoted in Lawson 54.

106. Coleridge told a correspondent in September 1800, "What W. and I have seen of the Farmer's Boy (only a few short extracts) pleased us very much" (*Letters* 1:623). In his essay, later a small book, on "uneducated" poets, Southey deliberately excluded Bloomfield because his poems could hold their own without special support (John Jones 163). For Byron's satirical remarks on Bloomfield and his brother Nathaniel, who was also a poet, in *English Bards and Scotch Reviewers* and "Hints from Horace," see his *Complete Poetical Works* 1:253–54, 314, 441–42.

107. Keegan discusses a "School of Bloomfield" (31–36), to which might be added W. H. Ireland's *The Fisher Boy . . . during the Four Seasons of the Year,* produced by Bloomfield's own publishers in 1806.

108. Coleridge, *Letters* 2:716.

109. Bloomfield, *Poems* 1:38–39.

110. Bloomfield, *The Banks of Wye* 132; *May Day with the Muses* 35, 46. Bruce Graver offers an interesting analysis of the early illustrations to *The Farmer's Boy* as evidence of the tussle between the publishers and the editor, Capel Lofft, for control of Bloomfield's public image.

111. Then called *A Ploughing Scene* and *Harvest Field, Reapers, Gleaners* (now *The Wheatfield*), these are both today in the National Gallery of Australia: http://nga.gov.au /exhibition/constable/Detail.cfm?IRN=143235, http://nga.gov.au/exhibition/constable/ Detail.cfm?IRN=145041.

112. For example, Birket Foster's *Rhymes and Roundelayes* (1857) and *Summer Scenes* (1870); Willmott's *Poets of the Nineteenth Century* (1857) and *English Sacred Poetry* (1862); and *Passages from Modern English Poets Illustrated by the Junior Etching Club* (1862)—all handsome volumes with embossed and gilt covers. A good American example is a Boston edition of *The Farmer's Boy* (1877) in a "vest-pocket series" designed to be "convenient for short journeys," which also included Emerson, Longfellow, Whittier, Gray, Browning, Milton, Pope, Thomson, "and others of equal fame."

113. Hopkins 300–301.

114. Bloomfield, *Poems* 1:i–ii.

115. Bloomfield (1800 3rd ed.) 114.

116. The Paris editor charged with abridging the biography for the "Sketch of the Author's Life" in 1804 grumbled openly about Lofft's long-winded prefatory matter and commented that "Bloomfield deserves a better Biographer, a more discerning critic, and a less partial friend" (18).

117. But they were admired in the best circles. In a letter intended to be made public, the Earl of Buchan described Bloomfield's recitation of his tales "accompanied with a symphony of broken expression and of frequent tears," by which his hearers were "highly pleased"; and the poet Samuel Rogers told Lofft, who told Bloomfield, that "The Miller's Maid" was a favorite with—of all people—the great but dissolute Whig

statesman Charles James Fox. See Bloomfield, *Letters,* 11 March 1806 (no. 179) and 24 October 1801 (no. 59).

118. Bloomfield, *Poems* 1:xxxvii–xxxviii.

119. Bloomfield, *Letters,* 2 October 1804, to Capel Lofft (no. 142).

120. Clare, *Selected Letters* 93–95.

121. These supplementary documents are not present in all copies, but they appear, for example, in two British Library copies, shelf marks 1467.c.45 and Bloomfield 164. The latter, still unopened in 2012, also contains a single printed leaf made up for presentation copies to (presumably) subscribers as "a token of gratitude" from the family, together with "Mr. Bloomfield's Autograph, taken from a letter to the Editor . . . which will appear in the Memoir and Correspondence."

122. His comments are judicious: "His want of vigour and passion, joined to the humility of his themes, is perhaps the cause of his now being little read; but he is one of the most characteristic and faithful of our national poets" (Chambers, *Cyclopaedia* 2:284).

123. Hazlitt 5:95–96, in "Lectures on the English Poets." His general view was that in contemporary society natural genius could not overcome the lack of a good education.

124. Saintsbury, *Short History* 717.

125. Saintsbury, "Lesser Poets" 132.

126. Lucas 2:40.

127. Blunden 120.

128. John Goodridge, a longtime champion of both Clare and Bloomfield, has always insisted on the centrality of aesthetic criteria. Remarks in a recent book reveal some signs of division in the ranks of supporters, when he declares that Clare resists "easy absorption into the tourist, leisure, ecological, educational and literary industries that have recently begun to lay serious claim to his legacy." Goodridge, *John Clare and Community* 4.

129. Peter T. Murphy has some thoughtful observations about the difficulty of making a case for once-popular Romantic poets and the kind of shift of standards that might bring them back into favor, in *Poetry as Occupation and Art in Britain;* his paper on Samuel Rogers suggests that Rogers is unreadable today because his poetry (like Bloomfield's) is unproblematic and "preempts the work of the critic" ("Climbing Parnassus" 51).

130. Harris 119 n5.

131. The quoted phrase is from Murphy, "Climbing Parnassus" 41.

Conclusion

1. *CPP* 613–14.

2. It's by W. S. Baring-Gould: "A goddess capricious is Fame. / You may strive to make noted your name. / But she either neglects you / Or coolly selects you / For laurels distinct from your aim."

3. Analogously, sociologists investigating the reputations of artist-engravers in the nineteenth and early twentieth centuries conclude that durable reputations in that field depended upon four factors: "the artist's own efforts, in his or her lifetime, to protect or project his/her own reputation"; "the availability of others who, after the artist's death, have a stake" in maintaining that reputation; "linkages to artistic, literary, or political

networks" with access to archives; and "symbolic associations with emerging cultural or political identities" (Lang and Lang 318–19). And Malcolm Gladwell, writing about renown, asserts that "no one . . . ever makes it alone"; that "it is not the brightest who succeed"; and that success is not a matter of merit or genius but is "grounded in a web of advantages and inheritances, some deserved, some not, some earned, some just plain lucky" (115, 167, 285).

4. Byron, *Don Juan*, in *Complete Poetical Works* 1:104.

5. Cowen 12.

6. Kermode defines a modern classic as "a book that is read a long time after it was written" because it contains "a plurality of significances" and thus lends itself to shifting uses and interpretations (118, 133).

7. Darnton, "What Is the History of Books?" (first published 1983). One proof of the usefulness of his model is the way in which other historians tinker with it or offer alternative models, for example Adams and Barker.

8. Frye, *Anatomy* 18.

9. *CPP* 44.

10. Coleridge, *Letters* 1:279.

11. For instance, Harris; Klancher; Stillinger, *Multiple Authorship;* Levy; and Clark and Goellnicht.

12. Miller 255.

13. Pierre Bayard tolerantly observes that talking about books from second-hand knowledge is unavoidable; see *How to Talk about Books You Haven't Read.*

14. The exhibition ran from 9 August 2010 to 9 April 2012. The associated website remains at http://www.tate.org.uk/whats-on/tate-britain/display/romantics.

15. With the rise of social media, the concept of popularity has been receiving much astute analysis. A recent long article by Adam Sternbergh in the *New York Times Magazine,* for instance, comments on both how the meaning of popularity depends on the standards of measurement applied, and on the way that modern-day popularity is no longer an indicator of uniform public taste but of its fragmentation.

16. Auden made the same point more eloquently: "In matters of artistic taste and judgment, we are all the children of our age, but we should not and need not be its slaves. Each of us must be loyal to his own taste, though always ready to enlarge it" (*Nineteenth-Century British Minor Poets* 17).

17. Lootens 9.

18. This is not to say that there have not been calls for reform before—that's what the canon wars were about—nor that they did not bring about revision of curricula, nor that there have not been reformist literary histories. The champions of individual "minor" writers, struggling to bring their discoveries to a broader audience, usually complain, with reason, that the system works against them. Many years ago, the eminent Romanticist Marilyn Butler, in her inaugural lecture at Cambridge, argued for the inclusion in the curriculum of underappreciated writers such as Southey, whom she described collectively as an "awkward squad" who did not easily fit the standard Romantic mould (22). But the changes have been relatively superficial in that they have added authors and created alternative canons without disturbing the immortals or the idea of the immortals.

19. Beard 163.

Bibliography

Adams, John, and Benjamin Rush. *The Spur of Fame: Dialogues of John Adams and Benjamin Rush, 1805–1813.* San Marino: Huntington Library, 1966. Print.

Adams, Thomas R., and Nicolas Barker. "A New Model for the History of the Book." *A Potencie of Life: Books in Society.* Ed. Nicolas Barker. London: British Library, 1993. 5–43. Print.

Ainger, Alfred. *Crabbe.* English Men of Letters Series. London: Macmillan, 1903. Print.

Altick, Richard D. *The English Common Reader: A Social History of the Mass Reading Public, 1800–1900.* Chicago: U of Chicago P, 1957. Print.

———. *Lives and Letters: The History of Literary Biography in England and America.* New York: Knopf, 1966. Print.

———. *Paintings from Books: Art and Literature in Britain, 1760–1900.* Columbus: Ohio State UP, 1985. Print.

Anderson, Chris. *The Long Tail: How Endless Choice Is Creating Unlimited Demand.* London: Random House Business Books, 2006. Print.

Anon. Rev. of *Marcian Colonna. London Magazine* 2 (July–August 1820): 81–83, 183–92. Print.

Armour, Richard Willard. *Barry Cornwall: A Biography of Bryan Waller Procter with a Selected Collection of Hitherto Unpublished Letters.* Boston: Meador, 1935. Print.

Arnold, Matthew. "John Keats." *The English Poets: Selections with Critical Introductions by Various Writers and a General Introduction by Matthew Arnold.* Ed. Thomas Humphrey Ward. London: Macmillan, 1880. 4:427–37. Print.

———. "Wordsworth." *Complete Prose Works.* Ed. R. H. Super. Ann Arbor: U of Michigan P, 1960–77. 9:36–55. Print.

Atherton, Carol. *Defining Literary Criticism: Scholarship, Authority and the Possession of Literary Knowledge, 1880–2002*. Basingstoke: Palgrave Macmillan, 2005. Print.

Auden, W. H., ed. *Nineteenth-Century British Minor Poets*. New York: Delacorte P, 1966. Print.

Auden, W. H., and Louis MacNeice. *Letters from Iceland*. London: Faber and Faber, 1937. Print.

Austen, Jane. *Letters*. Ed. Deirdre Le Faye. 4th ed. Oxford: Oxford UP, 2011. Print.

———. *Pride and Prejudice*. London: Partridge, [1896]. Print.

Austen-Leigh, J. E. *A Memoir of Jane Austen; and Other Family Recollections*. Ed. Kathryn Sutherland. Oxford: Oxford UP, 2002. Print.

Bacon, Francis. *The Essays or Counsels Civil and Moral*. Ed. Brian Vickers. Oxford: Oxford UP, 1999. Print.

Baldick, Chris. *The Social Mission of English Criticism, 1848–1932*. Oxford: Clarendon P, 1983. Print.

Ballantyne's Novelist's Library. 10 vols. London: Hurst, Robinson, and Co., 1821–24. Print.

Barbauld, Anna Letitia. "The Origin and Progress of Novel-Writing." *British Novelists*. London: Rivington, 1810. 1:1–62. Print.

Bareham, Terence, and Simon Gatrell. *A Bibliography of George Crabbe*. Folkestone: Archon Books, 1978. Print.

Barrell, John. *The Idea of Landscape and the Sense of Place, 1730–1840: An Approach to the Poetry of John Clare*. Cambridge: Cambridge UP, 1972. Print.

Bate, Jonathan. *John Clare: A Biography*. New York: Farrar, Straus and Giroux, 2003. Print.

———. *The Song of the Earth*. London: Picador, 2000. Print.

Bate, Walter Jackson. *John Keats*. Cambridge, MA: Belknap P, 1963. Print.

Bauer, N. S. *William Wordsworth: A Reference Guide to British Criticism, 1793–1899*. Boston: G. K. Hall, 1978. Print.

Bautz, Annika. *The Reception of Jane Austen and Walter Scott: A Comparative Longitudinal Study*. London: Continuum, 2007. Print.

Bayard, Pierre. *How to Talk about Books You Haven't Read*. Trans. Jeffrey Mehlman. New York: Bloomsbury, 2007. Print.

Beard, Mary. *The Invention of Jane Harrison*. Cambridge, MA: Harvard UP, 2000. Print.

Beer, John. *William Blake: A Literary Life*. London: Palgrave Macmillan, 2005. Print.

Bennett, Andrew. *Romantic Poets and the Culture of Posterity*. Cambridge: Cambridge UP, 1999. Print.

Bentley, G. E., Jr., ed. *Blake Records*. 2nd ed. New Haven: Yale UP, 2004. Print.

———, ed. *William Blake: The Critical Heritage*. London: Routledge & Kegan Paul, 1975. Print.

Bertholf, Robert J., and Annette S. Levitt, eds. *William Blake and the Moderns*. Albany: State U of New York P, 1982. Print.

Blake, William. *Complete Poetry and Prose*. Ed. David V. Erdman. Rev. ed. Berkeley: U of California P, 2008. Print.

———. *The Letters of William Blake, Together with a Life by Frederick Tatham.* London: Methuen, 1906. Print.

———. *Lyrical Poems.* Ed. John Sampson. Oxford: Clarendon P, 1905. Print.

———. *Poems.* Ed. W. B. Yeats. The Muses' Library. London: Lawrence and Bullen, 1893. Print.

———. *Poetical Works . . . Lyrical and Miscellaneous.* Ed. William Michael Rossetti. London: George Bell, 1874. Print.

———. *Selection of Poems and Letters.* Ed. J. Bronowski. Harmondsworth: Penguin, 1958. Print.

———. *Songs of Innocence and Experience, with Other Poems.* London: Basil Montagu Pickering, 1866. Print.

———. *The Works of William Blake: Poetic, Symbolic, and Critical.* Ed. Edwin John Ellis and William Butler Yeats. 3 vols. London: Bernard Quaritch, 1893. Print.

Bloomfield, B. C. "The Publication of *The Farmer's Boy* by Robert Bloomfield." *The Library* 6th series 15.2 (June 1993): 75–94. Print.

———. "Robert Bloomfield: A Provisional Checklist of His Published Work, with Some Bibliographical Notes and a Record of Later Editions." *Robert Bloomfield: Lyric, Class, and the Romantic Canon.* Ed. Simon White, John Goodridge, and Bridget Keegan. Lewisburg: Bucknell UP, 2006. 288–301. Print.

Bloomfield, Robert. *The Banks of Wye; a Poem.* London: Vernor and Hood, 1811. Print.

———. *The Farmer's Boy; a Rural Poem.* London: Vernor and Hood, 1800. [1st ed.] Print.

———. *The Farmer's Boy; a Rural Poem.* London: Vernor and Hood, 1800. [3rd ed.] Print.

———. *The Farmer's Boy; a Rural Poem.* 7th ed. London: Vernor and Hood, 1803. British Library shelf mark C.61.a.3. Print.

———. *The Farmer's Boy . . . Illustrated.* Boston: James R. Osgood, 1877. Print.

———. *The Farmer's Boy. With Notes for Teachers and Scholars.* London: T. J. Allman, [1875]. Print.

———. *The Letters of Robert Bloomfield and His Circle.* Ed. Tim Fulford and Lynda Pratt. Romantic Circles Electronic Edition. 2009, rev. 2012. Online.

———. *May Day with the Muses.* London: Baldwin, Cradock, and Joy, 1822. Print.

———. *The Poems of Robert Bloomfield.* Stereotype ed. 2 vols. London: Vernor, Hood, and Sharpe; and Longman, Hurst, Rees and Orme, 1809. Print.

———. *Poetical Works . . . Illustrated by Birket Foster.* London: Routledge, 1857. Print.

———. *The Remains of Robert Bloomfield, Author of The Farmer's Boy, Rural Tales, &c.* Ed. Joseph Weston. 2 vols. London: Baldwin, Cradock, and Joy, 1824. Print.

———. *Wild Flowers; or, Pastoral and Local Poetry.* London: Vernor and Hood, 1806. Print.

Blunden, Edmund. *Nature in English Literature.* Lectures in Literature Series. London: Hogarth P, 1929. Print.

Bode, Christopher. "Re-Definitions of the Canon of English Romantic Poetry in Recent Anthologies." *Anthologies of British Poetry: Critical Perspectives from Literary and Cultural Studies.* Ed. Barbara Korte, Ralf Schneider, and Stefanie Lethbridge. Amsterdam: Rodopi, 2000. 265–88. Print.

Bolton, H. F. *Scott Dramatized.* London: Mansell, 1992. Print.

Boswell, James. *Boswell's Life of Johnson, Including Boswell's Journal of a Tour to the Hebrides and Johnson's Diary of a Journey into North Wales*. Ed. G. B. Hill. Rev. L. F. Powell. 6 vols. Oxford: Clarendon P, 1934–50. Print.

Bourdieu, Pierre. *Distinction: A Social Critique of the Judgement of Taste*. Trans. Richard Nice. London: Routledge & Kegan Paul, 1984. Print.

———. *The Rules of Art: Genesis and Structure of the Literary Field*. Trans. Susan Emanuel. Stanford: Stanford UP, 1995. Print.

Brabourne, Edward Lord. "The Novels." *Letters of Jane Austen*. Ed. Edward, Lord Brabourne. 2 vols. London: Bentley, 1884. 1:81–111. Print.

Braudy, Leo. *The Frenzy of Renown: Fame and Its History*. New York: Oxford UP, 1986. Print.

British Poets of the Nineteenth Century. Ed. J. W. Lake. Paris: Baudry, 1828. Print.

Bronowski, J. *William Blake, 1757–1827: A Man without a Mask*. London: Secker & Warburg, 1943 [1944]. Print.

———. *William Blake, 1757–1827: A Man without a Mask*. Rev. ed. Harmondsworth: Penguin, 1954. Print.

Brooke, Rev. Stopford A. *Theology in the English Poets. Cowper—Coleridge—Wordsworth and Burns*. London: Harry S. King, 1874. Print.

Browning, Elizabeth Barrett and Robert. *The Brownings' Correspondence*. Ed. Philip Kelley and Ronald Hudson. 19 vols. to date. Winfield, KS: Wedgestone P, 1984– . Print.

Browning, Robert. *Poems*. Ed. John Pettigrew. 2 vols. New Haven: Yale UP, 1981. Print.

———. *Poems*. Ed. zJohn Woolford and Daniel Karlin. 4 vols. London: Longman, 1991. Print.

Brunton, Alexander. "Memoir of her Life, including some Extracts from her Correspondence." In Mary Brunton, *Emmeline, with Some Other Pieces*. Facs. of the 1819 ed. Introduction by Caroline Franklin. London: Routledge/Thoemmes P, 1992. ix–xcvii. Print.

Brunton, Mary. *Discipline: A Novel*. 3 vols. Edinburgh: Manners and Miller, 1814. Print.

———. *Self-Control: A Novel*. 2nd ed. 3 vols. Edinburgh: Manners and Miller, 1811. Print.

Butler, Marilyn. *Literature as a Heritage, or Reading Other Ways*. Cambridge: Cambridge UP, 1987. Print.

Byron, George Gordon, Lord. *Complete Miscellaneous Prose*. Ed. Andrew Nicholson. Oxford: Clarendon P, 1991. Print.

———. *Complete Poetical Works*. Ed. Jerome J. McGann. 7 vols. Oxford: Clarendon P, 1980–93. Print.

———. *Letters and Journals*. Ed. L. Marchand. 12 vols. Cambridge, MA: Belknap P, 1974–93. Print.

Carpenter, Humphrey. *Benjamin Britten: A Biography*. London: Faber and Faber, 1992. Print.

Catalogue of the Centenary Exhibition of Portraits, Books, Manuscripts, Letters and Other Things belonging to or connected with John Clare, the Northamptonshire Peasant Poet, who was born at Helpston, 13th July, 1792. Peterborough: Peterborough Natural History, Scientific, and Archaeological Society, 1893. Print.

Catalogue of the Genuine Library, Prints, and Books of Prints, of an Illustrious Person-age, Lately Deceased. Which will be sold by auction, on Wednesday the 9th of June, 1819, and the following days, by Mr. Christie, in his rooms in Pall-Mall . . . . London, 1819. Print.

Chambers, Robert, ed. *Cyclopaedia of English Literature.* 2 vols. Edinburgh: Chambers, 1844. Print.

———. *History of the English Language and Literature.* Edinburgh: Chambers, 1836. Print.

———. *Illustrations of the Author of Waverley.* Edinburgh: Chambers, 1822. Print.

Chartier, Roger. "Popular Appropriations: The Readers and Their Books." *Forms and Meanings.* Philadelphia: U of Pennsylvania P, 1995. 83–97. Print.

Cherry, J. L. *The Life and Remains of John Clare, the "Northamptonshire Peasant Poet."* London: Frederick Warne; Northampton: J. Taylor, 1873. Print.

Chilcott, Tim. *A Publisher and His Circle: The Life and Work of John Taylor, Keats's Publisher.* London: Routledge & Kegan Paul, 1972. Print.

Cicero. *De finibus bonorum et malorum.* Trans. H. Rackham. Loeb Classical Library. London: Heinemann, 1914. Print.

———. *De re publica; De legibus.* Trans. Clinton Walker Keynes. Loeb Classical Library. Cambridge, MA: Harvard UP, 1977. Print.

———. *Tusculan Disputations.* Trans. J. E. King. Loeb Classical Library. London: Heinemann, 1927. Print.

Clare, John. *The Early Poems of John Clare, 1837–1864.* Ed. Eric Robinson and David Powell. 2 vols. Oxford: Clarendon P, 1989. Print.

———. *The Journal; Essays; The Journey from Essex.* Ed. Anne Tibble. Manchester: Carcanet New P, 1980. Print.

———. *The Later Poems of John Clare, 1837–1864.* Ed. Eric Robinson and David Powell. 2 vols. Oxford: Clarendon P, 1984. Print.

———. *Poems.* Ed. Arthur Symons. London: Henry Frowde, 1908. Print.

———. *Poems Chiefly from Manuscript.* Ed. Edmund Blunden and Alan Porter. London: Cobden-Sanderson, 1920. Print.

———. *Poems Descriptive of Rural Life and Scenery.* London: Taylor and Hessey, 1820. Print.

———. *The Poems of John Clare's Madness.* Ed. Geoffrey Grigson. London: Routledge & Kegan Paul, 1984. Print.

———. *Poems of the Middle Period, 1822–1837.* Ed. Eric Robinson and David Powell. 5 vols. Oxford: Clarendon P, 1996, 1998, 2003. Print.

———. *Selected Letters.* Ed. Mark Storey. Oxford: Clarendon P, 1988. Print.

———. *Sketches in the Life of John Clare, Written by Himself.* Ed. Edmund Blunden. London: Cobden-Sanderson, 1931. Print.

———. *The Village Minstrel, and Other Poems.* London: Taylor and Hessey, 1821. Print.

Clark, David L., and Donald C. Goellnicht, eds. *New Romanticisms: Theory and Critical Practice.* Toronto: U of Toronto P, 1994. Print.

Clark, Steve, and Jason Whittaker, eds. *Blake, Modernity and Popular Culture.* Houndmills: Palgrave Macmillan, 2007. Print.

Colbert, Benjamin. "Popular Romanticism? Publishing, Readership and the Making of Literary History." *Authorship, Commerce and the Public: Scenes of Writing, 1750–1850*. Ed. E. J. Clery, Caroline Franklin, and Peter Garside. New York: Palgrave Macmillan, 2002. 153–68. Print.

Coleridge, Samuel Taylor. *Biographia Literaria*. Ed. James Engell and W. Jackson Bate. 2 vols. Bollingen Series 75: *The Collected Works of Samuel Taylor Coleridge*. London: Routledge & Kegan Paul, 1983. Print.

———. *Collected Letters*. Ed. Earl Leslie Griggs. 6 vols. Oxford: Clarendon P, 1956–71. Print.

———. *Marginalia*. Ed. George Whalley and H. J. Jackson. 6 vols. Bollingen Series 75: *The Collected Works of Samuel Taylor Coleridge*. Princeton: Princeton UP, 1980–2001. Print.

———. *Notebooks*. Ed. Kathleen Coburn, Merton Christensen, and Anthony John Harding. 5 vols. Princeton: Princeton UP, 1957–2002. Print.

———. *Shorter Works and Fragments*. Ed. H. J. Jackson and J. R. de J. Jackson. 2 vols. Bollingen Series 75: *The Collected Works of Samuel Taylor Coleridge*. Princeton: Princeton UP, 1995. Print.

Colvin, Sidney. *John Keats: His Life and Poetry, His Friends, Critics, and After-Fame*. London: Macmillan, 1917. Print.

———. *Keats*. English Men of Letters Series. Ed. John Morley. London: Macmillan, 1887. Print.

Corman, Brian. *Women Novelists before Jane Austen*. Toronto: U of Toronto P, 2008. Print.

Cornwall, Barry. *See* Procter, Bryan Waller.

Cowen, Tyler. *What Price Fame?* Cambridge, MA: Harvard UP, 2000. Print.

Cowley, Abraham. "The Motto." *Poems*. London: Humphrey Moseley, 1656. 1–2. Print.

Cox, Jeffrey. "Leigh Hunt's *Foliage*: A Cockney Manifesto." *Leigh Hunt: Life, Poetics, Politics*. Ed. Nicholas Roe. London: Routledge, 2003. 58–77. Print.

———. *Poetry and Politics in the Cockney School: Keats, Shelley, Hunt and Their Circle*. Cambridge: Cambridge UP, 1998. Print.

Crabbe, George. *Beauties of the Rev. George Crabbe. With a Biographical Sketch*. London: Effingham Wilson, 1832. Print.

———. *Complete Poetical Works*. Ed. Norma Dalrymple-Champneys and Arthur Pollard. 3 vols. Oxford: Clarendon P, 1988. Print.

———. *The Poetical Works . . . with His Letters and Journals, and His Life, by His Son*. 8 vols. London: Murray, 1834. Print.

———. *Selected Letters and Journals*. Ed. Thomas C. Faulkner. Oxford: Clarendon P, 1985. Print.

Crabbe, George (Junior). *The Life of George Crabbe*. Introduction by Edmund Blunden. London: Cresset, 1947. Print.

Cunningham, Allan. *Biographical and Critical History of the British Literature of the Last Fifty Years*. Paris: Baudry's Foreign Library, 1834. Print.

———. *Lives of the Most Eminent British Painters, Sculptors, and Architects*. London: Murray, 1829. Print.

Curtis, Jared, ed. *The Fenwick Notes of William Wordsworth*. London: Bristol Classical P, 1993. Print.

Darnton, Robert. "What Is the History of Books?" *The Kiss of Lamourette: Reflections in Cultural History.* New York: Norton, 1990. 107–35. Print.

De Waal, Edmund. *The Hare with Amber Eyes.* New York: Farrar, Straus and Giroux, 2010. Print.

Dibdin, T. F. *Library Companion.* 2 vols. London: Harding et al., 1824. Print.

Dorfman, Deborah. *Blake in the Nineteenth Century: His Reputation as a Poet from Gilchrist to Yeats.* New Haven: Yale UP, 1969. Print.

Elfenbein, Andrew. *Byron and the Victorians.* Cambridge: Cambridge UP, 1995. Print.

Elias, Edith L., ed. *English Literature in Prose and Verse: From Cowper to Landor.* London: G. G. Harrap, 1916. Print.

Eliot, T. S. "Shelley and Keats." *The Use of Poetry and the Use of Criticism: Studies in the Relation of Criticism to Poetry in England.* London: Faber and Faber, 1933. Print.

Elton, Oliver. *A Survey of English Literature, 1780–1830.* 2nd impression. 2 vols. London: Edward Arnold, 1920. Print.

Elwood, Anne Katharine. *Memoirs of the Literary Ladies of England, from the Commencement of the Last Century.* 2 vols. London: Henry Colburn, 1843. Print.

Emerson, R. W., ed. *Parnassus.* Boston: Osgood, 1875. Print.

Erickson, Lee. *The Economy of Literary Form: English Literature and the Industrialization of Publishing, 1800–1850.* Baltimore: Johns Hopkins UP, 1996. Print.

Estermann, Barbara. *John Clare: An Annotated Primary and Secondary Bibliography.* New York: Garland, 1985. Print.

Evans, John, ed. *The Parnassian Garland.* London: Cundee, 1807. Print.

Ezell, Margaret. *Social Authorship and the Advent of Print.* Baltimore: Johns Hopkins UP, 1999. Print.

Fergus, Jan. *Jane Austen: A Literary Life.* London: Macmillan, 1991. Print.

Ferguson, Frances. "Wordsworth and the Meaning of Taste." *The Cambridge Companion to Wordsworth.* Ed Stephen Gill. Cambridge: Cambridge UP, 2003. 90–107. Print.

Ferguson-Wagstaffe, Sarah. "'Points of Contact': Blake and Whitman." *Sullen Fires across the Atlantic: Essays in Transatlantic Romanticism.* Ed. Lance Newman. Romantic Circles Praxis Series. November 2006. Online.

Ferris, Ina. *The Achievement of Literary Authority: Gender, History, and the Waverley Novels.* Ithaca: Cornell UP, 1991. Print.

Fiedler, Leslie A., and Houston A. Baker, Jr., eds. *English Literature: Opening Up the Canon: Selected Papers from the English Institute, 1979.* Baltimore: Johns Hopkins UP, 1981. Print.

Fields, James T. *Old Acquaintance: Barry Cornwall and Some of His Friends.* Boston: Osgood, 1876. Facs. repr. Folcroft, PA: Folcroft Library Editions, 1974. Print.

Ford, George H. *Keats and the Victorians.* New Haven: Yale UP, 1945. Print.

Foster, Myles Birket. *Rhymes and Roundelayes.* London: David Bogue, 1857. Print.

———. *Summer Scenes.* London: Bell and Daldy, 1870. Print.

Foucault, Michel. "What Is an Author?" *Partisan Review* 42.4 (1975): 603–14. Print.

Franta, Andrew. *Romanticism and the Rise of the Mass Public.* Cambridge: Cambridge UP, 2007. Print.

Frow, John. *Cultural Studies and Cultural Value.* Oxford: Clarendon P, 1995. Print.

Frye, Northrop. *The Anatomy of Criticism: Four Essays.* Princeton: Princeton UP, 1957. Print.

———. *Fearful Symmetry: A Study of William Blake.* Princeton: Princeton UP, 1947. Print.

Ganz, Charles. *Souvenir of the Crabbe Celebration and Catalogue of the Exhibits, at Aldeburgh, Suffolk, 16th to 18th September, 1905.* N.p., n.d. Print.

Garside, Peter. "The English Novel in the Romantic Era: Consolidation and Dispersal." Peter Garside and Rainer Schöwerling. *The English Novel, 1770–1829: A Bibliographical Survey of Prose Fiction Published in the British Isles.* 2 vols. Oxford: Oxford UP, 2000. 2:15–103. Print.

———. "Politics and the Novel, 1780–1830." *The Romantic Period.* Ed. David Pirie. Harmondsworth: Penguin, 1994. 49–86. Print.

Garside, Peter, and Rainer Schöwerling. *The English Novel, 1770–1829: A Bibliographical Survey of Prose Fiction Published in the British Isles.* 2 vols. Oxford: Oxford UP, 2000. Print.

George Crabbe . . . Bi-Centenary Celebrations. Aldeburgh: Festival Committee, 1954. Print.

Gilchrist, Alexander. *The Life of William Blake.* Ed. W. Graham Robertson. London: John Lane, 1907. Print.

———. *The Life of William Blake, "Pictor Ignotus": With Selections from His Poems and Other Writings.* 2 vols. London: Macmillan, 1863. Print.

Gill, Stephen. *William Wordsworth: A Life.* Oxford: Clarendon P, 1989. Print.

———. *Wordsworth and the Victorians.* Oxford: Clarendon P, 1998. Print.

Gilson, David. *A Bibliography of Jane Austen.* Winchester: St. Paul's Bibliographies; New Castle, DE: Oak Knoll P, 1997. Print.

Gittings, Robert. *John Keats.* London: Heinemann, 1968. Print.

Gladwell, Malcolm. *Outliers: The Story of Success.* New York: Little, Brown, 2008. Print.

Godwin, William. "Of Posthumous Fame." *The Enquirer.* [1797.] Facs. repr. New York: Augustus M. Kelley, 1965. 283–97. Print.

Gooch, Bryan N. S., and David S. Thatcher. *Musical Settings of British Romantic Literature: A Catalogue.* 2 vols. New York: Garland, 1982. Print.

Goodridge, John, ed. *The Independent Spirit: John Clare and the Self-Taught Tradition.* Helpston: John Clare Society, 1994. Print.

———. *John Clare and Community.* Cambridge: Cambridge UP, 2013. Online.

Graver, Bruce. "Illustrating *The Farmer's Boy.*" *Robert Bloomfield: Lyric, Class, and the Romantic Canon.* Ed. Simon White, John Goodridge, and Bridget Keegan. Lewisburg: Bucknell UP, 2006. 49–69. Print.

Gregory, Gill. *The Life and Work of Adelaide Procter: Poetry, Feminism and Fathers.* Aldershot: Ashgate, 1998. Print.

Groom, Nick, ed. *Thomas Chatterton and Romantic Culture.* Basingstoke: Macmillan, 1999. Print.

Grumbach, Doris. "Tigers of Wrath at the MLA." *Commonweal* (31 January 1969): 564–66. Online.

Guillory, John. *Cultural Capital: The Problem of Literary Canon Formation.* Chicago: U of Chicago P, 1993. Print.

Hanley, Keith. *An Annotated Critical Bibliography of William Wordsworth.* London: Harvester Wheatsheaf / Prentice Hall, 1995. Print.

Harman, Claire. *Jane's Fame: How Jane Austen Conquered the World.* New York: Henry Holt, 2009.

Harper, George McLean. *William Wordsworth: His Life, Works, and Influence.* 2 vols. London: Murray, 1910, 1916. Print.

Harris, Wendell V. "Canonicity." *Publications of the Modern Language Association of America* 106.1 (1991): 110–21. Online.

Hayden, John O., ed. *Scott: The Critical Heritage.* London: Routledge, 1970. Print.

Haynes, Christine. "Reassessing 'Genius' in Studies of Authorship: The State of the Discipline." *Book History* 8.1 (2005): 287–320.

Hazlitt, William. *Complete Works.* Ed. P. P. Howe. 21 vols. London: Dent, 1930. Print.

Healey, George Harris. *The Cornell Wordsworth Collection: A Catalogue of Books and Manuscripts Presented to the University by Mr. Victor Emanuel.* Ithaca: Cornell UP, 1957. Print.

Hebron, Stephen. *William Wordsworth.* London: British Library, 2000. Print.

Herford, C. II. *The Age of Wordsworth.* London: George Bell, 1897. Print.

Higgins, David. *Romantic Genius and the Literary Magazines: Biography, Celebrity, Politics.* London: Routledge, 2005. Print.

Hillhouse, James T. *The Waverley Novels and Their Critics.* Minneapolis: U of Minnesota P, 1936. Print.

Hine, Joseph, ed. *Selections from the Poems of William Wordsworth, Esq. Chiefly for the Use of Schools and Young Persons.* London: Moxon, 1831. Print.

Hood, E. P. *The Literature of Labour: Illustrious Instances of the Education of Poetry in Poverty.* London: Partridge and Oakley, 1851. Print.

Hopkins, Kenneth. *English Poetry: A Short History.* London: Phoenix House, 1962. Print.

Horace. *Odes and Epodes.* Ed. and trans. Niall Rudd. Loeb Classical Library. Cambridge, MA: Harvard UP, 2004. Print.

———. *Satires, Epistles, and Ars Poetica.* Trans. H. Rushton Fairclough. Loeb Classical Library. London: Heinemann, 1926. Print.

Howitt, William. *Homes and Haunts of the Most Eminent British Poets.* 2 vols. London: Bentley, 1847. Print.

Hume, David. *Essays Moral, Political, and Literary.* Ed. T. H. Green and T. H. Grose. 2 vols. London: Longmans, Green, 1889. Print.

Hunt, Leigh. *Foliage.* London: Ollier, 1818. Print.

———. *Imagination and Fancy.* 2nd ed. London: Smith, Elder, 1845. Print.

———. *Lord Byron and Some of His Contemporaries; with Recollections of the Author's Life, and of His Visit to Italy.* London: Colburn, 1828. Print.

———. *Poetical Works.* Ed. H. S. Milford. London: Oxford UP, 1923. Print.

———. *Selected Writings.* General eds. Robert Morrison and Michael Eberle-Sinatra. 6 vols. London: Pickering & Chatto, 2003. Print.

———. *Selections in Prose and Verse.* Ed. J. H. Lobban. English Literature for Schools Series. Cambridge: Cambridge UP, 1909. Print.

———. *The Story of Rimini.* London: Murray, 1816. Print.

Hunter, John. *A Tribute to the Manes of Unfortunate Poets: in Four Cantos. With Other Poems on Various Subjects.* London: T. Cadell, Jr., and W. Davies, 1798. Print.

Huxley, Aldous. *The Doors of Perception.* New York: Harper, 1954. Print.

Jack, Ian. *Browning's Major Poetry.* Oxford: Clarendon P, 1973. Print.

Jackson, H. J. "A General Theory of Fame in the *Lives of the Poets.*" *Age of Johnson* 19 (2009): 9–20. Print.

———. "What's Biography Got to Do with It?" *European Romantic Review* 22.3 (June 2011): 357–72. Print.

Jackson, J. R. de J. *Jackson Bibliography of Romantic Poetry.* Online.

Jacobs, Edward. "Eighteenth-Century British Circulating Libraries and Cultural Book History." *Book History* 6 (2003): 1–22. Print.

James, Elizabeth, ed. *Macmillan: A Publishing Tradition.* Basingstoke: Palgrave, 2002. Print.

Jameson, Anna. *Loves of the Poets.* 2 vols. London: Colburn, 1829. Print.

Jeffrey, Francis. Rev. of *A Sicilian Story. Edinburgh Review* 33 (January 1820): 144–55. Online.

Johnson, Claudia. *Jane Austen's Cults and Cultures.* Chicago: U of Chicago P, 2012. Print.

Johnson, Edgar. *Sir Walter Scott: The Great Unknown.* 2 vols. London: Hamish Hamilton, 1970. Print.

Johnson, Samuel. *Johnson on Shakespeare.* Ed. Arthur Sherbo. Yale Edition of the Works of Samuel Johnson, vols. 7–8. New Haven: Yale UP, 1968. Print.

———. *Letters.* Ed. Bruce Redford. 5 vols. Princeton: Princeton UP, 1994. Print.

———. *The Lives of the Poets.* Ed. Roger Lonsdale. 4 vols. Oxford: Clarendon P, 2006. Print.

———. "Morin." *Works.* Ed. Arthur Murphy. 12 vols. London: J. Johnson et al., 1806. 12:160–67. Print.

———. *The Rambler.* Ed. W. J. Bate and Albrecht B. Strauss. Yale Edition of the Works of Samuel Johnson, vols. 3–5. New Haven: Yale UP, 1969. Print.

Johnston, Kenneth R., and Gene W. Ruoff, eds. *The Age of William Wordsworth.* New Brunswick: Rutgers UP, 1987. Print.

Jones, Ann H. *Ideas and Innovations: Best Sellers of Jane Austen's Age.* New York: AMS Press, 1986. Print.

Jones, John. *Attempts in Verse . . . with . . . an Introductory Essay on the Uneducated Poets, by Robert Southey, Poet Laureate.* London: Murray, 1831. Print.

Jones, Mark, and Karl Kroeber. *Wordsworth Scholarship and Criticism, 1973–1984: An Annotated Bibliography, with Selected Criticism, 1809–1972.* New York: Garland, 1985. Print.

Jump, John D., ed. *Lord Alfred Tennyson: The Critical Heritage.* London: Routledge, 2000. Print.

Justice, Donald Rodney. *Oblivion: On Writers and Writing.* Ashland: Story Line P, 1998. Print.

Juvenal. *Juvenal and Persius.* Trans. Susanna Morton Braund. Loeb Classical Library. Cambridge, MA: Harvard UP, 2004. Print.

Keats, John. *Poems.* Ed. Jack Stillinger. Cambridge, MA: Belknap P, 1978. Print.

————. *Letters.* Ed. Hyder Edward Rollins. 2 vols. Cambridge, MA: Harvard UP, 1958. Print.

————. *The Poetical Works of Coleridge, Shelley, and Keats.* Paris: Galignani, 1829. Print.

————. *The Poetical Works of John Keats. With a Life.* Boston: Little, Brown, 1854. Print.

Keddie, Henrietta. *See* Tytler, Sarah.

Keegan, Bridget. *British Labouring-Class Nature Poetry, 1730–1837.* New York: Palgrave Macmillan, 2008. Print.

Kelly, Stuart. *Scott-land: The Man Who Invented a Nation.* Edinburgh: Polygon, 2010. Print.

Kermode, Frank. *The Classic: Literary Images of Permanence and Change.* 2nd ed. Cambridge, MA: Harvard UP, 1983. Print.

Kett, Henry. *Elements of General Knowledge.* 2 vols. Oxford: Oxford UP for the author, 1802. Print.

Klancher, Jon P. *The Making of English Reading Audiences, 1790–1832.* Madison: U of Wisconsin P, 1987. Print.

Kramnick, Jonathan Brody. *Making the English Canon: Print-Capitalism and the Cultural Past, 1700–1770.* Rev. ed. New York: Cambridge UP, 2008. Print.

Lake, J. W. "A Biographical and Critical Sketch." *The Poetical Works of Thomas Moore, Complete in One Volume.* Paris: Galignani, 1827. i–xxii. Print.

————. "Memoir." *The Poetical Works of Walter Scott.* Paris: Galignani, 1827. vii–xxxiii. Print.

Lang, Gladys Engel, and Kurt Lang. *Etched in Memory: The Building and Survival of Artistic Reputation.* Chapel Hill: U of North Carolina P, 1990. Print.

Lawson, Jonathan. *Robert Bloomfield.* Boston: Twayne Publishers, 1980. Print.

Legouis, Émile. *The Early Life of William Wordsworth, 1770–1798: A Study of "The Prelude."* Trans. J. W. Matthews. London: Dent, 1921. Print.

Levy, Michelle. *Family Authorship and Romantic Print Culture.* Basingstoke: Palgrave Macmillan, 2008. Print.

Liu, Alan, ed. *William Wordsworth.* Illustrations by James Muir. New York: Sterling, 2003. Print.

The Living Poets of England: Specimens of the Living British Poets, with Biographical and Critical Notices and an Essay on English Poetry. Paris: Baudry et al., 1827. Print.

Lockhart, J. G. *The Life of Sir Walter Scott, Bart. Abridged . . . with a Prefatory Letter by James R. Hope Scott, Q.C.* Edinburgh: Adam and Charles Black, 1871. Print.

Lootens, Tricia. *Lost Saints: Silence, Gender, and Victorian Literary Canonization.* Charlottesville: U of Virginia P, 1996. Print.

Lovejoy, Arthur O. *Reflections on Human Nature.* Baltimore: Johns Hopkins UP, 1961. Print.

Lowell, James Russell. "Life." *The Poetical Works of John Keats. With a Life.* Boston: Little, Brown, 1854. vii–xxxvi. Print.

Lucas, E. V. *The Life of Charles Lamb.* 2nd ed. 2 vols. London: Methuen, 1905. Print.

Lynch, Deidre, ed. *Janeites: Austen's Disciples and Devotees.* Princeton: Princeton UP, 2000. Print.

MacCarthy, Fiona. *Byron: Life and Legend.* London: Faber and Faber, 2003. Print.

Macdonald, Gina, and Andrew F. Macdonald, eds. *Jane Austen on Screen.* Cambridge: Cambridge UP, 2003. Print.

MacGillivray, J. R. *Keats: A Bibliography and Reference Guide, with an Essay on Keats' Reputation.* Toronto: U of Toronto P, 1949. Print.

Madden, Lionel, ed. *Robert Southey: The Critical Heritage.* London: Routledge & Kegan Paul, 1972. Print.

Marcus Aurelius Antoninus. *The Communings with Himself of Marcus Aurelius Antoninus, Emperor of Rome, Together with His Speeches and Sayings.* Trans. C. R. Haines. Loeb Classical Library. London: Heinemann, 1916. Print.

Marggraf Turley, Richard. *Bright Stars: John Keats, Barry Cornwall and Romantic Literary Culture.* Liverpool: Liverpool UP, 2009. Print.

Martial. *Epigrams.* Ed. and trans. D. R. Shackleton Bailey. Loeb Classical Library. 3 vols. Cambridge, MA: Harvard UP, 1993. Print.

Martin, Frederick. *The Life of John Clare.* London: Macmillan, 1865. Print.

Martin, Philip W. *Byron: A Poet before His Public.* Cambridge: Cambridge UP, 1982. Print.

Matthews, G. M., ed. *Keats: The Critical Heritage.* London: Routledge & Kegan Paul, 1971. Print.

Maxwell, Richard. "Inundations of Time: A Definition of Scott's Originality." *ELH [English Literary History]* 68.2 (2001): 419–68. Online.

McGuffie, H. L. *Samuel Johnson in the British Press, 1749–1784: A Chronological Checklist.* New York: Garland, 1976. Print.

Miller, Lucasta. *The Brontë Myth.* London: Jonathan Cape, 2001. Print.

Millgate, Jane. "For Lucre or for Fame: Lockhart's Versions of the Reception of *Marmion.*" *Review of English Studies* 44 (1993): 187–203. Print.

———. *Scott's Last Edition: A Study in Publishing History.* Edinburgh: Edinburgh UP, 1987. Print.

Millgate, Michael. *Testamentary Acts: Browning, Tennyson, James, Hardy.* Oxford: Clarendon P, 1992. Print.

———. *Thomas Hardy: A Biography Revisited.* Oxford: Oxford UP, 2004. Print.

Milnes, Richard Monckton, ed. *Life, Letters, and Literary Remains, of John Keats.* 2 vols. London: Moxon, 1848. Print.

———. "Memoir." *The Poetical Works of John Keats.* London: Moxon, 1854. i–xl. Print.

Mitchell, Jerome. *More Scott Operas.* Lanham, MD: UP of America, 1996. Print.

———. *The Walter Scott Operas.* Tuscaloosa: U of Alabama P, 1977. Print.

Moir, David Macbeth. *Sketches of the Poetical Literature of the Past Half Century, in Six Lectures Delivered at the Edinburgh Philosophical Association.* Edinburgh: Blackwood, 1851. Print.

Mole, Tom. *Byron's Romantic Celebrity: Industrial Culture and the Hermeneutic of Intimacy.* Houndmills: Palgrave Macmillan, 2007. Print.

———, ed. *Romanticism and Celebrity Culture, 1750–1850.* Cambridge: Cambridge UP, 2009. Print.

Montaigne, Michel de. "De la gloire." *Oeuvres complètes*. Paris: Gallimard, 1962. 601–14. Print.

Moore, Thomas. *Letters*. Ed. Wilfred S. Dowden. Oxford: Clarendon P, 1964.

Murphy, Peter T. "Climbing Parnassus, and Falling Off." *At the Limits of Romanticism*. Ed. Mary A. Favret and Nicola J. Watson. Bloomington: Indiana UP, 1994. 40–58. Print.

———. *Poetry as Occupation and Art in Britain, 1760–1830*. Cambridge: Cambridge UP, 1993. Print.

Murray, Lindley, ed. *The Introduction to the English Reader*. York: Longman, 1801. Print.

Mylius, William Frederick, ed. *The Poetical Class-Book: or, Reading Lessons for Every Day in the Year, Selected from the Most Popular English Poets, Ancient and Modern. For the Use of Schools*. London: M. J. Godwin, 1810. Print.

Newlyn, Lucy. *Reading, Writing, and Romanticism: The Anxiety of Reception*. Oxford: Oxford UP, 2000. Print.

Noon, Patrick. *Crossing the Channel: British and French Painting in the Age of Romanticism*. New York: Metropolitan Museum of Art, 2003. Print.

Ostriker, Alicia. "Blake, Ginsberg, Madness, and the Prophet as Shaman." *William Blake and the Moderns*. Ed. Robert J. Bertholf and Annette S. Levitt. Albany: State U of New York P, 1982. 111–31. Print.

Ovid. *Metamorphoses*. Trans. Frank Justus Miller. 2nd ed. rev. G. P. Goold. Loeb Classical Library. 2 vols. Cambridge, MA: Harvard UP, 1984. Print.

———. *Tristia; Ex Ponto*. Trans. Arthur Leslie Wheeler. Loeb Classical Library. London: Heinemann, 1915. Print.

Owen, W. J. B. *Wordsworth as Critic*. Toronto: U of Toronto P, 1971. Print.

Pace, Joel. "Wordsworth and America: Reception and Reform." *The Cambridge Companion to Wordsworth*. Ed Stephen Gill. Cambridge: Cambridge UP, 2003. 230–45. Print.

Paley, Morton D., Morris Eaves, and G. E. Bentley, Jr. "Handlist of Works by William Blake in the Department of Prints and Drawings in the British Museum." *Blake Newsletter* 20 (1972): 224–58. Print.

Palgrave, Francis Turner, ed. *The Golden Treasury of the Best Songs and Lyrical Poems in the English Language*. Cambridge: Macmillan, 1861. Print.

———, ed. *The Golden Treasury of the Best Songs and Lyrical Poems in the English Language*. Facs. ed. with a preface by Andrew Motion. Basingstoke: Palgrave Macmillan, 2000. Print.

———, ed. *The Golden Treasury. Second Series*. London: Macmillan, 1897. Print.

Passages from Modern English Poets Illustrated by the Junior Etching Club. London: Day, 1862. Print.

Peek, Katherine Mary. *Wordsworth in England: Studies in the History of His Fame*. 1943. New York: Octagon Books, 1969. Print.

Perkins, David. "The Construction of 'The Romantic Movement' as a Literary Classification." *Nineteenth-Century Literature* 45.2 (1990): 129–43. Print.

Phaedrus. "Fables." *Babrius and Phaedrus*. Ed. and trans. Ben Edward Perry. Loeb Classical Library. Cambridge, MA: Harvard UP, 1965. Print.

Phelan, Joseph. *The Music of Verse: Metrical Experiment in Nineteenth-Century Poetry.* Houndmills, Basingstoke: Palgrave Macmillan, 2012. Print.

Pittock, Murray, ed. *The Reception of Sir Walter Scott in Europe.* London: Continuum, 2006. Print.

Pliny the Younger. *Letters; Panegyricus.* Trans. Betty Radice. 2 vols. Loeb Classical Library. Cambridge, MA: Harvard UP, 1969. Print.

Poems of Wordsworth, Shelley, and Keats Selected from "The Golden Treasury" of Francis Turner Palgrave. Edited for the Use of Schools by W. P. Trent and John Erskine. Boston, New York, Chicago, and London: Ginn, 1914. Print.

Pollard, Arthur, ed. *Crabbe: The Critical Heritage.* London: Routledge & Kegan Paul, 1972. Print.

Potkay, Adam. *The Passion for Happiness: Samuel Johnson and David Hume.* Ithaca: Cornell UP, 2000. Print.

Pratt, Lynda. "Family Misfortunes? The Posthumous Editing of Robert Southey." *Robert Southey and the Contexts of English Romanticism.* Aldershot: Ashgate, 2006. 219–38. Print.

Procter, Bryan Waller. *An Autobiographical Fragment and Biographical Notes, with Personal Sketches of Contemporaries, Unpublished Lyrics, and Letters of Literary Friends.* Ed. Coventry Patmore. London: George Bell, 1877. Print.

———. *Dramatic Scenes. With Other Poems, Now First Printed.* London: Chapman and Hall, 1857. Print.

———. *"Dramatic Scenes" and "Marcian Colonna."* Introduction by Donald H. Reiman. New York: Garland, 1978. Print.

———. *English Songs, and Other Small Poems.* London: Moxon, 1832. Print.

———. *The Poetical Works of Milman, Bowles, Wilson, and Barry Cornwall. Complete in One Volume.* Paris: Galignani, 1829. Print.

———. *A Sicilian Story, with Diego de Montilla, and Other Poems.* London: Ollier, 1820. Print.

Reid, Ian. *Wordsworth and the Formation of English Studies.* Aldershot: Ashgate, 2004. Print.

Ricks, Christopher, ed. *The Oxford Book of English Verse.* Oxford: Oxford UP, 1999. Print.

Riede, David G. *Oracles and Hierophants: Constructions of Romantic Authority.* Ithaca: Cornell UP, 1991. Print.

Rigney, Ann. *The Afterlives of Walter Scott: Memory on the Move.* Oxford: Oxford UP, 2012. Print.

———. *Imperfect Histories: The Elusive Past and the Legacy of Romantic Historicism.* Ithaca: Cornell UP, 2001. Print.

Robertson, Eric. *Wordsworthshire: An Introduction to a Poet's Country.* London: Chatto & Windus, 1911. Print.

Robinson, Eric, and David Powell. "Introduction." *John Clare.* The Oxford Authors. Oxford: Oxford UP, 1984. xv–xxvi. Print.

Roe, Nicholas. *Fiery Heart: The First Life of Leigh Hunt.* London: Pimlico, 2005. Print.

———. *John Keats and the Culture of Dissent.* Oxford: Clarendon P, 1997. Print.

———, ed. *Leigh Hunt: Life, Poetics, Politics*. London: Routledge, 2003. Print.

Rollins, Hyder Edward. *Keats's Reputation in America to 1848*. Cambridge, MA: Harvard UP, 1946. Print.

Ross, Trevor. *The Making of the English Literary Canon: From the Middle Ages to the Late Eighteenth Century*. Montreal: McGill-Queen's UP, 1998. Print.

Rossetti, William Michael. "Prefatory Notice." *The Poetical Works of John Keats*. Ed. W. M. Rossetti. London: Moxon, [1872]. ix–xxiii. Print.

Sabl, Andrew. "Noble Infirmity: Love of Fame in Hume." *Political Theory* 34.5 (2006): 542–68. Print.

Saintsbury, George. *A History of English Prosody from the Twelfth Century to the Present Day*. 3 vols. London: Macmillan, 1910. Print.

———. *A History of Nineteenth Century Literature (1780–1895)*. London: Macmillan, 1896. Print.

———. "Lesser Poets, 1790–1837." *The Nineteenth Century*. Cambridge: Cambridge UP, 1932. 95–139. Print. Vol. 12 of *The Cambridge History of English Literature*. Ed. Sir A. W. Ward and A. R. Waller. 15 vols. 1932.

———. *A Short History of English Literature*. London: Macmillan, 1898. Print.

Savile, Anthony. *The Test of Time: An Essay in Philosophical Aesthetics*. Oxford: Clarendon P, 1982. Print.

Scott, Sir Walter. *Letters*. Ed. H. J. C. Grierson. 12 vols. London: Constable, 1932–37. Print.

———. *Lives of the Novelists*. Introduction by Austin Dobson. Oxford: Oxford UP, 1906. Print.

———. *Scott on Himself: A Selection of the Autobiographical Writings of Sir Walter Scott*. Ed. David Hewitt. Edinburgh: Scottish Academic P, 1981. Print.

———. *Sir Walter Scott on Novelists and Fiction*. Ed. Ioan Williams. London: Routledge & Kegan Paul, 1968. Print.

Shelley, Percy Bysshe. *Letters*. Vol. 2: *Shelley in Italy*. Ed. Frederick L. Jones. Oxford: Clarendon P, 1964. Print.

Sher, Richard. *The Enlightenment and the Book: Scottish Authors and Their Publishers in Eighteenth-Century Britain, Ireland, and America*. Chicago: U of Chicago P, 2006. Print.

Simmons, Jack. *Southey*. London: Collins, 1945. Print.

Simpson, David. "Wordsworth in America." *The Age of William Wordsworth: Critical Essays on the Romantic Tradition*. Ed. Kenneth R. Johnston and Gene W. Ruoff. New Brunswick: Rutgers UP, 1987. 276–90. Print.

Smith, Christopher J. P. *A Quest for Home: Reading Robert Southey*. Liverpool: Liverpool UP, 1997. Print.

Southam, Brian, ed. *Jane Austen: The Critical Heritage*. Rev ed. London: Routledge & Kegan Paul, 1986. Print.

———, ed. *Jane Austen: The Critical Heritage*. Vol. 2: *1870–1940*. London: Routledge & Kegan Paul, 1987. Print.

Southey, Robert. *Later Poetical Works, 1811–1838*. 3 vols. Gen. Ed. Tim Fulford and Lynda Pratt. London: Pickering & Chatto, 2012. Print.

———. *The Life and Correspondence of Robert Southey*. Ed. Charles Cuthbert Southey. 6 vols. London: Longman, 1849. Facs. repr. St. Clair Shores, MI: Scholarly P, n.d. Print.

———. *New Letters.* Ed. Kenneth Curry. 2 vols. New York: Columbia UP, 1965. Print.

———. *Poetical Works.* 10 vols. London: Longman, 1837. Print.

The Spectator. Ed. Donald F. Bond. 5 vols. Oxford: Clarendon P, 1965. Print.

St. Clair, William. *The Reading Nation in the Romantic Period.* Cambridge: Cambridge UP, 2004. Print.

Stephen, Leslie. "John Clare." *Dictionary of National Biography.* Vol. 10. London: Smith, Elder, 1887. Print.

Sternbergh, Adam. "What Was, Is, and Will Be Popular: The Driving Forces of Popular Culture." *New York Times Magazine* (8 September 2013): 23–36. Print.

Sterne, Laurence. *Works.* 4 vols. London: J. Johnson et al., 1808. Print.

Stillinger, Jack. *Multiple Authorship and the Myth of Solitary Genius.* New York: Oxford UP, 1991. Print.

———. *Romantic Complexity: Keats, Coleridge, and Wordsworth.* Urbana: U of Illinois P, 2006. Print.

———. "The 'Story' of Keats." *The Cambridge Companion to Keats.* Ed. Susan J. Wolfson. Cambridge: Cambridge UP, 2001. 246–60. Repr. in Stillinger, *Romantic Complexity,* 112–28. Print.

Storer, J., and J. Greig. *Views in Suffolk, Norfolk, and Northamptonshire; Illustrative of the Works of Robert Bloomfield; Accompanied with Descriptions: to Which Is Annexed, a Memoir of the Poet's Life, by E. W. Brayley.* London: Vernor, Hood, and Sharpe, 1806. Print.

Storey, Mark, ed. *Clare: The Critical Heritage.* London: Routledge & Kegan Paul, 1973. Print.

Suarez, Michael F., and H. R. Woudhuysen, eds. *The Oxford Companion to the Book.* 2 vols. Oxford: Oxford UP, 2010. Print.

Suarez, Michael F., and Sarah M. Zimmerman. "John Clare's Career, 'Keats's Publisher,' and the Early Nineteenth-Century English Book Trade." *Studies in Romanticism* 45.3 (2006): 377–96. Print.

Suetonius. *Suetonius* [*The Lives of the Caesars* and extracts from *The Lives of Illustrious Men*]. Trans. J. C. Rolfe. Loeb Classical Library. 2 vols. London: Heinemann, 1924. Print.

Sutherland, Kathryn. "Jane Austen and the Invention of the Serious Modern Novel." *The Cambridge Companion to English Literature, 1740–1830.* Ed. Thomas Keymer and Jon Mee. Cambridge: Cambridge UP, 2004. 244–62. Print.

———. *Jane Austen's Textual Lives: From Aeschylus to Bollywood.* Oxford: Oxford UP, 2005. Print.

Swinburne, Algernon C. "Keats, John." *Encyclopaedia Britannica.* 9th ed. Repr. New York: Funk & Wagnalls, 1890. 14:22–24. Print.

———. *William Blake: A Critical Essay . . . with Illustrations from Blake's Designs in Facsimile, Coloured and Plain.* London: John Camden Hutton, 1868. Print.

Symons, Arthur. *The Romantic Movement in English Poetry.* London: Constable, 1909. Print.

Terry, Richard. *Poetry and the Making of the English Literary Past, 1660–1781.* Oxford: Oxford UP, 2001. Print.

Thomas, Edward. *A Literary Pilgrim in England.* London: Methuen, 1917. Print.

Tibble, J. W., and Anne Tibble. *John Clare: A Life*. London: Cobden-Sanderson, 1932. Print.

Todd, Janet M. *Jane Austen in Context*. Cambridge: Cambridge UP, 2005. Print.

Todd, William B., and Ann Bowden. *Sir Walter Scott: A Bibliographical History, 1796–1832*. New Castle, DE: Oak Knoll P, 1998. Print.

Tompkins, Jane. "Masterpiece Theatre: The Politics of Hawthorne's Literary Reputation." *American Quarterly* 36.5 (1984): 617–42. Online.

Tytler, Sarah [Henrietta Keddie]. *Jane Austen and Her Works*. London: Cassell, Petter, Galbin, [1880]. Online.

Virgil. *Eclogues; Georgics; Aeneid; Minor Poems*. Trans. H. Rushton Fairclough. Rev. ed. 2 vols. Cambridge, MA: Harvard UP, 1978. Print.

Walsh, Marcus. *Shakespeare, Milton and Eighteenth-Century Literary Editing: The Beginnings of Interpretative Scholarship*. Cambridge: Cambridge UP, 1997. Print.

Ward, J. P. "'Came from Yon Fountain': Wordsworth's Influence on Victorian Educators." *Victorian Studies* 29.3 (1986): 405–36. Online.

Watkins, John, and Frederick Shoberl. *A Biographical Dictionary of the Living Authors of Great Britain and Ireland*. London: Henry Colburn, 1816. Print.

Watson, Nicola. *The Literary Tourist: Readers and Places in Romantic and Victorian Britain*. Basingstoke: Palgrave, 2006. Print.

White, Simon J. *Robert Bloomfield, Romanticism and the Poetry of Community*. Aldershot: Ashgate, 2007. Print.

Wicksteed, Joseph H. *Blake's Vision of the Book of Job*. London: Dent, 1910. Print.

Willmott, Robert Aris, ed. *English Sacred Poetry*. London: Routledge, 1862. Print.

———, ed. *Poets of the Nineteenth Century*. London: Routledge, 1857. Print.

Woodmansee, Martha. "On the Author Effect: Recovering Collectivity." *The Construction of Authorship: Textual Appropriation in Law and Literature*. Ed. Martha Woodmansee and Peter Jaszi. Durham: Duke UP, 1994. 15–28. Print.

Woodmansee, Martha, and Peter Jaszi, eds. *The Construction of Authorship: Textual Appropriation in Law and Literature*. Durham: Duke UP, 1994. Print.

Woof, Robert, ed. *William Wordsworth: The Critical Heritage*. Vol. 1: *1793–1820*. London: Routledge, 2001. Print.

Wootton, Sarah. *Consuming Keats: Nineteenth-Century Representations in Art and Literature*. Basingstoke: Palgrave Macmillan, 2006. Print.

Wordsworth, Christopher. *Memoirs of William Wordsworth, Poet-Laureate, D.C.L.* 2 vols. London: Moxon, 1851. Print.

Wordsworth, William. *The First Book of the Excursion . . . The Wanderer. With Notes to Aid in Grammatical Analysis and in Paraphrasing by the Rev. H. G. Robinson*. Edinburgh: James Gordon, 1863. Print.

———. *Poetical Works . . . Complete in One Volume*. Paris: Galignani, 1828. Print.

———. *Prose Works*. Ed. W. J. B. Owen and Jane Worthington Smyser. 3 vols. Oxford: Clarendon P, 1974.

———. *Selections from Wordsworth's Poems. With Notes for Teachers and Scholars*. Allman's Classics for Elementary Schools No. 11. London: T. J. Allman, [1874]. Print.

———. *Wordsworth's Poems*. Uniform with Tit-Bits Monster Series. London: Newnes, [1902]. Print.

———. *Wordsworth's Poems for the Young.* London: Strahan, 1863. Print.

Wordsworth, William, and Dorothy Wordsworth. *Letters of William and Dorothy Wordsworth: The Early Years, 1787–1805.* Ed. E. De Selincourt. Rev. Chester L. Shaver. Oxford: Clarendon P, 1967. Print.

———. *Letters of William and Dorothy Wordsworth: The Late Years, 1821–1853.* 4 vols. Ed. E. De Selincourt. Rev. Alan G. Hill. Oxford: Clarendon P, 1978–88. Print.

——. *Letters of William and Dorothy Wordsworth: The Middle Years, 1806–1811.* Ed. E. De Selincourt. Rev. Mary Moorman. Oxford: Clarendon P, 1969. And *Letters of William and Dorothy Wordsworth: The Middle Years, 1812–1820.* Ed. E. De Selincourt. Rev. Mary Moorman and Alan G. Hill. Oxford: Clarendon P, 1970. [Distinguished by vol. no.] Print.

Wright, Beth S. "'Seeing with the Painter's Eye': Sir Walter Scott's Challenge to Nineteenth-Century Art." *The Reception of Sir Walter Scott in Europe.* Ed. Murray Pittock. London: Continuum, 2006. 293–312. Print.

Wu, Duncan. "Keats and the 'Cockney School.'" *The Cambridge Companion to Keats.* Ed. Susan J. Wolfson. Cambridge: Cambridge UP, 2001. 37–52. Print.

———. *Romanticism: An Anthology.* Oxford: Blackwell, 1994. Print.

Xenophon. "Agesilaus." *Scripta Minora.* Trans. E. C. Marchant. Loeb Classical Library. London: Heinemann, 1925. 60–133. Print.

Young, Edward. *Conjectures on Original Composition.* 1759. Facs. repr. Leeds: Scolar P, 1966. Print.

Index